Bad Beekeeping

by

Ron Miksha

Bad Beekeeping by Ron Miksha

Printed in Victoria, Canada

First Edition

Front Cover Drawing by Sandy Miksha
Back Cover Photograph by Erika Miksha

National Library of Canada Cataloguing in Publication
Miksha, Ron
Bad beekeeping / Ron Miksha.
ISBN 1-4120-0627-9
1. Miksha, Ron. 2. Bee culture--Saskatchewan. 3. Beekeepers--Saskatchewan--Biography. I. Title.
SF523.82.M54A3 2003   638'.1'092   C2003-903959-5
ISBN: 1-4120-0627-9

TRAFFORD

This book was published *on-demand* in cooperation with Trafford Publishing. On-demand publishing is a unique process and service of making a book available for retail sale to the public taking advantage of on-demand manufacturing and Internet marketing. **On-demand publishing** includes promotions, retail sales, manufacturing, order fulfilment, accounting and collecting royalties on behalf of the author.

Suite 6E, 2333 Government St., Victoria, B.C. V8T 4P4, CANADA

Phone	250-383-6864	Toll-free	1-888-232-4444 (Canada & US)
Fax	250-383-6804	E-mail	sales@trafford.com
Web site	www.trafford.com	TRAFFORD PUBLISHING IS A DIVISION OF TRAFFORD HOLDINGS LTD.	
Trafford Catalogue #03-0997		www.trafford.com/robots/03-0997.html	

10   9   8   7   6   5   4

Bad Beekeeping. Why 'bad beekeeping'? When I was young, back in the '70s and '80s, someone who was really 'hot' was pretty 'cool' and if you had a 'mean' car, smart and sharp looking, it was 'bad' which meant, of course, it was extremely good. So, one might conclude that this book, <u>Bad Beekeeping</u> is about really, really good beekeeping in the 70s and 80s. Well, in this case, the word 'bad' doesn't mean anything except the standard Oxford's definition – bad beekeeping on my part was simply very poorly executed beekeeping. I was a master of bad beekeeping.

This book started out as a manual. I thought I would write short essays about all the stupid things I'd done as a beekeeper. Swarms that fled from me, queen bees that danced upon my hat, honey tanks that leaked, bee trucks that wouldn't haul bees. It would have been quite a big book. But somehow, the project evolved into a memoir - a biography of a part of my adventures (1972 to 1987) when commercial beekeeping was my life.

I want to thank some special people for their help on this book. Particularly, those people who came along for the ride while I lived the story - my father, my brothers Joe, David, and Don. And my other six siblings. And people like Sandy, Buzz and Mary Trottier, Earl and Josephine Emde, the folks at Sand Lake Hutterite Colony, Stan Kanter, Mrs. Eleanor Dern. I want to thank Frank Andres for selling me the Canadian honey farm; the Fox brothers for buying it from me. Some of these folks have moved on, some passed on. Some are beekeepers whom I met only briefly, or knew but casually - they presented a life-time of encouragement and enthusiasm – Murray and Brian Hannigan, Keith Schwalenberg, Gary Oreskovic, Willi Van Herren, Ray Meyers, Chris Wariner, Steve Clifford. Also a word of thanks to those who answered my queries as I verified the facts and details in this book - correspondents throughout the United States, Canada and Germany; Vietnam, New Zealand, and Japan.

I had some incredible help in crafting this memoir – including the many people who read the drafts and offered their disparaging though constructive commentary. But especially the guidance of my editor, Rosemary Nixon, who turned this beekeeper's drivel into something less drivel-ish through her suggestions, comments, and pencil scrawlings in the margins. And Kenn Tuckey, Alberta's retired provincial apiary inspector, who smeared red ink over half the manuscript and made me check and re-check my sources and allegations until they were solidly proven and supported by documented footnotes. Thanks.

And special thanks to my wife, Eszter. She read revisions of this book and corrected them over and over again, helping me clarify and communicate my thoughts. Her support, encouragement, and unwavering belief in this project were ultimately the elements that brought this work to completion.

Ron Miksha
Calgary, Alberta, Canada
April 2004

Dedication

This book is dedicated to the people of Lake County, Florida and of Val Marie, Saskatchewan. Americans and Canadians from whom I learned and took so much.

Lake County is the center of Florida - its heart and heart-beat. The county hosts swamps, alligators, panthers, and some eccentric reclusive souls who have found solitude and peace amid the moss-covered live oaks. Lake County is gorgeous. But it is changing.

Some of the cultural and political changes have been in the direction of positive growth as the citizens create communities that welcome everyone. And services have improved. When my friend Eleanor Dern arrived in Florida, air conditioning in public buildings and refrigeration in grocery stores were rare. When I arrived, they were common. Today, cell phones and satellite receivers penetrate the isolation of the most secluded homesteads. In most ways, life is now easier and safer.

Other changes in Lake County are less welcome. Just as I had hacked a home place out of forty acres of pristine swamp and oak and pine-draped hummocks, so did tens of thousands of other recent settlers. Central Florida is becoming crowded and folks are transforming the rural landscape into the sort of place they have escaped.

Val Marie, Saskatchewan, is also changing. But your cell phone won't work in this isolated community. Too few people live here to support a cellular tower, a hospital, or even a gas station. You will need to drive an hour north, to Swift Current, to find such services. The village of Val Marie is not what it was twenty – or fifty – years ago.

My most significant observation, returning to the valley after a fifteen year exile, is the continued loss of people. Farms and ranches are growing ever larger as folks pack up and move away, selling their estates and their birthrights to those who somehow manage to stay. Val Marie has dwindled from a town of 500 people in the sixties to a village of perhaps 100 today. People have been uprooted by the incessant wind and its effect on the land - lifted and removed - to Regina, Saskatoon, Medicine Hat, Calgary.

One might not guess that this village and the farms and communities nearby produced a range of artists and artisans who changed the world. From Eastend, a Pulitzer Prize winner - Wallace Stegner's memories of growing up in southwestern Saskatchewan led to Wolf Willow. Cowboy Will James lived in the valley, just east of Val Marie. He was a novelist and an artist. Some of his stories became movies. Bryan Trottier - the super-star hockey player, the man who helped earn six Stanley Cups - roped calves and picked guitar on the family ranch, minutes south of Val Marie. The artist, Lise Perrault, has had grasslands landscapes gracing the walls of a federal art gallery in Ottawa. The village has produced lawyers, physicists, physicians, at least one member of Parliament, business people and research scientists. But that's not so evident as you cruise the dusty streets and gaze at the empty lots where their homes once stood.

The village is shrinking, people are fleeing, but Val Marie is not dying. Today it serves as headquarters for the new national park which promotes and celebrates the surrounding grasslands. Deer and antelope, snakes and cacti, teepee rings and petrified trees are protected. Val Marie is changing, and Val Marie's future may be in its past. But Val Marie will live forever.

CONTENTS

Arrival

Bright summer afternoon. Alfalfa and wild clover blooming. An excited young bee lands at the entrance of a hive. The bee's tummy is full of nectar, its small pollen baskets dusted with yellow powder. Confused, a novice, the young bee has landed at a wrong hive. It happens. Bees get lost. But the guard bees of this hive, overwhelmed by the sweet scent of fresh nectar becoming honey within the walls of their nest, ignore the mistake. Besides, the lost bee is bringing pollen and nectar. The new bee becomes a member of the hive. From now on, it will build new combs and store honey and pollen to profit the adopted colony. Life goes on for the bee and for the hive.

The same guard bees, on a windy day in late autumn, would not be so tolerant. With winter coming, they would drag old drones from the hive to their deaths. On a bad day, guards would reject a young lost bee as a thieving opportunist. They would grab the innocent insect, shred its wings and legs. And discard the mutilated body.

My truck rolled to a silent stop next to three wooden huts. I was a few feet - a *metre?* - inside Canada. Two thousand miles[1] from home. Home was green - forests of oak, maple, hickory. This place was also green. Sort of. But where were the trees?

At my window stood a tall man in a blue uniform, short blond hair. Big smile. I scratched my face, felt the stubble of three day's growth, and wished I had bathed and shaved before arriving for inspection. Would the border guard know I had slept on the seat of the truck last night? Would he care?

"Untie this tarp." The man pointed at the back of my truck. He called over a second officer, a younger man with very short black hair. I should have had a hair cut. Canadians wear hair short. I got out of the truck, fumbled with the rope securing the tarp.

"Did you tell Officer Mackenzie that you have a job waiting for you in Canada? You have a work permit, a visa?" Officer Macdonald[2] asked.

"I don't exactly have a job waiting for me. My friend had a business, I bought it from him." How much should I say? *The truth. Just the truth.* What did they see? A hippie? A deadbeat? Could they tell I was nervous? I had a visa. A self-employment visa. I handed Officer Macdonald the yellow sheet. He asked another question.

"I'll be here all summer," I answered, both hands gripping the tarp, holding it up so they could see my jug of drinking water, extra radiator fluid, steel tool box.

Macdonald looked at me and the visa. "If you're coming into the country as a visitor, you can't be paid anything. Wait here."

"I won't be getting paid anything. I bought a honey farm." I'm not sure they heard me. The guards were walking back to the door of their customs' house. A small white building. In a sea of grass. No trees. I looked up. Bright clear sky. The officers, not far from me, still outside their office. I saw Macdonald looking at my Florida license tag, he wrote something on a clip board, kept talking to Mackenzie. I couldn't hear them. They disappeared in their office, then were back in a moment, smiling.

"You're from Florida?" asked Macdonald.

"Not really. Pennsylvania. The family farm is in Pennsylvania. That's where I'm from."

"Your truck has a Florida tag."

"Yea, I live there in the winter. But I spend summers in Pennsylvania. And Wisconsin. Keeping bees." I was talking too much.

"Wisconsin?" said the second officer.

**My Hair was a Bit Long.
Canadians Wear their Hair Short.**

"OK," said Macdonald. "We're not going to stop you from giving your friend a hand on his farm. But if you've really bought a business, then this visa is in order. But don't stay longer than six months. Remember, those speed limits are kilometres, not miles, per hour. Have a nice day."

The truck started the first time I turned the key. I slipped the clutch, it rolled forward. I was in Canada. Past the border guards. And after the rough dusty gravel trail out of Montana, I was glad to be on a paved road.

I had seen this road before. Last year, I had worked for three weeks with Frank Andres. He had four hundred hives of bees in Val Marie. A little business that did well. We pulled off two thousand boxes of white honey from his beehives. We spun the honeycombs in his extracting machine. Filled almost a hundred barrels.[3] We were sitting in his kitchen, on plastic chairs with metal tube frames, when Frank squeezed the keys to the tiny house into my hand.

"Why do you want to sell?"

"I've got plans," Frank said. And he did. He was an Amway distributor. He showed me sales receipts of the hundreds of dollars he made every month. Selling soap. "Ron," he said, "when I left my government job to keep bees, I thought it was the smartest thing I could ever do. But you know what, Ron? Selling Amway's even better. So – you want my bees?"

"Yes, I want the bees. But I don't have any money." I was twenty-two.

"No problem. Just pay me a little every year. Nothing down."

Twenty-two. Any offer that included a house, a work-shop, and beehives - no money down - sounded pretty good.

I agreed to his easy terms. We signed some papers. Now, the following spring, I was back to see what it was that I had bought. I left some bees behind in Florida. My plan was to work Canadian bees in summer, American bees in winter.

Arrival

To reach my new bee farm, I followed the road north from the border. I drove past smooth hills of prairie grass, broken occasionally into brown soil awaiting spring seeds. I reached a stop sign. Left, west, looked almost the same as east. Short pale grass with bits of fresh green stretching from the crowns of plants. No houses; except for a tiny, abandoned homesteader's shack. Some fields captured behind fences. Far to the east, I could see rugged badlands. Seventy Mile Butte's bald and haggard face was dark against the cloudless blue sky. I drove east, towards the buttes, the badlands.[4] Towards Val Marie.

Grasslands Homesteader Shack
A Real Home on the Range

I traveled high on a plateau, though it was not obvious until the road curved from east to north again and plunged into the Frenchman River Valley. The bottom land was wide, smooth, black. Folks called it the flats. Full of plowed and terraced earth, planted in broad fields of clover and alfalfa. Two roads met at the valley centre, with the town of Val Marie at the junction.

Val Marie: Two Roads, Grain Elevators, the Bryan Trottier Arena

From atop the plateau, just before descending, I could see white grain elevators, a red brick school, and the Bryan Trottier Arena. Big structures, surrounded by small wood frame houses.

Mid-morning. The April sun was strong. Before I reached the flats at the valley's bottom, half-way down the hill, I slowed the truck, turned off the road. The summer before, Frank had put thirty hives of bees behind a thick caragana hedge. I was almost there, my first beeyard. Everything else - Val Marie, my little house

3

and shop, my Hutterite friends, the dozen farmers and ranchers I'd met the summer before - would have to wait. I wanted to see my bees.

I parked on a slick muddy trail near the apiary, after driving a few feet off the highway. Not too far. I didn't want to get stuck. I could imagine the ranchers in Val Marie. "Yea, that American boy drove up from Florida, then tried to drive on wet gumbo in an old two-wheel drive. Had to pull him out with the tractor, eh?" I stepped out of my truck, walked through sticky mud towards the beehives, my beehives.

It was April 30, 1977. I was barely twenty-three, about the same age my father had been when he set off on his big journey. Before Dad's adventure began, he'd kept a

California, 1945
Dad and Al Winn Move Bees to Onion Pollination.

few hives of bees on Grandpa's 50 acre farm in Pennsylvania. From a magazine ad,[5] Dad got a job working for the California beekeeper Al Winn in the Napa Valley. Winn lived near Petaluma and raised queen bees, sold them to Canadian beekeepers. Dad and Mr. Winn moved honeybees to onion farms for pollination and then into the foothills of the Sierra Madre for winter-time manzanita and sage honey.[6] Dad, Mom, and their first baby, David, took the train from Pennsylvania to Al Winn's California. In the dark, they dropped out of the high frigid Nevada mountains. "Those brakes screeched all night long," Dad once told us. "When it got light, we could see palm trees." A year later, he went back to Pennsylvania because Grandpa Miksha bought Dad a farm. He never returned to California. That was 1945.

I found my veil, smoker, and hive tool under the tarp that covered the back of my truck. I stuffed Florida pine needles into the shiny new smoker pot,[7] worked the bellows until clouds of cool white smoke drifted from its funnel. I tramped through the mud, up the hill to the hives that were wrapped in black cardboard. I blew smoke at the entrance of the first hive and pulled off the winter covering. I put the black cardboard box on the ground and placed two large rocks on it. The sun was warm, May was one day away, the bees no longer needed their winter protection.

With the black wrapper off, the beehive stood stark white against the yellow-brown grass, against the dark prairie soil. Along the banks of the river, a kilometre away, pussy willow must have been blooming because dozens of bees were flying back to the hive, each carrying big tawny wads of pollen tangled in the bristle-hairs of middle legs. The bees were confused. They were looking for a black hive, but now a white one stood in its place. They started to fly towards a neighbouring hive, still covered with its black winter wrapping. I quickly lifted and folded the cardboard from each hive, and as I did, more and more confused bees drifted about, lost at first, but no longer trying to enter the wrong hives. In an hour or two, the bees would forget that their homes had mysteriously changed colour. For the next six months, they would live in white beehives. Bees are confused for a short time when the environment changes; but they adapt, quickly forgetting their old circumstances.

I went back to the first hive. I lifted its cover, blew a tiny puff of smoke over the wax racks - the frames - that held honey, pollen, and brood. Thousands of bees, fuzzy brown and yellow, danced on the honeycombs. Life was good for this hive. It had a queen that had filled half a dozen big frames with brood. Fresh pollen and nectar surrounded the new eggs and larvae. The entire nest smelled sweet and clean. The bees hummed. They were not disturbed as I slowly shifted frames of honeycomb from side to side, inspecting their prosperity.

I drove from the apiary an hour later, reached Val Marie in five minutes. I was still heading north on Highway 4, past the church, the school, the arena. Almost out of town, I turned right on Highway 18. A row of houses on long, narrow two-acre plots lined the north side of the road. My home was the fourth house in the row.

Frank and the owners before him had parked their trucks on the patch of bald dirt in front of the house. Wheel ruts in dried mud were within inches of the only door on the small square shack. Grass grew to the sides of the house and in the back, but the front lawn was not a lawn at all. It was ugly brown dirt that greasy farm trucks had compacted into something like shale.

Bad Beekeeping

The Beekeeper's Square Little House in Val Marie

The house – shack – was simple. Years ago, someone had hammered yellow plywood to the square house as siding. They had shingled the steep roof with squares of grey and white tar. A big window looked south, out to the ball park across the street. But a grey curtain was pulled across the window. The house was empty. The single door at the front had a padlock.

From a pocket in my jeans, I pulled out the spare key Frank had pressed into my hand the previous summer. I unlocked and opened my new home. Stale air. Dead flies lined the window sills; the walls were cold and damp. The house had been closed for months.

I needed water. A drink. I turned on the kitchen faucet. Nothing came out. The sixty-five houses in Val Marie each had their own well, pump, and pressure tank. My pump was off. The tank was empty. I hoped that the well wasn't dry. I called Frank. He had moved to the city, Swift Current, a hundred twenty kilometres away. "I drained the pipes and the tank in the fall, so it wouldn't freeze over winter," he said. "All the pieces are on the basement floor. You'll have to put it all back together again. And Ron, there's a garden hose in the basement. Run it from the Laturnus' house to get water until you get things going."

Laturnus. My neighbours. Sounded French, but the elderly couple were speaking German when I tapped on their door. Catholic Germans from Russia. They gave me black tea.

"Please wash your hands and face."

I must have looked like a tramp, but they set silver spoons and cloth serviettes on the table for my tea. From the refrigerator, they brought carrot cake.

"Frank's gone?" Mrs. Laturnus asked.

She cut a second piece of cake for me. I hadn't met these people the summer before, but they remembered me, must have seen me working alongside Frank. "Everyone in town knows who you are," Mrs. Laturnus said. I should have thanked them by staying longer, talking more, but I had work to do, and as soon as I downed the last of my tea, I stepped back outside.

I connected garden hoses and led them across the yards, linking my thirsty house to the Laturnus' water system. I now had water to prime the pump in my basement. But I did not know how to prime a pump.

Arrival

"Ask Mr. Briand, he's good at that," called Mrs. Laturnus, pointing towards the house on the other side of my lot.

The Briands were my neighbours to the west. The name sounded German, I thought. They were speaking French when I tapped on their door. I was given black tea; was asked to wash my hands and face.

"Can you help me get my water going?" I asked.

"Of course. I have all the tools we'll need," said Yves Briand. We carried two pipe wrenches, pliers, and a pail through my kitchen, down the steep wooden basement steps. The check valve was on the floor.

"This really should be down in the well," Yves said.

He tapped it on the cement floor, showed me how water pressure and a spring keep the pump's water from draining back to the sand-point buried in the well.

Ron with Martha and Yves Briand

"Seems to be working correctly."

We put the check valve back in the series of iron pipes, used the heavy wrenches, tightened everything. The pliers opened a bung plug on the top of the pump. Yves dribbled water from his pail, through the bung port, until the pump reservoir was full.

"OK. Now we try the switch."

Air gurgled within the tank, some hissed out the bung hole. Then water started to come through the hole and Yves deftly screwed the stopper back in place. I had water.

"In the fall," he said, "I can help you strip this all down again. You're going to go back to Florida in the fall again, are you not?"

We let the water run for a long time, flushing out antifreeze that Frank had poured into the S-traps and into the toilet bowl in the autumn. The house had been empty for five months. The heat turned off. It reached minus forty in January, but with the drained pump and the antifreeze, there had been no frost damage. Water ran and ran from the faucets. White water. Flakes of white scale attached themselves to the spigot and knobs.

Bad Beekeeping

"Alkali," said Yves. "You can wash it off with vinegar. Water here has magnesium, too. Upsets some folks' stomachs, but we drink it all the time. Just let it run a few hours before you start using it."

I had water. I opened windows and the smell of dead flies blew out of the old house. I carried in my clothes and sheets and books and food. I opened the can of green beans I had bought the day before in Jamestown, North Dakota, ate them cold, right out of the can. I was still hungry. I would need to buy a meal, but first I had to get some Canadian money.

I didn't own a credit card. All my cash was American, I would have to exchange it. Val Marie had a credit union instead of a bank. Someone told me it was a sort of socialist thing. A bunch of farmers could not get loans from the bankers in far-off cities, so they built their own bank, a co-operative. Sounded like a good idea to me.

I gave the teller a check from my Florida bank. She reached out, not to take my check, but to shake my hand. "Mary. Mary Trottier," she said. She had short red hair, a hint of grey. Freckles. Slim build. She looked Irish to me.

I asked her to set up an account for me.

"How long do I have to wait before I can use this account?" I asked. The nice lady did not understand my question.

"I can give you some blank checks today," she said. I told her that I expected she would make me wait until my deposit cleared. "Heavens, no!" Mary said. "You can start using your cheques today!"

"What if my American check is bad?" I asked.

"Is it?"

"No."

"Then what's to worry?" Mary handed me my new cheques. "Do you want some cash?" Then she apologized. The exchange rate was 1.05, my thousand dollar US deposit was only worth nine-hundred fifty-two Canadian dollars. "The Canadian dollar has been ahead of the US all winter," she said.[8]

A lady standing behind me joined in. She wore rubber boots and a plaid parka. Instead of a purse, she held a wallet in her hands. "But it helps if you want to go shopping in the States," she said. Mary introduced me to Patsy and the other folks waiting in the credit union. I was Ron, the new honey-man. A young lady attached to a restless four-year old said I should drop by, meet her husband. But she didn't tell me her name or where she lived.

Before I left, Mary asked me if I would come to her house for supper. "Buzz is across the street at Wong's. Go meet him. He'll tell you how to find our ranch."

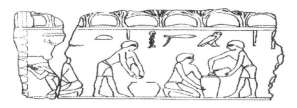

Egyptians, Packing Pharaoh's Honey

Buzz and Mary

A honeybee begins its life as an egg. A creamy white ovoid unceremoniously dropped to the bottom of a wax cell by a busy queen bee. The egg is ignored by the other bees for three days. Then the egg tips over on its side and a grub, a worm-like larva, hatches from the egg. Adult bees in the hive notice it immediately. They drip secretions from their hypopharyngeal glands to the larvae and later they drop bits of pollen and honey – bee bread – into the larva's mouth. It eats. The larva ingests so much and so often that she grows a thousand times bigger in five days. Just when the fat and plump immobile larva looks like it will burst apart while begging for still more food, an adult bee wanders by and covers the cell with a wax lid. In darkness, the larva becomes a pupa. It quits eating, molts from a grotesque white worm into a fuzzy baby bee. Twenty-one days after the egg falls from the queen, the new adult bee chews off the wax lid from her cell and emerges. A young adult with wings, huge eyes and six spindly legs. Her entire body is soft and hairy. This insect has a stinger, but it, too, is soft and wooly, and is not yet a weapon.

Wong's was empty, except for the four cowboys sipping coffee at the table nearest the cash register. Harry Wong smiled and the cowboys waved me over to sit with them. They slid their chairs around to make space and Harry brought a chair for me from the table behind us.

"You wanna eat?" Harry hopefully handed me his one page menu.

"Oh yes. I'm starving!" I said.

"How 'bout fried rice beef and broccoli. Very good. Or maybe you like hamburgers, gravy and fries?"

I had never tasted Chinese food. I ordered a hamburger. And I had never eaten gravy on fries, so I asked for ketchup. I looked at the cowboys. Real cowboys. I wondered which one was *Buzz*. The men were all fifty or sixty years old, wore broad-rimmed hats. Real cowboy hats. White, tan, brown, black hats. They drank their coffee with their coats on. Two smoked cigarettes, a package of Players on the table. One of the men was very thin. He had crooked black teeth and he chewed tobacco. Beside him was a big man, his chair pushed far back, his belly bumped the table. His coat was open and a coffee stain drew an arrow between the white buttons of his blue shirt. The youngest man had short black hair and a dark complexion. He sat very still. Looked shy. I was surprised when he spoke first. "Mary says you should come down for supper tonight." I had just crossed the street from the Credit Union a minute earlier. How did he know Mary had invited me to supper?

My hamburger arrived. Harry Wong leaned forward with the food as he presented it to the table. He nodded. I sensed he was bowing. "You like this, I know," Harry said.

The big man waited until Harry Wong was back in the kitchen. "We'll miss him," he said. "He's trying to sell. Wants to move to Swift."

"Yea, you'll miss your poutine. Not him," Buzz said.

Bad Beekeeping

The cowboys quit talking. "You want in?" The skinny man with black teeth was dealing cards.

"No, no. Don't play cards. Don't really know how," I said.

"We've heard that before. You'd probably clean up." Cards were dealt, none were handed to me, I was still eating. And then I had to go, I wanted to check the honey shop, see if I could find frames of honey to use as feed for the rest of the hives I'd be inspecting.

"Don't forget about supper," Buzz said as I left Wong's.

Buzz Trottier, on his Ranch, South of Val Marie

The Trottier ranch was five minutes south of Val Marie. Buzz had lived in the valley most of his life. He was an Indian, a native-Canadian. His ancestors had lived on the continent for thousands of years. His grandparents taught the English and French how to hunt and live on the prairies. They taught them games, sports. Buzz taught his own children to compete, to be tough, but fair. It was the way of the Indian. I knew nothing of this when I drove out to the ranch that day. Through the irrigated flats, up a butte, past red cows, black horses. I stopped in front of a modern ranch bungalow. A white house with brown trim.

Buzz and Mary

Mary opened the door. She was dressed in the same red slacks and white shirt she had been wearing at the Credit Union. I could smell a roast. Potatoes? Carrots? Onions? *How had she found time to bake a roast?* "Buzz'll be here in a minute. He's feeding the horses," she said.

Mary, Entertaining Grandchildren

I looked past the dining table. A guitar leaned against the wall between the kitchen and living room. A colourful mural was on the distant living room wall. I couldn't see it clearly, though it covered much of the wall. It was huge - some sort of drawing, or photo. It looked like a football player, someone in a blue sports uniform, racing across a field. Left of the mural, on the west wall, was an enormous window. Through it, far beyond leafless poplar trees, I could see the river.

Buzz came in. He still wore his jeans and leather boots, belt buckle and the tan cowboy hat. He was a cowboy. As the years went by, I would learn a little about ranching from him. I would brand his calves, load his cattle onto the trailers that hauled them to market. But I would never become a cowboy. Buzz was the cowboy.

Buzz hung his jacket on a post by the kitchen door. Over it, his hat.

"Found us?" he said.

He went to the fridge and got us both a Seven-Up.

"What's that?" he asked, pointing to the oven door.

Mary didn't answer, but put the roast in the middle of the round table in the kitchen. As we ate, they asked me about Florida and Pennsylvania. Usually, I was a bit

The Badlands - Scene from the Trottier Ranch, south of Val Marie

Bad Beekeeping

shy. When I was a kid at school, the shyness was painful – my face glowed bright red whenever I had to speak in the classroom. But these people made me comfortable. I chattered through the entire beef roast, told them about my bees, my father's farm in Pennsylvania. I told them how the eastern states were different from Saskatchewan. The big cities. The damp climate. We finished eating and I was still talking. Not very polite. "Mary works at the bank," I said, "You do any other work besides the ranch?"

Buzz rubbed his eyes.

"I worked for the highways," he said. Buzz stacked dirty plates in the center of the table. "Built some houses. Spent a lot of time getting my boys going at hockey. Used to do some picking and singing. Kathy, our youngest daughter, she and I made a record down in Nashville. But mostly, I take care of the cows."

Bryan Trottier: Hockey Superstar

"Nashville? You got kids? They play hockey?" I asked. I had not been very attentive.

"That," Mary pointed towards the mysterious mural on the living room wall, "Is our oldest son, Bryan. He lives on Long Island, in New York. Plays hockey with the Islanders. Carol is married, lives in Speedy Creek. Kathy is married, lives on a ranch. Monty is playing hockey in Indianapolis and Rocky in New Jersey, but I think he'll be playing in Norway this fall." I walked over to the wall and looked at the mural. Number 19 scoring a goal.

"You like music?" Buzz asked. "Western music?"

"I play a bit," I said. Buzz pulled a Fender out of a case and handed it to me. "Go ahead," he said. I was awful.

"You practice much? If you practice, you might get better," Buzz said. He lifted the guitar that had been propped against the wall. "I used to have a band. But not now," said Buzz. "Might do it again, someday."

Then he cradled his guitar, closed his eyes. Buzz played country songs and ballads - hurting songs, he called them. I followed his chord changes, watching his hands. Mary sat near by. "I don't sing or play," she said. She picked up a magazine, then got up and brought pretzels and another pop from the fridge, setting everything on the coffee table in front of us. I stayed late, ate all their pretzels. At midnight, Buzz played "One Day at A Time, Sweet Jesus" and I sensed it was time for me to leave.

"Don't get lost driving home," Buzz called from the door as I left. "You remember which shack is yours?"

The next morning I was back in the bees. The first beeyard I had unwrapped, on my first day in Saskatchewan, had been good. The bees had enough honey, only a few hives had poor queens, and only three hives out of thirty had died during the winter. Colonies of bees may die if they have foulbrood disease; if their collective community runs out of honey; if the queen is slow at laying eggs; if the hive is ripped open and exposed to cold and snow. None of the hives seemed to have any diseases. The winter insulation boxes had stayed on the hives, protecting them from the wind and cold. Most of the hives in the apiary behind the caragana hedge still had twenty or thirty pounds of extra honey to eat – a surplus. And now the bees were gathering fresh nectar from the willows along the river bank.

I had six apiaries in the irrigated alfalfa flats west of Val Marie, I wanted to begin my day with the beeyard farthest from home. A gravel trail twisted past sparse ranch houses, hay fields, and cattle pastures. The air was crisp. I drove with the window of the six-wheeled Ford rolled down, my left elbow greeting the bright sun. Fresh odours - from blue-gray sage, dry grass, cow pastures - filled the truck cab. A long brown trail of dust followed my truck to the first apiary, at the PFRA headquarters.

The PFRA, Prairie Farm Rehabilitation Administration, was a land assistance system established during the dust-bowl years of the depression. The government erected dams and wind-breaks, and it controlled pastures and irrigation canals across the Canadian prairies.[9]

**The PFRA Helped Irrigate Ten Thousand Acres of Sweetclover and Alfalfa
in the Frenchman River Valley – The Bees Loved it**

In Val Marie, one of the driest communities in Canada, PFRA folks in blue trucks patrolled the irrigation canals and ditches; men on backhoes and graders trenched and leveled fields; PFRA cowboys herded ranchers' cattle on the community pastures. To me, it seemed like a big and complicated industry. In reality, it probably employed only a dozen people who helped irrigate ten thousand acres of sweet clover and alfalfa and shepherded three thousand beef cattle in the government summer pastures.

My bees were behind small white wooden PFRA buildings. Although I had not been driving for long, I felt the need to stretch and shake myself when I stepped out of the truck. I had not slept well the night before, my house cold and mouldy smelling. And I had no bed. I had rested five hours, curled up on a blanket on the bare bedroom floor. But the water was still working and I'd been able to start the day with a hot shower, followed by cold cereal and instant coffee.

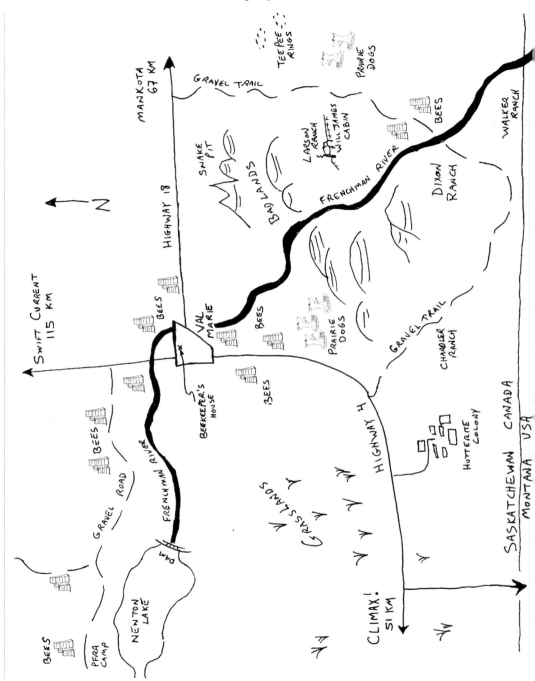

Val Marie Area in Southwest Saskatchewan

Buzz and Mary

I must have been yawning for a long time. I still had not lit my smoker nor put on my white coveralls. The PFRA manager's blue half-ton approached.

"Frank?" the man asked before I looked up.

"No, I'm Ron."

"Oh, yea... I heard you'd be the beekeeper this year." Tracy offered his hand. He had an interested, curious expression. "Can I watch you for a while?"

I didn't want an audience. I preferred that people wait until I was ready to show off. I had no idea what the bees would look like. The unexpected was exciting to me, but it was not something I wanted to share. What if all the bees were dead? What if I opened a hive and snakes or mice or something really strange came crawling out? Would the whole town know about it within an hour?

"Sure," I said, "Put this on." I handed him a bee veil.

"How does it work?"

I guessed Tracy had never helped anyone with bees before. "Put the helmet on. Pull the veil down tight, the strings go around your waist." I pushed the pith helmet firmly into his short hair. He stretched the strings, the veil fit snuggly on his shoulders. His face was protected from the bees.

"Keep your hands in your pockets, the bees won't bother you that way," I said. With hands in pockets, the bees do not have exposed skin to attack, should they become angry. But more importantly, the spectator stays quiet. In the past, I had friends watch me working bees and the folks would become nervous. Before long, their hands would be batting the bees that were casually examining them. Soon the flaying arms would attract more bees and the bees would go from curious investigation to aggressive irritation. Hands in pockets. Safer for everyone.

I lifted the black cardboard winter cover off the first hive, exposing the white beehive boxes. I used my flat pry-bar - the hive tool - to dislodge the hive cover. A pungent sweet-sour odour wafted up into our faces. Masses of wet, mouldy, dead bees were visible between the frames. Not a single live bee crawled forth.

"Something's wrong with this hive," Tracy said, helpfully.

"Yea," I said, "The bees are dead."

"Why? This normal?"

"I hope it's not normal," I said. I could see why the bees had died.

Without honey, bees die. The entire wintered colony - twenty thousand bees - starves. It is a democratic end to a social structure that shares food until all of it is gone. There are no remote enclaves of tough, superior bees fighting other bees for scarce food and watching their weaker sisters starve. The honeybee can only survive as a society, individuals perish. As their stores dwindle, each bee gets less and less to eat, until all the honey is gone. Then, within a few hours, all the bees die together.

I opened the next hive. It was also dead.

"Uh-oh!" said my new friend.

"Well, there are still twenty more hives to open," I said.

A few more dead hives; others were alive. By now, Tracy needed to head off to the irrigation ditches. "Stop by for lunch," he said pointing up the hill towards his white government house. "About twelve."

Bad Beekeeping

The bees at the PFRA site had not wintered well. They were in a location that held damp air. The dead hives all had mouldy bees, while the day before, the few dead hives at the Kornfeld beeyard had crisp, dry bee carcasses. No smelly mould. The live hives at this beeyard were in fair shape, but did not have the large populations I expected to see. A few hives, maybe five of the twenty, had old queens, perhaps three or four years old. Old queens are a problem. Queens mate only during their first few days. They fly out of the hive, find half a dozen bee boyfriends, then return to the colony and lay eggs. When the sperm they collected on the mating flights runs out, the queen is old and no longer produces fertile offspring. The entire hive suffers with a smaller population of bees. Unless the bees begin raising a new queen, the hive dies.

When I finished cleaning the beeyard and loading the dirty boxes of the dead colonies on the flatbed truck, I tied down the cardboard wintering cases. I counted hives. Eleven out of twenty-two were alive. All the colonies that were left had bees flying, bringing in big wads of brown pollen from nearby flowers. It was May, the alfalfa and clovers would not bloom until

Spring Beekeeping Chores in Saskatchewan

July. I could be optimistic, there was time to expect the remaining colonies to build up huge populations of bees and make a big honey crop.

The sun was warm. It was almost ten. I had time to unwrap and clean another apiary before stopping at the PFRA-guy's house for lunch. The next beeyard, six kilometres east of the first, was inside a pasture. I stopped the truck on the road and unhitched the gate.

Ranchers' gates were usually made of barbed wire and a couple of wooden posts. One of the posts latched to the fence. The latch itself may be a simple rope, but typically it was a wire hook that snuggly held the gate post to the fence post. Some ranchers kept loose, sloppy latches. On those, I could quickly unhook the rope or slip the gate post out of the wire loop. But other ranchers took great pride in the tautness of their gates. The gate at the trail to the Legault beeyard was constructed by a rancher of enormous pride. To get the gate open, I threw all of my hundred sixty pounds against the gate post. My muscles trembled as I squeezed the gate post closer to the fence post and worked the wire hook up.

By the time I opened the gate, I had an audience. Black cows, Aberdeen, had politely made a broad semi-circle around the inside of the fence. Gate open, I drove in. The cows thought about leaving, going through the open gate, out to the road. I quickly jumped from the truck and, long moments later, had tightly secured the gate. My disciples were no longer watching me. Their interest had shifted to my truck. Long, fat tongues touched and tasted the drips of honey on my wooden truck deck. I chased the big, dumb, harmless animals away. I was unaware that they were already seasoned connoisseurs of honey.

Buzz and Mary

The cows stayed by the fence. My old Ford bounced across the pasture to my beeyard. Here were forty-two hives. Half a dozen had been knocked over. Broken combs were scattered about. As if wrecked by some big, dumb animals. Cow tracks and cow paddies filled the spaces between the hives. I had never seen or heard of cow damage in a beeyard. But here it was. Big wooly tufts of animal hair hung on the broken hives. The cattle had been scratching off their winter coats, rubbing against posts, barb wire, and beehives. My hives had been pushed over by itchy cows. Their curiosity aroused, they began to taste the honey. This was not the only animal damage in the Legault apiary.

There were small piles of dead bees in front of a few hives. The dead bees were wadded and matted together. The same hives with the bee carcasses had tufts of soil and grass ripped up at the entrances. The work of skunks. A skunk prowls at night, scratching the ground in front of the insect nest to alarm the residents. As the bugs crawl out of the hive to investigate, the skunk laps up the hapless invertebrates with its long, agile tongue. In a few evenings, most of the adults in the colony have been eaten. The hive can become so weak that it never recovers. With the cow and skunk damage and two hives dead from starvation, the Legault apiary had only thirty hives left.

Before coming to Saskatchewan, I had kept bees on the family farm, back in Pennsylvania. I'd also worked in Florida with my brother David. And in Wisconsin, with my brother Don. Each area has its attractions, each its problems. In Pennsylvania, it was poor production. Bees seldom earn their keep in the north-east U.S.A. – too few nectar-bearing flowers; too much rain. In Florida, bees fare better – if the beekeeper is willing to put up with intense heat, drenching humidity, fire-ants, drug-dealers, tourists. And if the beekeeper doesn't mind moving bees from forest to field to grove to forest to seaside several times a year. Wisconsin is rural, holds pastures and hay meadows with nectar-rich alfalfa and white clovers. But Wisconsin has wet long bitter winters. Bee colonies often perish. And bees make only a half as much honey as they may make on the Canadian prairies.

I had kept bees in Pennsylvania, Wisconsin, and Florida, but I had bought Frank's honey farm because it was for sale, no money down. For sale in Saskatchewan - a place with enormous clover and alfalfa fields; sunny, hot weather and long summer days. A place with its own unique problems, but nevertheless, the best place for bees on the entire American continent.

Despite the huge potential, I felt neither optimistic not enthusiastic as I looked at my mouldy dead bees. The grass was still brown. From where I stood in the Legault beeyard, I could see no trees. Not one. I was only in southern Saskatchewan for two days; already I missed the trees. The green grass of the east. Two thousand miles from my five brothers, my four sisters. Sleeping on the floor in a cold, mouldy house; sharing a village with two hundred strangers.

It was almost noon. I left the Legault apiary and drove back to the PFRA compound. Climbed up the steps of the small, white government-issued house. At a crowded table, we ate soup. Ham sandwiches with butter. Tracy's wife politely asked me about the bees.

"Tracy says your bees are dead, eh? What are you going to do?"

Bad Beekeeping

"I've only looked at three yards. I've got seventy out of a hundred hives alive so far. That's not too bad," I said. I must have sounded defensive because the next question had nothing to do with bees.

"Have you met any of the folks in Val Marie?"

"Buzz and Mary," I said. "Had supper at their house last night."

"You must have heard of Val Marie when you lived in Florida? Because of hockey? Bryan Trottier's home town?" I had not. The lakes never freeze in Florida. Kids don't hang around Lake David in Groveland, ice skating. And although I grew up in Pennsylvania, we could skate only two weeks each winter on the family pond. Sometimes the neighbour's lake. We did not play hockey. The States had only a few hockey teams, the networks never broadcast a game - not even the Stanley Cup.

"Did you know that Bryan was the first hockey player to sign a million dollar contract?" I knew neither Bryan Trottier[10] nor hockey. Years since I'd last skated, I doubted I could even stand erect in skates anymore. My lack of ice talent did not matter, I was never tested on it. I suppose there are a few Canadians who believe that a fellow who's never played hockey isn't a real man. But I never heard nor felt anything of the like from the Trottiers. To them, hockey was an exciting sport, a profession at which they had quite a lot of talent. But not everyone has the same skills and interests, Buzz Trottier would say. I liked the Trottiers.

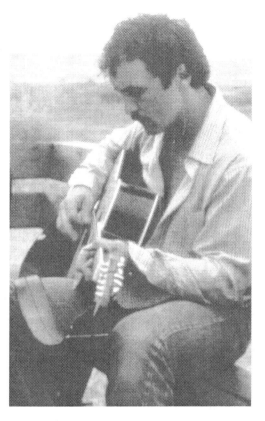

Bryan Trottier, at Home in Val Marie: Hockey Superstar and Cowboy

Tracy handed me butter. "For the buns," he said, waving his free hand towards a platter near his wife. "You must know that in his first NHL game, Bryan did a hat trick." *A hat trick?* I had no idea what that meant. Perhaps he skated onto the ice and performed a hat trick, pulled a rabbit from a tall black hat. I figured if I ever met him, I would like him. A sports star with a sense of humour. It sounded like the sort of thing I would want to do myself. In front of twenty thousand fans, something totally outrageous. A hat trick, for example.

"Hat trick. That means he got three goals in one game," Tracy's wife said, reading my face. "Most players never do a hat trick in twenty years. He did it his first game."

After apple pie with ice cream, Tracy walked me out to my truck. "Some of the boys here don't much like bees," Tracy said. "They figure they'll get stung. Me, I don't really care, one way or the other. I suppose it helps the ranchers, having bees around to pollinate their hay. But, I thought you should know, some of the fellows asked me to see if you'd move the bees away from here."

I didn't want to be anywhere I wasn't welcome. Most Saskatchewan farmers and ranchers liked bees on their properties, I could move my hives to a new place. But I didn't want to feel like I was being run off.

"Tell the guys I'll move them if anyone is bothered this summer, but I'd like a chance to keep them here. It's my first summer in Saskatchewan. If they're a nuisance, I'll move them."

"Yea, I know it's your first summer, I felt bad having to tell you. And it's got nothing to do with you being American, you know? Just one of the guys doesn't much like bees."

I drove away, not understanding why Tracy pointed out my nationality. One of his fellows didn't like bees; what had that to do with me being American?

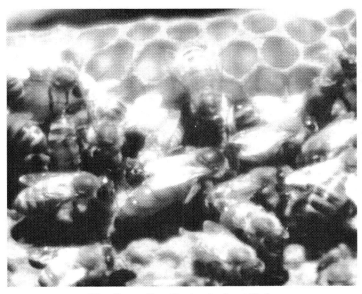

The Queen Bee, Center, is about Twice the Size of her Worker Bee Attendants

I continued working through the hives I'd bought from Frank. For a week, I unwrapped the insulation from my four hundred colonies, cleaned the hive's bottom boards, moved honeycombs from hives with too much honey and put the excess into hives with too little honey. I transferred extra bees from hives that were too strong into hives that were too weak, searched comb after comb for the single queen bee amongst the tens of thousands of workers - and when necessary, I removed old, failing queens and combined their children with the children of better mothers. And I picked up the messy equipment of the hives that starved during the winter.

The number of colonies was now only three hundred twenty - about twenty per cent had not survived the winter. This was not a shocking, nor even a particularly bad, result. It had been a bitter, windy winter on the prairies. And the losses included hives that actually survived the long, cold dark months, but were weak and not likely to make much honey during the coming summer - they were united with better hives.

Three hundred or so hives are not a lot. Most commercial beekeepers have one or two thousand colonies of bees. The largest honey farm in the world at the time was

Bad Beekeeping

Miel Carlota, started by two young friends on holiday in Mexico. Herr Wulfrath and Dr. Speck were from Germany. It was the autumn of 1939, and the Second World War suddenly began. They considered their options - and decided to stay in Mexico. They bought a few hives of bees, learned what they could about their new country, new climate, new culture. Twenty years later, with over 50,000 hives of bees, they were exporting honey all over the world.

I had bees. Not as many as most bee farmers, but it was a start, and they were Canadian bees. And some of the hives were quite good. Work was progressing.

During the week of cleaning hives and apiaries, I became more acquainted with the town and the folks living in Val Marie. I made new friends. And I met a few people who did not like me.

Queen   Drone   Worker

From L.L. Langstroth, <u>The Hive and the Honey Bee</u>, 1853

Canadian, eh?

Bees speak to each other. Their language is a blend of chemistry and motion – literally, body language. Bees with the most to say speak the most elegantly. They dance – graceful, circular, side-stepping twists and turns.

What does a bee talk about? Surely, some of their stories retell legends. Stories about a huge creature that once ripped the roof off their house and pulled out combs. The ground shook like an earthquake and there was a great fire – white smoke poured through the community. Then, suddenly, the tremors ceased, the smoke faded, and the giant disappeared.

Scientists, though, claim honeybees mostly talk about eating. How far to the nearest banquet? Which direction? What sort of meal is being served? Returning to the hive, a bee with a belly full of nectar will share a taste or two through a kiss with her hive mates. Then, in ecstasy, the bee begins a vigorous celebration dance. Round and round, over and over. The speed of the dance indicates distance. A fast dance means supper is not far from the table. The direction of the dance – up and down the comb or left and right along it – tells the other bees which direction to fly when they leave the hive.

When I moved to Val Marie, villagers could receive only three radio stations - country music from Swift Current, rock from Regina, and everything from the CBC.[11] Mostly, I listened to the CBC. I was not sure where the CBC signal came from, but I could always find it at the same spot on my radio dial, regardless of where I was in Saskatchewan. It seemed to follow me in my travels around the province, a kindly big brother teaching me how to be Canadian. The CBC avoided country music, except for occasional clips from a western yodeler named Wilf Carter or a guy from Prince Edward Island who stomped on a piece of wood with his boot and sang about potatoes. I liked the news, interviews, and talk programs the most.

I usually worked alone, so the CBC people - Don Harron, Peter Gzowsky, Barbara Frumm - became my buddies. They told me about themselves, their fellow Canadians. They taught me about Canada. I listened as they interviewed fishermen on the Atlantic, loggers on the west coast, and jazz musicians in Montreal. They gave me a feel for my adopted country. I wanted to know as much history and geography and sense of place as real Canadians. More, if I could.

I tried to speak Canadian; finished sentences with a well-timed, eh? I taught myself to say a-boot for about and shhedule instead of skedule. When I heard someone in Val Marie use a word differently from what I expected, I tried to learn the new word and use it right away.

Words like kee-kumber. A neighbour showed me her garden. Tiny, fragile cucumbers she had transplanted from her kitchen window to the cold May soil were barely surviving.

"We usually get hot weather in July and August," she said, "And with enough water, I should have lots of nice kee-kumbers."

Bad Beekeeping

Keekumbers. My new Canadian word for the day. I used it proudly and regularly - until I discovered that my neighbour and her one convert were the only people in Canada using this strange pronunciation.

I was equally guilty of mistraining people trying to learn American English. It was somehow assumed that since I was from the eastern states, my pronunciations were correct. Some of the older French-Canadians in Val Marie said my accent was colourful. Unfortunately, a second-generation North American with grandparents speaking obscure central European languages will likely mispronounce more than a few words. I was the one, after all, who accidentally taught the residents of the German-speaking Hutterite farm, south of Val Marie, to say "Inner-resting."

More communication problems awaited. That same spring, I had to fly to Florida to get a second truck, a vehicle I owned in the States that I wanted in Canada. I needed it to work with the bees that summer. I had to fly from Regina to Orlando.

I liked flying. I was served food. A nice young lady brought me a newspaper and pillow. I returned the favourable treatment by bathing, shaving, and sometimes even washing my hair before climbing aboard. And I would try to wear my cleanest dirty clothes.

Ron, Fishing in Saskatchewan. I Looked Like any other Twenty-Three-Year Old Long-haired Farmer.

In the end, though, I must have looked like all the other twenty-three year-old long-haired farmers traveling from Saskatchewan down to Florida to pick up a truck.

Connecting in Toronto, I had to pass through American immigration, then catch my Orlando flight. I'm not sure what the immigration officers found most suspicious - my unruly hair, my one-way ticket to Florida, or my accent. I was removed from the line.

I tried to be patient, but I had a Florida-bound plane to catch. I explained again to the American with the big gun that I owned a small business operating in both Saskatchewan and Florida. I had to fly south - with a one-way ticket - to get my other truck. He called over another guy with a gun. Tag-team time.

"You claim to be American."

Canadian, eh?

"I am," I said.

"You don't have a passport?"

"No, but I have my Florida driver's license. See?" I held the paper close to the officer's face.

"I'm sorry, Mr. Miksha, but anyone can get a Florida driver's license. This doesn't prove that you're an American. You could be a Canadian heading down to pick oranges. Taking a job from a real American."

Real Americans pick oranges?

"Where did you go to school?" They started their questions again.

"Sharpsville, near Pittsburgh."

"What grade did you finish?"

"Grade Twelve. I mean, twelfth grade." A real American would never say Grade Twelve. Too Canadian. Too late. I'd already said it. *Why had I made such a slip?* I'd only spent a few weeks in Val Marie, but I was trying desperately to fit in, constantly practicing my Canadian English. A third guy, older and wiser, showed up. The other officers explained that I had a one-way ticket, no passport, and sounded Canadian.

"Mr. Miksha," said the older and wiser gentleman with a gun. He paused, looked me square on. "Can you recite... the pledge of allegiance?"

Can I recite the Pledge of Allegiance?? For twelve years, every school day, facing the front right corner of the classroom, hand over heart, I had rattled off the words that did not begin to make sense until years after they were etched into my memory. *The American secret handshake!*

Quickly, loudly, with right hand pressed firmly against the left side of my heart, standing rigid, facing slightly to my right, I recited "I-pleg-allege-ants-to-theflag-of-the-united-states-of-america-and-to-the-republic-forwhich-itstands-one-nation-"

The third man lifted his hand; stopped me. "Mr. Miksha, welcome to America. Go catch your plane."

"They could never do something like that in Canada," Buzz told me later.

"Why not?"

"If Canadians had to sing more than the first seven words of 'O Canada' no one I know would ever get back into the country."

Early June. I was back in Saskatchewan with my second truck. The bees continued to gain strength. Early summer bee management requires that hives expand their brood nests - increase their populations - very quickly. The honeybees had to go from spring populations of fifteen or twenty thousand up to mammoth colonies with sixty to eighty thousand bees. The essence of good beekeeping management is getting a maximum bee population when a maximum number of flowers are in bloom. Nature takes care of the details, but there are things a beekeeper can do to help the bees expand in a big hurry. I learned some of the tricks from the most important beekeeper in the United States.

Bad Beekeeping

Jim Powers had 30,000 Hives of Bees and Wore a Bow Tie

A few months earlier, in Florida, I heard Jim Powers talk about commercial beekeeping. Jim Powers was a big beekeeper. Not particularly tall or fat. But big the way beekeepers measure each other. Most beekeepers tried to make a living from the craft with perhaps a thousand hives. Powers had thirty thousand hives of bees. He kept them in Idaho, where he lived. He had branch offices with thousands of hives in Florida, where I sometimes lived, and in Texas, North and South Dakota. A queen bee business in Hawaii. He was one of the few beekeepers in the world who amassed a large fortune from bees. And he was the only person I ever saw wearing a bow tie at a beekeeper's meeting. It was polka-dotted.

The meeting where Jim Powers told us how to succeed as beekeepers was interrupted twice by phone calls for Mr. Powers from the field. Between calls, he told the audience the secret of his success. "It's simple," said Jim Powers. "Good queens. Good locations. Surplus feed – honey and pollen – in the hives. Take care of that and you can produce lots of honey."[12] Feed, location, queens. Beekeeping in three easy steps. Genetics, environment, management. He gave us details, made the story entertaining. "But it's that simple," he said.

I did what I could to follow his instructions. *Feed.* I moved combs of honey from hive to hive, making certain that all the hives had enough feed. *Location.* I was in Saskatchewan, the best place in the world to keep bees. *Queens.* Oops. I had older queens. The hives I had were over-wintered colonies, headed by queens at least a year old, possibly two or three. Older queens lay fewer eggs, producing weaker hives. Hives that make less honey. I worked with what I had.

Bees Need Feed in the Hive, Good Locations, and Excellent Queens. But Saskatchewan Colonies Also Need Lots of Supers.

Canadian, eh?

In June, it was my job to assure that the hives had enough space to store fresh nectar and pollen - and enough empty combs for the queen to lay two thousand eggs each day. To give the bees enough space, I could keep stacking boxes higher and higher, erecting small skyscrapers in my apiaries. But this wasn't efficient management. Building beehive skyscrapers would require a lot of boxes. And the queen, looking for the warmest place in the hive to lay her eggs, would follow the heat up until her eggs and brood filled only the top boxes of the towers. The bottom boxes would be abandoned. The bees would feel crowded at the top, even though they had unused space below. Crowded colonies swarm. Swarms land in old barns. Old farmers who own old barns get upset and expect me to come gather my lost flock. So I kept the bees from swarming by reversing the order of the hive boxes every other week. The heavy box with the queen and eggs was shuffled to the bottom of the stack, the lighter bottom box moved up to the top to be re-used by the queen. I destroyed swarm cells – long wax cocoons the bees built to raise extra queens. I shifted excess bees from the strongest hives, put them into weaker ones.

I couldn't find and destroy every queen cell (some were cleverly hidden by the bees) and a few hives swarmed. One swarm came to town. A shaky voice, belonging to someone named Helen, called me one afternoon. "Your bees are all downtown. In a tree beside the post office." *All of my bees?* I avoided correcting her enthusiastic description and thanked her for the information.

Late in the evening, bees quit flying. About eight o'clock, I drove down to the post office with a hive body and nine frames, a cover and bottom board. People began to gather before I had shut off the truck. A handsome cluster of bees, perhaps twenty thousand, clung to a low branch. I methodically positioned my spare bee box on the ground, under the swarm.

"You plannin' to catch 'em?"

"Yea."

"But you got no veil or gloves. You'll get killed, eh?"

My audience was anticipating a great show. Sort of like the last few minutes before midnight on New Year's Eve, or the end of a Harrison Ford movie – everyone knows what will happen, but it's exciting anyway. I stood next to the swarm. Bees hummed softly, peaceful in the cool evening. But I knew they wouldn't stay that way. In a day or two, the bees would fly to a new home, better

**A Swarm of Honey Bees,
Clustered in a Tree**

sheltered. Perhaps in the wall of an old farmer's old barn. Or a house. I had dug bees out of the walls of houses. Stripping off siding, brushing angry insects into a net. Chopping out huge chunks of wax and honey and brood from between wall studs. Much easier to catch a new swarm in a tree. Especially on a low branch of a tree.

Bad Beekeeping

My box was positioned beneath the cluster. I reached slightly above my head with my right hand and got a solid grip on the branch that held the bees. A bee landed on my cheek. With my left hand, I casually flicked the bee into the box on the ground. My audience gasped. "He's gonna get killed," someone said. They admired my bravery. Or perhaps my intelligence. "God, is he ever stupid," someone said. The dozen spectators backed up, just in case. I tightened my grip and checked that my head would not be caught in a bee shower. Then I gave the branch one quick, hard shake.

The bees were locked, hand-in-hand-in-hand, into a tight wad that fell as a massive gray ball. The bees landed on the combs and quickly crawled down within the warm dark safe bee box. A few bees flew back into the air and a few still clung to the branch, refusing to relinquish their view. I gently set the lid over the combs and let the bees become quiet again. A few bees landed on my white shirt. "Look at him! He's covered in bees! My God! He's gonna shake the branch again!" And I did. The few remaining bees dropped alongside the beehive and crawled in through its entrance. The show ended, I'd demonstrated my talent to a new crowd. I couldn't skate and I couldn't rope calves, but I sure could hive a swarm of bees. I felt a warm glow of respect from the villagers. "He's crazy. You'd never catch me doing something stupid like that."

Most people left, walking away without speaking. Except for one young fellow in boots, jeans, a broad black hat. "Come here," he said. His back leaned against a grey outfit, rigged up with a bale lift. Attached to the lift was a round bale, the kind that weighs a thousand pounds and has to be moved by a fork-lift tractor. I approached, he turned away, reached through the truck window, came back around with a beer, handed it to me. "You're a stupid shit," he said. "You come here from the States, eh? Ain't there enough places to keep bees in the States? You know a woman was killed here last year by bee stings?"

I knew the story. She was a lovely young lady from England, a nurse who lived in Saskatoon before moving to Val Marie. But she'd died in the hospital from meningitis, not bee stings, though there was a persistent rumour to the contrary. I handed the beer back without figuring out how to open it.

"You're a dumb shit. You could've killed someone here."

"Bees aren't as dangerous as cows," I said, not sure what else to say.

"You got something against cows?"

"No. Look, I gotta go."

He moved away from the truck, a little closer to me. "You don't want my beer?"

"Another time, OK?"

Another truck stopped. Tracy from the PFRA.

"Hey, Ron," Tracy called out from his truck. "I heard you caught a swarm. Good work!" Tracy got out of his truck, walked up to me and my new friend. The cowboy went to his truck. "Good work?" he said and shook his head. The cowboy fired up his Dodge, revved the engine hard, then slowly drove away.

"New friend," I said to Tracy.

"Him? Don't worry 'bout Jerry, he's harmless. His Dad's losing the ranch, from drinking, I guess. And Jerry's off to the rigs next month. He's scared. Don't worry 'bout him."

Canadian, eh?

I had no more swarms to fetch. My bees were under control and the field work – rotating brood chambers, cutting grass near the hive entrances, inspecting for honey and queen quality – was progressing nicely. These beekeeping chores were not hard. With only three hundred twenty hives, it took just three days out of fourteen to keep my bees from swarming. I did this by cutting off swarm cells, reversing brood chambers, and shifting hives. Shifting was what I called moving hives around within the same beeyard. If I had a really strong colony, one with perhaps eighty thousand bees, I could expect it to swarm. So, I shifted its position within the apiary with the weakest hive, one with perhaps twenty thousand bees. The strong hive was moved to the weak one's location. The bees that flew out of the strong hives would fly back with legs laden in pollen, bellies full of nectar. In their haste, they'd return to the old hive location, now occupied by the weak hive. This cut the strength of the hive that was too strong, preventing swarming, while boosting the poor colony.

My oldest brother David had studied beekeeping thoroughly. He'd been a research assistant at Cornell University and at the federal bee lab in Madison. He taught me some of what he'd learned. David said, "In the spring, practice communism - each according to its need, each hive gets an equal economic opportunity. Move bees and brood and honey around so each hive is equal. But despite this treatment, some hives will still be laggards, so when summer comes, be a capitalist - knock out the weakest hives and give their bees and equipment to the strongest ones. That's how you'll make the most honey." It was spring; I was a communist. At least in the beeyard.

The work I did the first few weeks of June was quick and easy. Equalizing hives, mowing weeds and grass in the apiaries. I had time to clean and organize my warehouse, build more bee boxes and frames, meet more people, get into trouble.

The Hutterites were not trouble for me. Fifteen kilometres south of Val Marie was a religious farm commune called Sand Lake Colony. Frank had introduced me to the Hutterites the previous summer. We had gone to the colony several times, swapped honey for eggs and milk; paid to have their blacksmith weld a trailer hitch to the truck. To me, the Hutterites became something of a family. We told stories, drank wine. If you can imagine a twenty-three-year-old bachelor beekeeper spending Friday nights at a religious farm community where the ladies wear babushkas and do

Hutterite Children, Examining the Roof of a New Barn

not date outsiders, the men dress in black, no one owns a TV or radio, prayers precede coffee, and children recite Bible verses in low German on a bench a few feet away - then you know a lot more about me than I knew about myself. Yet I did not find it strange. It was pleasant. Comfortable.

The Hutterites did not try to convert me from my lack of religious conviction. But I was curious about their traditions, so I paid attention when they told me their history. The Hutterian Brethren began following the teachings of Jacob Hutter in the sixteenth century, I was told by the young minister David Kleinsasser. According to the Book of Acts, early Christians shared all their property in common. So Jacob Hutter taught that the practice of Christian faith requires communal living. Four hundred years ago, in Switzerland and Austria, the Hutterites were mostly craftsmen and artisans. They built towns and collectively farmed small plots. Each received according to need, gave according to ability. A Marxist experiment? Hardly. Their collective philosophy and communal living is not intended as a charitable lifestyle but rather as a requirement in the worship of God. When dealing with *the Anglish*, as English-speaking folks are called, the Hutterites are razor-sharp business folks. Shrewd business people, but nonetheless generous to outsiders. They helped townsfolk put out house fires and they built barns and plowed fields when neighbouring farmers were ill.

As Anabaptists in the sixteenth century, they taught adult baptism and encouraged all members to read the Bible.[13] This didn't fit well with the European counter-reformation. Jacob Hutter's followers were forced to move. From Switzerland, to Hungary, then Rumania and Bulgaria. Eventually, Catherine the Great invited the Hutterites into southern Russia. She gave them land; they built new Bruderhofs. They agreed to stay as long as their religion, communities, and pacifist beliefs were respected.

Two centuries later, Czar Nicholas the First, desperate for soldiers, began drafting Hutterites. The Hutterites couldn't stay. Nine hundred people moved to the States, where they were told they could farm in the Dakotas and never have to serve in the army. But thirty years later, the Americans began drafting Hutterites. Several young men, conscripted and sent to Camp Funston, refused to wear military uniforms – it was forbidden by their faith. They were imprisoned, beaten, starved. Two died. The US Army sent the dead young men back to their Dakota farms in wooden boxes. They were clad in the soldier uniforms they'd refused to wear while living.[14]

Josh Hofer, Beekeeper at James Valley Colony, in Manitoba

So the Hutterites moved to Canada, where they were invited to settle on the prairies. Canada has never drafted the Hutterites or other pacifist groups. But during the Second World War, because of their German-heritage and pacifist beliefs, young Hutterite men were collected from their farms and placed in work camps. The Trans-Canada Highway from Calgary to Banff was rebuilt by these German-speaking Canadians who were locked behind barbed wire fences each night near Seebee, Alberta. The older minister at Sand Lake Colony, Reverend Peter Kleinsasser, told me. He had been there. Four long years.

Canadian, eh?

Today, there are hundreds of Hutterite farms in Canada. Each has about seventy people. And ten thousand acres of land, most of it planted in wheat. Hogs, dairy cows, chickens. Hutterites drive big trucks and enormous tractors. They also have computerized auxiliary power generators. But they wear their traditional black clothes and do not have radios. Some of the colonies have beehives and skilled beekeepers. Modern, efficient; simple, plain. Families are large. As the population of a colony grows, there is less work for each person. Within twenty-five years, the group buys more land a few miles away; the members draw lots, divide their population. Half stay in the old houses, on the old land. Half move to new homes, work in new barns, plow new soil. In a hundred years, their communities grew from a handful of farms in the States to about six hundred Hutterite colonies today.

Sand Lake Colony was ten years old when I moved to Saskatchewan. The settlers had bought a couple of dry ranches south of Val Marie. For homes, they built condominiums – long row houses that ran together, each with a separate entrance. Storage and repair shops were metallic buildings with concrete floors. They dammed a creek, forming a lake for irrigation. They broke prairie sod and seeded four thousand acres with wheat. Much like an industrious swarm of bees colonizing new country, they created a massive, neatly organized nest and quickly filled it with food and babies.

Eager Student in Classroom at Sand Lake Hutterite Colony

They were successful in places where other farmers often were not. Some of *the Anglish* were jealous of Hutterite prosperity.

The Hutterites at Sand Lake Colony did not keep bees; I had no reason to be jealous. Instead, I admired much about them. Self-reliant. Courageous enough to be different – dress differently, act differently. Hospitable – strangers were welcomed, fed. Meanwhile, some of the folks on the colony seemed to admire me. I kept bees. Was American. I traveled. Drove a black truck. I didn't own a television. I didn't have a bed - slept on the floor in a tiny house. *Was I stoic? Perhaps spartan? A closet Hutterite?* I didn't go to the pub. Didn't follow sports. Worked ten, fourteen hours a day. On the other hand, I didn't go to church, either.

For the older preacher on the colony, I was a bit of a problem. Young people everywhere like to move beyond the familiar. Hutterite kids are no different. But Peter was able to keep most people on the farm by warning them of the dangers of the outside world. Until I came along.

Bad Beekeeping

I drove my black Dodge onto the Sand Lake Colony from the north, billowing up a cloud of dust as I raced along the kilometre trail from Highway 4. The path curved around the dammed creek that fed the farm's gardens and geese. Three kids, perhaps ten years old, held willow twigs with strings that dangled into the murky lake. They waved their black caps as I slowed down. The road curved back again, and immediately past the dairy barn, abruptly ended to the right in an unpaved parking lot. Mine was the only vehicle, the only visitor at the colony that evening. I waved at girls with their noses pressed against the window at the community kitchen. They quickly disappeared. I parked, took my keys. ("Always take your keys," Ben the Hutterite Welder had warned me, "or the kids will be sitting in your outfit all night, listening to your radio. Then your battery will sure be dead.") I tapped on David Kleinsasser's door, he pulled me in to join his wife, kids, and the older preacher, Reverend Peter. I sat down.

"On the outside, all the young people take drugs, right, Ron?" Peter asked me in front of some young Hutterites. He pulled on his beard, waited for my answer.

"I don't."

"But, it is a big problem. Your friends, they take drugs, yes?"

"Not that I know. Probably not."

"Well, they sit in the bars, they listen to their loud music." Peter stroked his grey beard, then dropped his hands to the table.

"I like a bit of wine like this," I said. "And I like music,"

"Yes. See, see," said Reverend Peter.

I Tried to Photograph my Friend, the Reverend David Kleinsasser, but he quickly turned away. "Photos are forbidden," he said.

David Kleinsasser, the fellow whom I had raced out to the colony to visit, was also a preacher. Hutterite colonies have two ministers for the hundred or so people who live on a colony. The younger minister was quiet. His wife Annie refilled our wine glasses. It was a strong, sweet wine. Yellow. "Honey-coloured," said young Reverend David. He changed the subject. David asked about my bees. "Do you think this year there will be a good crop?"

"I don't know. But I saw the first sweet clover blooming by the railroad track in the flats. Usually the bees start making honey when the clover's been out for a couple of weeks. And it's been raining a lot, there should be enough moisture. Yea, they'll probably make lots of honey this year."

"You doing all the work alone?" David asked.

"I'm not sure. My father called yesterday. He wants to send my youngest brother up here. Sounds like there are some problems at home."

"How old is he?"

"Fifteen, I think," I said. "Yea, fifteen."

Old Reverend Peter leaned forward. "Yes, teenagers on the outside can be trouble." Then he smiled. A warm and friendly smile.

Canadian, eh?

The next morning, Dad called again from his farm in Pennsylvania. How were my bees doing? Did it look like I would make a good crop? Did I plant a garden? It was June. School was out in Pennsylvania. Could Joe come up for the summer? I told him I'd think about it.

I drove out to Buzz's ranch, up the long clay and gravel trail, past a muddy spring that dribbled alkali water across the road. Past some of the cattle that Buzz and Mary kept. We had supper. Picked guitar.

I said, "My dad wants Joe to come here for the summer."

Buzz said nothing. I thought he hadn't heard me.

Buzz looked out the huge window towards the badlands, then turned back towards me. "Do you want him to?" Buzz asked.

"Well, sure," I shifted in my chair to face Buzz more directly. "I'd like to have some family around. And when the crop comes in, I'll need the help."

Buzz scratched his face with a guitar pick. I wasn't thinking so much about Joe as I was concerned for myself. I was a bit lonely. I was a long way from friends and family. But, in a way, so was Joe. All of our brothers and sisters had left the farm. They headed for Florida, Kentucky, Wisconsin. I was settling into Saskatchewan. Joe was the youngest of ten, alone with our father and step-mother on the family farm.

I was still waiting for a response from Buzz. He scratched his face again.

"Do you really need the help?" Buzz asked me.

"Yea, but I'm hiring a couple of local kids. It just sounds like Joe needs to get away."

"Who's left on the farm?"

"No one, really. Dad's new wife. All the older kids and I have been gone a few years. And the younger ones. JoAnn is married. The twins moved to Cincinnati. Fred left home. Only Joe is still there. A fifteen year old kid, the last of us still on that farm."

Buzz Trottier Thinks before Answering

Bad Beekeeping

Buzz looked at me. "Do what you need to do," he said. He moved the pick from his right hand to left. "It might be good for you. You come to Val Marie and all you do is work, unless you're here, eating Mary's cooking."

Buzz laughed, then sat silent a while. "A lot of people come and go in this valley. It changes them all. Sometimes for the better. Might be a good thing for the kid."

Hiving a Swarm,
from <u>The Beekeeper's Guide Book</u>,
by Professor Cook 1883

Into the Land of Rape and Honey

Bees go through stages. Emerge, grow, change. Typically these are slowly evolving stages. From fuzzy baby bees that scrub and clean, to nurse bees that feed the young, to attendants that cater to their queen. Most of these changes are caused by hormones, stimulated by age and nutrition. These changes are usually gradual. For example, the bee doesn't suddenly drop house duties and become a forager. She engages in learning, recreational activity – play flight. The bee stands at the entrance of the hive, feeling the fresh air, the warm sunshine. She takes short little flights, swooping around the apiary like a kid on a first bicycle. Wobbly at first, then moving smoothly, quickly, with purpose.

The next morning I called a travel agent. Joe would arrive June 25. There was a beekeeper's meeting in Tisdale on the 21st. I wanted to go to the meeting. Saskatchewan beekeepers were famous for the huge crops they made, I wanted to meet some famous people. After the meeting, I would visit the fellow who introduced me to Saskatchewan. Earl Emde lived in Big River, kept bees there in the summer, kept more in Florida during the winter. I had met Earl in Florida, at the Central Florida Beekeepers' meeting. It was Earl who introduced me to Frank on one of Frank's trips to the south. Earl had encouraged me to buy the honey farm in Val Marie. I wanted to visit Earl Emde and his wife; see their house on the lake in Canada's far north. After my five-day foray, I'd find Joe at the Saskatoon airport, on my way back to Val Marie.

My colonies were getting stronger. In two months, their populations grew from twenty thousand to fifty. Fifty thousand bees packed into two boxes. I had over three hundred of these hives. Sixteen million bees. They worked willow when it bloomed in April, dandelions in May, goat's beard, Russian olive, and caragana in June. Now the clovers were starting to bloom, but not yet yielding nectar.

Three hundred hives is not a lot. Not for someone who has no other means of support. It takes about a thousand hives to make beekeeping a real business. But three hundred were enough for my first year in a new country. I could learn a little about the climate, gain some experience in Canadian beekeeping. But I would need more bees the following year.

I owned some hives in the United States. Those bees were in Wisconsin for the summer. In November, I would haul them from Wisconsin to Florida. I spent my winters in the south, making a little honey from the orange groves and raising new bees and queens. My plan was to raise extra bees in Florida and bring them up to Saskatchewan. I would use my American bees to make orange blossom honey, then stuff them into cages with new queens. The citrus bloom ended in March or early April, so I could remove the extra bees that finished making honey in Florida, put them in cages, drive three thousand miles, and drop the packages of bees into my equipment on the Canadian prairie. To make all this work, I would need more equipment - more boxes and honeycombs. And I would need to figure out how late in the spring I could bring bees to southern Saskatchewan and still harvest a good crop.

Bad Beekeeping

It was time for me to begin the drive from the short-grass prairie of southwest Saskatchewan north to Tisdale. The day before leaving, I assembled new boxes for the hives, hammering inch and a quarter nails into pine boards. I worked late into the night, trying to finish five hundred new boxes before the bees would need space to hold new honey. I quit working before midnight, then slept four hours.

I began driving in the morning dawn, the dull red horizon to my right. I drove north from Val Marie towards Swift Current. I had adjusted my seat belt and the mirror. Turned on the CBC. I gazed ahead into long shadows. Suddenly a floppy-eared deer stood on the highway, eyes blinded by my headlights. I slammed on my brakes, was almost stopped when the radiator grill of my Dodge wrinkled into the animal. I had not gone thirty kilometres from home and I had struck a mule deer. But, apparently, little damage was done to doe or truck. The animal staggered backwards; suddenly awake. I, too, was suddenly awake. I climbed out of the truck. The deer and I stood ten feet apart, each wondering why the other had chosen this moment, this place to meet. The deer was disgusted by my rudeness. She staggered to the road's edge, jumped across the ditch and vanished into the predawn murkiness. She left me standing, shaken, beneath the stars, the blood-red morning sun.

There were no other accidents as I drove from Val Marie to Swift Current. But I kept thinking about the rare coincidence that could bring two creatures together. We had a hundred kilometres of isolation to share; a half dozen hours of night to hide from one another. Yet, we met. Another unlikely meeting would happen at this same spot, nine years later. It would not be so innocent.

It was after five when I skirted around the edge of Swift Current and began traveling the nearly deserted Trans-Canada Highway, east towards Regina. I reached the capital in three hours. A loop road around Regina helped me miss what Saskatchewan calls an eight o'clock rush hour. North of Regina, on the road to Tisdale, stood a Husky truck stop. My first stop since the deer. I stretched, ate pancakes and bacon and eggs. Drank coffee. I paid three dollars for breakfast, ten for gasoline, and drove on.

The scenery changed. Trees. I missed the forests of the east. Here, in the Saskatchewan parkland, groves of poplar trees separated farms. The trees had a soft spring glow, baby green leaves quaked in the slight morning breeze. The grass was tall, thick, dark. The lush land rolled gently. Farmers seeded huge fields of black soil. The fertile black earth of the parkland, far north of Val Marie, supports a wide variety of crops. The dirt around Val Marie was pale brown, except in a few places along the river. Southwest Saskatchewan was hot and dry; the soil brown and weak. Not suitable for much other than wheat. Only the fertile river valley supported alfalfa and clover.

Much of the rich earth north of Regina sprouted small plants that looked like cabbages. Rapeseed, canola. Canola produces tiny black seeds that millers crush into cooking oil. For a month each summer, twelve million acres of canola brandish yellow nectar-producing flowers. During the 1970's, ten thousand tonnes of honey came from the rapeseed blossoms on the Canadian prairies. But a hundred times as much honey was lost because there were not enough bees in the country to visit all the flowers.

Into the Land of Rape and Honey

Wasted food. Each year, millions of pounds of honey dripped out of those flowers to the ground or evaporated into the air, forever gone.[15]

An hour north of Regina, the ground turned black as tar. And looked as thick and heavy. Farm houses and farm yards shone with cleanliness. New trucks and big tractors parked themselves proudly on paved driveways near quonset sheds. This was clearly a wealthier place than Val Marie. Many years earlier, my father had taken me to Ohio to deliver tomatoes we had picked on our Pennsylvania farm. I noticed big houses and new cars. As he drove along, my father pointed to the black soil. "People here are no better or smarter than the people where we live. Except they happen to live here, where the soil is better. When you see nice houses, study the land. It's not the people who made themselves rich. Their land. Their land did it for them."

A big, colourful sign greeted my entrance to the town of Tisdale - a billboard with a grain elevator, a hill covered in yellow flowers, and a skep beehive. Big block letters across the bottom of the billboard proclaimed: "Tisdale – Land of Rape and Honey." Perhaps the local chamber of commerce thought the sign was a cute way to introduce their town to the world. It is certainly memorable. But rape is the out-dated word for *canola*, its genetically altered offspring. Canola grows a bit like turnips, *rapus* in Latin. When *rapus* was a minor specialty crop, rapeseed oil was sold in a few health food stores. Now that it had become a billion dollar business, the same stuff was labeled canola oil. [16]

I reached Tisdale shortly after noon. The beekeepers' meeting would start at two. I drove around the town, looking for evidence that this town of rape and honey would soon host a bee meeting. I passed St. Paul's United

I am Welcomed to Tisdale:
"The Land of Rape and Honey"

Church, Jake's Bait and Tackle. A big warehouse with a sign - The Honey Co-op – indicated the place members traded honey for beekeeping supplies. Then I found the town hall. A cluster of four-wheel drive trucks, some with flat wooden decks, indicated a beekeepers gathering.

I parked on the street, half a block from the hall. Walked up six unpainted cement steps to a set of double doors held ajar by a chair. It took a moment for my eyes to adjust to the dim lighting. I began to see Beekeepers. Mostly tall, thin, young. Healthy looking folks. Jeans, cowboy hats, hiking boots, long-sleeved blue and grey shirts were everywhere. Clean shaven, except for two gentlemen with beards. Caps proclaimed "Bee Maid Honey," and "John Deere." A hundred men, only a dozen women. More people entered from the doors behind me. I did not know any of these beekeepers; I felt awkward as folks were gathered in chatty clusters while I was an obstacle on the floor that new arrivals darted around as they waved towards old friends and called their names.

Bad Beekeeping

A loud voice invited us to find seats. Our meeting started with a slide show. The chief apiary inspector, Ed Bland, spoke. The bee inspector's job is to look into people's beehives and check for bee diseases. The inspector also enforces laws dealing with buying and selling beekeeping equipment. Ed Bland was an important person.

Two hundred beekeeping folks sat in uncomfortable silence, waiting for the first slide. They had been to these meetings before; they knew what the first few slides would be about. I looked around. To me, it seemed everyone had grown much too quiet. The first picture flashed up on the screen. Then I understood the hushed anticipation. Ed Bland started his meetings by showing a few slides of someone's honey farm. He did not show the best farms. He brought pictures of the worst. Places where buildings needed paint. Where old rusty barrels leaned against the outside walls of rugged wooden sheds. Where beehives were stacked carelessly, in need of mending. If possible, Ed Bland would include one or two shots from inside the poor beekeeper's warehouse. Usually the audience would get to see floors messy with spilt honey. By the time the second and third slide flashed up on the big screen, people were breathing again. They had not been the one selected as a bad example. Not this year, anyway.

Ed Bland took the issue of honey house cleanliness very seriously.

"One of the best answers to an untidy, unsanitary extracting set-up would be to get the man out of the extracting plant and put a tidy, neat, authoritative woman in charge," claimed Ed Bland. "I maintain that women have a penchant or inclination towards tidyness and cleanliness. It is both part of their nature and part of their training."[17] I was shocked. People don't say things like that - not in public, anyway.

I studied Ed Bland's face. He looked pretty old to me, but what did I know? I was barely past my teens. Ed was probably only sixty. Thin. With a wise and wrinkly face. Years earlier, I'd heard of him, read some of the things he had written in beekeeping journals – how to build up huge colonies from packages[18] and how many empty boxes a strong hive needs in mid-summer.

After the slide show, but before the real beekeeping stuff started, someone decided we should have some fun. A game. A quiz contest of sorts, with beekeeping trivia. Two small teams battled their wits with things like bee anatomy and types of bee equipment used in remote parts of the world. "Skeps!" "Hive boles!" and "Vases – clay vases!"

People were relaxing, laughing, spilling coffee from little styrofoam cups onto the oak floor. I was not competing, I was sitting in the back, listening. The one topic that seemed most exciting was the least important. Contestants had to name as many famous beekeepers as they could in two minutes.

This was an exciting time for beekeepers. For over twenty years - from the late forties into the seventies - people who made honey had been poor. Honey sold for ten cents a pound. Big commercial bee farms grossed only twenty or thirty thousand dollars, as late as 1972. Beekeepers kept bees because they loved the insects, not because it was a short-cut to riches. They often held another job and gave the bee business their spare time and spare cash. Then honey prices started going up. Fast. Very fast. By 1975, honey sold for fifty cents a pound. The same depressed businesses were suddenly grossing a hundred and fifty thousand dollars. Beekeepers spent money. More beehives were built, new warehouses. People bought cars, perhaps for the first time ever. Houses were remodeled.

This excitement spilled over to the game played at the Tisdale meeting that afternoon. As beekeepers shouted out the names of famous people who had kept bees, there was a sense of arrival, a sense that we, too, were famous and important people.

"The actor, the actor... Henry Fonda!"

"Sir Edmund Hillary!"

"Aristotle, Pythagoras...."

The next two minutes were like this. Beekeepers struggling to identify themselves with important people. A catharsis for some. After years of existence as strange adults playing with bugs, these folks now felt in good company. And they were making good money.

The game ended and the meeting began. We listened to expert beekeepers. After two hours of discussion about raising queens in Saskatchewan and techniques for successfully wintering bees, a panel of experienced beekeepers answered questions from the audience. My own question had not yet been asked. All talk was about wintering bees (indoors, in climate-controlled sheds), raising queens (feed the bees extra pollen in March), honey prices (high, and going higher). I found myself shy and uneasy in this big crowd of important people, but I wanted their expert advice.

When my raised hand was acknowledged, I felt too awkward to stand. I stayed in my seat, face flushing. "How late in the spring can packages be brought up from America?" *from America?* Why did I say *America*? I had been living in Canada for two months. I had never heard anyone call the States, *America*.

The first person on the panel smiled knowingly. "You can bring bees in from the States any time of the year," he said. Everyone laughed.

"I mean," I said, "So the bees will catch up with wintered hives and make a good crop."

The fellow answering my question did not look unkind. He had a friendly face. Bushy dark hair, a full mustache. He looked about thirty and very much in charge. "Package bees will never catch up with wintered bees," he said. More laughter, but restrained. I was being eaten alive and did not even know it. Fewer people chuckled now, some were apparently sympathetic towards the foolish young man from America.

A lanky fellow stood up. "I only use packages. Never have much luck with wintered bees. Try to get them in by mid-April, you'll do fine..." He said this in a gentle voice, then sat down. People shuffled their feet. Moments later, the meeting ended. People stood, stretched.

Another chatty circle formed, this time around me. A long-haired blond man and his pretty wife introduced themselves to me. "You really stepped into the lion's den, welcome to Canada," Steve said. He invited me to supper with his wife and some friendly looking beekeepers. While we were talking, Ed Bland approached and asked if we could speak together, alone.

"You're buying the Andres' business, down in Val Marie?" he asked me.

"Yea," I said.

Bad Beekeeping

"I don't think you should," Saskatchewan's chief apiarist said. My mouth felt dry. *Why not?* Were the bees full of diseases? Was Val Marie outside an approved beekeeping area? What was the kindly, old bee inspector trying to warn me about? I said nothing.

"I'd rather see a Canadian buy that farm," he continued. "We already have enough Americans keeping bees in Saskatchewan."

"I think Frank tried to sell to a Canadian," I said. "He advertised. No one made any offers."

"Well," said Ed. Bland, "what does that tell you about his business?" Saskatchewan's chief apiary inspector walked away. He retired that summer. I never spoke to him again.

At supper that night, Steve clued me in on the politics of beekeeping in Saskatchewan. In Val Marie, I had been living my life and working my bees in a social vacuum. I was in a remote, unsettled part of the province, the only commercial beekeeper for two hundred kilometres, the only commercial beekeeper in the southwest corner of Saskatchewan. The other sixty thousand hives of bees in the province were in the north. I had been blissfully and peacefully working my bees without realizing that a war was raging among beekeepers in distant parts of the province.

"*Package* is a dirty word," said Steve over a bowl of steamed vegetables and egg noodles. I sat among a small group of beekeepers occupying a large table at the Smoking Dragon. "Package bees used to cost beekeepers eight bucks," Steve continued. "New queen bees were a dollar. That was only three years ago. Now prices are three or four times that. Saskatchewan beekeepers are trying to winter their bees, they see it as a patriotic statement, a way to demonstrate independence from pushy, greedy American bee salesmen – plus, of course, they think it'll save them some money."

A small man across the table said, "If an American had invented the wheel, some Canadians would rather walk. Of course, other Canadians would open tire stores and get rich. But we'd all complain about American tire companies."

"Package is a dirty word. "American" is another," Steve's wife added. She had a relaxed smile, wore a loose poncho, and kept her long brown hair pulled back into a pony tail. "People here think Americans are going to move in and harvest all their honey, ehhh?" She exaggerated the 'eh'. I guessed she was also an American.

"We both are. So is Jack Charen's wife. And the Kings, they're from California. Matt Freisen is from Minnesota. And there are a lot of beekeepers here from Holland - the Bolts, the Vandens, the Groots. Some others - like Derek Alen - are from England. I think the beekeepers who were born here feel out-numbered sometimes."

From Tisdale, I drove further north, then west towards Big River. Number 3 Highway was wide and new. It took me through Prince Albert, called P.A. by people who live in P.A.; the town was gorgeous, built on steep green-forested hills that dropped down to the North Saskatchewan River. A city of trees. It was an old town, begun as a fur trading post two hundred years earlier. But after its early start, it did not grow fast. About thirty thousand folks lived in P.A.

Into the Land of Rape and Honey

I stopped to get some oil and a tire pump. My front right wheel was slowly leaking air. I'd had the truck in a garage twice, but we weren't able to figure out where to patch the tire. Upon climbing out of my truck, I understood one of the reasons why P.A. was not attracting a lot of new settlers. The air stank. It was foul. Wretchedly foul. The rank odour, I was told, came from a huge paper mill a few kilometres down river. "It doesn't usually smell this bad," the man at the Canadian Tire said, "except when we get an east wind. And whenever we get an east wind, we get rain – that clears the acid out of the air pretty fast." I was doubtful.

I left P.A., continued on Number 3 to Shellbrook. From there, it was another hour north to the Emdes' home. I needed to see Earl and Josephine Emde, to make arrangements to buy some of Earl's beekeeping equipment. But I also enjoyed their friendship. They were kindly and gracious hosts. And the Emdes were interesting people. They had traveled the world, and Earl sure knew a lot about beekeeping. I was eager to visit them.

It began to drizzle. I drove in the cold, light rain, past more canola fields and scattered patches of alfalfa. The scenery was changing again. There were fewer farms, more bush. Swamps of tamarack and hills with scrubby pine replaced some of the quivering poplar trees. Most of the country was still virgin aspen forest, some recently cleared by homesteaders. Bulldozers had gleaned the trees from the black earth and piled logs and stumps in huge windrows where the wood rotted and remnants were later burned. Between the rows of fallen trees, farmers scooped massive boulders into buckets attached to their John Deere and Belarus tractors. Within a year or two, the new ground would be tilled and planted into canola. Saskatchewan was turning forest into field; a thousand acres of new farmland every day. Planted into honey-producing alfalfa and canola, Saskatchewan could add thirty thousand new hives of bees a year to collect nectar from these new fields.

The highway was paved to Debden, but I still had another thirty kilometres. Beyond Debden, the road turned into dirt and gravel, slippery from the rain. Farmers and truckers hurled mud and gravel at my windshield. They approached me from the north and hugged the center of the slippery road until we nearly collided, slowing and easing to the opposite side an instant before we passed. I reached a construction site. All traffic was stopped. The road was being widened and packed and made ready for paving. But near the spot where traffic was being held, a ditch had been dug across the road. I watched as the trucks ahead of mine were made ready for the murky trip through the ditch. Highway workers hooked huge chains on the front bumpers of the travelers' vehicles and caterpillar tractors jerked them and their passengers across the void. When it was my turn, my truck slid sideways and bounced hard, but arrived on the other side, bumper still attached to frame. Ten minutes from the Emdes'.

But first, I had to drive through Big River. The frontier town stood beside a small dam that turned the narrow sinuous Cowan River into a long and skinny lake. For decades, farmers worked in the bush during the winter - cutting timber, hauling it to the frozen lake. In the spring, the logs floated downstream to Big River's saw mills. The mills still operate, but by the seventies, lumber was delivered by truck. It was a mill town, though other commerce was trying to eclipse Big River's forestry business. Merchants bought fish and wild rice from the natives; mechanics fixed bulldozers and farm tractors; stores provided groceries, clothes, beer. Some of the streets were paved, but mud slopped everywhere. It fell off my truck in great clumps and was smeared along the street. The rain continued. Big River, at first sight, was dismal.

Earl and his wife, Josephine, were beekeepers. Seventy years old. They had come up to Big River fifteen years earlier. "To retire," Earl had told me. Some retirement. They bought property along Cowen Lake, on the north edge of Big River. Flower gardens surrounded the house they built on their estate. Retired. But Earl still produced a hundred thousand pounds of Saskatchewan honey every summer. And each fall, he and Josephine drove a big truck to Apopka, Florida, where he raised thousands of queen bees and produced fresh packages for his Canadian farm. In Florida, he was a well-known and highly regarded queen breeder. He wrote for the bee journals[19] and he trained beekeepers from around the world in the art of queen rearing.

The Emde's Home
Big River, Saskatchewan

Until their move to Canada, Earl had five thousand hives of bees in the Dakotas. He moved those hives to Florida each winter. He and his sons had figured out how to strap hives to pallets and move the pallets of beehives with forklifts. Before that, all beekeepers in the world moved their hives by hand – lifting the heavy boxes on trucks, one at a time. By the late fifties, highways and trucks were getting better and migratory beekeeping was becoming common. Forklifts hit the market. The Emdes may have been the first to put these things together; hundreds of other beekeepers caught on within a few years. Soon, millions of beehives maneuvered through the swamps and groves of the south – Florida, Texas, California – to the clover fields of New York, Wisconsin, the

Dakotas. North in the spring; south in the fall.[20] Earl Emde and his sons David, Mark, and Tom pioneered this whole system.[21]

Earl had worked with bees for nearly sixty years. Still a teenager when he left Whittier, California, he already had a few hundred hives. Earl never finished high school; got too busy, he said. A classmate of his at Whittier High was Richard Nixon. Nixon, the one elected president of the debating club became president of the United States. Earl remained a beekeeper. There were other differences – when Earl Emde went to the Soviet Union in the 1970's, it was to study how the Russians produced honey. Richard Nixon went, not to learn, but to reprimand. Sliding through the muck on that north Saskatchewan highway, I wondered what the world would have been like if Earl had been president, and Richard had kept bees.

Earl was my role model. At a Florida bee meeting, people whispered to me that Earl was a millionaire - made all his money from beekeeping, nothing else. Earl himself once told me that he could go into any store, any time, anywhere, and buy anything he wanted. I realized that meant he had money; but also it meant that he never really wanted anything. Earl was frugal. He lived simply on home grown vegetables and slept comfortably in a modest home. Except for his habit of traveling the globe and supporting his church, he spent little money. I admired his austerity.

**Earl and Josephine Emde,
Fifty Years Together**

I also admired how Earl kept himself fresh and alert by turning his world upside-down every few years. After his start in southern California, Earl and Josephine had kept bees in Oregon, then Nebraska, South Dakota. Then Florida and North Dakota. They hauled several semi-loads of bees to Florida each winter. Their business grew. Earl owned five thousand hives of bees, made a million pounds of honey each year. He became middle-aged, had adult sons. Earl felt the urge to start over again. Something small. No hired help. A new part of the world, a frontier somewhere. He found his spot a thousand kilometres north of the States, in Saskatchewan's bush country, along a narrow river teeming with beaver and loons. At age seventy, Earl now had only five hundred hives of bees, a mere hobby compared to his previous scale. He wanted to let some go. Again.

Josephine met me at the door. "Ron!" Her arms reached for me. Josephine had beautiful hair. White and shiny. She smiled and shook my hand, hugged me again. "Welcome to Big River!" She was as happy to see me as I was to see a friendly, familiar face. "Earl is in the bees. He'll be back by five, unless he's totally rained out. You hungry?"

41

Bad Beekeeping

I was always hungry. I was twenty-three years old. Josephine brought out spinach and asparagus from the garden. And tiny orange carrots, steamed. Her house smelled like a home, she had baked a seedy bread cake and offered it to me as dessert.

"You guys weren't at the beekeepers' meeting in Tisdale yesterday?"

"Yesterday was Saturday," she said. "We were in church. Was it a good meeting?"

"Sort of, I guess. There were a lot of people there. Mostly talked about wintering bees."

"Earl wintered some hives last year. Two yards, I think. I don't know how they're doing." She looked at the window towards the lake. "Looks like it quit raining. Want to take out our canoe?"

Josephine led me out through the basement, finding a yellow life-preserver vest. She had me put it on even before we got near the water. Two canoes were lying, inverted, on lawn grass that was mowed to the lake's edge.

"Take the smaller canoe," Josephine said. "The paddles are under it."

I was alone on the lake. For two hours. I crossed its narrow width to the opposite side, worked my way to a heron's nest. Birds scolded me and I retreated. I drifted mid-lake for a long time, the only human within a mile. *How much does anyone really need?* It occurred to me then that it would be nice to share the canoe, the lake, with someone.

Lynn, in a Pennsylvania Field of Buckwheat, 1976

I'd had a girl friend, a year earlier. Lynn had three hives of bees on the family acreage, next to an organic garden and a pit where she grew earthworms. Lynn was a petite and very pretty girl with long brown hair. Didn't smoke; didn't drink; didn't cuss. Smiled an awful lot.

Lynn helped me with my bees when I'd kept about three hundred hives in Pennsylvania, north of Pittsburgh. She helped me super hives in the huckleberry swamp where I'd kept twenty colonies, and in the middle of a huge buckwheat field where thirty (somewhat aggressive) colonies of bees bounced against our veils when we removed the reddish-black buckwheat honey from those hives.

She was a sweet girl. But her church had taught her that "unequal oxen can't be yoked together, the righteous and the unrighteous." I couldn't accept her beliefs, the ones that included Garner Ted Armstrong, a World Wide Church of God, and claims that the ten lost tribes of Israel had been discovered in England by Garner Ted's dad, the living prophet Herbert W. Armstrong.[22] I couldn't believe this; or anything else - I really had no religion. And Lynn couldn't forsake the things God had revealed to her family through the Armstrongs.

It all seemed trivial as I floated along the shore of that cold northern lake. Lynn was a perfect match six days a week; but not the seventh. I could have pretended to believe, but instead I argued my case and went away, leaving her in peace. And me alone. The last time I saw her, she had helped me load three hundred hives of bees in Pennsylvania. She waved goodbye as angry bees batted her veil, then she walked to her car and left. I fired up my truck and drove south, towards Florida.

The air grew chilly. I glided back across the reservoir, past willows that grew in the water, then I spotted the wooden dock at the Emdes' home. I pulled the canoe to the grassy shore, hid the paddles under the boat, walked the hundred paces back to the front of the house, was barely in the door when I heard a truck pull up.

Cowan Lake from my Canoe. The Emde Home is Far Ahead, on the Right.

"Earl is here now," Josephine said. She was in the kitchen, chopping carrots. Earl entered his house through the basement, where I met him as he hung up his coveralls and changed out of his mud-covered boots, pulling slippers over his socks. "Ron!" He shook my hand. "You should have been here this morning, you could have been in the bees with me all day! Tomorrow, for sure?"

We went up the steps to the main floor of the house. Earl and Josephine led me to the living room where I sat on their huge couch and looked out the picture window at Cowan Lake. It had begun to drizzle again, but through the misty rain, a gorgeous view of placid blue water, framed by green hills, filled our glass-lined view of the world. Near the middle of the lake, where I had been half an hour earlier, a beaver made a small water trail. Earl pointed it out to me.

"A lot of animals here - moose, bear..." said Earl.

"And Loons," added Josephine and she made a playful trill that sounded like the bird.

"How's David?" Earl asked. The Emdes knew my oldest brother well. During the winter months, they lived in the same part of Florida. There were only a few beekeepers in central Florida in the early sixties when my brother David showed up to raise queens. Earl also produced queen bees. And packages. Earl brought his own bees to northern Saskatchewan every spring, all the way from Florida. He would make a big crop of honey, kill the bees in the fall so he wouldn't have to feed them, wrap them with insulation, re-queen them, or worry about them for six months. Then he'd go back to Florida to raise more bees and queens for the next season. It was Earl who'd told me that Frank Andres was trying to sell his bee farm in Val Marie. Earl had introduced us when Frank was in Florida buying packages two years earlier. Earl told me he had some money invested in Frank's business. Frank wanted out, but couldn't find anyone to buy his operation. Earl found a buyer. Me.

"You went to the meeting in Tisdale." Earl told me.

"Yea, it was pretty interesting."

"Ed Bland called me

Ron with Earl and Josephine

last night. He said we shouldn't be selling to you. He said you are not a nice person, not very diplomatic. You need to watch how you talk to people, Ron." I stood before Earl, my mouth hanging open. *What had I said to anger Ed Bland?* And now Earl was upset. But Earl wasn't scolding me. I felt he was offering fatherly advice. I apologized, but was unsure how I might improve my behavior. I hadn't realized I was pushy and arrogant. "You know," Earl told me, "I've lived here fifteen years and a lot of my neighbours don't even know I'm American. They think I'm from Ontario, or something. You want people to think you're from Ontario, too, Ron."

"How about B.C. I like B.C. better."

Earl was not amused. "Are you missing my point?" he asked.

Into the Land of Rape and Honey

"I understand you," I said. "Do you still want to sell me some of your equipment?" I asked Earl.

"Of course," said Earl, "You're a good beekeeper even if Ed Bland doesn't like you."

We made an arrangement, that evening in the living room with the big window and the glorious view of the lake with its beavers. Earl would sell me enough brood chambers, stocked with honey and pollen, to start four hundred more hives. I wouldn't be picking up the equipment that I was buying until fall - Earl would use it all one more summer. I would then haul the bee boxes south to Val Marie in September.

The next morning we walked through Earl's honey shed. A simple building. Much concrete - loading docks, floors, basement, all made from cement. Wooden walls and wood siding. The wood was gathered from the Big River sawmill. Earl cut and planed it, hand-built the trusses, framed the windows and doors. Then he painted it white with red trim. Most beekeepers were building sterile steel sheds. But wood was the right material for a honey shop sitting on the shore of Cowan Lake.

Earl showed me his extracting equipment. His machinery only had a few moving parts. There was simplicity, symmetry, and organization in his operation. Boxes full of honey combs had wax cappings scratched off. Combs were loaded into a centrifuge, the extractor, which held the frames upright. Gravity pulled thousands of pounds of fresh honey through pipes to a big reservoir in the basement. From there it was pumped back up into a huge tank on the main floor. When the tank was full, Earl wheeled drums under the tank and tapped the honey into barrels.

I opened the lid to the extractor. It could hold fifty deep frames. About four hundred pounds of honey could be separated from the combs each time Earl loaded the machine. A switch turned on a motor. The motor rotated a rubber belt. The belt looped around a pulley at the top of the extractor. A shaft down the center of the machine turned as the pulley and belt turned. The shaft was bolted to a metal cage that held the honey combs. When the motor ran, the metal cage whirled around and honey sprayed against the walls of the extractor. Then it drained down through the pipes to the collecting tank in the basement of Earl's honey house.

"It's so simple," I said.

"Has to be," said Earl. "If I had equipment that wasn't simple, eventually it would break. No one in Big River would be able to fix it. So I'd have to order parts from Toronto or Los Angeles or somewhere. Do you know how long it would take to get repair parts in? Meanwhile, I'd lose thousands of pounds of honey because I wouldn't be getting the boxes emptied and returned to the hives on time."

Here I was, in the best beekeeping place in the world, and the equipment that handled the honey was simple and inexpensive. Elegantly unsophisticated. Earl did not use anything more advanced than a couple of electric motors. Beekeepers in other parts of the world might make a quarter as much honey using much more complicated tools. I liked Earl's system. I did not have a mechanically adept mind. His operation was easy to understand, operate, maintain. Even for someone like me.

Bad Beekeeping

I offered to help Earl put honey boxes – supers - on his hives. To put supers on, we had to wheel empty honey boxes out of his shed and onto his truck. I thought about the idea of extracting all the honey that these boxes might hold. The boxes were now empty, except for raw wax comb. Filled, they would hold thousands of pounds of honey. Bees gather nectar from flowers, one mouthful at a time. Beekeepers put the honey into barrels, one drop at a time. Handling thousands of honey boxes, tens of thousands of honeycombs. All that work. Simply to get enough honey to pay enough bills to be able to keep bees again the next year.

Almost all the honey that a beekeeper makes and sells starts out as a fluid. The bees bring watery nectar to their hive, reduce it to liquid honey, packed into wax cells. Beekeepers don't strain the fluid honey from the wax combs – it is whirled out.

The idea of an extractor is relatively new. About a hundred years before I arrived in Saskatchewan, the Austrian beekeeper Franz von Hruschka thought of the technique. He was watching his favourite milk maiden returning from the barn, swinging her milk buckets. As she walked, the pretty girl swung those milk jugs around and around. Franz was fascinated. Spellbound. The buckets were upside down, then right side up, then upside down - and not a drop of milk spilled out. At this moment the extractor was invented. If centrifugal force could push the liquid against the bottom of the bucket while it spun, would the same force push liquid honey out of a comb?

Franz cut a chunk of comb honey and centered it in an empty bucket.

**The 1883 Honey Extractor
- Less Fun than a Milkmaid's Bucket**

The girl whirled and whirled.

Apicultural historians report that the milk maiden and the beekeeper spent an enjoyable summer, spinning honey.

Maybe the milk maiden grew tired of the sport. Eventually, Franz von Hruschka built a machine to hold the combs in place. He attached a crank. He turned honey rendering into efficient, but hard work. But he invented a way to empty honeycombs so that the wax combs could be returned to the hive. This was a tremendous advantage to the honey producers and the bees. Until 1865, combs were always destroyed to get the honey, forcing bees to continually repair and rebuild their wax – suffering a great loss in efficiency and productivity. Thousands of others must have watched milk maidens swing their pails; von Hruschka was the first to connect this sight with the invention of a honey extractor.

Earl and I loaded four hundred and twenty boxes onto his truck. I stood on the ground, on the passenger side of the truck. One after another, Earl tossed long sisal ropes over the load. Each row needed a rope to keep the boxes in place for the trip along the Saskatchewan backroads to the apiaries.

Simple, practical inventions fascinated me. The extractor. Then the hook that looped Earl's sisal rope to the truck. People saw a problem, a need, a necessity, created a solution, sometimes with surprising results. Franz von Hruschka was not likely trying to find a way to package liquid honey - the idea leapt at him unexpectedly. For tens of thousands of years, humans chewed wax honeycombs whenever they wanted to eat honey. Or they smashed the combs, squeezed out the honey, and saved the wax to make candles.

Almost certainly the candle was invented in a similar way. Serendipitously. And almost certainly, it was invented by a cavewoman. Caveman sat with woman in front of the fire.

"Nice," says caveman. He pulls some burnt mammoth off the fire. "Where's the honeycomb?"

Cavewoman points out that it is right beside him. Any closer and he would be sitting in it. Caveman breaks off a piece. He bites and chews. It is good. Inspiration. Caveman has an idea. Meat tastes better after being burnt. Honey is very good. It will be even better burnt. He tosses a big chunk of honeycomb onto the fire. The wax ignites into a brilliant, white blaze. The honey melts free and disappears into the dirt and ashes. Gone. "Not good idea," says Caveman.

But Cavewoman thinks about that bright flash of light. She rolls a small handful of another honeycomb into a taper, touches one end to the fire and it burns brightly. She wanders off to the far end of the cave, candle in hand. For the first time in her life she can clearly find her way to bed without tripping over the bones and rocks in the middle of the dark cavern. She stops to move the rubbish. Civilization has made a great advance. Artificial light has suddenly extended normal working hours.

Earl was wondering why I was not in the truck. He was ready to go. I was thinking about Cavewoman. I got in. We drove south towards Debden, then east. We entered a pasture that belonged to Denis Jean. Earl quickly jumped from the truck and lifted lids from hive after hive. It reminded me of how my father would examine bees, except Dad was better at it. Dad would walk from hive to hive, placing his open palm on each hive's plywood lid. He showed me how the feel and sound of a hand against the hive told the beekeeper what each hive held. A tight contact meant that the hive was full of honey and needed another honey box. A hollow thud meant the hive was not making

Bad Beekeeping

much honey. A hollow thud accompanied by an angry buzz from the bees meant that the hive was doing poorly and probably had no queen. A hollow thud and absolutely no sound probably meant the hive was dead, or nearly so. Earl had no time for hive touching. He raced from hive to hive to hive and tore the lids off.

The bees at Denis Jean's were doing very well. They needed the empty honey boxes we had brought on the back of Earl's truck. It was my first view of hives in the far north. It seemed to be cool and it rained a lot in northern Saskatchewan, but these bees had filled their chambers and desperately needed more space to hold the honey that was coming in. The air was thick with flying insects. Earl grinned. He punctuated the air with a series of "Good Night!" and "Oh! Good Night!" exclamations as he saw bees overflow from the tops of the hives he had opened. (Good Night? – that was the way Earl cussed; it surprised and confused me the first time I heard the expression. I never heard Earl Emde use stronger language, but he certainly put a lot of energy into those two words.)

We stacked five and six honey boxes on top of each hive. The apiary grew tall, brushed tree branches. Earl had raced ahead to open all the hives, he told me, because it would keep the bees from attacking each other. If only one or two hives are open at a time, the undisturbed bees smugly sneak around looking for a chance to steal honey from the open, exposed hives. But as soon as all the lids are open, the bees have more immediate concerns and are less likely to begin robbing. That was likely true, but I suspected Earl was simply excited and wanted to quickly see how well all his hives were doing.

Earl Emde at the Denis Jean Beeyard, 1977

This apiary was fenced inside a cattle pasture. The ground was littered with dry, hard cow paddies. Halfway through the beeyard, Earl did something unexpected. Normally, as fuel for his bee smoker, Earl used sawdust and tiny scraps from wood that he turned into new beehives. But I caught him hefting a dry, hard cow paddy. He dropped it into his hot bee smoker. I gave him a puzzled look.

"You're wondering what I'm doing?" he said. He puffed the bellow vigorously, thick white smoke gushed from the bee smoker.

"Seems a bit weird," I said. "Why stick a cow pie in your smoker?"

"Well, reminds me of when I was a kid - a smell I don't get to enjoy, except a couple times a year."

"When you were a kid - you had a job burning manure?"

Into the Land of Rape and Honey

"No, I kept bees in the California desert. No trees, no wood, nothing to burn in the smoker except dried cow dung. Fifty years ago, I used this all the time." He breathed, his lungs ballooned out. He grinned. "Nothing like it."

Back in Big River, Earl introduced me to Clive Fetterman. At the time I was getting started in the honey business in southern Saskatchewan, this young beekeeper was also starting. Clive worked with his father in the north, near Blaine Lake. Clive was kind, generous, soft-spoken, polite. Earl told me that Clive worked slowly, carefully, diligently.

It was the perfect little things about Clive that were particularly nauseating. Some time later, I helped him with his bees. He wore a pith helmet and wire veil for six hours. At the end of the day, he took off his hat and revealed perfect hair. Worse, he did not sweat. Cool, calm, non-sticky. He could work in his father's honey shop all day, extract twenty barrels of honey, and his clothing would be completely clean. No dripping wax and honey coated his uniform. No dirt, dead bees, nor tree twigs clung to his khakis. If Clive had any faults at all, he hid them from people like me. So, it frustrated me immensely that he and his father could make a nice living messing with a few hives of bees, working only six days a week, and walking - not running - as they worked.

Clive had come up from Blaine Lake in the morning to deliver honey to the IGA. We sat in Rex's, eating rice, talking about beekeeping. Clive handed me a religious pamphlet, a little tract of Bible verses, born-again stuff, which I did not keep for long. He wanted to talk about it, I steered our conversation towards beekeeping.

Clive asked how much honey a beekeeper in the States might produce from a hive of bees. In Saskatchewan, with the huge fields of canola and alfalfa, the long sunny summer days, and the healthy, new soil, flowers were abundant and secreted much nectar. Bees were scarce and had much more food than almost anywhere else on earth. So, Saskatchewan hives of bees made two or three hundred pounds of honey a year.

I answered Clive's question. "In the States? About fifty or sixty pounds." Then I explained about geography, climate, and how a lot of the hives are not kept for honey, but are used only to pollinate crops. Other beekeepers raise queens for sale, they do not make honey from their hives. Averaged together, all these things result in the States having a much smaller honey yield. About twenty percent of a Saskatchewan crop.

I thought my new friend understood. "Well, maybe, Ron," Clive said. Clive stirred sugar into his coffee, bent his neatly kept head of hair forward. "But my guess is that Americans don't make as much honey as Canadians for another reason. Bad beekeeping. You guys just don't know how to keep bees as well as we do. It's not geography, it's bad beekeeping, don't you think?"

At about the same time, some American beekeepers journeyed through western Canada, looking at honey farms and beehives. They told me that they were surprised the Canadian colonies of bees were so weak at the start of the year. I explained that the colonies always look bad at the start of the season - they had survived eight months without fresh pollen or nectar and the bees were only starting to become active. These were smart Americans from California, they could understand what I said, but could not appreciate it. "If we kept bees that poorly, we'd go broke," they concluded. "If Canadians

Bad Beekeeping

kept bees as expertly as Americans have to keep bees in order to survive, they'd really be making some big crops." They shook their heads.

"Bad beekeeping," the shorter gentleman said, "is keeping you guys behind."

The words from Clive stung as did those of the touring Americans. They both manifested a truth. But it was not a truth about beekeeping at all. It was one of those broader truths about how we need to see ourselves and how we see our neighbours. How we go through life making judgments about each other based on things we know little about; how we live our lives comparing our insides to other peoples' outsides. It was a lesson I hadn't fully learned and didn't have time to discuss with my new friend Clive. I had to head on to Saskatoon. My brother Joe was waiting at the airport.

Partial of Sketch by Durer, 1500: Cupid does some Bad Beekeeping

Brother Joe

Honeybees in a colony are sisters. Elderly, grizzly-looking bees are only a few weeks older than their soft fuzzy siblings. But the elders have been flying out of the hive for days, collecting nectar and pollen, aging rapidly in the process. Meanwhile, woolly new sister bees are learning to walk. It will be a while before they test their wings. Old and young are the same generation. There are no grandparents, no wizened ancestors providing sage advice. Older bees are greasy and shiny, the soft fuzzy brown hairs of youth fallen out; flexible skin has become tight and hard.

Some of the old, experienced bees use their skills to scout for new sources of flowers. Weeds, bushes, trees. Anything growing in abundance and secreting an excess of nectar from easily accessed flowers. Scout bees may leave the home hive early in the morning, as the sun's heat begins to make the air comfortable for flying. Scouts fly for hours, tasting nectar from a variety of flowers, getting a sense of the density of the blossoms in the patch, the bounty's location. North? East? Two hundred meters? Caragana hedge? Alfalfa field? Willow trees? All is remembered, the information is brought back to the hive, shared with siblings who trust the news, then fly out to forage.

Joe was sitting on his suitcase, outside the *Arrivals* door at the Saskatoon airport. When he saw my truck, he jumped up and ran to the passenger door, throwing his bag into the truck box. He looked skinny. He moved quickly.

"Want to eat?" I asked him. We pulled into the Husky Truck Stop along the ring road, south of the airport.

"So, they let you into the country?"

Joe sat across from me in the booth at the truck stop. He ordered a hamburger, loaded. Fries. With ketchup.

I hadn't seen him for seven months, not since November, Thanksgiving, when I was last in Pennsylvania. His hair was turning from dirty blond to brown. He sat tall, confident. He didn't pick at the food on his plate the way I did, he ate it quickly, determined to finish the task at hand.

"No problem from the guys at the border?" I asked again.

"No," Joe said. "I told them I was going to be working on my brother's farm for the summer. One of the guys that let me in at Winnipeg said he has a brother keeping bees in Saskatchewan."

"Yea, beekeeping is a big business here. If you were going the other direction, into the States, to work for a beekeeper, they'd never believe you."

Joe nodded, kept stuffing in fries.

"How was Dad?" I asked.

Joe looked up from his plate, looked down again, then reached for his fork. "He was OK. He drove me to the airport in Pittsburgh."

"Did he give you any money or anything?"

"No." Joe looked away.

Bad Beekeeping

I wasn't surprised. Our father felt that by the time a person was old enough to hold a shovel, they were on their own. Dad had lived at home until his mid-twenties, then his father bought him a neighbouring farm. He'd been spoiled, and wanted to spare his ten kids a similar fate.

I was glad to see Joe.

"How is Florence?" I asked. Dad's wife. She had married our father two years after Mom died. We all agreed it was a good thing, at the time. Dad seemed happier, cut back on his drinking for a while.

"She doesn't say much. I didn't see her this morning, she was in the back of the greenhouse when Dad took me to the airport."

Joe's long skinny arm placed the fork back on the table. He took his hamburger, ate the last bit without looking up. I wondered how Joe felt, so far west, traveling alone on the plane. In another country. "What do you think, so far?" I asked.

"Can't say," said Joe, using his fork as a toothpick. "Haven't seen anything much yet."

After we ate, we hit the road, heading south of Saskatoon. In no time, the grain elevators of Elrose were in sight. "How far are those?" I asked. A trick question. Joe had arrived from Pennsylvania where the air was thick with smog.

"Two miles." He guessed.

"Nope," I said. "Nine."

Joe, Getting a Better View of the Grasslands

The sun glared down from high above us, a single point of light. Everything we saw stood out in sharp, crisp, two dimensional focus. The edge of the sky did not blend into grain elevators. Grain elevators did not blend into earth. Earth remained separate from sky. Everything distinct, sharp and clear.

The only exception to the clarity was the occasional water-mirage on the highway. The heat, the pavement, and the dry air created phantom water puddles on the road. These formed and dissolved, then formed again.

Brother Joe

"Dad was feeling OK?" I asked.

"I guess so." Joe tapped open the glove box, dug for a map.

"Didn't he have enough work for you on the farm?"

"Yea, there's lots of work. I finished rebuilding his old geranium house the day before I left. We planted about ten acres of tomatoes. I don't know how he'll get it all picked."

"Still drinking?"

Joe took a big breath.

"Oh, yea."

After five hours of guessing distances and driving through mirages, we reached the hill north of Val Marie. I had been gone for five days. I wanted to look at my hives before reaching the house. We drove west six kilometres, to the beeyard with the difficult gate. Joe unhitched it easily, using part of the rope as a pulley, giving him an edge with the gate that I hadn't figured out. I drove through. I touched a few lids, then, without using a smoker, carefully lifted the cover off a hive that I guessed would be doing well. It was. The bees had added new white bridge comb between the frames. A sign of prosperity. The late afternoon air was thick with bees. The honey flow was on!

We drove into Val Marie. Barely stopped at the house to offload Joe's bag, then ran up to the extracting shed. I pulled the old Ford up to the cement loading dock. It was time to take the first honey supers out to the hives. We carted the honey boxes, eight wax combs in each, onto the truck's wooden deck. Stacked the supers one on another, into piles eight high. Four stacks across the width of the truck. Eleven rows back. Three hundred and fifty-two honey supers, enough for two beeyards. It was late in the afternoon, but it was only slowly growing dark.

"We'll wait until morning to put the boxes out," I said. Joe looked like he had energy. Had it been his choice, we might have driven to the bees in the dark to continue working.

We were both hungry. I had nothing except eggs, canned soup, some potatoes, spaghetti, and ketchup in the house. Wong's was still open. I took Joe for his first Val Marie meal. He ordered a hamburger, loaded. Fries. With ketchup. I took the broccoli and fried rice. Two girls with long straight hair and Prairie Dog blazers sat beside us. I'd seen them before, but didn't know them.

"Got a cigarette?" one asked.

"Don't smoke," I answered.

They got up and left. Joe said they were cute. I shrugged. Certainly not Lynn-caliber. Harry brought the bill.

He stood before us, smiling, waiting for money.

I studied Harry's face, his short black hair. "You're from China?" I asked Harry.

"Oh, no. Canadian. Born in Moose Jaw. My father, mother, they was Chinese. They come here to work, like you, eh?"

I glanced at our dinner bill. It didn't look right. He had undercharged me. Harry Wong sat with us, went through the bill. He apologized, made the correction, thanked me.

Bad Beekeeping

"Never good with numbers," Harry said. He looked at Joe, "What you think about Canada?"

Joe wiped the last fry through his ketchup.

"Can't say," said Joe, using his fork as a toothpick. "Haven't seen anything much yet."

I was pretty tired. Joe sat in the tiny living room on my old couch. I had no TV, but the radio was on. Joe's bare feet pointed towards my chair. I noticed a scar across his right sole. I asked.

Joe, Child-Labourer
on the Farm in Pennsylvania

"You don't remember this?" Joe held his foot straight, giving me a clear view.

I'd forgotten.

"I stepped on glass, out near the barn." A moth clamored her wings against the window, trying to join us in the dimly lit livingroom. "Same summer Mom died. You and Dad took me to the hospital." Joe looked incredulous. "You really don't remember?"

He continued. "You picked me up and ran into the house..." I thought back to when Joe was ten. I remembered. Blood gushing from the deep gash. I was in such a hurry that I banged Joe's foot against the door, spraying more blood, making Joe scream again.

Joe brought his foot down, out of sight. "At the hospital, you and Dad got into a big fight. Dad kept saying that I wouldn't be able to go in the pond all summer because I was so careless." Dusk slid in the window, Joe's face grew dark. "You told Dad to shut up. When we got home, you guys argued all over again. You said it wasn't my fault I'd cut myself. He said I was careless. He said the hospital bill was eighty dollars."

I looked at Joe – so young, skinny. It wasn't that long ago. Why had I forgotten so much?

The next day, driving out to the bees, we continued our conversation. Joe said, "I went looking for the glass." We were still listening to CKSW, I turned the radio down. The truck bounced through a ditch, up to the hay meadow where my bees sat. "I wanted to find the glass and throw it away before someone else got cut. Halfway between the barn and the house, I found a bloody, broken beer bottle." Joe reached for the truck's door handle. "Had to be Dad's. No one else drank."

We stacked supers on hives for three days. I would lift a lid, then announce "Four" or "Five," even "Six" if I thought the hive was really strong. Stronger hives - colonies with more bees - make more honey. Five shallow supers could hold one hundred twenty pounds of honey. The hives were bearded, that is, there were so many bees in the two storey hives the excess population sat at the hives' porches, covered the fronts of the hives, brown beards on square white faces. Hives like these could easily fill five boxes. Joe ran back and forth from the truck, putting the right number of empty supers on the inverted lids I had set beside each hive. I lifted the supers, one at a time, eased them on the hives, and spaced their combs evenly. It took less than five minutes to take care of each hive, then replace the lids. Joe delivered boxes quickly - faster than I could stack and adjust the frames.

The bees would need three weeks to fill the supers. Three weeks for the bees to be left on their own, gathering honey. Three weeks for Joe and me to build more equipment. Clean the honey shed. Explore Val Marie.

Joe, Stacking Supers on Bearded Hives

So far, Joe had been in Saskatchewan one week. Now I had a chance to show him a good time. A big celebration - a homecoming in Val Marie. Canada Day. I told him we were taking part of Tuesday off to hang out downtown.

There would be a parade. Val Marie's main street was paved. Lucky thing. It made the parade go by more smoothly.

Bad Beekeeping

In 1905, when Saskatchewan became a province, Val Marie didn't even exist. Fifty years before the province had a name, the Palliser Scientific Expedition struggled across the badlands near Val Marie and declared the whole area unfit for agriculture and settlement.[23] Too dry. Too isolated. Too windy. On the Expedition's advice, southwest Saskatchewan stayed wild for a long time – it had been scientifically described as an uninhabitable desert. But a few isolated ranch houses survived along the river valleys, seasonal homes for rich Americans who brought cows in from Montana. The animals would eat Canadian grass all summer, then the cowboys herded them south for winter.

When Saskatchewan became a province of Canada, it was less than twenty-five years after Sitting Bull led the Sioux into the valley of the Frenchman River, seeking refuge from the revenge of the American cavalry. In 1910, Father Passaplan, Louis Denniel, and the brothers François and Léon Pinel founded the village of Val Marie. Valley of Mary. Most of the early settlers were ranchers and farmers from Quebec and France. A few years later, the government decided to give away small chunks of prairie to anyone without enough sense to move on. Serbian lumberjacks, Norwegian fishermen, and English machinists turned over the sod and built little stone, grass, and wood houses with dirt floors. And the French Canadians kept coming. The French dominated the Val Marie culture. They built extensive houses, filled them with children, erected a tall church, a school, hospital, convent. Somewhere along the way, the government added a railroad, an irrigation system, police barracks. People built stores, a bakery, a pub and restaurants. But things had changed by the time I entered the valley. Cable brought American television, people forgot how to speak French. Families grew smaller, farms larger, people moved away. With fewer folks, the hospital and bakery closed. That's when the remaining folks at Val Marie started the parade.

And it was truly impressive. Showing off seventy-five years of Saskatchewan history. Someone found an old fire engine. Someone else decorated a grain truck with pitch forks and shovels, tied on with baler twine.

**Lise and Fernand Perrault Guide
their Democrat Buggy in the Val Marie Parade.**

The Seniors' Centre folks covered a flat-bed trailer with century old artifacts, assembled in a very convincing domestic scene, complete with a slender young woman who scrubbed clothes using a wash tub and brush.

The Mounties ambled by on tall, quiet horses with wet noses. Cowboys in black hats rode by atop wild-looking horses. The manager of the Credit Union drove past with all the members' money in a safe. That car was followed by more cops on big, runny-nosed horses. Music. Eight kids, the entire Grade Eleven class, marched by, pounding on drums. A farmer led draft horses pulling an ancient thrasher; a rancher and his wife bounced about in a Democrat buggy. Some hockey playing teenagers marched past us, waving skates and sticks.

Joe and I stood along Main, east of the Bryan Trottier Arena. Joe, just fifteen, had never seen a live Saskatchewan parade before. Eighteen floats drifted by. We cheered for every one of them. People must have worked for a week to prepare for the ten minute show. We watched the last clown on a bicycle pass. Then the parade was out of sight, having gone west along Main, then south on Highway 4. Joe and I clapped. Loudly. There were not many of us on the street, most of the people of Val Marie were in the parade. We felt this had all been done for Joe and me. We turned to leave.

"Don't go yet." A voice said from behind.

We stayed. Unsure why. But in a moment, the parade that had passed us by was back, having completed the short loop around the village. The music started again. The fire engine clanged past, followed by the decorated truck, the seniors' flat bed trailer, the whole parade.

Everyone on the street waved and cheered, as if they had never seen a parade before.

My honey house was similar to Earl Emde's in Big River. This was because Earl had helped to build the shop in Val Marie, five years before. It was wooden, with a concrete floor and loading dock. But it was tiny. Not much bigger than a two car garage. The walls were unfinished, uninsulated. Nothing but two-by-four studs. No ceiling, no insulation above. The outside was also incomplete. Plywood, no siding. There was no basement. No running water. Frank had carried a bucket of hot water up from the house each day for washing hands. Cold running water, for washing the floor, came from seven garden hoses, cobbled together, anchored to the house a hundred metres away, at the base of the gently sloping hill.

As soon as the honey boxes were on the hives, Joe and I began digging a trench for a real water supply from the house to the shed. With shovels. By hand. It did not need to be deep, about two feet would be enough. It took us a few days to dig and then bury a black plastic inch and a half pipe to carry water from the house to the extracting shed. The garden hoses that the previous beekeeper used always froze in September. And in the summer, the sun's heat made them swell and leak. The buried pipe would give me water for the entire honey season, from May through October. The shed was uphill, so I could drain the water out in the fall. The water pipe did not have to be buried seven feet deep to escape the frost; it would be empty before the ground froze.

We finished the trench and led the pipe into the west side of the shed. We attached more pipes and tubes and connectors, installed a hot water heater and sink. I bought soldering equipment, but did not know how to use it. Joe did. He pieced together the sink, water heater, and drain for me. Then we bought scratchy pink insulation and stuffed it between the two-by-fours. Four-mil plastic covered the insulation, over which we tacked thin sheets of masonite. We painted our new walls white. The building was a little warmer, the prairie wind could not blast through the siding. The shed still had no heat, but now I was out of money. Further construction would wait until the bees had made some honey and I had sold a bit. But we had turned the little shed into a honey factory.

"What do you think Dad would say?" I asked Joe.

"He'd think it's OK," Joe said. He reached up to dab a bit of white paint across a spot I had missed. "You didn't spend too much money fixing it up. We did all the work ourselves. Nothing too fancy or expensive." Joe landed back on his heels. "He'd think it's OK."

I was glad that I was getting our father's approval, even if it arrived second-hand. Dad once said I was the smart one in the family of ten, but not smart in a way that mattered. I'd once tried to help him line up pipes, tried to screw them together in his greenhouse. I couldn't keep my end straight. "You got an A plus in physics, but you sure don't know shit about anything practical, do you?" he asked. Dad was right.

It was a defect I seemed to battle all my life. Practical skills evaded me; but less important talents – scholarly, cultural, even perhaps social – came a bit more easily. I knew that if I were to succeed, I needed to suppress the latter, reinforce the former. I was realizing Joe, with his practical common sense, could help me. I might not be gifted with practical common sense, but if I could produce a huge honey crop, I might be vindicated.

Bee Hive Thieves, from Pieter Breughel the Elder, 1565

Honey Crop

Bees do not think about making honey. They simply do it. There is no big bee accountant in a yellow and black bee suit allocating resources, urging the bees to gather more or to stop gathering when the balance sheet reaches perfection. Bees need no command to do what comes naturally. They exit the hive when flowers provide nectar and pollen; when the weather is fine enough to allow flight. They stop foraging when the flowers dry up, when the weather turns sour, or when their wings have fallen apart from over-use.

My father said, "Bees don't fill honey boxes stacked in the back of the shed. You gotta get them out on the hives." Joe and I were getting the boxes out. All beekeepers optimistically place empty honey supers on hives. Hopeful that the empty combs in those boxes will be full of honey when it's time to remove them. On the western Canadian prairies, beekeepers are almost never disappointed. Bees can make a lot of honey. In Saskatchewan, the average crop was about two hundred pounds per hive. That's why I was there.

My goal was a gigantic honey crop. I wanted three hundred pounds of honey from each hive. This would not be a world record. Back in the fifties, a fellow named Rob Smith had his bees working Australian eucalyptus when he produced an average of seven hundred sixty-two pounds from four hundred sixty hives.[24] Many of his hives made a thousand pounds of honey - each. One thousand pounds. The bees were all in one big apiary, in a remote forest. He set up a small camp, complete with an extractor, and he lived among his bees in the apiary for a year. He would extract almost every day and put the emptied boxes back on the hives. The empties refilled over and over again. This went on for a year. Finally, after months without rain, the blossoms on the eucalyptus trees dried out and stopped secreting nectar. The bees quit making honey. Rob Smith moved his bees away.

With our honey boxes on top, many hives stood taller than me. Seven feet of honey and wax and boxes and bees. I had to reach my arms high to remove the lids from some of the better colonies. New wax sealed the lids tightly to the hives, it took an effort to peel them off. Almost every comb in every box was full. The bees had even built clean white burr comb between the frames to hold their excess honey. Each box was thirty pounds heavier than it was when placed on the hives three weeks earlier. Some of the hives had made a hundred fifty pounds of surplus honey and the season had barely started. Ten pounds a day for each day with good weather.[25] The few rainy days gave the soil moisture, the moisture freshened the plants. Weather, flowers, and bees cooperated; the boxes filled.

For a beekeeper, hives jammed full of honey is pretty exciting. It may only happen once a year. Maybe once in a lifetime. A gift from the gods. Pure, sweet ambrosia. A big honey crop tells the beekeeper everything is working. He chose the right place at the right time. His bees are in the right condition - good queens, healthy bees, exemplary

Bad Beekeeping

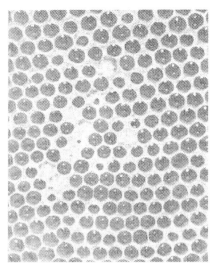

Pure Honey Comb

apiary location. A tangible, material validation of success in at least one aspect of the beekeeper's life. It also means money, but only the most desperate beekeeper stands among the filled hives in the field, counting boxes and guessing the dollar value of the unharvested crop.

I needed money, but I wasn't desperate. I pulled out a comb, poked my finger into fresh honey and stuck the sticky finger into my mouth. My mouth squeezed down on the wax comb. Honey oozed out, on my lips, my tongue. The sticky liquid dripped down my throat, sweet and choking. Joe interrupted my love affair.

"Where's the stink stuff?" he asked.

"In the side-box. Behind the smoker." Beekeeping was about to get real. The boxes full of honey had to be loaded onto the truck. Bees, millions of bees, were in the honey boxes. It was part of their homes - their upper floors. We needed to chase the bees from the top storeys of their houses, displacing those millions of insects to the bottom boxes. The bees would not know that we were stealing their honey, but they would know that we were pushing them around. They wouldn't like this. For the next few hours, the work would be hard. Heavy lifting. And lots of stings.

Charlie (foreground) and Joe Stacked Honey Supers on the Hives until the Apiaries Looked Like Miniature City-Skylines

Some beekeepers call it *pulling honey*. In the southern states, they more rightly define it as *robbing the bees*. I liked to think I was pulling. If the hives were full of honey, and if I did not pull the excess and then place empty combs back on, my hives would become too crowded. If they were crowded, the bees would swarm. If they swarmed, they would be a nuisance to the people who lived in Val Marie, a nuisance to themselves. I pulled honey to help the bees. I wasn't really robbing; I was rationalizing.

Honey Crop

I had a system that eliminated some stings and reduced the time we spent wrapped in hot veils, canvas bee gloves, and thick coveralls. In Earl Emde style, I raced around the apiary, ripping off all the hive covers. At the same time, I gave each hive long, cool puffs of white smoke from the bee smoker. The smoke helped mask our bad human odours. More important for us, when bees smell smoke, they gorge their tummies with honey. It is part of an eat and run response, similar to the performance of humans at all-you-can-eat buffet bars. Preparing to leave their burning home, the bees eat quickly, stuffing themselves. And a bee with a fat tummy is a happy bee. Or at least, a bee with a flabby stinger. So, a person doesn't get stung. Much.

By the time I had all the lids off and the hives smoked, Joe had the stink boards sloshed with chemicals.[26] They are called stink boards because the acids dribbled on these wooden pads smell pretty harsh. Some people say it affects the nose like sour vomit. The cotton padding on the boards absorbs the puke scent, slowly releasing the bad odour when the trays are placed on top of the hives. Understandably, the bees scurry as fast as they can to the bottom of their nest, escaping the bad scent and leaving the honey boxes nearly free of bees. A wicked chemical. Probably not healthy if taken internally. But not as bad as carbolic acid, which was the stink chemical used in the fifties and sixties in North America. The FDA had conducted tests on the stuff Joe and I used and said the chemical did not get into our honey. Nor did it increase the risk of cancer - at least not in any statistically meaningful way. The food industry, in fact, used the same foul stuff to artificially flavor almond-banana bread. Perhaps it was safe. But still, it stank. After a few years, most of us would discover less smelly ways to separate bees from honey.[27]

But on that day, we chased the bees from the honey boxes with stink boards, then we stacked the supers of honey on the truck's open, flat deck. I organized the outfit so there was always space at the front for boxes full of honey. Piled towards the middle and back of the truck were new boxes with empty combs. As full boxes came off the hives, they were stacked near the front. Empty boxes went back onto the stripped hives immediately, giving the bees more combs to fill and freeing more space on the truck to stack even more honey. It took the bees only a few hours to recover from the rude interruption. They could continue gathering honey and filling the new set of boxes. Once the apiary had been stripped and empties put back on, we drove away, the truck groaning under the weight of a few hundred boxes of sweet, ripe honey.

**The Val Marie Honey House:
Almost Clean Enough for Photographs**

On the trip back to the honey shed in Val Marie, bees stranded in the honey boxes took flight and drifted back to their colonies. The stray bees made a trail along the highway, little flying insect crumbs. When I reached my shop in Val Marie, I backed the truck to the concrete dock and we offloaded the boxes. Then the really hard work started. Honey had to be separated from wax in the big extractors.

The first honey in the first extractor on the first day of extracting was an exciting event. The Swift Current newspaper never sent a photographer, but they should have. The floor and extractors were photogenically clean on that first day. But within hours, the floor and machines were sticky and dirty-looking, covered in wax and honey.

We mounted the fresh white combs into slots within the extractors, and threw switches. Machines whirled and hummed. Honey dribbled through the pipes of the extractors and within a few hours the holding tank filled with honey and the automatic float balanced in the tank switched on a big honey pump. Honey was sucked from the reservoir in the pit below the extractors and pushed up to the huge settling tank. A few ounces became a few pounds. Many pounds filled the lower tank. After the lower tank filled and emptied a few times, the big settling tank was full. One moment, bees gather microliters of nectar from within a soft blossom's petals; another moment, the beekeeper dumps tonnes of honey into rugged steel drums. Bit by bit. It all adds up.

Charlie Dumont started working for me the third day of extracting. He had helped Frank the year before. Charlie was good, not quite like Joe, but still a keen worker. Most sixteen-year-olds would not take the stings, the heavy lifting, the smell of the chemicals, the long hours, the sticky mess. Most sixteen-year-olds? Most thirty-year-olds wouldn't do what we did to make a living.

Charlie worked hard, willingly. He needed the money. Joe and I could have easily handled all the work - I only had a few hundred hives - but I was glad to have the extra set of hands - and I was training permanent staff. Charlie had three attributes which made him an ideal beekeeping apprentice: he needed money; his father had kept bees; and Charlie took stings well.

A willingness and ability to suffer bee stings is certainly a beekeeping assistant's asset. Dr. Mark Winston, a bee scientist at Simon Fraser University, describes three levels of bee sting reaction.[28] The worst results in death – bee stings kill about fifty people in North America each year.[29] Winston attributes most bee sting deaths to rapid, systemic allergic reactions. Body chemistry is at odds with the injected bee proteins. A similar and sometimes fatal reaction occurs in people with peanut allergies, for example. In the bee case, a single sting may result in death. But only for the unfortunate dozen people who suffer this severe systemic reaction each year in North America.

A more common, but less severe sting reaction results in localized and painful swelling, sometimes immobilizing a limb for several hours. In this case, it is the poison that causes problems. Enough stings, several hundred actually, can result in death from envenomation - poisoning. Less than five percent of bee sting deaths (perhaps one a year in North America) are due to massive stingings, all the rest result from hypersensitivity – the allergic reaction. Even after the arrival of the Africanized stock in Texas and California, these figures haven't appreciably changed.[30]

Winston's third level of response, he says, is the most common. The sting is painful and irritating but not health-threatening. It passes quickly, resulting in minor swelling, redness, and perhaps itchiness – the result of the worker bee poking her barbed stinger into soft skin, leaving behind a throbbing sac of poison anchored by a stiff hook.

I would add a fourth level of lessening severity to the three that Dr. Winston

Gophers by the Side of the Road

describes. A pin-prick reaction. Most of us who keep bees receive dozens of stings each day. They hurt, but only for a few seconds. No redness, swelling, nor itchiness. Sort of like getting a hot, clean needle. That's all. A moment's irritation, then on with the job at hand.

I kept Charlie working most of that summer. He laboured full-time for the next several years. He worked hard, usually showed up on time, and never refused a chore. He had a few - very few - disconcerting characteristics. The first day I allowed him to pilot one of my trucks back to the shop, he maintained a safe distance behind the outfit I drove. But I occasionally saw him swerve towards the ditch, then he recovered quickly and reached town safely. After we parked the trucks, he thanked me for leaving the gophers at the side of the road – for him to run over. "Most people want to run them down themselves, hardly any farmer leaves them for the hired help. Really. Thanks," he said.

Charlie's extra help allowed us a bit of free time we would not otherwise have had. On the first Saturday of the honey pull, Charlie told us we should quit early and go to the movies.

"In Swift Current?" Joe asked. Swift Current was the nearest big town. Fifteen thousand people, an hour away in a fast truck.

"No," Charlie said, "We have a theatre in Val Marie. Didn't you know?"

We quit work early that evening. We showered and scrubbed and removed most of the smell of the chemical we had been bathing in. We walked from our house on River Road, on the remote north edge of town, to the heart of Val Marie, one block away. Twenty people, mostly kids, were standing on the street and sidewalk in front of the show hall. They were neatly dressed, in leather boots and long-sleeved cotton shirts. Everyone – male, female, old folks, small kids – wore blue jeans. Levi's mostly. Some of the young men had big black hats on their heads and skinny girls on their arms.

We tried to figure out where the line ended so we could wait our turn. Then we realized there was no line. The kids on the street were simply waiting on the street. They were out in the cool evening air, waiting for the movie to start. We went in.

We each handed a dollar to the boy taking money at the door and walked into the dark, stuffy hall. We found seats near the center of the theatre, sat up tall so we could see over the cowboy hats and the kids skipping rope up near the screen. "Shut up!" someone yelled, not at us, but at the world in general. "Sit down!" a woman's voice boomed towards the pre-schoolers at the front of the hall. The first reel was rolling. Like a big, rowdy, and very familiar family, people ate, drank, scolded their (and other peoples') children until all the folks slowly settled down to watch the movie.

It was a boxing movie. Rocky was nobody, but he had a chance at the big time. Rocky Balboa versus the Greek God Apollo. "Hasn't this movie been out for a few years already?" Joe whispered. "Shut up!" someone behind us suggested. It had been out for four years. Already had won its Academy awards, but neither Joe nor I had seen it. And it only cost a dollar. "Shut up!" This time the words were hurled at some cowboys standing near the wall. They'd been bouncing their hats off the ceiling, laughing when they missed catching them.

Our evening ended when the show ended. We walked back onto the dimly lit Main Street, still crowded with parked trucks, with young people on foot, with kids leaning out of truck windows. A young cowboy, someone we had never seen before, invited us to fight him, but we declined the offer. Sunday was a few hours away, and it was just another workday in the middle of the first pull of the honey season.

Over the next several days, we continued bringing in honey, extracting, filling the tank. After spinning honey out of the frames, we put the combs back into their boxes and rushed back to the hives. I had fifteen apiaries. Some in alfalfa fields, others in the buttes near the fields.

The Dixon Beeyard - Sage Brush, Cacti, Rattlesnakes, Badlands, and some Alfalfa - Almost Everything Anyone Could Ever Want

Years ago, my father had eight hundred hives of bees. He had thirty outyards. He told me to always keep at least one apiary just for the scenery, even if it didn't make much honey. His favourite beeyard was at the Andrews place. Off a narrow Pennsylvania country road, down a tree-lined trail, into a dark narrow valley. The tiny gorge was cut from slate and metamorphic gneiss by a fast moving creek. The bees rarely performed

Honey Crop

well in the little Andrews hollow, but this was a place where a glistening stream always rustled and bees always hummed sweetly.

My scenic beeyard was at the Dixon Ranch. It was far from Val Marie, about an hour with a fully loaded truck, but the trail twisted past prairie dog colonies[31] and bob cat dens, a rattlesnake covey and an alkali flat populated with scrubby sage brush, wild clover, and the occasional prickly pear cactus. The bees I kept at the south end of the Frenchman Valley, on the Dixon Ranch, never did as well as the bees near Val Marie. There was less water for irrigation, alfalfa fields were smaller, and wild sweet clover was sparse on the hot parched buttes near these bees. But the sage brush and cacti, the steep-sided buttes and the slow moving river made Dixons' my favourite apiary.

We usually carried a lunch when we went to the Dixon ranch. Carrots, salami sandwiches, and coke. We worked the bees first, then drove for ten minutes and parked in a field full of holes. With the truck engine cut off and our windows rolled down, we listened to the chirps, squeaks, and barks of prairie dogs as they warned each other that beekeepers were near. The plump rodents had learned to fear trucks. Trucks sometimes brought young ranchers with rifles. And prairie dogs presented a way to sharpen hunting skills, by targeting the fat dumb animals as they popped in and out of their burrows.

We never carried guns. If we had, neither Joe nor I could have fired on those fuzzy creatures. Or any other inedible animal. I doubt if the young cowboys ate their kill. But a hundred years earlier, the Sioux may have, as an alternative to starvation. We thought about this as we sat within earshot of the barks, next to rings of stones set on the ground by the Sioux to hold their teepees in place.

Sitting Bull
Had Lived Here

Those Sioux were visitors. Other Indians, including Cree and Blackfoot, had lived on the Canadian prairie for thousands of years. But the Sioux, led by Tatanka Iyotake – Sitting Bull – immigrated into this Canadian valley. They sought amnesty after their victory against General Custer at Montana's Little Big Horn, two hundred miles south of us. Two thousand people fled to this spot. They felt the same wind, saw the same landscape, listened to the prairie dogs. But there were few buffalo in Saskatchewan in 1895. Not enough antelope or mule deer. The Sioux were hungry. Starving. Perhaps they ate prairie dogs.

The Sioux were fed by the Canadian western patrol, the Royal Canadian Mounted Police. At the same time that the Americans sent soldiers to tame the wild west and move Indians off farmland and onto reserves, Canada put together a national police force to protect the natives from the whites, and to shut down whiskey trading posts that had been built by Americans. The Canadian Mounties brought in food, but finally persuaded the Sioux to return to the States. The people were settled on reserves in South Dakota. Sitting Bull got a job with a Cowboy and Indian show. He did rope tricks and rode a horse around a big arena. Signed autographs for ten cents. But he died in an uprising, one last fight for dignity.

The Indians - the ones with tents and long bows - were long gone now. Joe and I finished our carrots and drank our iced colas. I started the truck and began the long drive back to Val Marie.

"Your honey is the best in the world," said the Reverend David Kleinsasser. He was a preacher; he was telling the truth.

Reverend David was my biggest fan, my best honey customer, and my most diligent unpaid spokesman. He was also an important and respected Hutterite. David had come to my house every second day in late June and early July, checking the status of the crop. He wanted the first honey. He told me that the first honey was the best, the whitest, the clearest. It sparkled like pure water in a mountain stream, glistened like fresh snow crystals. It was mild, sweet, thick, he had said, and smelled like a bouquet of summer blossoms. The young Hutterian preacher had a way with words. Reverend David wanted to buy five hundred pounds of fresh honey for the Sand Lake Hutterite Colony. He also wanted samples he could give to other Hutterite ministers and farm managers.

Out of three hundred Hutterite farms on the western prairies, only a few had honeybees. Most had chickens and turkeys, vegetables and wheat, cows and hogs. But bees were a nuisance on a Hutterite farm. Keeping bees is messy and sticky. Bees sting. Beekeepers usually need to spread their hives out over many kilometres, Hutterites like to do all their farming close to home. Hutterites wear dark clothing and bees tend to sting people dressed in black. Most Hutterites don't keep bees.

This creates a bit of a dilemma. The founder of the faith, Jacob Hutter, wrote sermons that cited the thrift, cooperation, prosperity, and harmony of the honeybee colony.[32] In the sixteenth century, he cited honeybees as a model for the Christian community that Jacob's followers, the Hutterites, developed. Twentieth century Hutterites were still reading and studying those sermons. If bees are so good, shouldn't the Hutterite colony keep bees?

The colony's gardener solved this dilemma. He built a small glass hive and I stocked it with bees. He put the observation hive in the garden shed. The children who worked in the garden checked on their bees every day. A tiny colony, housed in a glass hive, is small and weak and not aggressive. Too small to make honey, there is no mess to tend to. Too few bees to rudely chase the people working nearby. Meanwhile, the little cluster of bees lived in exemplary harmony as they pollinated the garden's squash and cucumbers. The Hutterite children pressed their noses against the glass cover on the little hive, saw bees sharing nectar, saw them cooperatively building new comb, participating in the care of the brood. The kids saw these things and learned their lessons. They didn't see bees at their worst – bees stinging passersby, bees robbing honey from weaker hives, queens killing queens. Lessons best left untaught.

While my first bit of the honey crop was filling the lower tanks, David Kleinsasser insisted it was time to sell. I told him we had to wait until the upper settling tank was filled to the top. At that time, I opened the valve at the bottom and drained off a pail of clean white honey. I put some in a small jar, held it up to the light. It looked cloudy. Tiny air bubbles hung in it. I wasn't happy.

"It's just air," David said.

Reluctantly, I gave him the jar.

"When will you fill my pails?" David asked. I wanted to think about a way to get the air out of the honey. "Give me a day or two," I said. David agreed, as long as I would fill one of the smaller pails immediately. The honey did not look too foamy. But it wasn't clear. Why was the honey full of air bubbles? When I was kid, our Pennsylvania honey was never clouded like this. Later that day, holding a nearly full glass jar of Saskatchewan honey in my hand, I solved the problem. When I turned the sealed jar upside-down, the air was trapped at the bottom of the inverted jar. It formed a single, huge air bubble which very slowly rose upwards. If the jar had held water instead of honey, the air bubble would rush upwards. If it had held Pennsylvania honey - thin honey from a humid climate - it would have also quickly risen. But the desert climate of southern Saskatchewan produced honey that was so thick, dry, and heavy that it trapped air. Air bubbles moved sluggishly through this thick stuff. Now I understood the problem. Air mixed in while the honey was flung from the combs to the sides of the extractor. It was locked in the honey. Thick honey is a good thing. It tastes better, lasts longer. My bees in Val Marie produced too much of a good thing.

I figured the air bubbles would float out of the honey if the honey was warm. My solution was to put honey into a steel barrel, heat the barrel a bit - not too long and not too hot, else the honey would darken - and let the air bubbles float to the top. Then I tapped honey out of the bottom of the drum and quickly cooled it again. It was a lot of extra work. But I had superb results.

I filled a dozen pails of the clear honey and hauled them out to David Kleinsasser at Sand Lake Hutterite Colony late in the afternoon. He ladled off a bit, putting it into a clear glass jar. He held it up to the light. No air bubbles. He nodded, then suggested we unload the truck. We carried the honey pails into a walk-in freezer, stacking it next to frozen beans and fish. In the deep freeze, the honey froze solidly without crystallizing. Whenever the cook needed more honey, she took another big pail out and let it thaw. It turned as liquid as when the bees stored it in their combs. Not all the honey went into the freezer. One pail went directly from my truck to the work-room in the community kitchen. David Kleinsasser scooped out a dripping spoon full. "Ron, your honey is the best in the world," he said.

I hadn't seen much of my friend Buzz for a few weeks. I saw Mary a few times in town, at the credit union, at the post office. She told me Buzz wasn't partial to all the bees floating around in my back yard. So he wouldn't come to see me. But I called him, insisted the bees weren't that bad, and he came to tour my honey house.

"What are you going to do with all this honey?" Buzz asked as he walked through the shop.

"I'll try to sell what I can't eat," I said.

Bad Beekeeping

"Lot of eating," Buzz said. "How's Joe doing?" Buzz had only seen Joe once, at Wong's. We'd been too busy to respond to Mary's invitations to come to the dinner, I hadn't played the guitar in a long while.

Joe had come into the shed balancing a stack of honey trays in his hands. "Ask him yourself."

"He making you work hard enough?" Buzz asked Joe. "Gotta work hard. Won't have anything if you don't." Joe grinned, dropped the sticky trays at Buzz's feet and a bee flew off the top tray. Buzz backed up to the wall, swatting.

"Work is OK. Keeps us busy," Joe said. "Better than sitting around."

We had a lot of honey. Within a week, we had stripped the boxes from well over half the hives and put empties back on. There were two hundred boxes in the shop waiting to be extracted. A thousand boxes had already been emptied, yielding twenty thousand pounds of honey. Work was grinding us, making us weary. We pulled honey all day, extracted into the night.

Finally, one day, all the honey was removed from my three hundred and twenty hives. Empty boxes replaced filled ones and the bees were storing honey in them. I would wait before extracting the next batch of honey, wait until the boxes were nearly full again. It was now the third week of July. I had fifty-five barrels of honey, thirty-five thousand pounds. And the various Hutterite colonies had bought thirty-five big pails - two thousand pounds of honey. Farmers, ranchers and other neighbours came to the shop, mostly bringing plastic gallon-sized ice cream pails. I filled these with hundreds of pounds of honey, one dollar a pound. I had enough cash for groceries, even a little extra. We had a couple of weeks to build equipment, clean the shop before the hives would be full again. I decided Joe and I should go and see some mountains.

Early on a Tuesday morning, we drove along paved and gravel country roads from Val Marie through Climax, Frontier, Maple Creek. The roads were straight and smooth, only occasionally bending around dry sloughs and small lakes with white alkali salt lining their edges. The occasional creek cut deep sandstone walls. Along some rangelands, shale and sandstone hoodoos - small anthropomorphically-shaped creatures - stood as sentinels before small gravel hills. It had taken us three hours to reach Maple Creek, near the Alberta-Saskatchewan border. We were half-way to the mountains. We were certainly not the first to have driven the route, but we felt like explorers. There were very few fellow travelers on the roads.

We were close to the Cypress Hills now. These hills were high in elevation, speckled with pine, poplars, and aspen - not cypress. The name was a mistake, someone told me. The first settlers thought those trees high up on the surrounding hills were cypress, but apparently no one bothered to go find out for sure. The name stuck. There are no cypress trees anywhere near Saskatchewan, but tucked into the southwest corner of the province, you can find a group of big hills named after trees that don't grow there. I wondered why we call things by the wrong name. Inertia? Maybe laziness. I wondered about this even more when we approached Maple Creek, the town without maple trees.

We entered Maple Creek, north along Highway 41; drove past irrigated alfalfa and sweetclover fields. These fields were similar to the ones around Val Marie. But we saw no

Honey Crop

beehives, no beekeepers. Over a hamburger and fries at the Star Cafe, we asked if anyone kept bees in town. One person, a carpenter, had a few hives. No one else. Twelve thousand acres of irrigated clover and no honeybees. A million pounds of honey lost, every year, because no bees were there to collect it.[33]

Joe and I continued along the Trans-Canada Highway towards Medicine Hat, across more range lands, past huge wheat fields and equally large chunks of fallow land. We listened to the CBC and learned that the first cross-Canada auto trip, from Halifax to Victoria in 1912, passed by the same spots we drove along. It had taken a 1912 REO four days to go from Swift Current to Frank, Alberta - about the distance we would cover in six hours. Obviously the roads were a little better, over half a century later. But we wondered if much else had really changed. The wind blew and antelope still lined the road. We drove along the Trans-Canada, parallel to the Canadian National railway track, same as a million other vehicles had done in the hundred years since the train line had tracked itself, enduring the prairie, heading towards the mountains.

We had a chance to talk, but we didn't say much. Joe seemed to be enjoying his Canadian adventure and rarely mentioned Dad, Florence, or the family farm in Pennsylvania. We got along well, never argued. Mostly because Joe and I worked so hard. He was only grumpy when he'd been awake too many hours. He'd get a bit anxious, but it always passed with a night of sleep. We traveled without talking, scanned the horizon for signs of the foothills. Our destination was a place called Banff, where we had been told mountains could be seen.

We found Banff. We saw the mountains. On the twenty-fifth of July, we hiked up a trail to the continental divide and kicked at crusty brown snow. We drove north from Banff, saw water tumbling hundreds of feet down rock walls. We touched the toe of a glacier, stood on its ice. Spent two nights in a cabin at Johnston Creek.

By a grey river in a forest of thick evergreens, we tried to eat a picnic lunch but were chased back into our truck by a small and haggard grizzly bear. The bear ate our bologna and mustard sandwiches, threw our squeeze bottle full of honey on the ground. I blew the horn a few times when the cub banged a paw against the tail gate, then I started the engine and rolled forward, causing the bear to amble off towards the river. We might have stayed and played with the forest creatures in the mountains for weeks, but after only four days we felt closed in by rock and tree; we needed to see farmland. Flat, pragmatic, arable. Farmland. And I missed my bees.

The Grizzly Searched our Picnic Lunch for Honey

Bad Beekeeping

The first of August. The bees had again filled the empty boxes on their hives. Time for the second pull. Work became a drudgery. Monotony replaced excitement. Wild sunflowers distracted the foraging bees – the August honey was slightly darker and less tasty than the honey from July. It was still light-coloured and mild-flavoured, but not as perfect as the first honey of the season. Our honey collection system continued to work well. We stripped three or four honey boxes off the top of each hive and left one, two, or three empty boxes behind, in case the season allowed even more honey. But we were going through tedious physical motions now, fighting exhaustion, forcing ourselves to work sixteen hours a day, getting stung, lifting heavy boxes, sweating in sticky coveralls under the harsh Saskatchewan sun; standing on concrete in front of the extractors, dropping sticky combs into noisy, whirling machines. In ten days, Joe, Charlie, and I had another forty barrels of honey. A hundred drums from three hundred and twenty hives of bees. And I was still expecting more.

Most commercial beekeepers stow honey - six hundred sixty pounds at a time - into steel barrels. It takes sixty-five barrels of honey (about forty-three thousand pounds) to fill a semi-truck. The drums are sent to agents in big cities – Toronto, Montreal, Chicago, Berlin, Tokyo. The packers establish business relationships - and sometimes even friendships - with the beekeepers who supply honey.

Honey in Barrels - We Sold What We Couldn't Eat

Two of the big competing Canadian honey packers were Paul Doyon in Montreal and Jack Grossman in Toronto. I didn't know much about either. But I had heard that Don Peer, one of the most successful beekeepers in Saskatchewan, had met Jack Grossman at a bee conference. Don Peer asked, "Can I see the note card you have on me?"

He expected that Jack's note cards had lengthy descriptions about terms of payment, quality of product, ability to deliver on time. But when Don Peer read the note card about himself, he was surprised to see it simply said "Doesn't need money." *Doesn't need money.* I wanted that written on my note card one day, instead of *'desperate'* or whatever else Jack may have penciled under my name. "Doesn't need money."

Power and independence in three little words. My father had lived much of his life from that side of the financial fence. Dad never earned much money. But he became wealthy. His secrets: rarely borrow money (and only for business - never, never, never for pleasure); and make everything you can by yourself. In other words, don't spend money and you won't need money. I was trying to learn this system of independence and self-reliance, but I was a slow student.

I figured I should research Canada's honey packers. I asked Keith Groot, a Meadow Lake beekeeper, what he did with all his honey.

"I sell what I can't eat," Keith said. I knew that.

But Keith produced three hundred thousand pounds a year. "Should I sell to Grossman or Doyon?" I asked. Mine was not an idle question. I needed to know where I should sell my honey - whom could I trust?

"They're both good," Keith said. He meant that these packers honoured their agreements – paying on time, paying the agreed price. So I phoned Jack Grossman and Paul Doyon. They both made offers on my crop. They'd pay fifty-five cents a pound, half when they got the honey, half two months later. Each said they'd send a big truck, pay the freight for me. The driver would help wheel my honey barrels into a van, then give me a slip of paper. The honey would arrive in Montreal if Paul bought it; Toronto if the sale went to Jack. The Val Marie honey was so good I decided that if I had enough honey, I'd split the crop in half. Send one or two loads to Ontario and one or two to Quebec, so as not to cause friction between the provinces.

But my very first load had to be sold. Montreal? Toronto? I flipped a coin. The Queen's face was down. I sent the honey to Quebec. Within days a huge van backed up to my little concrete loading dock and Joe and I and the lady truck driver rolled the heavy honey drums into the trailer. I was given a bill of lading and the enormous truck lugged away. Our honey was heading east. Three weeks later I got my first cheque in the mail. Ten thousand dollars.

We had collected most of the honey that the bees could produce for the season. Days were getting shorter. And cooler. The bees flew less each day, but continued to carry in a little honey every afternoon. Joe and I slowed our pace to match the efforts of the bees. We hiked the badlands, looking for rattlesnakes and prairie dogs, collecting the fossilized remains of trees. We sat on our butts on the tops of craggy buttes and slid down the loose dirt to the bottom. We spent a little more time with the farmers of the Frenchman Valley, helping the Waldners build a basement, the Syrennes shovel grain. We ate often at the Sand Lake Hutterite colony where Joe would sit quietly as young ladies in babushkas poured yellow wine for him.

For suppers, we mostly ate what I could dig from a can, but occasionally we went to Buzz and Mary's ranch or over to Wong's. I always checked the bill at Harry Wong's cafe, found he continually undercharged me. He started to give me the bill to add up myself. Harry often sat at our table, told stories about how he worked at the family restaurant in Moose Jaw, growing up, learning to work, instead of going to school. "Don't you do that!" he shook a finger at Joe, then me. "You go to school! All my kids go to school, two in university."

Twice during the summer I rescheduled Joe's return ticket to Pennsylvania, each time Dad said Joe should stay in Canada a little longer. Joe was keen to return home; resigned to stay longer. I enjoyed having my little brother in Saskatchewan, he was good company, and he worked hard for his supper. But fall was coming and he was already missing high school. Joe finally packed his small bag with clothes, a jar of honey, and a bottle of home-made wine the Hutterites wanted to send to our father. Then we loaded fifteen barrels of honey - which I would later deliver to Earl Emde in Big River - on the back of my big flatbed truck and we drove north to the airport in Saskatoon.

**Barrels of Honey for Export to the USA,
Havana, Cuba in 1902
From *American Beekeeper Magazine*, May 1902**

First Frost

Bees know when their season has ended. In tropical climates, after the avocado and citrus blooms have withered, the bees turn listless, unruly. Suddenly unemployed. Their energy and attention are directed towards defending the crop they have gathered. With fewer flowers, sweltering heat and heavy rainfall, pollen is scarce. The queen quits laying eggs. Any new bees would be hungry bees. The hive population shrinks and the remaining bees survive by eating the stored surplus.

In Canada, bees similarly adapt to changing fortunes. Days grow short as autumn approaches. The air is cool; the bees fly only a few hours each afternoon. Pollen becomes scarce. The bees jealously guard their surplus honey. Then one morning, the flowers are covered with ice. The first frost of the year blackens the clover blossoms – the honey season has ended. The bees survive months of snow and frigid winds, eating hoarded surplus honey. Sleepy, docile bees settle in for inevitable winter.

Joe was in the air, flying to Pennsylvania, toting some honey, his clothes, and the bottle of Hutterite wine. I was on the road, heading north from Saskatoon towards Big River. I was glad Joe had spent the summer, but the season was ending. In a few weeks, I'd be heading back to the States myself.

I drove alone now, the radio playing loudly, tuned to CBC 540. Peter Gzowski kept me company, he was interviewing single parents who were raising families and working at professional jobs. Men and women - journalists, doctors, and lawyers - who had found themselves alone with children. I switched to the Saskatoon radio station. It was playing rock. I drove faster, the tires of the truck singing with the rhythm from the radio.

I had fifteen barrels of honey on the back of my truck. The honey was barter, exchange for four hundred beehive boxes that Earl Emde offered to me. I arrived at his home as the sun set on Cowen Lake. We carted the drums into his shop. I was exhausted, but Earl and I worked late into the evening, loading heavy boxes of comb, pollen, and honey on my truck. After we tied the load down with thick ropes, we ate Josephine Emde's rice and cooked vegetables.

The next morning, after I'd had a short outing with the canoe, Earl told me I should meet someone. Murray Hannigan wanted me to stop by and see him before I headed back to Val Marie. He was my age, had as many brothers as I, and was born into a beekeeping family. He lived in Shellbrook, a town I traveled through after I left Big River, on the route back to Saskatoon. I would like Murray.

There were three flatbed beekeeper-trucks in the yard when I pulled into the Hannigans'. A visiting beekeeper, Gerry, had arrived from a town northeast of Prince Albert, an hour away. He had finished extracting his crop and was traveling around northern Saskatchewan, trading stories with beekeepers. Murray invited me in. I hung my jacket on a peg by the door, next to a long line of heavy, padded winter coats. I threw my runners on top of the pile of boots. It was September and winter coats were waiting by the door. We had coffee and bread and I asked about the coats. "Goodness, no," Murray said. "Our winter coats are a lot heavier than those!" The weather had been mild in Val Marie, but in Murray's part of Saskatchewan, it could be pretty chilly even in the summer. And I had no concept of what a cold Saskatchewan winter might be like.

"You're a beekeeper?" Gerry asked me.

"I guess so," I said. I had met a lot of successful beekeepers during the past few months. Could I claim membership in their group?

"Well," Gerry said, "Did you have any problems with bears this year?"

"There aren't any bears where I live."

"Oh? I thought you were from Saskatchewan," Gerry said. He looked at me, my cup of coffee. "You're from Saskatchewan, no?"

"Southern Saskatchewan. The badlands. No bears."

"Well, we have bears here!" Gerry said. "You have bear trouble, Murray?"

Murray looked up from his coffee and smiled. "Not usually. We use electric fences. We started using the solar charged ones this year, work really well. You also have to keep the beeyard clean - no wax or combs left lying about. We keep most of our yards fenced and close to farm houses. If the farmer has dogs, it's even better. Dogs scare the bears away."

Attacking Bears Will Schlep a Hive, Run into the Bush, Then Eat Lunch

"Well, I keep my bees near the bush," Gerry said. "Lots of bear problems."

"What do you do?" I asked.

"Kill 'em. We kill 'em. I know, lots of people think black bears are just smelly Winnie the Poohs. We kill 'em, especially if they get near our bees. A big bear can rip up ten hives in a night... scatter 'em to hell and back."

"It doesn't seem fair to shoot a bear for eating its supper," I said, "while not being allowed to kill the idiots who drive over beehives with four-wheel drives."

"Yea, I hear ya'," said Gerry, scratching his hair. "Should shoot those bastards, too. I had one yard near P.A. smashed to hell by someone in a truck, eh? At least you're allowed to track and shoot the bears. And I always give the teeth and claws to the Indians." He sat back in his chair, hands in lap. "But I'd probably get in trouble skinning cowboys."

"I heard you got a really big bear this year," Murray said.

"Well, yea, we did. I had a yard up near Christopher Lake. Big bear was ripping hives apart, carrying the boxes off into the woods. I sat up all night and finally he showed up. I shot him, three, four times. Must have weighed five hundred pounds. So I drove home. Missus catches me at the door. Farmer called, the one that owned the land where my bees were, madder than hell. Said I couldn't leave no dead bear laying in his field.

"So I went back with my boy, Tom, and we try to load the bear into the half ton. Can't do it. Can't budge it. Tom says, 'Let's drag her.' Tom's a smart boy. Hope he goes to university. Anyway, we pull a tarp out and roll the bear onto the tarp, tie ropes around it and hitch up to the bumper. Start dragging her. In half an hour, we're almost home, but we notice the bear's gone. So is the tarp. We were just dragging ropes now.

"So we turn around, head back. We come around a corner, there's our bear, sitting up in the middle of the road. But blue lights are flashing, the Mounties had come by already and the cop is standing there with a flashlight.

Murray and Ruby Hannigan and a Baby Hannigan

So, we drive by real slow and have the window down. 'Havin' a problem, Officer?' I says to him. He asks if it's my dead bear. Of course I says, 'No... But the tarp's mine.' So he lets me take the tarp. Real nice guy, that cop."

"You didn't get in trouble?"

"No, but after a while I felt bad about leaving the cop with five hundred pounds of bear meat."

"I think you should use solar fences," Murray said.

"Well, I got a better way, now. Lots cheaper and easier than solar fences, too. Almost always works," said Gerry.

"Better than fences?"

"Well," Gerry said, "Almost always works. Bears don't like human smells, scares them away. So now I always pee in pop bottles, leave one laying half over in each end of the beeyard. Sometimes I use beer bottles. Depends on my mood, eh?"

Bad Beekeeping

I was back in Val Marie. David Kleinsasser invited me to his house for supper. I drove out to the Hutterite colony and parked by David's door. He wasn't home. Annie wasn't home. But Rachel, in the house next door, saw me, called me over. Rachel was Joe

At the Rev. David's House - his Wife Annie is in the Middle

Kleinsasser's wife. Joe was David's brother. Joe managed the hog barn, a big, multi-million dollar business. I sat at Joe and Rachel's table and had a glass of wine. Rachel set out noodle soup, thick white buns, warm pork. I protested, I had been invited to supper next door. These people were too nice, too friendly. I ate and David walked in. "When you finish eating here, you come to my house to eat," he said. My mouth was full of bread, so I nodded. I was young, I could eat two suppers. I sat there among those wonderful people, my mouth full of food.

I didn't want to upset anyone, to make a social blunder. I wanted to be liked. So I was compliant. Agreeable. What the heck, it meant an extra free meal.

When I finished eating his food, Joe Kleinsasser and two of his sons followed me to his brother's apartment. They sat on a long bench at one side of the kitchen, black hats held in their hands, dark clothing merging together in the distance. David, Annie, and I sat at the table. Annie set out noodle soup, buns, warm pork. The people on the bench watched me eat again.

"You were up north?" David asked. "Big Beaver?"

"Big River, it's north of Prince Albert."

"I know P.A." David said. "We go up every fall and buy fish from the native people. A thousand pounds of white fish for the colony. What did you do in the north, buy fish?"

"I took my brother to the airport, then traded fifteen barrels of honey for beehive equipment. I was only gone two days."

"That's a long way, a thousand miles – round trip. That's all you did?"

"Yea. I drove up, made the trade, drove back."

A little voice from the distant bench called out: *"Vini, vidi, vici!"* Everyone laughed. I was stunned. I was sitting in a simple kitchen at a religious colony five hours from a city, gazing at an eight year old child who did not learn to speak English until he started school. And the little kid in the black pants and black coat knew about Julius

First Frost

Caesar and the efficiency of his conquests. "I'm not Caesar," I said. "I slept overnight in the north."

Annie looked up from her coffee. "You slept in a bed?" Her voice was stern. I did not understand the purpose of her question.

"At the Emdes', yea, I slept in a bed," I said.

"But you sleep on the floor in Val Marie."

How did she know? For months I had been sleeping on blankets on the wooden floor.

"Bring it," Annie said to someone in another room. A shy, dark-haired teenaged girl brought a small mattress out. It was a foam pad, about four inches thick, seven feet long, three feet wide. Annie had sewn some checkered red and green cotton over it. "Take it," she said. "Don't sleep on the floor anymore."

Early September, Removing the Last Honey Supers for the Year

The weather in southern Saskatchewan had been pleasant throughout August. The big sky was clear, pale blue. And the sun was warm, not hot. Grain fields turned yellow. Farmers plodded across their land with big red and green machines. In a few days, brown and gold wheat transformed into white stubble. I saw farmers working long hours, late into the night. Headlights, flashlights, and brilliant spotlights lit trucks, tractors, and machinery in dark wheat fields.

My bees made a lot of honey in July, but by late August they'd turned lazy. The air was no longer scented by sweet nectar becoming honey. The bees flew more slowly as they left their hives. When I drove into the apiaries, the bees met my windshield with interested curiosity. In July, I had been ignored by the busy bees, except for the few that absent-mindedly banged their heads into the truck windows. By the middle of August, I had taken honey from each hive twice. Five shallow boxes the first time, three the second.

Bad Beekeeping

A hundred pounds, then sixty pounds, from each hive. Most of the hives still had one extra box for surplus honey as September approached. I left two empty boxes on a few exceptional hives. But it looked like autumn was coming quickly.

My first season in Val Marie ended with a big freeze. On the second morning in September, the dry air of the high plains chilled to ten degrees below frost. I quickly gathered the four hundred honey boxes that were still on the hives. The bees were evil, viciously wicked. Flowers that had distracted them when I formerly rampaged through their hives were blackened and dead. This angered the bees. They aggressively defended the boxes of honey that sat above their brood nests. I was stung a lot. It hurt. I was tempted to take all the honey from some of the hives, so they would starve and die. But I didn't. I left enough honey with each colony so the bees might survive the long winter ahead, only pulling the surplus. Soon, the last of the crop was extracted and drained into drums. I had twelve more barrels, seven thousand extra pounds of honey, another four thousand dollars. With all the steel barrel lids hammered and bolted into place, I had one hundred twelve drums - seventy thousand pounds of honey. Enough to fill a big swimming pool.

I had made enough honey to earn enough money to buy trucks, gasoline, equipment, and machinery so I could keep bees again the following year. The season had been good. I'd be in business the next summer. I had learned a lot. Next year would be better. I had equipment from Earl, enough to start four hundred new hives. I had three hundred hives that would be wintering on the prairie. I'd have seven hundred hives the next summer. More work, certainly, but it had been an easy year, I knew I could work harder next season. Twice as many bees, twice as much honey, twice as much money. And I wanted to make more money.

It was late September. I built hive equipment. The blade on my table-saw spun for hours as I trimmed spruce boards and plywood sheets into new covers and bottoms for new hives. I sorted combs, arranging pollen and honey and empty frames so that the new bees I would bring from Florida the next spring would have the things they needed to call a box a home. I cleaned, washed, rewashed, then painted my extracting shop. Getting ready for the next honey season, nine months away.

With the honey season behind me, I had more time to visit friends. I was back at the Trottier ranch, eating Mary's roasts and potatoes, playing Buzz's guitar. Buzz asked if I would come by the next morning. He had seventy calves to ship out, wanted my help to herd them into the trailer.

"The boys used to help me, they're all gone now," Buzz said.

He couldn't keep the young cattle over winter, only their mothers. A buyer sent a semi-tractor from Swift Current. We chased fuzzy animals into it. They cried for their mothers, the cows cried for their calves. We cried for them all. But we bolted the trailer door shut and a truck load of veal left Buzz Trottier's farm yard.

First Frost

Buzz Takes a Break from Being a Cowboy

"Your life's easy, you ship honey, not bees." Buzz said.

"No, I move bees all over the country."

"But not off to slaughter, right?"

Buzz was right, of course. I didn't slaughter my bees. But if it were necessary to make a living, I probably would have. For fifty years before I arrived in Canada, beekeepers on the prairies killed their bees every fall. After the first frost, beekeepers would quietly dump a spoonful of cyanide into each hive. The poison quickly killed the bees. Bees spent six months establishing a home, raising their young, producing beautiful combs of honey for their masters. Then they were snuffed out, season over. I didn't do this. I gave every colony a chance to survive the winter; but I introduced new bees in packages from Florida each year to expand my small bee business.

Economics indicated package beekeeping was a good thing, and most Saskatchewan beekeepers in the 1970's killed their bees in the autumn. They sold all the honey the bees made, except for a small amount used as feed for new bees the next spring. New bees arrived from California (or Texas or Florida) in small screened boxes – packages - each April. Bees from the south were cheap. It cost about fifteen dollars to buy three pounds of bees and a queen – enough to start a new colony. If a hive was killed in the fall, an extra forty dollars worth of honey would be extracted. Then the equipment was stored in a clean dry building. Packages were a good thing.

Using packages made good sense in some ways – trying to keep bees alive over winter on the prairies is risky. To winter bees, surplus honey has to be left on the hive. And the equipment stays outside, freezing, getting wet, aging quickly. Wintered hives are wrapped in expensive insulation material, and the work is tedious. Some of the wrapped hives die during the winter, after eating a hundred pounds of honey left by the beekeeper. The queen in an over-wintered colony becomes old, doesn't lay enough eggs. There were a lot of reasons to kill bees in the fall and start fresh each spring, but few beekeepers found pleasure in the slaughter. I decided I would winter all my bees, but also bring new bees in from the States every spring, to increase my numbers and to replace any hives that died during the winter.

Buzz and I watched the trail of dust left by the cattle truck. Buzz told me that I worked too hard. "What's a smart boy like you doing in a place like this?" he asked. I didn't answer. Meanwhile, his calves were gone, the cows stood in the pasture near the corral, bawling. I headed for my truck.

"You want to eat?"

"What are you having? Beef?" I asked.

"Chicken," said Buzz.

He grinned and headed for Mary's kitchen.

After six months in Val Marie, I was feeling somewhat Canadian. I had survived the winds, dust in the nose, cacti needles in the knee. And I had listened to the CBC almost every day. Of course, I had not yet experienced a prairie winter. Nor should I. By December, I would be in the southern states. Even that seemed pretty Canadian to me.

October. Various friends invited me to their homes to share the Thanksgiving meal. Canadians planned ahead, but inviting guests six weeks before Thanksgiving? I was impressed. I typically could not guess what I might be doing an hour into the future. Then I started to see the Thanksgiving Day ads on the store window, fliers in the mail. The crass commercialization was even worse than in the States, where Thanksgiving is only advertised for two or three weeks. Dinner invitations kept coming.

"Thanks, but I'm having Thanksgiving in P A with my family."

"We thought you were from the States?" A young lady retrieving mail at the post office asked. I didn't know her well, her mom had bought a pail of honey, then sent Sue over to the shop to buy another.

"I am from the States," I said. "You really plan ahead."

"What do you mean?" she asked. "Thanksgiving is in three days! If you're not going up to P A, you can have dinner at our house."

Non-American Canadian Holidays:	
May 19:	Victoria Day
June 24:	St. Jean Baptiste Day
July 1:	Canada Day
August 4:	Heritage/Family Day
October 13:	Thanksgiving
December 26:	Boxing Day
(Some Holiday dates vary year-to-year)	

This was getting confusing. Saskatchewanians say P A when they mean Prince Albert. I said P A because I meant Pennsylvania. In the States, Thanksgiving is on a Thursday in late November. I had no idea Canadian Thanksgiving was on a Monday, in early October.

First Frost

I ate at the young lady's house on Monday. Her mom, dad, three sisters, two brothers, grandparents – on both sides – found it easy to squeeze one more chair up to the table. "It's not a bother," her dad said. "We just throw a little extra water in the soup."

The food was great, the folks were nice, but it was noisy, everyone grabbed from big bowls in a great hurry. The food was good, but I was uncomfortable. I was reminded too much of the crowded table I had left back on the family farm in Pennsylvania.

**The Val Marie Back Yard was a Winter Wonderland
– my Neighbours Did Not Share my Exuberance**

One night, the windows of my tiny house shook, a north wind rattled the panes. The glass whitened. Snow - wet and heavy - replaced leaves torn from the trees during the night. The prairie looked fresh and clean, clad in white.

I enjoyed the crisp cold air. But I was leaving for Florida in a few days to raise queen bees and produce orange blossom honey. I kicked at the snow with my boot; the Val Marie villagers tramped upon the slosh. They would be staying in this winter-wonderland, it would be months before they would enjoy long sunny days again.

**A Hive, with Bees Snug as Bugs,
Wrapped for the Long Winter in
Pink Insulation and Black Tar Paper**

The morning after the first snowfall of winter, I began wrapping wintering material around my hives, brushing snow off the hive covers, replacing it with fuzzy pink fiberglass. I stretched kolomax - heavy, black, water resistant paper - over the boxes and insulation, then looped baler twine around everything. It took three days to wrap my hives. They wouldn't be touched again for six months.

I had no reason to spend the winter in Val Marie. Other bees I owned, in the States, had finished their season in Wisconsin. I needed to cart them to Florida. I drained water from the pipe that led up to the honey shop. I emptied the water pump in the basement, dumped antifreeze into the toilet and sinks, as Frank had done a year earlier. Then I went to Wong's for lunch.

Harry Wong was selling his restaurant and moving to Swift Current. He smiled at me and took my order. Then he came out of the kitchen with something in his hands. He handed me his abacus. He hadn't used it in years, he told me, it had sat idly above the stove in his café kitchen. His grandfather's abacus had a thin layer of grey rust, the beads longed to be dragged across their wires, to count and add. "You like numbers," Harry said. "You keep this now."

The American agents who worked the border apparently weren't paid enough money. They had to make up the difference on their own. I learned about this my first year in Canada. When I left for Florida, I had four hundred pounds of honey in the back of my truck. Fifty neatly packaged clean white pails. Gifts for family, friends, and people in Florida who let me put bees in their orange groves.

The American officer looked in my camper. "I heard about you," he said. "The Hutterites say your bees make the best honey."

I started to thank him for the compliment. He interrupted me.

"We wanted to buy some honey from you this summer, but never made it up to Val Marie. Can I get some now?"

First Frost

I was going to say no. All the honey pails had previously assigned homes. But he was wearing a gun.

"I don't have any cash on me," he continued. "I'll pay you next spring, when you come back. You are coming back, right?"

I gave him an eight pound pail of honey.

"What else ya' haulin'?" he asked.

Did he want some of my clothes? "Clothes."

"OK. How many pounds of honey are you haulin'?" He was counting my pails.

"I had four hundred pounds. Now I have eight pounds less."

"The duty on four hundred pounds of honey is eight dollars."

I knew that the tax was one cent a pound, four dollars, not eight. I told him. I had become bold because it looked like he wasn't going to take any of my clothes.

"Is it?" he said. "OK. Maybe you're right." I gave him four dollars. He stuffed the cash into his shirt pocket. I wondered if he'd still be working there the next spring. He wasn't.

Winter Apiary of FJ Miller, London, Ontario
Wrapped in Wood Shavings and Wooden Cases,
From AI Root's 1913 <u>ABC and XYZ of Bee Culture</u>

ANNUAL HONEY BEE MIGRATIONS

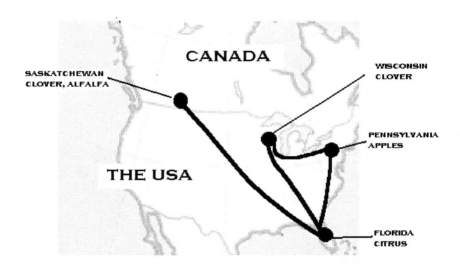

Florida Hives Went to Apple Orchards in Pennsylvania,
then on to Clover Fields in Wisconsin.
Meanwhile, I Hauled Packages from the Florida Groves to Saskatchewan.
The Entire Annual Migration Kept Four People Employed at Exxon,
Looking for Gasoline for my Trucks.

On the Road

It's evening. Nearly dark. The autumn air, crisp. Frost coats the clovers, bees cluster tightly for warmth within their nest. A cloud of white smoke drifts into the hive entrance. It's too late in the day for the bees to take flight and flee the smoke. But, instinctively, they gorge honey, anticipating escape from the fire. The beehive shakes, tilts. Not quite upside down, but down becomes left, up is to the right. Another hard shake and the nest is level again. Bees try to crawl out of the hive, to investigate the cause of the commotion, but they are overwhelmed by a new odor. The foreign scent of bees from other hives. Other colonies are stacked above and below and on each side of their wooden hive. A low rumbling begins and everything vibrates again. This time, though, a soft, soothing quake, a cradle's lullaby. It lasts for two days. The bees are on a truck, traveling across the continent.

Suddenly the rumbling ceases. It's quiet and the bees begin to crawl out of their hive, investigate. A quick jolt sends the colony into warm air and bright light. A rebirth. The hive is far from the snowy pasture; it drops onto warm sand. The bees are greeted by a blazing sun, scouts fly out of the hive, mark their colony's new location using a towering, moss-clad live oak as a reference, and dart off to small yellow flowers in a meadow. They rush back to their sisters with wads of pollen. The earth is fertile; the colony will eat well again.

I left Saskatchewan November sixth. Away from the prairies and plains. As I drove east, the short grass on the high prairies of the dry west was replaced by tall grass. The arid western air ceded to muggy humidity, the taller grasses transformed themselves into dense collections of trees. Strange to see the thick, dark trunks with branches growing out the top, branches towering high above the road. For a boy escaping the bald prairie, trees seem parasitic. Blights upon the earth, sucking water and nourishment from the soil, shading the grass from the sun's energy. It took days to recover from this distorted interpretation of the ecology.

Becoming comfortable with the nearness of neighbors took even longer. Villages were towns and cities now. As I drove farther and farther east, farm houses, barns, and silos were perched so close to the highway I thought I would hit them with the side mirror of my truck. I parked, stretched my arms out. My fingers could almost touch the buildings that surrounded me. I had been in Saskatchewan for only six months, but depth and breadth were disturbingly rearranged. The east was scaring me.

I arrived in Wisconsin the eighth day of November. My older brother, Don, had used my American bees for the summer. They had made sixty-two barrels of clover honey. Don gave me twenty barrels, my share for his use of my bees. Selling the honey gave me enough money to move the American bees back to Florida and buy sugar to feed them. I spent only a day in Wisconsin with Don.

When I was child, this brother who was eight years older was my favorite sibling. We played board games, chess especially. Don was brilliant at the game. Unforgiving, unyielding. I never beat him. He couldn't allow anyone to win against him. At this or any other game. "If you beat me, it will be because you're better; not because I let you win."

He was physically the biggest, tallest, strongest of my five brothers. When he was twenty, and I was twelve, the US Army snatched him from the family farm, dressed him in drab olive green. Instead of dropping him in Viet Nam, they sent Don to patrol the demilitarized zone in Korea. He came back a sergeant, won the Army's highest service award. But he put all his medals, his stripes, and his uniform into a steel box that he rarely opened.

"You can't stay here longer?" he asked.

"No, gotta get these bees to Florida. But I'm leaving the Dodge here. I'll be back in a month to pick it up. Maybe I'll stay a day or two then." I was wound up tight. Needed to keep moving.

**My Brother Don had Gathered Together my Wisconsin Hives
into One Enormous Apiary, Ready for Loading and Hauling to Florida**

I swapped vehicles; parked my half ton beside Don's greenhouse, took my big three axle truck with its trailer from behind Don's shed. My ten-wheeled truck had stayed in Wisconsin while I was in Saskatchewan. Don used the big truck to harvest our Wisconsin honey crop. He kept the vehicle serviced and running. Now it was ready to transport my bees to Florida.

Don had collected all the hives together from their summer pastures and arranged them in a corner of a dairy farm pasture. Wind swept crusty flakes of snow off the hives as we lifted bee boxes into the big truck. My fingers ached from grasping the icy boxes, but the bees stayed inside their hives - too cold to fly. We quickly loaded three hundred forty double story hives onto my mammoth GMC. I drove south with my bees. Away from Wisconsin winter.

On the Road

November is a good month to move bees from the north to the south. By late autumn, northern hives have begun to prepare for winter. The queen, no longer stimulated by heat, long sunny days and fresh pollen, quits laying eggs. The bees cluster tightly together in the cool weather.

If one lifts the bees from their cold slumber and

Hives of Bees Loaded in my Truck and Trailer - Leaving the Snowy North for Florida

drops them into a warm southern climate, the bees get active again.

Moving bees in November is good, but the best time to make the move is late December. Then the bees reach the tropics only a few weeks before southern springtime. The warm air and bright Florida sunshine stimulates the bees; they expand their brood nests. Maples, oaks, and willows yield pollen and nectar; the bees soon develop big populations. They become powerful hives by the time the citrus bloom starts in March. Winter solstice is a good time to move bees from north to south.

But I was moving my bees from Wisconsin to Florida in November.

Florida. The name means florid, covered with flowers. This is what the Spanish found. It's what beekeepers still find today. But strangely, the Flower State, with its year long blossoms, is not the best place to keep bees. Saskatchewan – with its brief three month flowering season – is better. Seems odd, but think of it this way: a parcel of earth has flowers growing on it. If a wide variety of flowers blossom, a few each month, for twelve months, there is no great flood of honey. Saskatchewan, with relatively few types of flowers but all blooming simultaneously, yields a huge amount of honey. Instead of one pound of honey a day for a year (which the bees would consume because they stay active), Saskatchewan may tender twenty pounds a day for twenty days. The bees have so much they can't eat it all. They store a huge excess.

Nevertheless, Florida beekeepers can be successful. If they move their hives around the state, taking colonies to places where there is an abundance of flowers of one type all blooming the same month. Natural and man-made monoculture zones. The gallberry marshes near the Georgia border in May; mangrove along the coast in July; pepper bush and melaluca in the far south in October; citrus in central Florida in March. Less progressive beekeepers let their hives sit in the dormant orange groves all year - idle in their stupor until the citrus blossoms again the following spring. But the honeybees that did the best were moved away from Florida for the summer, then back again in late December, a few days before southern spring.

Even though later is better, most northern beekeepers haul their bees into Florida during November. The reasons for the less optimal timing are partly practical, but mostly regulatory. In Wisconsin in late December, hives sitting on the ground have a bad habit of freezing to the icy soil or being buried under snow drifts. Welded to the ground, they can't be lifted again until after the spring thaw. Of course there are solutions. The hives could be stacked on pallets and covered with loose tarps to protect them from the weather. We did that one year in Wisconsin. A beekeeper might out-smart the weather, but the government made it even more difficult to move bees late in the year.

Florida's strict importation regulations meant that a government inspector in Wisconsin had to look at the bees before winter started. *"While the bees were still active."* The officer had to open hives and examine the bees and brood. After being certified healthy, the bees had to reach Florida within thirty days. Wisconsin would not inspect past October. Most years, the bees didn't have brood to inspect after October. And the state didn't have enough money to inspect later in the year – they had to get their seasonal inspectors off payroll and out of the field as early as possible. Government money for bee inspection is scarce. So, examinations ended in October, Wisconsin bees arrived in Florida in November.

Trucking bees is not complicated. Load the hives in an hour or two, try to drive without stopping until the trip is over. I liked driving. All the physical work was done, the human energy spent. Time to relax in the cab with music and coffee, one hand on the steering wheel. Wisconsin, Chicago, Nashville, Atlanta, Florida. About two days for a truck load of bees to reach its southern destination. Then offload as quickly as possible. Don't stop. Stopping, especially if the weather is warm, can suffocate the bees. The migratory beekeeper doesn't want problems, trouble, delays.

Trouble started south of Chicago. The snowfall and light breeze that kept the bees quiet while Don and I loaded them in Wisconsin became a huge blizzard in Indiana. Interstate 65 was reduced to a single south-bound line of traffic. Ice and snow pelted my truck's windshield. I followed an Exxon fuel tanker. Snow and ice caked over the letters on the tail end of the huge pot of oil. I followed, watched as the red letters disappeared under white snow, until only two big letters, the X's, guided me.

The tanker driver blew snow off the slow lane of the highway; I humbly rolled along behind the great beast, grateful that a professional driver was cutting trail. Grateful that the tanker had slowed to twenty-five miles per hour. Not all the traffic that day could afford to travel south at such a restricted pace. I watched as cars and pick-up trucks occasionally attempted to pass my truck and my small trailer. Travelers in a hurry, with important things to do. I marveled at their courage as they shot their small chariots around my truck. I watched as the deep snow in the unused passing lane flooded their windshields and the erring drivers slid off the road, engulfed their vehicles in cold snow drifts off the highway's edge. I stayed to the path.

My fists hurt as I clenched the steering wheel. My eyes were runny, bleary from staring into the swirling white flakes that tried to obscure my view of the giant cargo truck a few hundred feet ahead of me. I decided that if the tanker pulled off the road, I would also quit driving. But on we went. Through a white blur for three hours. Then the storm ended. Snow left the highway. The sun shone. We drove sixty again. The patient cars that had stayed in line behind us were now free to blast around on the clear passing lane. Life was good. For a while.

Late afternoon. Clouds again darkened the sky. I was still on Interstate 65, approaching Nashville, entering the city during a light rain. Traffic was heavy, stalled at times. The rain became sleet, then ice. A happy man with a smiling voice on the A.M. station said, "It's a good night to stay at home! What a mess on our roads tonight! A tanker truck fell over and spilled gasoline all over Interstate 65." The accident was a mile ahead of me. Flashing road signs urged traffic in my lane to exit, detour. Obediently, I got off the highway and found myself driving on a busy parallel side street in the big city. I fought red lights, struggled against merging traffic and cars sliding on ice in front of me. I continued to drive south. I could see the accident on the highway below me, to my left. I wanted to get back to the relative comfort of Interstate 65. I looked longingly at the main route.

Past the accident site, traffic was moving much more quickly on the freeway than it was on my side road. At the next red light, possessed with uncontrolled inspiration, I swung my big truck and trailer load of bees into the left lane, turning my truck back towards Interstate 65. Unfortunately, my road and the Interstate did not converge. Instead, I found myself on an overpass, above the coveted highway.

My shortcut to the Interstate ended abruptly in a parking lot, surrounded by gray apartment buildings. A few people stood in the rain, amid graffiti, old cars, trash. They saw my old truck, saw me through my windshield, must have recognized how confused and weary I looked. Windows on the floor above the spectators were shattered. Bad neighborhood. Folks watched idly as I attempted to turn my rig around in their crowded car lot. Tight fit. I couldn't see behind my truck. *Bad neighborhood.* I imagined a small article in the following day's *Tennessee Tribune*. Something about a farm boy getting lost in the wrong part of town. My story involved a knife. No, a gun. A gun, a bad neighborhood, and a very dumb farm kid. I sat in my truck, the engine quietly idling. I ignored the sound of fingers tapping on my truck door. I was trying to figure out how I would get out of this mess. But the elderly gentleman in the yellow raincoat persistently rapped on my truck's door, tried to get my attention. I rolled down my window.

"Ya want me to spot for you?" the old black man asked.

"What?" I said.

"Wan' me to spot? I'll watch so you don't hit nothing."

After he got me turned around, he asked where I was going. He told me I would need to go out of the parking lot and turn right, left in two blocks, then left again. This would put me back on the Interstate. Soon I had escaped the parking lot, turned right, and was about to turn left. I wasn't far from the dangerous parking lot and I'd driven painfully slowly, not wanting to make another mistake. My window was still rolled down. I realized that the old man in the yellow raincoat was now walking beside me on the slippery sidewalk.

"You doin' fine, son," he said, "Your highway's just ahead."

Bad Beekeeping

I continued to do fine, arriving in Florida the next day.

The warmest part of Florida begins about a third of the way down the long sandy peninsula. Drivers must cross one of the rivers or swamps that separate the tropics from the cooler zone to the north. Tributaries of the Suwannee, to the west, and the St. Johns, to the east, meet in a swampy area north of the Ocala Forest in Putnam County. To reach the hot part of Florida, drivers have to cross a bridge. At the bridge is an agriculture inspection station. Armed guards check every truck entering and leaving south Florida. Grain, fruit, milk, vegetables, cattle, hogs, bees.

Compared to the relatively relaxed border patrol protecting Canada, these agricultural inspectors looked pretty grim. Guns. Patrol jeeps. Guns. Mirrors to look under trucks. Log books, wireless radios. Guns. These rigorous inspection efforts may help curb the flow of drugs into Florida, but the inspectors work for their state's department of agriculture. Their main job is to control the spread of exotic pests that might thrive in the isolated tropics. A bug or weed that is only a casual pest a hundred miles north may grow monstrous populations in the subtropics. Such pests would cost fruit and vegetable growers billions of dollars. Every living thing – except humans and pets – must be inspected and accompanied by proper paper work before entering or leaving sub-tropical Florida.

Hundreds of truck loads of bees pass through the Florida entry points every fall.[34] Beekeepers return from cranberry bogs and blueberry fields in Maine, clover-covered dairy farms in Wisconsin, basswood forests in Pennsylvania, alfalfa draped prairie in the Dakotas. California, Arizona, Texas, Georgia, and Florida host a million colonies of exiled bees a year. Bees carried south to enjoy winter heat. Heat that allows colonies to survive the winter while generating some income for their owners. Orange blossom honey is harvested, new queen bees produced, new beehives established.

**Dad's Bees, Heading South in 1959
Sans Nets for 3 Days on the Road**

The system of moving bees to follow the bloom is called migratory beekeeping. A hundred years ago, one pioneer put bees on a barge and followed the seasons along the Mississippi River.[35] But migratory activity was rare until the 1950s when roads and trucks became better. Fifty years ago, my father was one of the first beekeepers to haul hives a thousand miles. He loaded his bees on a red six-wheeled International that pulled a flat bed trailer. The trip from his farm in Pennsylvania's

Appalachians to Florida's swamps took three days, four hundred miles a day. None of his journey was on four-lane highways. His route crawled through towns and cities along the eastern seaboard. Today's interstates by-pass city traffic lights and stop signs and turn the trek into a relatively quick and easy journey.

Now, billions of honeybees are moved around North America every year. It's the way modern farming is done. In the west, beekeepers haul bees from Montana's hay meadows to California's almond groves every fall. In the center of the country, bees leave Ruby Red Grapefruit trees behind in Texas' Rio Grande Valley and relocate on summer sunflowers in Kansas and Nebraska. The beekeepers usually move with their bees, sometimes dragging families and kids to new schools and new playmates in new climates.

My Father and Grandfather, Tending Bees in a West Virginia Apple Orchard, April, 1948

Monoculture farm production - thousands of acres of uniform crops - requires dramatic intervention to compensate for the disruption of the natural ecology. In an undisturbed area, there are enough wild pollinating insects to satisfy a half dozen crab apples and some elderberry bushes growing on the edge of a forest. But when a farmer strips out the forest to plant a thousand acres of tightly spaced Grannie Smiths, five hundred colonies of honeybees must be trucked in from a thousand miles away to replace banished indigenous pollinators. As soon as the apples set their fruit, the commercial bees are dislocated so the orchard grower can soak tree mites and worms with insecticide.[36]

Poisons, of course, further reduce the natural pollinating population. It's how we farm in North America. My reproach is not meant as a condemnation of the way we grow our food. I participated in the process for years and it may be the cheapest way - in the short term - to feed the billions of folks around the world who would like to eat. Agribusiness has increased the food supply and kept costs low, or at least deferred the real price to the next generation. Cheap food allows North Americans to spend more money on their car than they spend on food.[37] It is a choice we all have made, not only the farmers and chemical companies. All of us. Even the neighbor lady, who wants to drive to the supermarket in an Oldsmobile to buy three perfectly spotless apples.

I was at the Florida entry inspection station. Five in the morning. The grizzled and weary agriculture inspector looked more haggard than I. He took my entry permit and slowly read it. We walked around my truck.

"Three hundred fifty hives. Extra covers. Excluders? What's them? And *extra bottoms*?" He read the paper again. I didn't answer.

It was dark. But warm. The bees, riding quietly for almost two days in their cool hives, were beginning to notice the Florida heat and the bright floodlights of the inspection station. A few bees found a crack in the screen that covered the load. They flew aimlessly around our heads. "Can I use your phone?" I asked. The guard pointed to a pay phone.

"Pull up to them weigh scales first. Then you can use the phone. But park your truck over there, we got enough strays flying round here already."

After passing the weight test, I hopped down from the cab, walked past a limp sago palm, then waited for my turn at the phone. I called my oldest brother. David was glad to hear I was on schedule, said he'd meet my truck and help me offload. He said I still had about four hours of driving, but it was supposed to be cool all day. High of seventy.

**My Hives, Off-loaded using the Armstrong Technique
in a Florida Pasture, beside an Orange Grove Awaiting Pollination**

David, Clifton Barnes, Jay Stewart, and Ron Nichols waited for me at the Micheloni Ranch. David was a beekeeper. The other guys weren't. The other fellows were his friends, some decent folks who slipped on bee gloves and veils twice a year to help load and off-load beehives by hand.

They took quite a few stings. The hives were heavy and the fellows groaned and complained with each box. But they lifted them off the truck and staggered away, scattering the bees around the pasture. Jay found a clump of Wisconsin snow still stuck under the handle of a hive. Everyone took turns tossing the snow ball. But the work went on. In an hour, my hives were spewed along the warm ground. Bees flew from the boxes, out into the bright Florida sunshine, and returned with tiny wads of pale pollen stuck to their legs. "Spanish needle," David said. "It's the only thing blooming." Job done, we drove to the Rainbow in Mascotte for breakfast.

White corn grits and hot buns. Three eggs each. Six strips of bacon. It was the only pay these men received. Breakfast. And the satisfaction of helping someone through a tough job. It had been hard physical work and everyone had been stung a few times. We did our work by hand; other beekeepers owned gasoline-driven forklifts and loaded palletized hives onto flat-bed semi-trailers.

On the Road

But to move my bees, ham and eggs powered the human machinery that did the work. We called it the Armstrong technique – it worked as long as the arms were strong. My helpers were used to hard work. Jay worked for the county, building roads. Ron owned a greenhouse and nursery. Clifton tended an orange grove. David had always been a beekeeper. Now he was past thirty. He had a reputation as the best queen bee producer in the state. He had worked at university and government entomology labs in New York and Wisconsin, and he had been employed by a variety of beekeepers. Then he shrewdly cobbled together a big honey and queen breeding business.

"I still remember when you drove your dad's truck into Mascotte," Ron Nichols said to David. "You weren't even eighteen."

"Yea, you went from station to station, looking for the cheapest gas."

"Whatever happened to that old Chevy?"

David looked across the table at me. "I sold it to him last fall for a hundred bucks!" Everyone laughed. "It was a good deal for Ron, still ran fine, only had two hundred thousand miles on it."

"Shoot man," said Clifton to me, "You got a good deal. Can't get anything that'll fire a spark for under five hundred."

Within a couple of days, I moved my bees off the Micheloni Ranch and into a dozen different locations – pastures, woods, groves. These Wisconsin hives now sat amid scrub oaks, palmetto, gallberry. The weather was mild, but the high humidity was uncomfortable. Even in the shade, sweat beaded on my forehead. My thick dark hair curled and kinked into tight ringlets. Despite the warm damp air, I had a lot of energy - partly due to the lower elevation. The thinner atmosphere up in Saskatchewan was replaced by Florida's warm, thick, oxygen-rich sea-level air. And the change in scenery and culture gave me a boost of energy.

Beekeeping was so different in Florida from Saskatchewan. I had no neighbor beekeepers in Val Marie. There were dozens around Groveland. But things in the USA were rougher, even hostile. Beekeeping is occasionally a rude business. For several years, thousands of hives were stolen in Florida by a band of rogue beekeepers who drove into isolated apiaries, loaded equipment at night, hauled it home. They killed the bees, removed the honey, melted the wax. Allegedly to buy cocaine with the cash. They were caught. Other beekeepers, irritated by new hives entering their old neighborhoods, sometimes dumped gasoline into the imported hives. The gas fumes quickly killed the competing bees and spoiled the hive equipment. Beekeeping could be a rough sport.

When beekeepers aren't stealing, burning, or poisoning other beekeepers' bees, the competition may instead be friendly and stimulating. We compare ourselves to other beekeepers, then we try harder. I was familiar with friendly competition. For my family of ten siblings, the struggle started early when we tried to find ways to get our father to remember our names. An easy way to get noticed was to pick potatoes faster than the next kid in line. For beekeepers, it was more hives, a bigger crop, newer trucks. Rarely, a nicer house. Always, more hives.

The most successful beekeeper, the yardstick we stand erect against, may be a local beekeeper with three thousand hives and four trucks. In southern Saskatchewan, in the late seventies, there were no other commercial beekeepers within a hundred miles. No one to learn from, no one to compete against, to compare my results. But in central Florida, beekeepers were as thick as, well, bees on honey. Within minutes, I could visit my brother, with his thousand hives. Or Keith, a Wisconsin ex-history teacher keeping fifteen hundred hives. Or Larry, the former psychologist. Leon, the former banker. Or Gary, Mel, Bob, Randy, Joel. Stan, Willi, and Ray lived in Johnny Stieffel's Trailer Court, the same place I rented a house for the winter. All these people moved bees down from the northern states and kept hundreds or thousands of hives of bees. Other beekeepers stayed in Florida all year – Jim Ely, a local guy with three hundred hives. The Randall's.

A dozen commercial beekeepers in and around Groveland, Florida. Average age: 30. Average number of hives: 800. Average net worth: $50,000. Average net income: $10,000, probably less. Most beekeepers lived well below the poverty-line, preferring to re-invest profits in new trucks and new beehives. The financial rewards of beekeeping are not impressive.

My Wisconsin bees were now Florida bees. I spent a few days opening hives and checking food supplies. Colonies would need forty pounds of honey to survive from November until March in Florida. Most of the hives had enough food. I dusted the top bars with a mix of antibiotics and powdered sugar. I dumped chlordane under the hives to keep fire ants away. After these chemical treatments, the bees could be left on their own for two months. I moved sheets, pillows, clothes, and books into the furnished two bedroom mobile home at Stiefel's on Highway 50 in Mascotte. I parked my truck at my brother David's farm, then flew back to Wisconsin to get my half ton truck.

I drove the smaller truck back to Florida, taking my time. Hiking in the Smokey Mountains; wading in a bay in North Carolina. Sleeping on the seat of my truck behind a gas station right outside Charleston, South Carolina. Arriving at my rented Florida trailer home late on a December afternoon. Hot again. When I snapped on the light switch, roaches scurried across the kitchen floor, disappearing into air ducts cut into the linoleum. I was back.

Moving Bees a Few Miles
Photo from Al Root's 1913 <u>ABC & XYZ of Bee Culture</u>

Ron on the Radio

When the weather is fine and nectar drips from flower blossoms, bees work until their tattered wings fall off through over-use. But bees are smart. When it's too hot, too cold, too windy, too dry, too rainy, too something, bees relax at home. When the weather isn't nice, they don't build new combs, they don't raise children, they don't even eat very much. Perhaps they read good books and listen to music, or have radios tuned to the CBC.

Driving across Florida from the west, it's Mascotte first, then Groveland. No one would call Mascotte and Groveland twin cities. Separated by a mile or two, depending on who holds the survey chain, the towns merge in a mix of trailer courts, hardware stores, restaurants and bars. Groveland is wealthier, almost upscale. Mascotte has more rural roots, older buildings. Approaching from the west on Highway 50, from Tampa, a driver passes Stuckey, sometimes called the Quarters or the Negro Quarters by older folks. A few dozen shacks and some nice, modest homes. And a *"Good Time Party Place"* according to four-foot tall purple words scrawled on an orange cement-block dance hall.

Black people lived in Stuckey, so I don't think it was actually a part of Mascotte. The absence of people of color in Mascotte is a remnant of a tradition that goes back at least to Theodore Ruff, the town leader who forced the Taylor brothers to locate the area's first industry outside the village, back in 1895. The Taylor brothers were tapping pine trees and distilling turpentine. They wanted black laborers to work in their shop. Mayor Ruff said he wouldn't allow it, not within the village of Mascotte. So the Taylor brothers set up east of town. They founded Taylorville, which became Groveland.[38]

Groveland grew into a center of business and commerce; Mascotte didn't. Years passed; the south changed. White and black kids were joined by Hispanics at the Groveland High School; their parents shopped together at Edge's. By that time, I lived in the cheapest place I could find. On State Route 50, in a trailer court that straddled the city limits of each community. A location slightly more a part of Mascotte than Groveland.

Surrounding both towns were a half million acres of orange trees. Valencia was the big crop, but thousands of acres were planted in grapefruit and Navels. In March, the citrus trees held a billion white blossoms and the air stank with the thick odor of nectar dripping from flowers. It was this nectar that lured beekeepers to Lake County. At a time of the year when spring was still an uncertain promise on the Canadian prairies, bees were sucking millions of pounds of honey from Florida citrus trees.

My bees were settled in swamps near the orange groves that surrounded Mascotte and Groveland. Prior to the March honey flow, the winter bee chores were light and easy. I had time to meet people, visit family, tour Florida, while I waited for spring.

Twelve hundred miles north, in Pennsylvania, my father had vineyards. Orchards. And twenty acres in row crops – potatoes, tomatoes, bell peppers, sweet corn. This kept him busy all summer. Years earlier, when he had ten kids living at home, the farm kept us all busy. We would weed and hoe and pick and pack. Weeks might pass without any of us going ten miles to Greenville, Sharpsville, or any other bustling community. We were rural hermits - hillbillies, perhaps. But our isolation was occasionally broken by city-folks who came to our farm to buy the apples and tomatoes and honey we produced.

Mom and Dad Working in their Greenhouse, Spring of 1971

In the family greenhouses, Dad had an acre of bedding plants – flowers and vegetables raised from seed and sold to people who wanted their own gardens. This kept him busy all winter. He was almost always busy. Gardens in summer, greenhouses in winter. His only break was a few days between seasons.

In early December, Dad left Pennsylvania and came to visit Florida.

He was a visitor, not a tourist. Anyone who has once lived in a place, bought a house, planted a few trees – can never be a tourist there again. Dad had kept bees in Florida for several winters, back in the late 50s and 60s when Yankee beekeepers were unwelcome novelties in the south. He wrestled hives onto trucks and trailers and carted them across the country to get a second season. He raised a few queens, split two hundred colonies into four hundred, made a little orange blossom honey, then trucked the bees back to Pennsylvania. But after a few years, he quit. He and Mom started the greenhouses that gave them a change of seasons without traveling on a narrow thousand mile road.

Dad was waiting for me at the Orlando Airport, smoking his corn cob pipe under the big 'No Smoking' sign. He was dressed in dirty work boots with long leather laces - long enough to wrap around the ankles of his khaki pants so that honeybees crawling on the ground couldn't work their way up his legs. His head was shielded by a faded brown hat with a thin broad brim, designed to shade his dark face from the sun, but strong enough to support a wire-mesh bee veil.

The khaki clothes, boots, and hat were the garb of a beekeeper. Fashion Dad started wearing thirty years earlier. Even though he no longer worked with bees, his uniform never changed. It was the same style he had worn when he had walked me through one of his Pennsylvania apiaries, late in March, when I was five years old. I saw the air thick with fuzzy brown bees gathering pollen from pussy willow along the muddy creek where Mr. Reno watered his Guernseys. Dad in khakis. The same clothing he wore when we drove his big trucks into the hilly West Virginia apple orchards ten years later, setting heavy beehives among the white blossoms. Same clothing he wore in his little honey shop while we dropped yellow honeycombs into his rusty extracting machines.

Ron on the Radio

Dad visited Florida for seven days. He said he wanted to stay longer but he didn't wish to bother my brother David or me. He came to help us, he said. I needed the most help. I was storing some beekeeping equipment at David's farm, keeping bees on the Micheloni and Kuharske ranches, living in a house trailer in Mascotte.

Dad figured I needed a place to clump everything together, a place of my own. Everywhere we went, he asked people if they had any land for sale.

Ron and Dad

We went to Billy Howard's hardware store in Groveland. Billy sold everything I needed to stay in the bee business except trucks, gasoline, and sugar. Tom Booth was there. Visiting. Dad knew Tom. They talked, Dad wanted to ask if Tom or Billy knew of any farmland for sale, but Billy Howard was on the phone. We heard only one side of the conversation. We listened.

"I highly recommend Mister Evans. He's a good plumber. One of the best. And cheap," said Mr. Howard to the voice on the phone. "But, do you know Mister Evans? No? Well, Mister Evans is a gentleman of color."

My father explained to me. "Billy Howard doesn't know if he's talking to a colored or a white," Dad whispered. "Billy can't recommend a colored plumber without letting the person on the phone know. The caller might be a little old white lady who wouldn't want a colored in her house." Billy Howard was a fair man living in a changing south. He wouldn't want his black friend to lose a plumbing job, but he couldn't send him over to someone's house without advance warning, just in case.

We were waiting for the conversation to end, so Dad could ask about land. I continued to listen in on Billy Howard's conversation.

Bad Beekeeping

Living in Florida was complicated. About a quarter of the folks residing around Mascotte and Groveland were people of color. Another quarter were Hispanic. The white half was partly new-comers, many of them Yankees, but many from other parts of the south - Alabama, Georgia, Tennessee. Others of the white people were old-family - descended from settlers who reached central Florida a hundred years earlier. We were white, black, Hispanic. By 1980, an uneasy truce had replaced much of the racial animosity that led to the naming of Gallows Lake and the torching of one of the Quarters during the 1950s.

I was white, but southern European. I had dark curly hair and skin that tanned deeply in the bright Florida sun. I was occasionally greeted in Spanish by my neighbors. These people of Spanish ancestry had not arrived five hundred years earlier with Ponce de Leon - they were largely, but not exclusively, immigrants from Mexico. They came during the past twenty years, seeking their fortune through hard physical labor. In that way, I wasn't so different from them.

Phone conversation ended, I was buying Billy Howard's nails; Dad was learning about Tom Booth's farm. Tom owned forty acres, deep within the Bay Lake swamps. He drew a simple map, showing us how to find the sand trail opposite Mac Kuharske's barn.

**Part of my Florida Farm was Low, Wet and Swampy.
But it Included an Alligator.**

We found the trail. It led across a nematode barrier – a broad track of uncultivated sand that kept parasitic worms from following the infected roots of grapefruit trees from one grove to the next. The trail turned sharply right, to the edge of a shallow lake. A three foot alligator gazed up lazily from the shore and slithered into the water as we drove past. Tom Booth's farm included an alligator.

The acreage began in a thicket of tall straight pines that shaded the path. Squeezing through the small forest, a field opened up before us, exposing rich black muck that had been harrowed smooth. In the middle of the field stood a small cypress barn with a tin roof. Somewhere for me to store bee boxes. Tom Booth wanted to sell the farm, but said he'd already agreed with a man in Stuckey that he could plant the field into pole beans. As he had every year for the past ten years. I could have the farm if I let the man have his beans.

Ron on the Radio

Tom's terms were easy. I gave him a down payment of four thousand dollars, money from the sale of fifteen barrels of honey. And I agreed to pay two hundred dollars a month for seven years. That worked out to about sixteen thousand dollars. Cheap for forty acres of Florida. But half the land was under water, or at least covered in cypress and swamp. And the access road was an issue. A big issue.

I talked to the people who owned the land that my trail crossed. They grumbled about me coming and going, building a house back in the swamp beyond their groves. They wouldn't sell me an easement. But they didn't stop me from entering my property, crossing their land every day. And they were likely relieved the acreage was being sold to a beekeeper instead of a land developer. Access or not, I bought the farm.

Later that week, I took Dad with me to south Florida. He had never been to Miami, five hours away. A climate away. Central Florida, where I bought Tom Booth's farm, is semi-tropical, which means it can freeze hard, and usually does, at least once every winter. Miami and the farmland south of it rarely feels a frost of any sort. Dad was fascinated with the tropical vegetation. He pointed out cassava farms, their tall leaves bending in the breeze. Australian pines, weeping like willows, lined irrigation and drainage ditches between sugarcane fields.

"You might try keeping bees down here," Dad said to me when we passed a melaluca grove, covered in white bottle-brush flowers. "Bees would do well here," he said. But the flat terrain, the poor-looking farms and crude cement-block houses with tin roofs did not appeal to me. And it was much hotter here, near Miami, than it was back in Groveland.

I left Dad wandering around a tropical park beside the ocean. Nearby, I entered a tall steel building that housed the Canadian consulate.

I had an appointment, an immigration interview. Unless I became a landed immigrant, I risked being turned away by a Canadian border guard when returning to Canada in the spring. To run a business in Canada, I either needed to apply for temporary business visas every year, or I needed to become a resident of Canada - a landed immigrant. I chose to become Canadian. So I had to have an interview with the consulate. I collected the necessary papers and tried to make myself look Canadian. I cut five inches of curls from my head, my first short hair cut in years. I wore green polyester pants with a matching jacket. A white shirt and yellow tie. I looked good.

"This is really just a formality," said the consulate agent. "As you know, we've already tentatively approved your application to become a resident of Canada." I knew. The conditional approval letter had arrived after I submitted my high school report card, a credit statement from People's State Bank, a business plan for my honey farm, the results from my physical, a letter of recommendation from the corporal at Val Marie's police station, and two hundred dollars. Apparently, the people in charge of approving immigration requests liked me. Or at least they liked the idea that I would be moving to Saskatchewan. The consulate guy was still talking.

"So, we just need to have a quick interview. Gives me a chance to see what you look like and to ask a few questions. But I really don't have any questions, except I am curious about you keeping bees. Why do you want to keep bees in Saskatchewan?"

Bad Beekeeping

I told him about the climate, the farms and ranches, and how it all made Saskatchewan a great place to keep bees.

"Do you know that Saskatchewan lost four thousand people last year?" he asked. "I mean, the population went down four thousand because more people moved out of the province than were born there. And almost no one moved in. But you say you want to move there?" The agent scratched an ear.

Then he asked me about my family. About my high school. In fifteen minutes, he was out of questions. I was a bit upset that I had driven so far to do so little. He tried to wrap it up.

"Ron," the agent said, "it's been a pleasure meeting you. I get so many different kinds of people wanting to move to Canada. All different colours. It's nice to meet an English-speaking white person like you who wants to come to Canada."

English-speaking white person?

I felt I was in trouble. Were race, color, and language the barriers for entry to Canada, my new country? I wanted to tell him I thought he was a bit stupid. But then, perhaps he'd refuse my visa. Maybe he wasn't stupid at all, maybe he wanted me to agree, to show I was prejudiced, backward. Was this a trick? Either way, he could refuse my application, saying I was unlikely to be a good citizen. I didn't know what to say.

I didn't say anything. I waited for my status. He looked at me. I looked at him. He looked at me. I looked away. Finally, the agent opened a drawer, pulled out a square rubber stamp, and hit the application paper. "APPROVED."

My father was back in Pennsylvania a few days later, tending his geranium and poinsettia plants. My brother David was adding to his workshop. I was cutting brush at my forty-acre farm and moving bee equipment into its old cypress barn.

A week later, I headed up to the Central Florida Beekeepers' Meeting in Eustis.

Beekeepers are among the most crudely individualistic characters on earth, and seldom gather in clusters. Rarely, they may come together in loosely organized events called beekeepers' meetings.

When I was a teenager in Pennsylvania, I attended an oddly memorable beekeepers' meeting. A hobby beekeeper - someone with few hives and little experience - was demonstrating his hive management expertise with a real live hive of angry bees. His lack of skill was impressive. The quick-moving man ripped off the hive cover and fumbled the top super to the ground. Forty spectators stood chatting and watching - a semi-circle of beekeeping disciples - none wearing bee veils, gloves, or other suitable armor. A black buzzing cloud of hostile bees shot out of the dropped box.

I stood at the edge of the gathered crowd and quietly retreated behind a fat oak tree. Others, standing much closer to the learning event, were less lucky. People slapped their faces and ran in circles. Running in a bee-line from clouds of angry insects is helpful, as long as you have some destination in mind. But running in circles is a bit counter-productive – bees are attracted to quickly moving targets. The more circles, the larger an entourage of bees one collects. Some members of the audience had dozens of followers, their whole body made a buzzing sound as they darted past.

Ron on the Radio

Beekeepers' meetings seldom include live hive demonstrations, probably because of the famous Pennsylvania incident. Instead, beekeepers tend to be found sitting on rows of folding chairs, drinking cold coffee from Styrofoam cups, and listening to bee experts - entomologists and various pestologists.

The Eustis gathering was one of those sitting-on-folding-chairs-drinking-cold-coffee meetings. The Central Florida Beekeepers' Association had a meeting every month, at least during the winter when migratory beekeepers were in the state. There were two hundred beekeepers at this meeting as it was held during a slow period on the beekeepers' usually hectic calendar - before the citrus bloom, but after the interstate trucking was done.

We used this time to constructively compare ourselves to each other. We'd ask "How many hives are you splitting, how strong are your colonies?" Little attention met the replies. When it was your turn to answer, you were expected to exaggerate. "Two thousand hives. They're so strong I'm worried they'll all swarm before the citrus bloom."

Beekeepers didn't usually come to these meetings to hear the speaker, they came to brag and to be bragged at. A charming orator was a bonus. We seldom knew who the speaker would be, though it was probably announced the month before. We'd show up, brag for a while, eat something from the pot-luck buffet, and hold on to some coffee until it was too cold to drink. I especially enjoyed the food. A young farmer can eat a lot of food from a pot-luck buffet table.

There we sat. Patiently listening as the club secretary told us what had happened at the last meeting. Patiently hearing how much money the treasurer had treasured and how much of that had to be used to rent the meeting hall for the evening. The club president spoke. He kept bees as a hobby; had a real job, made real money - a situation some of us full-time beekeepers envied. He introduced the guest speaker. The evening's speaker was the bee club president's boss in real life. The two of them worked together at a missile factory near Orlando. They built guidance systems that could deliver nuclear bombs to the Chinese and Russians. Perhaps to Chinese and Russian beekeepers similar to us, sitting around drinking cold coffee at their beekeepers' meetings.

"We have a different sort of guest speaker tonight," the President said, without exaggerating. "Instead of boring you with details about bees and beekeeping - you all know about beekeeping - we have something really exciting and different. Please welcome Mr. James Grossbomb, spokesman for one of central Florida's most exciting industries - armaments." Until then, I didn't even know Florida had bomb factories.

Mr. Grossbomb told us the history of the arms race, from a bomb builder's perspective. The audience began an uneasy shuffle. Some of us did not want to hear how Jimmy Carter was weak on communism and how his proposed cuts would leave America defenseless. We had not realized that Secretary McNamara, under John Kennedy, had invited the Russians to develop nuclear weapons so that the world's powers would be evenly armed. We didn't really care that Mr. Grossbomb's job was on the line if we didn't telephone our congressmen that evening. More feet shuffled. The hippies from the Lady Lake colony looked very uncomfortable. Seventh Day Adventists and other pacifists studied their shoes. Some beekeepers showed their disappointment by going to the back of the room, fetching more coffee. We had come to the meeting expecting to hear bee talk

Bad Beekeeping

- how drones find mates, not how nuclear warheads find Moscow. An old man seated near me looked the most uncomfortable.

It may have been the free food. It may have been the speaker. Or maybe the poor, elderly, gray-bearded gentleman in the green shirt was sick even before the meeting started. But as the speaker approached his thundering, spell-binding conclusion, as rockets soared in defense of the homeland, as Mr. Grossbomb shouted, "We are talking about the survival of democracy! No less is at stake than the *sacred* lives of your *children* and your *grandchildren!*" - the vomiting started. The poor old green-shirted gentleman jumped up and darted towards the washroom at the back of the meeting hall. The audience turned away from the admonishments about the sanctity of our unborn grandchildren, focused instead on the vomiting grandfather by the restroom door. He was projecting some pretty impressive missiles of his own.[39]

A few days after Christmas, Dad called from Pennsylvania. He asked if I could use Joe's help for the winter. Joe was in high school, 10th Grade. Did I want my fifteen-year-old brother in Florida? I wasn't certain, but I assumed that Dad wanted Joe gone. It was winter, cold and wet in Pennsylvania. No farm work. Too early in the season for Joe to be busy in Dad's greenhouses.

I bought Joe a plane ticket. He lived in the spare room of my rented house trailer. I enrolled him at Groveland High School. He caught a bus to school each morning, walked home in the afternoon. We both cooked. I signed his report card, he helped me with bee-work after school. It was a good deal for both Joe and me. Especially me. Joe found the class work a lot easier than it had been in Pennsylvania, so he seldom brought school work home. Weekends, we hammered together boxes on my farm, fed the bees, checked for diseases. But it was slow season, the bees weren't demanding much attention or energy. And I had spare energy. I was looking for something else to do with my time. A job?

For five years, almost all my income - all the money I needed for food, for dandruff shampoo, for sock and shirts, for everything - came from selling stuff that honeybees made for me. I sold their honey and beeswax. I sold bees and queens to other beekeepers. I didn't need the money which steady employment might bring, but there were a few slow periods and I was willing to trade my time for extra shampoo.

I would take a job if it was challenging and unusual. And if there wasn't too much heavy lifting. I lifted heavy hives all day as a beekeeper. I wanted a less physical job. A job like Joe's high school friend Larry Freeman had - talking on the radio. I had never seen a broadcasting station, but I thought I might like to work in one.

WWFL was on the west edge of Clermont, on Highway 50, ten minutes from my rented house trailer. Clermont was attractive. Bigger and cleaner than Mascotte and Groveland. It had culture. A drive-in theatre. The first MacDonalds I had ever seen. It was in the center of Florida, heart of citrus country. Halfway between Georgia and Cuba. Halfway between the Gulf and the Ocean. It even had a tourist attraction. A big tower. In those days it was called the Citrus Tower and tourists would ride an elevator up twenty storeys and gaze out at millions of orange trees. You can still ride the elevator to the top of the tower, but most of the citrus are gone. The orange trees froze and their dead roots were ripped out. Replaced by mobile homes, pavement, and shopping malls. But Clermont also had WWFL, the radio station. Joe and I stopped to watch Larry Freeman at work one evening. The studio manager was there.

"I'm Howard," the manager said.

He was a tall thin man with a voice like a sack of gravel.

"I'm Ron."

"You have a good voice, Ron. Would you like a job here?" Howard asked.

My voice must have been outstanding. A job offer three minutes after arriving at the studio. And I had spoken only two words.

"I've never worked on radio," I said.

"You're a natural," said the deep-voiced man. "We'll train you. We pay three and a quarter an hour. Minimum wage. We have a shift starting next week. You can work five hours a night, three or four nights a week. What do you think, Ron?"

Ron on the Radio

I liked the deejay job. It required wit and clear speech - characteristics I had been trying to acquire for years. I sat at the microphone and chatted between Hank Snow and Anne Murray tunes. I announced myself as "Ron on the radio... You've got Ron on the radio tonight." With a feeble five hundred watts, I might have shouted louder than the radio station could broadcast, but WWFL had a mission - entertaining a few dozen farmers and country kids. It was good work. No heavy lifting. All indoors. I could work at night, when my beekeeping day was finished. When I no longer had enough energy to stand and lift heavy things, I could sit and chat. And I worked alone in the broadcasting studio - no boss, no manager.

Bad Beekeeping

The equipment was simple. I lined up a needle on vinyl records and spun them half a turn backwards before flipping the play switch. If this was done correctly, the record reached forty-five revolutions per minute before the first note was played. Otherwise, the record would be heard gaining speed on the air, which was considered rather poor form.

I spun records and said incredibly witty things about the time, the weather, or the bean bags on sale at Edge's. I read the news from sheets I tore from the AP machine in the engineering room. Mostly, I'd introduce a song, then I'd have two and a half minutes of down time. I worked five hours, seven to midnight, then powered the station off for the night, locked the door when I left. It was fun. Friends would visit and drink WWFL coffee and make me play their favorite country tunes. I was getting involved in the community. I thought it might even be a way to meet girls.

While I worked the evening shift, Joe did projects at home. Sometimes he assembled cages for queen bees, sometimes he wrote essays. His high school didn't give him enough work, so I assigned reports for him to do while I was gone. He used my encyclopedias and *National Geographics*. He wrote a page or two while listening to me - or one of the better radio stations. The next day, I marked his work.

I liked radio well enough to come back to the job five more winters, quitting each spring to head off to keep bees in Saskatchewan. I studied the broadcast rules, earned an FCC license which claimed I was a "radio-engineer." I propped it up on my desk next to Joni Mitchell's picture.

I had a good practical education, on the job training that taught me the difference between three seconds and five. I trained my voice, the records, and the AP news wire to all begin and end at the right moment, counting time in my head. A good show was a tight show, no dead air space, no awkward moments. I liked the work. And I met some unusual people. A beekeeper named George called the station to request a song by Porter Wagoner. I ended up at George's homestead later that week.

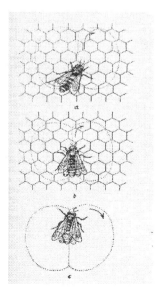

People Talk.
Bees Dance.
Everyone
Communicates.
Original
Sketch by Karl
von Frisch,
Awarded the
Nobel Prize
for Unraveling
Bee Speech.

Florida Beekeeping

Some bees are scout bees. Path finders. They navigate miles and miles. Across rivers, through forests and gardens. They search for fresh fields of blossoming flowers.

Scouting is expensive. It ties up a bee that might be tending to the queen, defending the hive, or storing honey. It also tires the bee, shortens her lifespan. And before the bee leaves on a scouting expedition, she tanks up on honey – the fuel she'll need for the long flight ahead. If every bee in the hive were a scout, the bees would all die young and would exhaust the colony's food supply.

The scout bee must also be smart enough to describe the new location to her sisters. Only a few keen bees get to be scouts. Perhaps they take a written exam. The brightest and the best with an enviable sense of direction and formidable memory. And bees don't usually get lost. Expanded to the human scale, their feats match a person carrying lunch in a small backpack, walking five hundred miles, remembering the route, returning home, telling friends how to find their own way.

George called me at the radio station and requested *A Satisfied Mind*. A song about a man who loses everything, but "is richer by far with a satisfied mind." It was old, from 1955, but my father had once owned the Porter Wagoner album, so I knew the song. I found it on a lower shelf of the WWFL stacks and I queued it up.

While the song played, I chatted a while with George. He asked me about my bees. I had mentioned the bees on the air a few times. I would say something subtle like, "87 beautiful degrees here in central Florida this evening. And tomorrow should be another great honey day for all the beekeepers listening," or, "Hey, have you tried oatmeal with honey? It's far out." I was not particularly clever as a D.J.

George asked me to come to his homestead. He gave me directions – off a clay road south of Clermont, through a pasture planted in timothy, to a brown cypress house with a tin roof and a wide front porch.

I parked in the grass. A frail gentleman with leathered skin and thin gray hair was poised near a small wooden barn. He was standing amid stacks of beehives, paint brush in hand. I sat in my truck a moment, got out and walked towards him. Angry bees swirled in the air between George and me. Nasty bees were robbing George's honey barn – the door was open wide.

I remembered Clive's comment about bad beekeeping - the American way - as I watched thousands of bees fly in and out of the barn. Frenzied bees, wild and vicious. Occasionally, they paused to attempt to sting. I picked nasty bees out of my hair, off my shirt. These bees were visiting from neighboring colonies, hives belonging to other beekeepers and kept in the surrounding swamps. The bees had discovered an open back door to George's honey barn. The floor of his shed was sticky with dirty honey and burnt wax. The robber bees had come to clean the floor.

I introduced myself. George waved his white brush at the bees.

"How ya get them to stop?" asked George.

Bad Beekeeping

"Well, start by keeping the door shut," I replied.

"Can't," George said. "If I shut the door, can't hear the radio while I'm painting."

What radio? The drone of the robber bees was louder than George's country music.

George had been painting hive boxes. He'd piled tall stacks of rectangular boxes in his yard behind the old barn. Homemade equipment, cut from local cypress. He smeared oily white paint on everything. Some errant bees hit the boxes as they flew past to rob the shed, their little bodies became glued to the wet paint. "You've got to shut the door," I said.

"Only been open half an hour. Where you reckon they come from?"

Beekeepers kept thousands of hives of bees in the groves and swamps near George's farm. With few flowers blooming in late January, the messy shop with the spilt honey was an irresistible invitation to the bees of the neighborhood to steal what they couldn't honestly gather from plants. We closed the door, then set up a garden sprinkler on the end of a leaky green hose. The water soaked the siding and the closed door; saturated the sand in front of the shed. Party over, but it would take days for the wet bees to forget about this picnic spot. It grew quiet.

"Want ice tea?" George asked. He had a glass gallon jug sitting on the steps of his house. Tea bags floated in the water, sunshine pushed the tea out of the bags, into the warm water. He came out of the house with two tall plastic glasses. There were a half dozen ice cubes in each glass. We poured warm tea from the glass jug. "Hold these," George said. He ambled back into the house, returned in a minute with a magazine, a sugar bowl, and one spoon. We dumped several spoons full of sugar into the brown tea. The ice melted quickly.

"Sun tea. Good, ain't it?" George drank quickly and refilled his glass. "Gotta show ya some stuff I done read about bees." George handed me his magazine. It was a popular magazine, a news magazine, with an article about beekeepers' problems.

"You think this stuff is true?" George asked me.

"Probably."

"Really? Why would tigers eat beekeepers?"

I hadn't seen that part of his magazine story yet. I'd been reading the piece about rising costs and third world imports. "Here it is. Twenty-nine honey gatherers eaten by tigers in India.[40] Well, George, these aren't beekeepers. These are people who go out into the jungle and pull combs of honey out of trees and off the sides of cliffs. They go into some pretty bad places. It's probably true. At least we don't get eaten by tigers, do we?"

We sat in the shade and watched the water spray against the barn door. Robber bees were still coming, but not as many as before.

"What about the cows?" George asked.

"You have problems with your cows?"

"No, in the magazine. It says cows were killed by bees. Read it."

"1898. Three hundred cows plunged to their death in Nebraska. Stampeded when chased by swarms of wild bees[41]... I don't know George, just because it's in a magazine, that doesn't mean it's true... Why you reading this, anyway?"

"You think I'm a bad beekeeper?"

Florida Beekeeping

"How long you been keeping bees?" I asked George.

"Coming on forty years now."

"You never had any other job?"

"No, sir, just messin with these bees."

Only a few bees were flying around the honey barn now. George said he was tired. I studied his leathered and weary face. He was at least seventy. I left.

George *thought* he was a bad beekeeper. As I struggled with old trucks, poorly built equipment, and weak hives, I *knew* I was. And so were many of my contemporaries. But after thousands of years of recorded beekeeping history, I recognized we didn't invent bad beekeeping in our generation.

The earliest evidence of a bad beekeeping experience may be attributed to a cave dweller. She lived along the Spanish-French frontier ten thousand years before that border was created.

The archeology community was buzzing with excitement last century when wall paintings of a cave dweller gathering honey had been discovered. The dark ochre rock-sketching shows a beekeeper on a tree branch over-extending her reach for a handful of honeycomb, apparently falling.[42] One of the oldest murals in the world - and the theme was a honey harvest gone bad.

Jumping ahead several millennia, I once found myself using an aluminum ladder propped against an electric transmission pole, fetching my own swarm. I was swinging a wide-blade stainless steel knife. We really haven't learned much in a hundred centuries. Technology has improved. We now have more efficient ways to make

Honey Harvest, 6000 B.C.E., Spain

mistakes. But as I tried to stretch beyond the reach of my grasp, I ended up on the hard ground. I don't know if the cave girl fell off her ladder. Maybe she was eaten by a tiger. But she once lived, once gathered honey from a wild bees' nest. We know this because cave girl's beekeeping was recorded in art. Thousands of years after the honey harvest, long after her food was consumed, long after she was buried by her family in the Pyrenees, her story survives.

By the end of February, my hives had large bee populations. The warm winter had brought a heavy pollen yield from swamp trees and weeds. Some of my hives were in citrus groves, others were parked in swampy apiaries where the bees found pollen during the winter. The swamp bees had to be moved to the groves before the citrus bloom.

Two of the largest grove holdings belonged to two of the most interesting families in south Lake County. The Kuharske family traces part of its roots to a Kuharske who came from Poland and was a hunter's guide in Wisconsin. He led President Grover Cleveland around the north wood and somehow ended up marrying the president's niece. Kuharske was frugal and adventurous and ended up owning quite a lot of land in the center of Florida a hundred years ago. His descendents cultivated orange groves covering thousands of acres on those swamp lands.

The Micheloni family, my father told me, came from Italy. The first Micheloni settler took any work he could get - pruning other people's oranges, hoeing and mowing between trees. In the back yard of his rented house, he experimented with grafting and growing his own citrus. Soon he had a nursery, then groves, then ranches. He worked incredibly hard for each penny he deposited into the bank he eventually directed.

The Micheloni and Kuharske families owned some of the land that was offered to my father, then my brother, then to me, as free rental space to stash our hives of bees. In return, their groves were well pollinated.

Beekeepers couldn't possibly afford all the little plots of land, spread over hundreds of square miles, where their beehives are placed. The beekeeper depends on the kindness of friends and strangers - usually farmers - for spots to set out bees. Sometimes the farmers are wealthy land barons who get a farm tax reduction if bees make agricultural use of their speculation lands. But usually, the land owners are poor, hard-working farmers. They tell the beekeeper where to place the bees - somewhere out of sight, but close to crops that might benefit from pollination.

Some bee spots are near gorgeous lakes and babbling brooks, snow-capped mountains in sight; other spots are wedged between dead cars and discarded Pampers. Sometimes a farmer allows bees in the grove or hay meadow because the bees will give a bigger and better crop of fruit or will help the clovers re-seed themselves. People sometimes called me to say that they have a nice place for my bees; but I'd find it wouldn't quite work – too windy; too close to a highway; too wet; too soggy; too something. Then they'd ask what sort of location would work best for me. "I'd like a good, all-weather road, a gently sloping south exposure, close to the fields, away from human traffic, maybe a nice view." One farmer told me there was only one place like that on his five-thousand acre ranch – and he'd already built his house there.

A beekeeper takes any reasonable place he can find. It works best for the beekeeper to scout the place first – to drive into the farmstead and tell the owner where he'd like to put his bees. Beekeepers probably have a better idea of all the trails and backroads in the nearby countryside than even the folks growing and smuggling marijuana do. The beekeeper knows which trail leads to which oak hammock and somehow talks a rancher into allowing forty hives of bees to be parked there for a few months. But sometimes, there is little choice. The farmer makes the decision. The beekeeper takes what he can get.

Not only must the commercial beekeeper find and use a hundred or so locations spread over dozens of miles, he usually remembers how many hives are in each spot, what attention those hives need. A really good beekeeper rarely forgets a bee location, never gets lost.

I know only a few beekeepers who have a poor sense of direction and occasionally end up in the wrong county. I am one of them. I envy the beekeeper who can be blindfolded, spun in circles, dropped out of a moving truck, land on both feet, and then point out north; recognize some distant landmark, flag down a passing police cruiser and end up at home in front of the TV before I could find my way back driving the fast moving truck. I have had trouble finding west while facing the setting sun. Put me on a straight road, I may be safe. But if the road has the tiniest little curve in it, you may never see me again.

Florida Beekeeping

I had to move several apiaries out of the swamps, into the orange groves. Each time, I was awake two hours before sunrise, long before the bees began flying for the day. I'd park my truck next to the bees in the swamp. Lift the hives, one at a time, onto the flatbed. Forty colonies. Two tons of bees, boxes, honey and combs. I'd throw ropes over the loose load, fire up the truck and drive through the early morning fog to the grove locations, thirty miles away.

Part of my North Mascotte Beeyard, Tucked between Orange Trees

My Platlakaha apiary was tied tightly to my flatbed truck. I was rolling north on Highway 33, about half a mile out of Mascotte. I passed Joel's truck, loaded with bees, heading south. Joel was moving his bees south while I was moving my bees north. We waved at each other through our respective windshields. Apparently he thought the direction I was heading was not as good as the direction I was leaving.

And I guess I thought the same thing about his choices.

I should have followed Joel.

I was trying to find a new location for my bees. The person who gave me the new apiary site was the manager of several large orange groves; too busy to meet me in the field at six in the morning. No one lived in the area; I was on my own. My instructions led me north of Mascotte on Highway 33, then west on a red clay trail. Then I went left, left, south again, and maybe east. But I wasn't sure. After east, I was supposed to find a tall, moss-covered live oak tree by a wire fence. "Go past it, through the orange grove by a canal." Driving along the canal, I was to see a young orange grove. "Look for navels, about two years old," I was told. The guy giving me directions didn't know I couldn't tell second year navels from third year grapefruit. I was to see a big clearing near the drainage canal. There I could unload my forty hives of bees. If I could find the clearing.

It was early morning. I needed to find the spot and set my hives off before it became light and warm, else the bees would become active and fly away from my moving truck. I almost succeeded. I think I ended up where I was supposed to be. But in the foggy sunrise, as I crossed the sand and drove closer to the clearing near the drainage canal, I could see the shape of beehives in the spot I was going to use. Other hives were already sitting there.

This meant one of three things. Perhaps some other beekeeper - a rude, mindless, arrogant outlaw, had done a 'drop' - put bees in a nice apiary spot without anyone's permission; or, the grove *manager* who gave me permission to put my bees in the spot didn't know that the grove *owner* had already given someone else permission to do the same thing. But it was also possible I was in the wrong grove – completely and hopelessly lost, wandering aimlessly among alligators and mosquitoes with my impatient flock of bees.

But then, a fourth explanation emerged. As I drove closer to the hives, I was surprised to discover that the errant hives, hugging my new beeyard space, belonged to me. How could some of my own bees be here already? I had used an unfamiliar, back entrance to this unrecognized location. I was given permission by a manager to use a place that the owner had already asked me to stock with hives. I had beaten myself to my own beeyard, meeting hives I had set out only a few mornings earlier.

If my orienteering was a disaster - groping through unfamiliar terrain - I did even worse at vehicle maintenance. If something seemed amiss under the hood – flames, for example – I might perhaps unscrew the air filter, then put it back on again. Sometimes this was enough to fix the problem. After my Chevy truck's starter-motor fried, I began hauling stout wooden planks everywhere I went. I'd assemble a tiny platform, park the truck up a few inches above the flat Florida sand. When I needed to start my old truck, I'd turn the key, place the seasoned machine in low gear, push the clutch in. The truck would roll down the home-made hill. I'd pop the clutch out, and the truck engine would ignite. No need for a starter. Worked every time. Almost every time. I finally fixed the burnt motor when I was stalled on a flat road and couldn't roll; then I crawled under the truck and swapped the gadget for a used one from Harb's Equipment.

My 25 year-old pick-up had no spare tire. This was not an issue until I got a flat tire. I stood at the tail-end of the truck, parked in a sunny apiary on the edge of a remote orange grove, rear right tire flatter than a hive cover.

I jacked up the axle in powdery soft sand, unbolted the wheel, pulled it loose, then put an empty wooden honey box in the middle of the axle. I lowered the truck and removed the jack, hiding it behind the truck seat. I locked the truck door, else I'd come back to the Chevy and perhaps find someone had stolen my jack. Not likely, of course, but without a jack, the axle would sink into the sand and I'd have no way of putting a repaired wheel back on.

The tire was a little too heavy to carry for long. Off the truck, it became a bit round again, so I rolled it in front of me, running to keep up. A beautiful spring day, eighty degrees. Fun to chase the tire along. I wondered why someone hadn't invented a competition sport based on wheel rolling. We count the number of hits it takes to knock a small white ball into a hole in the ground. We measure how high a person on a stick can bound up into the air. Why not wheel rolling?

I was soon out of the orange trees and on Highway 27 - the four lane state road south of Clermont that carries visitors towards Disney World and beekeepers to orange groves. Tourists raced past me. Some waved. One car stopped.

It was from New York. An excited group of young women jumped out, cameras in hand. "You-speak-English?" the one with big hair ventured. Then, "Can-we-take-your-picture? We want to show people back home what Floridians look like." I didn't tell them I looked like an ex-Pennsylvanian just back from Saskatchewan. They saw a scraggy young man in dirty jeans, dark face shaded by a black Stetson. "We don't want the tire in the picture, just stand by the orange tree, don't look into the camera." One of them finally asked why I had the tire. I explained about the Olympic tire-rolling try-outs. They accepted this, clambered back into their Chrysler, and left me, my tire, the orange grove, and the state of Florida.

I was still rolling my tire, far from a service station. But I was enjoying this newly invented sport, and was getting good at it. A vigorous blast from a trucker's air-horn disturbed me, brought me back to the sun, the heat, the paved highway. The trucker waved at me from the opposite side of the four lane highway. He drove his rig - loaded with grapefruit - across a paved spot in the medium, making a wide illegal turn that brought him beside me.

"I'll give you a ride," he said.

"But you just turned around the wrong way from where you're going."

"I'll give you a ride, friend." His face was beaming, a huge smile that showed off a scary inner happiness. Jehovah's Witness?

"Look," my new friend continued, "One night I rolled a tire for five hours in Georgia. You think anyone would stop and give this nigger a lift? I swore I'd never pass up anyone who needed help again. And I won't. I'll give you a ride."

He took me to the service station, waited while I repaired the tire, then took me back to the edge of the orange grove. He didn't give me any church literature. Another smile, a handshake. Then he was gone.

More truck trouble. Another fire. After supering bees in Polk County, I reloaded my equipment. Smoker and hammer went into the steel tool box bolted to the underside of my truck. The one hive tool I didn't lose that day went on the truck's dashboard. I tied ropes over the boxes that were stacked on the home-made wooden flatbed of my old truck. Then I drove north half an hour to the next beeyard. As I approached my stop, I saw my friend Stan Kanter pulling his honey truck up behind mine. He jumped out and ran towards my vehicle. "Get out!" he shouted. I got out. He pointed to a very tiny fire, with wee little yellow flames, burning in the middle of my truck bed. Now that the truck had stopped, the fire began to spread. Stan pulled a flat hive cover from my loosely piled cargo. He quickly smothered – or, rather, squished – the fire out for me.

Stan probably saved my life. If I had sat in the truck, eating my Moon

Left to Right: Ron, Stan, Willi

Bad Beekeeping

Pie and drinking my Squirt, the truck would have been blazing before I even knew I had a fire. Stan saved my life, keeping me in the bee business a few years longer.

The truck fire remains an unexplained mystery. But my long series of vehicular mishaps had a clear significance; undoubtedly I needed to get out of the bee business. Or, buy a new truck.

I found a new truck in Orlando. The dealer had seven, identical. All had white exteriors, leather bucket seats, huge 454 engines. Cheap. Buy one or buy all seven and get a discount. I asked for the story – *why would any dealer have seven identical trucks?*

"We ordered 'em up for an ambulance company. The company went belly-up before they picked 'em up."

I parked my ambulance at David's farm, south of Groveland, for a few days. He helped me build the bed for it. Then I spent a week shaping a van out of plywood and two-by-fours. Small windows with screens and a funnel-shaped wind scoop would allow fresh air to pass through the home-made contraption, cooling the bees that the van was intended to carry. The van was removable, not a permanent part of the truck. I could slide it off and park it on stilts when I wasn't moving packages from Florida to Saskatchewan.

The new truck and specially designed van gave me some confidence that I may succeed in the next big milestone in my beekeeping career. In a few weeks, I would be making one of the longest solo migratory treks with bees that anyone had ever attempted. I felt I might actually drive the twenty-five hundred miles from the southeast USA to northwest Canada in three days.

Citrus blossoms were opening up, beekeepers had stacked honey boxes on their hives. We were all waiting for the flow to start. Once the crop was on, everyone would be too busy to talk or visit. I decided to entertain my beekeeping friends. I hosted a honey-flow party. My house-trailer at Stieffel's Trailer Court was full of khaki-dressed beekeepers in work boots. Almost everyone brought beer, almost no one was drinking. I had WWFL on

**My Yard at the Kuharske's – Citrus was Just Opening Up.
Colonies were Strong;.
It was Time for a Beekeepers' Party.**

the radio and had arranged for Larry Freeman to mention my party every half-hour or so.

"Big party over at Ron's tonight... a honey-flow party. All the beekeepers in the Groveland-Mascotte-Clermont area are invited. *B.Y.O.B. – Bring Your Own Buzz.*"

Of course, I had already invited all the beekeepers in the area. Everyone ignored the radio and the beer. But the chips and pretzels were gone in an hour. When not eating, the beekeepers obsessed about their hives, their trucks, their summer homes in the north. These were bright people, but conversation never strayed beyond beekeeping.

We talked about how people get into beekeeping. Some people fall in love with the business after keeping a few hives as a hobby. I kept bees because my father did, because two brothers did, because I learned to like it. Ray Meyers also kept bees because his father had been a beekeeper. Ray had been a beekeeper a long time, but he didn't want to stay with it. However, he didn't change careers, either. At the party, Ray said, "Thirty years ago, I told my mother I quit - I was through with bees. I told her there sure as hell are better ways to make a living than keeping bees! But here I am, still keeping bees, damn it!"

We talked about the orange trees and the coming honey crop. We all decided that the orange bloom would probably not yield much nectar. Beekeepers always predict poor crops. Boastful predictions result in the disastrous wrath of angry honey gods. A conservative prediction avoids future disappointments ("I knew we wouldn't make much honey.") – but if the crop were actually good, it allowed us to feel pleasantly surprised.

"Not enough rainfall in January," said the oldest beekeeper, "Never seen a good flow in a dry year."

Another added, "Bloom is starting too early. We could still get a frost. That'll kill the flow."

The only Florida-born beekeeper at the party didn't move his bees north for the summer. He said, "Too many bees, not enough flowers. Crop was better when there weren't so many bees here." What he didn't say was 'too many bees because too many Yankee beekeepers moved here.'

Stan Kept Bees, as Did Almost Everyone I Knew

Everyone felt a bit embarrassed, especially the young fellow who offered the observation. I found another bag of Doritos. I figured that if I were responsible for his poverty, I could at least give him some chips.

Stan Kanter was the last to leave the little party. He rented a trailer nearby, didn't have far to walk. He was running about a thousand hives. He hadn't said much all evening. "You worried about making a crop?" I asked.

"You bet I am," said Stan. "If we make a crop, we make enough money to keep on keeping bees. I think a bad crop would convince us to quit the beekeeping business."

I had trouble with this reasoning. Should I be keeping bees, or not? I knew I had a lot to learn about running a company. Stan's father had been in business, owned and managed a furniture factory. I asked Stan if his father taught him anything about business. "Not really, not directly, that is."

"Well, did he have any advice for you? You know, some parting shot as you left the house?"

"Oh, yea, one thing. He once told me, 'Never kick a piece of shit.' You know, it's just lying there, minding its own business. Kick it and it starts to stink. Sticks to your shoes. You track it around with you. Never kick a piece of shit. Walk around it." That's what Stan's father told him. My father gave me little bits of advice, too. My father said be fair to everyone. What goes around, comes around. Always be good to your customers. Well, that's what he meant. What he said was, "Ron, never piss in a honey barrel."

Stan and I had a few things in common. About the same age. Started keeping bees about the same time. Wisconsin and Florida, like me. He had taken in his younger brother, Robert. I had Joe. We both thought too much, worked too hard. I invited him to the house of a family friend, Eleanor Dern.

Eleanor Dern's grove was south from Mascotte, east at Gallows' Lake, on a sand trail that dropped off the pavement, wound past oaks draped by Spanish moss. The trail ended at her flat-roofed house near a shallow lake. A few hundred orange and grapefruit trees hugged the shore. Eleanor managed the grove alone, doing most of the tractor chores herself. She hired out some of the work, but at nearly seventy, she was both proud and grateful that Juan Gonzalez showed up every year to give her a hand. She bought postal money orders for Juan, sent the cash to Mexico. "He's got nine kids, and he's only thirty-five. Can you believe it?" she'd say.

I met Eleanor because of my brother David. He kept bees along the edge of her grove. He and Linda spent a lot of evenings visiting Eleanor, giving her a hand, fixing things, like broken light switches and stalled tractors. Linda often carted over pasta salads or casseroles. Twenty years earlier, Dad kept his bees on the Dern Ranch. Dad would speak Croatian to Eleanor's husband Bill; Bill Dern would answer back in Polish. I never met Bill, he died too soon. I was told that he swung a sword while perched on a horse during the last cavalry charge in the history of the world, a poor match against Hitler's Panzer divisions. Bill spent six years in a German prison, then twenty years as proprietor of a hardware store on Chicago's south side, and ten years as a grove owner in Florida. Then he died.

Stan, Eleanor, and I sat around a small square table, Scrabble board centered amidst us. We talked about Ronald Reagan.

"No one ever called him Ronnie!" Eleanor said. "Dutch! Dutch! We all called him Dutch. That was his name."

Eleanor Dern set out four tiles. E-C-H-O. The E turned STATE into ESTATE and connected the new words together at a Double Word square. Her score was 132; Stan had 92. I was at 78.

Florida Beekeeping

Stan looked at me, probably wondering the same thing as I. "Dutch?" I asked. She snapped her 1931 Eureka College yearbook off the top of a small maple bookshelf. Eleanor Dern flipped to a picture of a handsome twenty year old. Ronald Wilson Reagan. "Dutch" was neatly written below the photo. "You called him Dutch? Was he Dutch?"

"Irish. They called him Dutch because he was careful with his money. The Reagans were poor people. His father drank. But Dutch wasn't cheap. He was frugal. He had to be."

"Wilson. His middle name was Wilson?" Stan asked.

"From Woodrow Wilson. His family was Democrat. My sister and I gave him a hard time about that, joking around, you know, because most all of us going to Eureka in those days were Republicans."

Eleanor Dern Would Puff Hot Smoke into the Eyes of Her Scrabble Opponents, if She Need the Edge.

It was interesting, knowing someone who knew someone. Someone running for President of the United States. Later Eleanor received an invitation to his Inaugural Ball. She didn't go. I was stalling for time. It was my turn. I owned six vowels and an N. I could put the N down, attached to Eleanor's ECHO, creating the word NO. That would give me two points. But I'd done something like that earlier in the evening. Eleanor had told me my effort was pitiful. "Try again," the former Eighth Grade English teacher from Peoria said.

"How well did you know him?" I asked, picking up tiles, then putting them back into my tray.

"I dated his brother. He dated my sister. We were friends." Eleanor released blue smoke from her cigarette. She told us that Dutch's pants were always too short because he and his brother shared pants. I wasn't sure if she meant one of the boys went to the prom in jockey shorts, or stayed home instead. "His brother was shorter," Eleanor told us as she shook ice, added rum and coke to a short fat glass. "Dutch's socks showed most of the time."

Jet had his nose at my crotch again. I slapped the big black lab and it cowered. "Rude!" she said, not to me, but to the animal. Eleanor lived alone. Her four dogs were friendly, but huge and scary looking. They growled viciously, hungrily. Certainly, they kept bad guys away from her farm.

I lost the game. Eleanor walked Stan and I out to my truck. Except for dozens of frogs calling from a distant lake, it was quiet. Stars filled the black sky. Chilly, but still comfortable, in long-sleeved shirts. Eleanor's citrus trees were beginning to bloom, the air carried a faint hint of honey. I told Eleanor and Stan that my Canadian beehives were frozen to the ground. It would be months before they made any honey.

"You'll probably make a lot of honey this winter?" Eleanor asked.

"Hope not," said Stan. Eleanor looked at Stan, shook her head, turned to me.

"I heard you on the radio. You're pretty good. If you don't get a honey crop, you should work in radio full-time. And maybe go back to school."

I wasn't interested in working full-time on the radio, or working anywhere full-time. I had no time for school. I was trying to build a bee business; trying to live my own life. The retired school-teacher's suggestions did not appeal to me.

I had a quarter of my hives in queen bee production, the rest were prepared to make honey. After honey production, I would shake extra bees from those hives, stuff them into the package cages, and cart them off to Canada. I liked honey production – much easier than raising queens. Making honey is like boxing; queen rearing is like Tae Kwon Do. Making honey requires big hives and big trucks; making queens requires a sharp, disciplined mind, keen eyesight, steady hands.

Honey Bee Working on Orange Blossom

Joe and I set two or three empty honey boxes on each hive. If the oranges bloomed well, if the weather co-operated, each hive might hold a hundred pounds of citrus honey. But that would be exceptional.

Beekeepers accepted fifty pounds of orange blossom honey as a reasonable crop. After the boxes were set on the hives, we had a few weeks to wait before harvest, time to try to raise some queens.

Florida Beekeeping

My queen business provided me with the new bees I'd need in Saskatchewan. Producing 3000 queens did not take much of our time, so Joe and I took a break.

With a few free days before honey harvest, we decided to go exploring. We packed a lunch, drove away from Mascotte. We used part of his spring school break to visit the east coast. We strolled around the gutted spacecraft lined up at Canaveral; we counted waves on a quiet beach, waded in cool salt water.

I drove aimlessly along the cape. Past an irrigation ditch bordered with Brazilian pepper bush, past a large grove of kumquats, then along a sand trail through thick palmetto and gallberry brush to the edge of a mangrove swamp. This was a rare mix of flora. Most places in Florida exhibit mono-silvaculture – partly by natural design (some swamps have only gallberry to offer the beekeeper); partly by human design (the bees can only work citrus in the heart of citrus country). The east coast environment appealed to me. Four major food groups – citrus, gallberry, mangrove, pepper bush – side by side by side by side.[43]

I wasn't the first person to note the potential – nearby were a dozen hives of bees. Someone else's bees. These hives were on permanent stands, built to keep the bees above fire ants and bee-eating Buffo toads.[44] The equipment was new, or at least very well maintained. Sheltered from the wind, surrounded by flora that could offer a nearly continuous supply of nectar, this bee location was the best I'd ever seen.

From these hives, the beekeeper might harvest some very dark and foul-smelling honey in November from maleluca and Brazilian pepper bush. The nearby citrus grove would yield sweet white honey in March. Mild gallberry and saw-palmetto would come in May. At the end of July, this lucky beekeeper might find salty, green-tinged mangrove honey in his surplus boxes. In an exceptional year, which would never happen, the dozen hives of bees would store five thousand pounds of honey, in four different flavors and colors. I wanted to move my bees here to the Cape, erect a tent, live forever by the sea.

We were back in Groveland. It began to rain the first week of March, stopped five days later. The sun became intense, the air sticky. White flowers exploded on the citrus trees. Huge blossoms lured billions of bees. Big drops of nectar fell to the ground. The air was nauseatingly sweet with orange blossom perfume. The honey flow had started.

Joe had helped me feed bees, move them, build boxes for the colonies. He helped me stack those supers on the hives. But he wouldn't see the boxes full of orange blossom honey. It was time for Joe to leave. Dad said he could come home – to work in the greenhouse.

"I like the bee work, but I like the greenhouses better," Joe said. I got his school transcript – he'd be leaving Groveland High School with nearly perfect marks to finish his school year in Sharpsville.

We drove to the Orlando airport, hardly talking. In a few hours, my young brother would be in Dad's Pennsylvania greenhouses. Transplanting petunias, watering geraniums, selling trees.

I worked alone now; I boiled potatoes and opened cans of beans for one person, not two. Harvest was approaching. Joe would have enjoyed seeing the combs filling with

Bad Beekeeping

sweet orange-blossom honey. But Joe was transplanting peppers and tomatoes and was probably happier. Perhaps not in our father's house, but at least with the work.

I wasn't looking for someone to replace Joe, but I met an earnest fifteen-year-old at the monthly beekeepers' meeting. Paul had ten hives of bees in Orlando. He wanted part-time work. "Any weekend," he said. I called Paul near the end of the flow, to see if he'd help me peel honey boxes off the bees and get packages and queens ready for Saskatchewan. "Sure thing," he said.

Paul Greene and I removed honey from bees in the orange groves near Clermont. The boxes of raw honey were tied to the wooden deck of my new one-ton. A few bees buzzed around the cab, mostly near the truck's windshield. More bees were stranded in the honey boxes on the flat bed. The rest of the bees that once owned the honey had already settled back in their homes, the hives we'd robbed among the citrus trees. By the time my truck was near Deland, an hour had passed; Paul and I were only dim memories for the bees we had disturbed and robbed.

We were taking the honey supers to a small town about half an hour north of Deland. At the edge of the village, on The-Little-Brown-Church-in-the-Pasture Road, stood a new honey warehouse where a man and his wife used their extracting equipment to remove honey from my combs, draining it into new barrels.

In Florida, I never owned an extractor or honey shop. I would pay someone else to handle the small amount of honey my bees made. Some years, I would only get a few thousand pounds of sticky sweet orange blossom honey. I paid two or three hundred dollars to have someone spin the combs and handle the boxes for me. It would have cost me thousands of dollars to own the equipment to do the work myself. Of course, it required faith in the honesty of the folks doing the processing. I would never know exactly how much honey was in my boxes, though I could guess. I had to trust that no one forgot one of my honey barrels in the back room, accidentally – or intentionally – confused with their own honey. I don't think they did.

With our honey cargo, Paul and I drove through pine forests and swamps towards the Little Church Road, passing few other vehicles. Blighted gallberry bushes, palmetto thickets, and scrub pines occupied the poor, damp, sandy soil. Few farms, few houses, few people. We saw a man walking beside the road. I usually picked up hitch-hikers. I stopped.

He was a tall black man. With a torn army jacket, dirty boots. It was hot, but he had a wool knit hat pulled over his ears. When he opened the door and began to crawl into my truck, an empty bottle fell to the ground. It didn't break. He found his bottle under the truck, buried it somewhere within his fatigues, tucked in with others he had been collecting. He climbed into our truck again. His face was scarred; he smelled of beer; he smelled worse than we did – and we'd been working with the rancid bee chemical.

"Got any money?" he asked as he settled onto the seat. He was direct.

"No. Don't even carry a wallet."

"Ron?" whispered Paul. He slid away from our new passenger and tried to make himself small. I drove faster.

"Not even a little money? For some wine?" He was honest.

Florida Beekeeping

"No," I said as a bee flew from my shirt and landed on the dashboard. Maybe I had a way out. "We have bees in the truck. We have more bees in the boxes on the back of the truck. Hope you're not afraid of bees?"

The big man gazed straight ahead at the bees collecting on his side of the cab, between his sun visor and the windshield. He didn't answer. I could see that he was thinking about the bees.

"You're not afraid of bees?" I asked again. Another pause. The man reached a huge fist out and tapped the window, right next to the bees.

"Hell, no. When I worked on the chain gang up in Alabam', I seen bees all the time. Never bothered me none."

My foot hit the brakes. I swung fast and sharp into the 7-Eleven that suddenly appeared at a country crossroad. "This is where you get out," I said. "They'll take your bottles and give you some money for wine." He climbed out without answering. Without turning to look at us. I saw his face reflected in the big truck mirror. Tired eyes. Unshaved face. Dirty clothing. He didn't look that much different from me.

Two hours later, after offloading our boxes of honey, we drove past the 7-Eleven again. Nearby, the man in the army fatigues and woolen hat walked along the edge of the road, searching for more bottles.

Apiary on the Indian River in Florida
July 1902 *American Beekeeper Magazine*

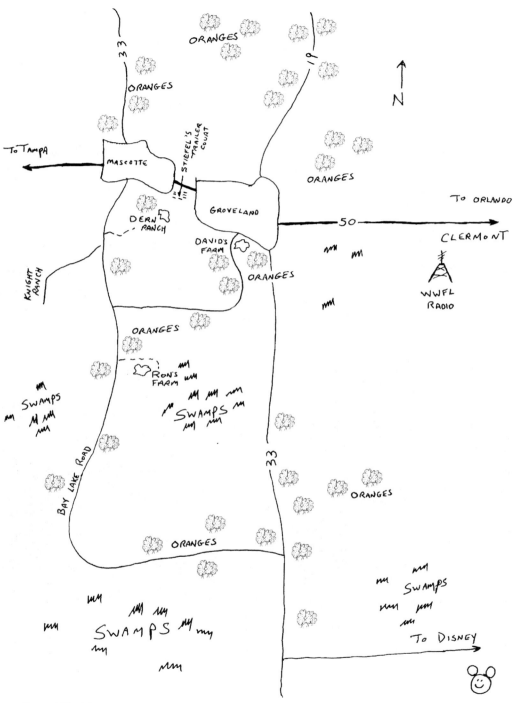

Central Florida: Bee Locations are not Shown - There were Hundreds within this Map Area

Raising Little Queens

Spring. Nature provides. Pollen and nectar flow in abundance. The hive, full of bees, grows heavy with honey. Nearly every comb is jammed with food. The bees become restless. The combs are filled, but flowers still beckon. Biology drives the bees to horde more and more honey. The queen finds few vacant cells to drop her eggs. Because she is not laying many eggs, she shrinks. The bees believe this is a sign their queen is failing in her duty as mother of the hive.

The huge, restless population of idle workers has another problem. Fresh pollen and nectar have forced glands in their heads to fill with creamy white food – royal jelly. Royal jelly is magic food. The tiniest larvae are fed royal jelly for only their first few hours of life. But a few special larvae continue on the diet and the food transforms them from the worker bees they were born to be into queen bees they are destined to become.

In a crowded hive with few places to lay eggs, the old queen is not hungry and there are few new tiny larvae to feed. Reeling with painfully swollen hypopharyngeal glands, the workers unload excess royal jelly in the few remaining cells of freshly hatched larvae. These infants swim in thick pools of rich royal food. The enhanced diet stimulates their bodies, triggers the growth of organs, switches on hormones. Instead of growing into worker bees, they will be queens.

Drones die when they mate with a queen. Drones that never mate live until fall, then they are tossed from the hive, left to starve and freeze on the doorstep. "Damned if they do; damned if they don't," my father would say about the drones' options.

The mating occurs on wing, high above the apiary; sometimes far from the apiary. When the young queen engages her nuptial flight she is pursued by a horde of excited males. The drones vie for the opportunity to die in service of their queen. It took humans a long time to figure out that the Queen is not a King. This discovery and subsequent observations were recorded by Butler in his book *Feminine Monarchie* in 1609,[45] and then again in Swammerdam's *Biblia natura* in 1773.[46] These beekeeper-scientists were among the first to piece together that man had the sex roles of the bees out of order. In 1771, a Slovenian beekeeper named Anton Janscha discovered that honey bee mating is done outside the hive, up in the air.[47]

Usually.

More recently, humans have played a role in the fragile mating ritual of the bee. It was E.B. White, in his poem "Song of the Queen Bee" (*"Let old geneticists plot and plan, They're stuffy people, to a man; ...love-in-the-air is the thing for me - I'm a bee."*[48]) who introduced the world to Dr. Harry Laidlaw's system of artificial insemination of bees. By 1945, Laidlaw had taken the randomness of drone encounters out of honey bee mating, using surgical equipment that guaranteed the parentage of the queen's offspring.[49] Professor Laidlaw's system is still used by research scientists, geneticists, and a few commercial queen breeders, but the majority of bee producers opt for the open-air natural breeding system that bees have enjoyed for nearly forty-five million years.

121

Bad Beekeeping

I never attempted injecting drone sperm into a virgin queen. I was much too clumsy. And shy. But my oldest brother, David, used a stereo microscope, tank of carbon dioxide gas, and the right set of tweezers and tools to accomplish this feat many times. For a while, it was an integral part of his queen breeding program. He showed me how it was done.

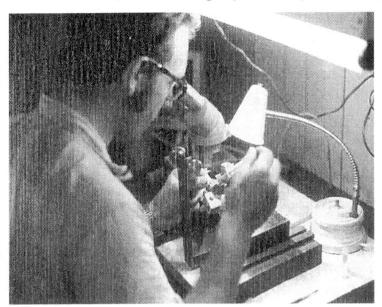

David, Using Artificial Insemination to Assure
the Genetic Heritage of his Bees

But still, I followed the song of E.B. White. My bees might have told you:

"I wish to state that I think it's great,
Oh, it's simply rare in the upper air,
It's the place to pair
With a bee."

Surely the most important insect in the hive is The Queen. A very important title. Aristocratic. Top of the hierarchy. Or is she? Granted, the queen bee lives longer than the workers and drones. A unique creature - only one queen per colony, please. And she gets to experience sex. But it is sex without romance, followed by a long life of monotonous drudgery. She becomes an egg-laying machine, confined to the cramped quarters of the hive's brood nest. Better to be the short-lived worker bee, a forager, flying miles and miles, carting home food for everyone, stopping to taste the flowers.

Humans became excited when scientists discovered that the queen is nothing but a worker bulked-up on royal jelly.[50] Beekeepers began to squeeze tiny vials of royal jelly from their hives. Health food fans gobbled up the expensive goo, expecting it to increase longevity – or at least to improve their fertility. Undoubtedly, people who eat royal jelly live longer, healthier, and happier lives than people who do not. But it is probably because they also eat less fat, less meat, less sugar. They probably sleep better and they probably meditate. Probably have regular bowel movements. The correlation between health and people who eat royal jelly is more likely a correlation between health and health-conscious people. Royal jelly, effective in stimulating the female bee's hormone system, has failed to conclusively enhance any other creature's body. Nevertheless, millions of pounds of royal jelly are marketed and consumed by millions of loyal fans, especially in Asia,[51] where it is widely held that the extra proteins and enzymes in the bee cream will help them live healthier lives.[52]

Raising Little Queens

I never sold royal jelly, though I worked with it every winter - it was an essential part of the queen breeding business. Never sold it, but I tasted it. Once. It felt slimy, left a coating in my mouth. But it made me taller. Smarter. Handsome. I also ate raw pollen, sometimes tugging tiny pellets from the bees' legs as they entered their hives. I sucked on wads of propolis, the bee glue that bees use as an antiseptic in their hive. And I scooped up fresh honey before the bees sealed it under clean white wax. I ate almost everything the hive had to offer. But I didn't eat bees. My friend George did that.

He was in the kitchen. Something smelled good.

"What are you cooking, George?"

"Brood," said George. He stood at the stove, right hand holding an iron skillet, left hand slowly stirring with a wooden paddle. In a nearby ceramic bowl were white drone pupae. A brood comb and saw blade lay on the counter. George had stripped the wax capping from the brood, then shaken the pupae into his bowl. In the frying pan, half a cup of drone pupae were simmering in olive oil.

"Be ready in a couple of minutes," George said.

I declined.

George spooned up a mouthful.

"Just like shrimp without the tails," he said. 53

I was getting busy, but I still dropped in at WWFL every few days to work a shift. I told Bill Bond that I would soon quit for the summer.

"You gotta come in and work Friday night, hear? We're trainin' a new girl. You can show her the ropes."

I dropped by on Friday night. Met Sandy. She was on the air. I stopped at the studio door, watched her work. She looked about twenty. She spoke quickly into the microphone, exhibited a natural confidence and a thick rural accent. Bill started up a turntable for her. The mike went dead. I introduced myself.

"I'm outta hear," Bill said.

I put the headset on. My turn to be on the air. "Stand over there," I said to Sandy. I pointed towards a corner of the studio. It was my show.

I was less rude as the evening wore on.

"You're working somewhere?" I asked her.

"No, I'm in eleventh grade," Sandy said. She sat down on the stool near the microphone. "I got this job because the radio station called Groveland High School, asked if there was any student who wanted to go into the job experience program. Mrs. Pecins recommended me. She's my English teacher. So here I am."

So, she wasn't twenty years old. She was a kid. About Joe's age, seventeen?

"You live in Groveland?"

"No, with my grandma and grandpa, down on Carter Island Road. They got a cattle ranch." I knew Carter Island. South of Mascotte. Very rural.

"My grandma's listenin'," Sandy said. She moved a hand through her blond hair.

"What does she like?"

"She really likes Jerry Lee Lewis, but he's not really country."

"Sure he is," I said. I looked into her brown eyes, she looked away, towards the turntable. I dropped a vinyl album in place, expertly spun the record back half a turn.

"Here's an oldie and a goldie from the thumpin' piano pounder himself! Here's Jerry Lee!" I said into the live mike, and *Great Balls of Fire* blasted through Clermont, Groveland, Mascotte, and down the clay road towards Bay Lake where Grandma Knight was listening.

A cattle ranch. On Carter Island Road.

"So, how many cows on the cattle ranch?" I asked.

"I don't really know. Forty. Fifty. I don't know. I don't have to work with them. I don't count them."

I liked the way she talked, her accent was disarming. Carter Island Road. Not too far from where I lived in Mascotte.

"You getting picked up? I can give you a ride home if you want to wait until my shift ends at ten. I live in Mascotte."

"My grandma would never let me ride home with someone she hasn't met," Sandy said. She gave me an appraising look. "But I'll call her."

"You eaten? We could get something at the Pizza Hut." I surprised myself. It had been a long time since I'd asked anyone to join me at a place like Pizza Hut.

Sandy left the room, used the phone in the manager's office. I spun up the next record. Sandy was back in a minute.

"Grandma says, 'Sure.' She says you got a nice voice and since you like Jerry Lee Lewis she thinks you're probably OK." Sandy looked more surprised than pleased to be reporting this to me. "But I've gotta be home before midnight."

Later that evening, Sandy's grandmother met us at the door of her brick ranch house on Carter Island Road. She said I should come by for supper. Sandy gave me her grandmother's phone number. I walked back to my truck, drove back to my trailer home at Stiefel's and went to bed. I would see her again.

Sandy

Raising Little Queens

February in Florida is queen breeding season. Queens are produced by southern beekeepers, sold to northern beekeepers. Those in the northern latitudes would mail five dollars to the southern breeders. Southern beekeepers would ship back a hardy young queen bee enclosed in a screened cage with food and an attending royal court of worker bees. The northern beekeeper would take possession of the little mother in April or May, when northern beekeeping is just starting for the year. By April, the northern beekeeper always has a few dead hives – from the winter's cold, or due to some mistake the beekeeper made in preparing the bees for winter. But the northern beekeeper also would have some very strong hives by late April. Hives that would swarm after a few weeks of mild spring weather. The beekeeper could split the strong colonies, some bees staying with the old queen, others transferred to a new box with the new southern belle. This prevented swarming and allowed the northern beekeeper to maintain a live hive inventory at a reasonable cost, while the southern beekeeper made a few dollars.

During the winter, I was a southern beekeeper, so I felt compelled to be a queen breeder. But not everyone can make their bees raise extra queens. It takes special talents - a combination of intelligence, observation, and manual skill, which some of us go through life without.

I fumbled to produce a few queens. At great expense and not without minor disasters. It would have been much worse had I not spent my first few Florida winters working for my brother David as a sort of queen breeder's apprentice. David showed me how to split big hives into small mating nucs, how to trick the bees into mass-producing queen cells, how to identify and capture new queen bees.

My first fall in Florida, some years earlier, I arrived at my brother David's farm and he shook my hand. "Careful," he said. "These are million dollar hands." I thought he was joking. But later I watched him swiftly, deftly, hoist dot-sized larvae from the bottoms of dark brood comb and transfer them with a supple wooden stick into home-made wax cell cups. He could move five hundred larvae in an hour, placing the new queen cells between combs of pollen in powerful hives.

He used a swarm-cell building method. Other breeders put their cells into queenless hives. "Queenless bees don't raise the best queens," David said. "They're in a big hurry - demoralized. Don't have enough food, enough royal jelly. Better to use strong hives, where the bees want to swarm. Makes the best queens. The bees take their time and they have lots of extra royal jelly." His method made the best queens, but it was also the most expensive and most time-consuming way to produce them. My brother David and his wife Linda were able to make it economical by working with skillful speed – and doing most of the work themselves. They produced more queens, even with their complicated system, than beekeepers who employed large crews. Quality production paid off. Every year, they harvested ten thousand queens and sold a hundred thousand cells.

The adult queens were mailed north to beekeepers in Montana, Wisconsin, Maine. The immature queen cells were purchased by southern beekeepers who divided their strong hives, using the cells to start new queens. David and Linda could have sold more queens, with hired help, but David was afraid unskilled assistants would lead to lower quality. Rather than recklessly expanding, David seemed satisfied with a business that more than paid the bills and he put extra cash into feeding his orange groves and his six kids. So he retained his labor-intensive, high-quality swarm cell building technique and did most of the work himself, with his wife and children as assistants.

I was not as skilled. I used the simpler queenless-box technique. My new queens weren't as plump or fecund,[54] but were adequate.

Thankfully, the queenless-box system was almost fool-proof. A small wooden box with thirty thousand bees trapped inside were given extra honey and pollen, but no brood and no queen. The bees were desperate to feed royal jelly to any living larvae I was willing to provide.

**David and Linda, Entertaining their
Security Dog with Laps Around their Farm**

I transferred larvae to the wax cell cups. Slowly. I used a metal hook, slid it under the grub which lay in the cell where it had been deposited three days earlier by a queen. I lifted the larva, moved her to a starter frame. My hands shook nervously, so I anchored them against the wooden rim of the frame. I clutched the big metal hook, like a child holding a crayon. I damaged some of the larvae – puncturing some in their side with the hook, flipping others upside-down - their breathing spiracles drowning in royal jelly. But I managed to graft enough cells to raise the queens I needed each year for replacing colonies in Saskatchewan - even sold three thousand a year. After grafting, I set the larvae into my queenless boxes where the transplanted larvae could become queens.

For this to work, the swarm boxes must be queenless. Occasionally an old queen would appear in one of my swarm boxes and ruin everything – all my work of transferring the dozens of larvae and preparing the swarm box would yield no result. I'd repeat all the steps again, hoping I could get it right. But usually, nature and the bees would surprise me. My queen cells would start. A few hours after the swarm box bees began saturating the larvae with royal jelly, the worker grubs would be on their way to becoming queen bees.

Stan Kanter helped me one day. We lifted racks of started queen cells, moving them to finishing hives. Finishing hives were strong colonies that had sixty thousand bees and a queen.

"Where is your queen?" asked Stan.

Raising Little Queens

"In the bottom of the finishing hive." I pointed out the excluder - the wire mesh screen that separated the old queen, at the bottom of the hive, from the new queen cells, which Stan and I cautiously perched in the top of the hive. Forty-eight of them at a time.

"Let's get this right," Stan said. "You graft three day old larvae..."

"The larvae are twelve hours old," I interrupted. "The eggs are laid by the queen three and a half days earlier."

"I know. You know I know. OK, you scoop up larvae, put them in a queenless hive, get them started. You wait a day, move them into these finishers. You wait - what, ten more days? - then you cut the cells off the racks and you put the cells into little mating hives. One cell in each mating hive, right? Then you go back to the mating hive two or three weeks later and dig around, find the queen and stick her in a cage. And you find a buyer who puts her into another hive, a new split of his own. Right?"

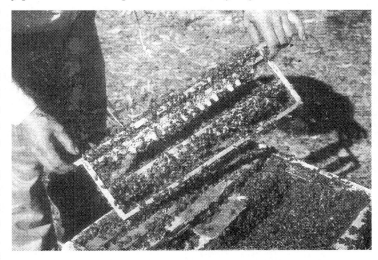

Moving Uncapped Queen Cells into a Finishing Hive from the Starter Swarm-Box

"Yea," I said. I stood there holding another rack of cells. "Yea. And I do it all for five bucks a queen."

"I wasn't going to remind you of that," Stan said.

We put all the started racks of queen cells into the finisher hives which continued to feed and care for the larvae. A few days later, nourishment was complete, the cells fully encased in wax, the larvae molting in their pupae stage. At this point, they were like butterfly cocoons – a wormy looking larvae starts the journey, an elegant winged insect completes it.

Shortly before the wax cocoons would open, I had to remove all forty-eight queen cells from the finisher hive. If one of the queens emerged inside the finisher hive too early, she would destroy the other forty-seven cells. This glitch happened several times each year. One queen would emerge too soon. Maybe I grafted an older larva, maybe the cell was kept too warm by the bees, maybe there was a genetic predisposition for early emergence. Whatever the excuse, there were always a few hundred nearly completed queen cells lost each year. But if the cells developed properly and if I removed them from the hive on time, I had a finished product – a marketable queen cell. Each sold for

Peanut-Shaped Cocoon Housing a Maturing Queen in her Pupae Stage

a dollar, but the shelf life was incredibly short – one day. If a buyer hadn't pre-ordered the bug, I would quickly use her myself in a small mating hive.

Ron, Nuking a Hive -
One Frame of Brood, One of Honey, One with Extra Bees:
This Establishes a Three-Frame Mating Nucleus.

My unsold queen cells were put into small queenless hives, one cell to each mating hive. Small hives were more manageable, it was easier to locate the new queens. Many small hives could be made from one big hive – a better use of equipment resources. The small hives are called mating boxes, nuclei, or more commonly, *nucs*. Taking one big hive and splitting it into six small nucs was a procedure that we called *nuking the bees*.

Beekeepers have a strange vocabulary. We *smoke* our hives when they are unruly; *shake* our bees when we need packages; *nuke* colonies that are too strong. In season we do hive *drops* and if those were successful, we come back later to *rob* the bees.

Friends and I discussed the best way to nuke our bees while we sat in an open booth on an all-you-can-eat night at the Pizza Hut in Clermont. The next table was occupied by a group of technicians passing through from the Crystal River Nuclear Power Station. They asked why we would nuke our bees. "Easy," said Stan, "It's either nuke 'em or watch 'em melt down." The fellow in the yellow uniform at the next booth said that in their business, a melt down would probably be preferable.

Nuking bees does keep the hives from melting down, or at least from being congested and overheated in the Florida sun. After nuking the bees, one colony becomes many. Each nuc had two thousand bees and one comb each of brood, honey, and pollen. The queen cell was gingerly suspended among the bees, though occasionally I would accidentally crush the cell when I placed it into the nuc. In about two weeks, the queen that emerged from the cell would enjoy her mating flight and even lay a few eggs.

Raising Little Queens

Some of the queen cells, though, would never emerge – these represented diseased larvae, chilled pupae, or cells that were jarred or dropped by an inept beekeeper. But most queens chewed off the wax tip of their cocoon and emerged alive. Some of these freshly arrived, unmated queens would be killed by jealous 'laying' worker bees in the little hive. Laying workers are wickedly rude creatures that try to be queens, but can't mate, so they produce unfertilized eggs that always develop into drones.[55] Out of spiteful vengeance, laying workers sting and kill real queens that are introduced into their pseudo-realms.

Some of the queens that survived the chilling and the jarring and the skirmishes with angry laying workers never left the nucs to mate because the weather was cool or rainy or because the little virgin queen was shy. Some of the successful queens that did take to the air to mate got lost. Others were not lost, but were eaten, swallowed whole by purple martins and dragon flies that patrolled the air-space above the mating nucs. Some of the queens survived the mating flights and returned to their cozy little homes. But a small number of the returning mated queens would not lay eggs because these queens were sick or malformed.

In the end, only about half of my nucs with new queen cells would yield healthy, mature, fully functional queen bees. Once the queen had mated and was laying eggs, I would open a small hive and chase the young queen around the box with my clumsy hands. Finally, I would snatch her wings, push her head-first into a tiny wooden cage, a prison, that held her until she was put to use in another hive. A hive belonging to a northern beekeeper who paid me five dollars.

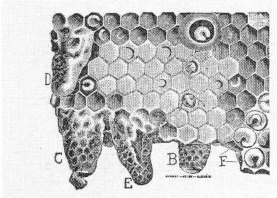

Queen-Cells, from A. I. Root Co.

A Queen-cell from modified worker-cell just started.
B Incomplete cell.
C Cell, after queen has emerged, showing cap hanging.
D Thinned cell.   *E* Cell cut into from side.

**Natural Queen Cells, from Prof. Cook's
1883 Beekeeper Guide Book, but
First Appearing in a Book Published by A.I. Root**

If the caged queen bees weren't sold, they were kept trapped until I was ready to drive north to Saskatchewan. There I'd use them in my Canadian hives. Most years I would sell only two or three thousand queens. Real queen breeders, able to focus their energy with amazing skill and discipline, might harvest fifty thousand queens.

I sold adult, mated queen bees. I also sold queen cells, the wax cocoons. One April afternoon, Ray bought a hundred twenty-five queen cells. I dropped them off at his rented trailer at Stieffel's. They were hanging like little wax candles in a wooden rack. A damp towel was wrapped around the cells.

Bad Beekeeping

"Can't use them today," Ray said.

I told him he had twenty hours before the queens would start to chew their way out of the cells.

"Should I keep them in the 'fridge?" he asked.

Cooling the cells off so they would delay emerging is sometimes a useful trick, but I told him some of the pupae might not have fully developed wings. I suggested he keep them somewhere warm and shaded. He told me he had the perfect spot for the wax cells. Ray left me standing outside, took the cells in, came back a few minutes later with a hundred twenty-five dollars. Fair exchange. He had also changed his shirt.

"Going out?" I asked.

"Yea," Ray said. "It's too late to use the cells today. I'm meeting a friend at Curtis'."

Ray called the next morning. Early.

"Got anymore god-damn queens cells?" he asked.

"How many?"

"Same as yesterday, a hundred twenty-five."

"I thought you wouldn't need any more."

"Got home last night. 'Bout eleven," Ray began. "Hadn't eaten, but I'd picked up some chicken earlier. Cold. So I turned on the oven, went to take a shower. Came back out. Damnedest smell in the house. Smoke, too." Ray paused. He wasn't sure he had to say anything else.

"You stored my queen cells in your oven?"

"Yea. What a mess. Melted wax, some queens running around in the oven. Some wax dripped on the coils, burning. What a mess. A few cells are probably still OK."

I got another sale from Ray. Another hundred twenty-five dollars. He used the queen cells that morning.

Other beekeepers bought mated adult queens from me. To catch a queen, the beekeeper snoops through the hive, one comb at a time, looking at each bee. The nicest looking bee is the queen. She has a long elegant body with long slender legs. Very sexy. At least to other bees. Maybe to some beekeepers. Once located, the able-fingered beekeeper swoops down on the queen, snatches her four opaque wings, lifts her from the comb, nudges her head into a tiny wooden cage. The entrance to the cage is a drilled hole, barely wide enough for the queen to squeeze through. Inside the cage, half a dozen workers await the queen, eager to be her attendants. The beekeeper provides some food, a ventilation screen, a cork over the entrance hole. It's cramped, but sufficient. Eventually, in a few days or weeks, the queen is released from the cage into a big new box of queenless bees. There she commands new subjects as queen and master egg layer for the enterprise.

Caging queens was tough. I was awkward. I'd grasp wings between thumb and finger. Guide a queen into the cage. Once the queen's head was centered, I had to release my fingers so she could crawl forward. This was the queen's last chance to jerk free and fly away. If she gained her freedom, she'd fly back to the tiny mating hive where she'd been captured. But now she was educated. The next time I looked for her, she'd run when the hive's lid opened. She would see fingers swooping towards her thorax and she would flee, perhaps fly into the air.

Late on a Friday afternoon, I sought a renegade queen for an hour. My brother David stopped by at my apiary. "Looking for the queen?" he asked. "She's sitting on your hat."

David reached out and snapped the bug from the brim of my black Stetson. "Here." He placed the queen in my hand.

Although many beekeepers kept hives in the northern states and moved them south each winter, only half a dozen people kept bees in both Canada and the States. There were different issues and problems affecting me than the migrants who stayed within the American border. In

Ron, Searching for an Elusive Queen

addition to visas and customs concerns, I couldn't haul large hives with combs between the States and Canada. I could only truck small cages of bees.

I had to invent a management system of my own. My American bees were separate from the Canadian outfit, the two operations barely intersected. Canadian law did not allow hives of bees – combs, wax, used equipment – to enter the country. Some nasty bee diseases are carried in wax combs and the prohibition against moving used equipment was originally to prevent transmitting brood diseases. Of course, years after cures were developed to disarm these diseases, the laws remained in effect. "Keeps out a lot of foreign competition," said Mike. "Can you imagine how many American beekeepers would be here if we let them load up their hives and supers and come bouncing across the border? They'd run us right out of business, eh?" Mike should know, he was born in the States.

Complete hives were forbidden, but live bees and queens could enter Canada in small combless cages, called packages. This reduced the chance of spreading diseases, but didn't eliminate it. It also slowed the spread of American beekeepers within Canada, but it didn't eliminate it.

A package of bees is a wooden box, twice the size of a toaster. Most of the box is wooden, but the walls include wire screen. The screen allows fresh air to cool the six thousand bees and one queen that occupy the cage. I built wooden cages, filled them with bees, hauled them across the continent. This is how I expanded my Saskatchewan honey farm and replaced bees that died during the winter. The bees were dumped from the cages into honey boxes. American bees set free on the Canadian prairie with their new American queen.

From about 1900 to 1980, billions of honeybees rode the rails of North America each spring. They migrated out of the hot climates to milder and greener pastures in the north. Beekeepers in Georgia, Alabama, and California made a modest living selling bees and queens to honey makers in places like Montana, Michigan, and Manitoba. In Dixie, queens and packages could be produced a few months earlier than in the north. Meanwhile, beekeepers in the far north found it expensive and sometimes impossible to keep bees alive through the long cold dark winter.

According to a book written by A.I. Root,[56] A.I. Root was the first person to think of shipping bees in packages. He published his ideas in the 1880's, following experiments that showed the bees and queens could survive without combs of honey. Mr. Root was a brilliant business man, abandoning his business of making earrings, necklaces, and other jewelry, preferring beekeeping as an enterprise.

A.I. Root,
Founder of the Root
Beekeeping Dynasty

He worked out the economics of raising and selling southern packages to northern beekeepers at the turn of the last century. Marginal economics. The biggest part of fixed overhead was transportation charges. He convinced the U.S. postal service to handle live bees – something they still do a hundred years later – but he realized that the express bills had to be reduced. Hence, the light-weight, combless package. Unfortunately, Mr. Root never shipped many packages. An unexpected secondary problem interfered with his success. The bees tended to starve to death in transit. Ever the thinker, A.I. Root worked on substitute food for the bees. He tried various sugar syrups and soft candy - sometimes the bees survived the long journeys, more often they did not.

The first person to get the food right was a beekeeper in Montgomery, Alabama. W.D. Achord shipped hundreds of packages north in 1912.[57] All survived. Surprisingly, he shared his tricks with his neighbors. In three years, thousands of packages of bees were leaving Alabama. The concept continued to spread. Beekeeping was boosted tremendously for southern beemen who had a new product and northerners who acquired a reliable source of quality bees for their apiaries and orchards.

Raising Little Queens

Most packages are supplied with a small tin pail of sugar syrup. The lid of the quart-sized pail has holes poked into it. Inverted, the syrup drips out for a few minutes. Then physics takes over – a vacuum forms inside the sugar pail and the rest of the syrup comes out only when a bee stuffs her proboscis into the punctured hole and sucks out lunch. Such a food supply may last three or four days for an inactive cluster of bees. Long enough for most modern deliveries.

The inverted syrup pail system was thought to be satisfactory for long international flights as well. Until the first long international flight. A Canadian beekeeper chartered a small cargo plane from Sydney, Australia. They had to turn back when the plane reached ten thousand feet. In the rarefied cargo bay, the vacuum in the inverted cans suddenly became a positive pressure. Lids popped off the tin cans and sticky syrup oozed to the floor. The bees, soaked by the unexpected banquet, were wet and dying. Their food, anticipated to last three days, was gone. The next flight out of Sydney had package bees with hard crystalline sugar candy, like a child's lollipop. Syrup was eventually used again by some of the shippers, but the pail was kept up-right.

Beekeeper with Package Bees,
ABC-XYZ in Bee Culture, 1929

Having the right food in the package cage does not solve all transportation problems. In the past, long rail trips were occasionally disastrous. The postal service, even though staffed by diligent employees of the United States federal government, simply could not guarantee delivery within three or four days. Well-stocked packages ran out of food if a railcar was forced to a sidetrack. The car would sit in the sun, the bees would become hot, their little bodies would dry out. They'd drop like flies.

Then the American interstate road system was built. This encouraged the use of private trucks to haul goods, delivery was quicker. Fewer packages starved, but heat remained a problem. Hundreds of packages were lost every year by beekeepers driving their own trucks. Long delays in snarled traffic, mechanical breakdowns, and accidents often left huge loads of bees cooking inside aluminum vans under bright southern sunshine.

Bad Beekeeping

To keep bees cool on long distance trips, beekeepers sometimes rig up sprinkler hoses in the van. Green hoses with tiny holes, once common on the sort of suburban lawns that beekeepers seldom own, are suspended from the ceiling of the truck's van. Flipped upside-down, water dribbles from the hose onto the bees, keeping their little exoskeletons from going crispy. But unless the beekeeper can invest in several hundred miles of garden hose connected to a water faucet in the south, an auxiliary supply of water is carried on board.

I built my own van for hauling bees. It had to be small, to fit on my one-ton truck, but also big and airy – to ventilate the packages and prevent overheating. With my brother David's help, I hammered together two-by-four studs to build a cedar frame. I sheathed the box with exterior-grade fir plywood. We designed an air-scoop to draw in fresh air. With the air scoop, the unit was a strange-looking contraption, a square wooden head with a big chin jutting forward. The van was six and a half feet tall inside. No one had to stoop to stand and stack packages. We strung up a water hose. I painted the inspired box white, to reflect the sun's heat, but also to match the white Chevy truck upon which it was chained. So it looked nice. Sort of.

SB Knight Clowns for the Camera, Thelma is to his Right
We Ate Okra and Greens, Black-Eye Beans and Roasted Chicken

I was busy with my bees, getting ready to head north with packages. But I had not forgotten about the girl I had met at the radio station.

I remembered Sandy, the ranch on Carter Island, her grandmother standing at the kitchen door. I called the number Grandma Knight had given me. Sandy met me at the door.

Sunday dinner was on the table. Sandy's Uncle David, Aunt Betty Ruth, and their three kids were in the dining room. Across the hall, Grandpa – known as S.B. - had a baseball game on, volume cranked up. S.B. sat back deeply in his rocking lounge chair, chewed a fat unlit cigar. He nodded at me, said nothing. T.K. and Claire entered from a side door, behind S.B.'s chair. There were a lot of people in the house.

"Ya'll get round the table now. Get in here," Sandy's grandmother called from the kitchen.

A huge table, with two extra leaves, held eleven chairs. Uncle David took several minutes to thank the Lord for the friends, the food, the nice weather, the healthy calves. I was especially grateful for the food. I hadn't eaten a real meal in a week.

134

Raising Little Queens

Baked chicken. Creamed okra. String beans with bits of pork. Sour turnip greens. Black eye peas. Golden sweet potatoes. Corn bread. I ate well.

"Brother J.B. done got a nice brood of calves comin' on," Grandma said.

Brother J.B.? Someone's brother? Or monk?

Sandy explained. "Most of the older folks and elders in the church are called 'Brother', especially on Sunday. But in this case, J.B. is Grandma's brother, and he's an elder. J.B.'s got the ranch across the road."

I hadn't heard of elders called brothers or brothers who were elders. Seemed strange. But there was much food on the table still to be eaten.

"Ron, you gotta take more okra. You hardly got a taste. There's a whole kettle on the stove." Grandma put more okra on my plate. I did my best to eat these strange foods, at times too bitter, at times too sweet. I was the only one at the table who had not acquired the taste. But I had the appetite.

"Grandma works at Mascotte Elementary. She cooks there."

"How long have you been there?" I asked Grandma.

"Oh, dang, it's been a long time," S.B answered for her. He held his fork in his right hand, reached out to the aluminum pan centered on the table, stabbed a chicken leg.

I knew the Mascotte Elementary. "I went to that school for a little while. When I was in Grade Five. Almost twenty years ago," I said.

"I worked there then. I'd a seen ya," said Grandma. With this she heaved sweet potatoes and chicken on my plate, perhaps as she'd done when I was nine. I kept eating.

"That boy sure can eat," S.B. said.

After dinner, some of the family were getting ready to go back to Sunday evening church. Grandma invited me to join them, but I had to get work done. It was almost time to haul packages to Canada, I had a thousand things to do.

Before leaving, Sandy led me around the yard. Purple bougainvillea and pink geraniums lined the front of Grandma's red brick house. Tidy citrus trees – grapefruit and small, sweet tangerines - stood between the house and the unused tin-roofed dwelling that stood behind. Sandy showed me the cattle, the corral. We exchanged addresses, my Canadian address, her Florida address. I told her I'd write. I'd phone. And I'd stop in when I got back from my first trip to Saskatchewan.

Previous years, I had helped beekeepers install packages – a messy, tedious chore. The traditional bee cage, designed in 1912, was troublesome to fill; difficult to empty. To get the bees out, the tin syrup can was removed, exposing a hole in the top of the cage. Angry liberated bees blew up into the face of the installing beekeeper. Next, the beekeeper reached a bare hand into the buzzing hole and pulled out the queen cage. The package cage, with its six thousand irritated bees, was then inverted, pointing the buzzing hole to the ground, above a beehive. The caged bees were jarred loose from the package, shaken back and forth until most had been centered on the open hole. Then they were thumped downwards, into the hive. Designed in 1912. Still used in 1980.

My brother David and I decided to design a better cage for carrying bees. We figured there should be a gentler way to free the bees.

Bad Beekeeping

Our cages were big. Clunky, one beekeeper called them. They had one and a half times the space of a standard package. Three toaster-sized. Into this cage we put twice the usual number of bees. If I were stuck in a blizzard in North Dakota, the large bee population would keep the cluster warm. But the boxes were also airy - if I were stuck in a traffic jam in Georgia, the extra air space would keep the bees cool. Each over-sized package had two queens, instead of one, sealed in separate queen cages.

Paul, Stan, and Willi Shaking Bees from the Blower-Box into Package Cages

Instead of leaky sugar syrup, we made lollipop candy, like the Canadian beekeeper who freighted bees from Australia. We heated granulated sugar with a wee bit of water. While the thick syrup was hot and runny, we poured it into a wooden tray at the bottom of each cage. It quickly hardened. The tray had a coarse wire mesh, fat enough for bees to freely pass through, but skinny enough to keep the candy from falling out of the tray. A few hours before injecting bees into the packages, I mounted the queens – in their little wooden cages – next to the cooled and hardened candy.

Bees were added and removed through a sliding door. During transport, the cages were flipped upside down so the food and the queens hung from the ceiling where the bees made a natural cluster, like a swarm in a tree. Once loaded into the cages, the bugs had a comfortable trip.

Convincing the bees to leave their Florida hives and enter the Saskatchewan-bound package cages was not easy.

Paul ran through the beeyard, "Canada! All aboard for Canada!"

The bees were not so easily tricked.

Beekeeping guide books list three ways to collect bees for packages.[58] The preferred method is the catch-the-queen technique. A skilled beekeeper opens each hive before the shaking crew comes along. She looks for the queen, puts it into a little cage, places the cage on top the hive. A less-skilled shaking crew follows behind, removes combs of brood and bees. Each comb is vigorously shaken over a huge metal funnel. Bees fall off the brood frames, slide through the funnel, and land in the package cage. The frames are put back into the old hive, the caged queen set free. Not all the bees are removed from a hive – enough bees are always left to allow the colony to recover.

The second shaking method doesn't require a skilled beekeeper. Instead, bees are dropped through a funnel, but the funnel has a screen at the bottom. The excluder screen has holes big enough to allow worker bees to crawl through, but the holes are too small for the big queen and drones to pass. After each hive is shaken, the residue bees stuck in the bottom of the funnel are dumped back into the old hive – returning queen and drones to their home. The problem with this method is that the bees tend to clog the screen. That is, they pass through it very slowly, doubling the amount of time it takes to get bees into cages. A bigger problem is that sometimes the queen gets squished or ends up in a wrong hive.

I helped a beekeeper shake bees using the third preferred system, an exciting method the book calls 'drumming.'[59] We lifted the lid from each hive, placed an excluder over the frames while adding an extra box of honey combs. Then we blew huge puffs of thick gray smoke through the bottom entrance of the hive, up into the brood nest. The exciting part was beating on the lower boxes with heavy sticks. This drumming chased angry bees up to the top box while the queen and drones and a few workers were stuck below the excluder. Although the book suggested that the excessive smoke would make the bees gorge honey and become calm, the drumming seemed

Beekeeper Drumming Bees Upwards, Above an Excluder, for Shaking into Shipping Packages

to have a very adverse effect. Instead of rolling like fat gerbils into the package cages, they attacked us viciously.

To gather my bees for Canada, I used a new method. One not in the book. While removing the top supers of orange-blossom honey, I chased all the bees down to the lower hive body. Then I cracked the double-story brood chamber apart, separating its two boxes. Slipped in an excluder, closed the hive. The queen was in the bottom box, below the wire barrier. All of this took very little time - two minutes per hive. The colonies were being worked to remove their honey; inserting the excluder was a minor extension of that chore. It took me four days to get all the honey boxes off my hives and to haul them to Deland for extracting.

Shortly after the last honey was off, I spent a day putting queen cages into my empty package boxes and plopped the home-made moving van on the back of the Chevy. The next day, Stan, Willi, Clifton, Paul, Ray and I stripped the top boxes from the honey producing hives and set them on a steel frame with a funnel. We used a blower – a wind machine – to dislodge the bees from the combs. It agitated the bees, but the chore progressed quickly. The fierce wind blew bees out of the brood chambers, down through the funnel, into cages - like Toto leaving Kansas.

Our package-collecting lasted two days. After dark on the second day of blowing bees, everything was loaded into the homemade van. I immediately began the twenty-five hundred mile drive. Half way through Georgia by sunrise.

**With Butler's 1609 "Feminine Monarch" a New Page
in Beekeeping was About to Turn**

On the Road Again

Frustrated with the lack of space for laying new eggs, the old shrunken queen flies out of the hive. A swarm, lured by the queen's pheromone signal, if not her boldness, follows her out of the hive. Scout bees quickly search for shelter. The swarm needs a warm, dry cavity – a hollow tree trunk, a vacant building. Scouts now lead the queen, the swarm following her. The settlers occupy once empty space. Idle bees are now busy bees, building new combs with fresh cells for the old queen to lay eggs. They gather pollen and nectar to feed the eggs which hatch into larvae, become pupae, emerge as fuzzy young adults.

I was conducting one of the longest livestock drives in history. Solo. My plan was to travel through central Florida and Georgia in the dark, while it was a bit cooler for the bees. The Appalachians, though not high mountains, were usually mild in April. I could cross them during the day. Then Indiana, Illinois. In Wisconsin I'd sleep in my truck. Minnesota, North Dakota, Montana, then a night at a cheap motel. At the start of the third day, a final push north, crossing into Saskatchewan at the Port of Monchy.

In Florida, my friends and I had loaded the bees in the evening, as the sun was setting. I drove out of Florida's suffocating heat during the night, so the insects wouldn't be exposed to bright sunlight.

Leaving Florida Sunday night with a big load of packaged bees in a truck that had a new-truck smell was exhilarating. Somewhere in the glove box were my immigration documents. I expected to present them at the border on Wednesday. I was alert, keen, excited. The radio was cranked up. Five hours later I entered Georgia. The excitement was fading. It was dark, no scenery to study. It was warm, making me drowsy. Midnight. One. Two. Two thirty. Two thirty-five. My eyes were bleary. I hit my face with the palm of my hand. Hard. Harder. Awake. Gotta stay awake. I rolled down the window, pushed my head out into the warm night wind. Turned the radio up. Louder. A truck stop was in sight. It wasn't part of my schedule, but maybe I could sleep a few minutes, in the parking lot of the truck stop.

I was sound asleep, sprawled across the seat of my Chevy one-ton. Someone was pounding on the driver's side door. He was looking in at me.

"Mr. Bee-man. Mr. Bee-man, wake up!"

I sat up at the steering wheel. It took me a few minutes to recognize where I'd been sleeping. The dimly lit truck stop was noisy and crowded. Trucks were hissing air from brake compressors and huge diesel engines were noisily idling. People darted around the sprawling complex that offered to the road knights hot showers, coffee, bacon, and sometimes companionship. Three a.m.

I was tired. I slept through the noise and flashing headlights. I remembered that I'd spent the previous eighteen hours rounding up the packages from orange groves and palmetto scrub around the swamps of Lake County. Then I drove, alone, with my cargo. I headed north, towards cool air, so my bees would become quiet. Allowing a truck load of bees to overheat would kill the colonies. And make me broke.

I look out at the small, bearded man with the cowboy hat.

"Wake up! Yer losin' bees!" he told me.

Losing bees? Probably. Some of my bees were on the outside of the cages. They were flying around the truck. Tiny bugs chasing big ugly truck drivers. The bees wouldn't go far. They could smell the odor of their traveling mates, their homes. Once free, they tended to hang onto the outside of the screen, trying to stay close to the truck. But a few broke loose, drifted towards the mercury vapor glow where the bees joined others in a circular orbit until daybreak. I knew that a handful of liberated bees - as few as five or ten, out of a cargo of several million - would be too many for most folks.

"Mr. Bee-man," the cowboy said again.

I rolled down the window.

"You need some bennies?" he asked.

"No," I replied, "I'm OK."

I knew bennies. The army fed them to fighter pilots to sharpen their senses, to keep soldiers awake for hours and hours.

"You can't stay here, they'll call the police. These pills will keep you awake until you get further north."

I bought two pills, for ten dollars. I had never seen 'bennies' before, but I knew they were supposed to keep a person awake. I didn't want trouble from the Georgia State Patrol, somehow I figured if I was drugged up driving down the highway it would be better than letting some bees drift around a busy truck stop. I was tired; the logic worked at the time. There were, in fact, a lot of bees flying around my truck. Maybe one of my cages was leaking. And it was really warm. If I didn't continue driving, over-heated bees might die. The cowboy pressed two big black pills into my hand.

"You better get out and walked around your truck first," he said.

I got out, walked around my truck. Warm. Too warm. Hundreds of bees were flying towards the truckstop's big spotlights. My new friend gave me a jolt of strong black coffee to wash down the first pill. The medicine was black and soft, jelly-like, I thought. I couldn't really tell. I was tired and swallowed it quickly. He told me to save the second pill for later.

As ordered, I walked around the truck again. I felt a lot better. My body became tense. My mind, alert. I fired up the truck.

I drove with my window rolled down, radio turned up - as the friendly drug dealer had told me. He also said that I may be tired again in a few hours and that I should probably sleep. He was right. I drove for three hours. It became much cooler. I had reached the Appalachian mountains. I sprawled across the truck's seat, slept for two hours. In the early morning, I awoke and looked at the remaining pill. It was then that I realized that I had spent ten dollars for two black licorice jelly beans.

As appealing as peering at North America through a bee veil may sound, there are always issues and problems trucking bees. Permits, inspections, safety issues. A worrisome part of moving bees is the weigh-station inspection stop. In the morning, I

On the Road Again

was comfortably driving along the wide, smooth Tennessee interstate, enjoying country music and mountain scenery. Suddenly a flashing sign warned "WEIGH STATION. ALL TRUCKS EXIT." My heart sank. An inspector in a glass booth wanted to weigh my truck. I couldn't see his face, but his voice boomed through a speaker. My truck's weight passed, easily. Package bees are not heavy. He asked me to flash my lights, lock brakes, display my turning signals. One bulb was uncooperative. I promised to get it fixed.

Bees were beginning to fly around the truck.

"Tennessee has a loose-load law," the voice through the loud speaker told me. Most states had 'loose-load' laws, which meant you shouldn't have cargo falling off the truck while you drive. Probably a sensible law if I were carrying plutonium, but some highway inspectors assumed that the rules included bees escaping from a bee truck.

"Yea?" I said.

"You have loose bees. That's a loose load."

"I see the bees," I said. "But mine are all in cages. Those bees must belong to the last beekeeper who came through here."

"You're the first beekeeper this morning," the voice in the speaker said.

"I think those bees are from a swarm of wild bees that were going across the road south of Mount Eagle. Some of them must have settled on my truck." I suppose he knew I was lying. I waited for the voice

"OK. Get out of here." Most truck inspectors are afraid of bees. Most people are afraid of bees. But most of the road inspectors I met were kindly folks who really didn't want to harass a poor farm kid.

Days before I left on this trip, my brother David told me he was once stopped by police as he drove a semi-load of his bees along Interstate 75. There had been a lot of bee thefts that winter. To try to stop the thefts, cops were stopping bee trucks, asking drivers to prove ownership of the property.

David told me that the state trooper stood beside the truck cab door. "Please get out and bring all your papers."

They walked around the big rig, past the fluorescent screen covering the huge load of bees. They stood in front of the officer's car. David handed the man his papers. It was hot, the bees were buzzing angrily. As long as David drove, air blew through the net, the bees kept quiet. Stopped alongside the road, the bees were no longer quiet. The policeman went into his car. David waited. The officer came back out.

"Okay, Mr. Misk-misk-miks-mik-sa. Your proof of purchase?

**Truck Load of Branded Bees,
Covered by a Fluorescent Bee-Net**

141

Sales receipt? Anything to prove you bought these bees? Where is it? What have you got?"

"I didn't buy the bees. I own them, I built the equipment myself. Raised the queens and bees myself. I don't have purchase papers."

"We need proof these bees are yours."

David was anxious. He wanted to drive, let fresh air blow through his hives. But he didn't have the papers the cop wanted. Then he remembered that all the equipment – boxes, frames, everything – was branded. Branded with his own name. "The bees are branded. They're all branded," David told the police man.

"All of them?"

"Yea."

"All of them?"

"Yea, they're all branded."

"All right." The traffic cop was silent a while. "I guess I'll have to believe you. Go ahead, get out of here."

Half an hour later, much further down the road, David realized that the cop didn't know that David was talking about the brands on the wooden equipment. The cop would have thought David meant each individual little bee had a tiny brand burnt into her side.

It took me most of Monday to cross Tennessee, Kentucky, Indiana. I got around downtown Chicago's eight lane race track, the Van Ryan Expressway, when I was tired again. This was probably a good thing. I was less alert; less nervous. Traffic weaved in and out of my lane as everyone moved along, bumper-to-bumper, sixty miles per hour. Soon I saw a sign. *The Cheese State. Welcome to Wisconsin.*

Monday night. I slept on the seat of the truck at an all-night gas station in Wisconsin. It was chilly in the morning, white frost outlined grass blades. I was cold. The bees were quiet. None flew from the van. I nailed plywood over the screen windows on the sides of the van - the bees would get enough fresh air from the wind scoop at the front, they wouldn't need icy air hitting them through the side of the box.

Tuesday was more leisurely, a fourteen hour drive across the western states, into Montana. I treated myself to an inexpensive room - hot water, a shower and a shave. Early the next morning, I dropped the room keys in a slot outside the motel office door, and drove the last few hundred miles. Into Canada.

I was at the border, twenty minutes from my home in Val Marie.

The fellow at the border studied my papers.

"You're moving here? Here?"

Of course I was moving here. Here. He was amused.

"I get paid bonus isolation pay working here," he said. "Most inspectors prefer bigger centres. Best job in the west is the Calgary Airport. I've got a transfer approved for Calgary."

I congratulated him.

I reached Val Marie. It was afternoon. I put as many of the bees out in the field as I could before dark, dumping the bugs from their screen cages into boxes with honey and combs. The bees gratefully settled into their new homes and gathered fresh pollen the next morning. By the end of my second evening in Canada, I had installed all the bees and I was ready to get back to Florida to move my other bees. The Hutterites had a van heading for Saskatoon. I hitched a ride, they dropped me off at the airport.

In Florida, I had six hundred hives of bees. These included the smaller nucs that raised queens and were now recombined to make larger hives. Those bees needed to visit an apple orchard in the center of Pennsylvania. Other hives, the ones I used to get my packaged bees for Saskatchewan, were rebuilding their decimated populations with the emergence of young brood. Those bees had to reach Wisconsin within a few weeks.

I prepared the pollination hives by removing the wooden dividers which had turned the single depth colonies into three individual nucs, each with three frames. Each separate section had its own queen, three mating queens in each single hive. Excess queens were captured and sold. Removing the dividers combined the bees and turned each hive into a standard nine-frame colony with one queen. These full colonies with combs and honey were much heavier than the light little screen packages that went to Saskatchewan.

I was still tired, having arrived two days earlier from the long trip north with packages, but the fellow who owned the apple orchard near Gettysburg, called to say his "buds were breaking". Could I get bees there in three days? I could, but it meant I had to race around to twelve beeyards, gather up four hundred hives, nail each lid in place, move the bees to one central load-out yard, and do that in one day.

I congregated the hives in a Kuharske pasture. Paul, Stan, Jay and I loaded four hundred single storey colonies, forty pounds each, by hand. In two hours we filled the big truck that had brought my bees south from Wisconsin in November.

I Gathered my Florida Hives at one of Chuck Kuharske's Pastures.
The Valencia Orange Grove Nearby had Lost its Bloom.
It Was Time for these Bees to See the North Again.

Bad Beekeeping

After finding my hives, parking them in a huge apiary, and enlisting friends to help load them all by hand, I drove the thousand miles from Florida to Pennsylvania and arranged the bees, ten hives to a cluster, in an apple orchard, among white blossomed Macintosh and Red Delicious. For three weeks, these bees transferred pollen from flower to flower, so the orchard owner could get a big set of apples. The happy farmer paid me three thousand dollars for my bees' services. Enough cash to cover spring moving expenses – including the trips from Florida to Saskatchewan.

I left those bees in the hilly, damp Pennsylvania orchard. I turned my big truck back towards Florida. I had not slept five hours any one night in two weeks. But the truck was empty, I was heading back south, drinking coffee. Black, with extra sugar. I tried cigarillos as an insomniac on my all-night trucking expeditions, expecting the nasty smoke to keep me awake. I tanked up on various legal stimulants to push my reluctant body along. But no more licorice bennies. Instead, I bought caffeine chewing gum and little white caffeine pills at the truck stops. A thermos of foul-smelling, coarse grind coffee and a couple sticks of Big Buzz Gum were enough to push me through the dreary early morning hours when my brain and muscles wanted to quit. The legal dope made my hands tremble. My heart pounded. It was exhilarating.

This wouldn't be a bad mental or physical state if I were operating a chain saw or some heavy equipment on my own farm. But during those brain-dead-over-stimulated hours, I drove thousands of miles with huge trucks loaded with tens of thousands of pounds of equipment and millions of honeybees.

I was in North Carolina. Driving back to Florida from the Pennsylvania apple orchards, after unloading the four hundred hives of pollination bees. I stopped to rest. I'd been awake for forty hours. I'd loaded bees in Florida, driven eleven hundred miles to the orchards on the eastern slopes of the Appalachians, distributed the bee boxes, and begun the return trip. For more bees. And more driving. The caffeine had quit working. I shut the truck off, lay down on the seat. It was seven, becoming dark. If I could sleep for two or three hours, traffic would quiet down. I would make up for my time off, driving faster, later at night. I could still get to Florida and move the next load of bees on time.

I slept. When I looked at my watch again, it was eleven. Four hours later. But it was light out. If it were eleven at night, it should be dark. I looked at the sun. High in the sky. OK, I'd slept for sixteen hours. On the seat of the truck. Alongside a busy American Interstate Highway in North Carolina.

I was hungry, but I needed to get moving again. Hunger won. A truck stop, more caffeine pills with bacon and eggs and pancakes and toast and hash browns and grits and lots of coffee. A father and his son entered the restaurant and walked over to me.

"I'm Bill Nelson," Bill Nelson said. "You own that beekeeper's truck parked out there?"

""Yea, it's mine." Was I in trouble?

"Can we join you?" They sat down. "This is my son, Tom. Tom Nelson. We're moving bees ourselves, heading back to Florida to get a second load for the apples in Maine."

I was suspicious. The father, about forty, had a clean shave and neat, short hair. His clothes were clean. Even his hands were clean. He smiled. Sat casually across the table from me. He wasn't wound up tight like a clock running on a caffeine battery. He smiled some more. He looked at his son, nodded.

"Tom thinks he wants to be a beekeeper. He's on this trip with me because he's got Easter week off from school."

Easter? When was that? This week? Last week? I wasn't sure.

"Beekeeping is a good business, Tom," I said, anticipating his father's next question. "You get to travel, be your own boss. It's hard work, the pay isn't very good, but it's a great lifestyle."

"That's not what I've been trying to tell him. He *wants* to be a beekeeper. He doesn't want to go to college... But he's a smart boy, not like you and me." Father looked at son, he continued talking to the boy. "Tom, look at this fellow's eyes - they're beet red, blood-shot. And he's driving an old truck. He probably even slept in his truck overnight. Do you want to end up like this?"

The boy shrugged his shoulders, looked away from me.

They got up and left.

I reached Florida a few hours later. My eyes still red.

I was back in Florida, back at the Knight ranch and Grandma was serving okra again. After supper, Sandy and I drove to Leesburg to see a movie. But first, we tried to find her father. She hadn't seen him in over a year. He lived on the south side of Leesburg, twenty miles from Mascotte. We parked on the road in front of a house. A tiny white house shedding its paint. And its windows. Up two steps. On the porch was a freezer, a plastic GI Joe, and a tricycle with only one wheel. To the left of the door were stacks of newspapers, moldy from rain that had dripped on them. The doorway was between the freezer and newspapers. The screen door was ripped, I shook it to knock it, and a bony lady appeared at the door. Her bare feet had purple-painted toe nails. She flicked her cigarette out into the lawn.

"Neil? I don't know no Neil. And I done been here two years. You got the right house, girl?"

Sandy knew it was the last house where she'd seen her father and brother. They were renting, must have moved on. We left. The search for her father made me feel closer to Sandy.

I had to move more bees north. My third big load of hives were the two-storey colonies. These had donated bees to the Saskatchewan packages - three weeks earlier, we had removed most of the young bees from the brood nests. But I'd left the queen and all the eggs, larvae, and pupae in the hives. The brood continued to develop and emerge in the warm, incubating Florida sun - these hives were full of bees again. They were even heavier than the hives that went to the apple orchards near Gettysburg. Heavier and bigger – two-storey instead of singles. My truck could only carry half as many.

The bees were loaded; I was heading through Georgia again.

I was tired when I crashed into Bud Tifton's gas station in Tifton, Georgia. It was shortly after midnight. I pulled up to the pumps. Unscrewed the cap from the 50 gallon gasoline tank and reached for the fuel hose. A long-haired young man stopped me from putting diesel fuel into my gasoline tanks.

"That's diesel! You need to drive over there!" he yelled, pointing to the gasoline pumps which were somewhere else - over there.

I backed up my truck and trailer and cut sharply towards the gasoline pumps. The pumps were shielded overhead by a wooden structure, meant to keep rain off customers. It stood 11 feet above the concrete. My truck was almost 12 feet high. I tore apart Bud Tifton's verandah as I attempted to approach his gasoline pumps.

People scattered when chunks of plaster board and cypress rafters dropped to the ground. I stopped trying to squeeze the truck into the place where it wouldn't fit. I backed out and drove into a small field behind Bud Tifton's gas station. I was in the town of Tifton, the county of Tifton. In Georgia. And I had just wrecked Bud Tifton's gas station. Not a very diplomatic thing for a visiting northerner to do.

"Should we call Bud?" someone asked.

It was five a.m. I suggested that they call the Georgia Patrol, and let Bud sleep.

"You got insurance for this, Mr. Beeman?"

"Yes, I think I do."

So, I sat in the tiny restaurant while a waitress offered me coffee. I had already drunk about ten cups earlier that night.

"Milk, please," I said.

The Georgia patrol arrived in about half an hour. The witnesses - including the hairy young man who had suggested that I pull up under the 11 foot verandah with my 12 foot truck – were gone. Someone had swept up the mess. It didn't look too bad, but I guessed that my insurance company would be building a new roof for the gas station.

The deputy sheriff was a nice guy. He told me he had an uncle who coached the high school basketball team in Eustis, Florida. He knew Eustis was near Groveland, which according to my driver's license, was my hometown.

"They had a great season last year." I volunteered.

"No, they didn't," said the young officer. "Don't worry, I'm not going to charge you. I can write this up as a non-moving violation."

Non-moving violation? I didn't explain that the verandah was standing still and the truck had done the moving. There was no ticket. No fine. A suggestion that I get some sleep. And even a "Come back soon," from the waitress in the coffee shop.

I drove for another hour, wanting to be well beyond Bud Tifton's Service Station, the city of Tifton, the county of Tifton, before I closed my eyes to sleep.

Next day, I saw the *Cheese State* sign again. My brother Don and I offloaded the bees, placing them in cow pastures amid clover. Then I drove the rig back to eastern Pennsylvania (nine hundred miles) because the apples had finished blooming. These bees had to be gathered up before the orchard owner started to spray insecticides on the trees (and bees, if I were tardy). I loaded the bees alone. They were much heavier than when they'd arrived from Florida. They were filled with dandelion and apple blossom honey. I began driving west. These bees would join their cousins in Wisconsin for the summer. Once all my American hives were located in Wisconsin, I would fly back to Florida one last time and get my pick-up truck. I'd need it in Saskatchewan during the summer.

On the Road Again

I was back in Florida, getting my second truck, loading it with personal stuff – junk, mostly - that I would be able to carry to Canada as part of my duty-free immigrant's effects. I invited Sandy to my brother David's for supper. Linda made baked chicken, twice-baked potatoes, and a huge tomato, lettuce, cucumber salad topped with avocados and a home-made honey dressing. I noticed that Sandy was picking at her supper.

"I love the chicken," she said, "but we never have this kind of salad." Northern cuisine. Sandy told Linda about her boy friend. He was off at college using a football scholarship. She'd met him when Sandy was a cheerleader, Eddie was an offensive end. Linda looked at me. "We're just friends," I said. I wasn't very convincing.

David opened a bottle of red wine. It was the last evening I would see them for months. I left Florida the next day.

Sandy and one of her Best Friends

Another drive back to Saskatchewan, my bottom glued to a truck seat for another three thousand miles. But more leisurely. I visited my sister in Cincinnati, spent a few hours at the Field Museum in Chicago, stopped to see Stan near Madison, hiked among the hoodoos west of Glendive, Montana. In five days, I arrived back in Val Marie – in time to tend the bees I had set out a month earlier. It was mid-May and the Canadian hives needed a second brood box to hold all the new bees that the young queens were producing.

That spring, I had driven eleven thousand miles in twenty-eight days. While not navigating and bumping into trouble, I was busy shaking packages, preparing hives for moving, loading and off-loading. I followed a similar routine for ten years. Luckily, I never rolled a truck load of bees on its side; nor ran down a nice, normal, station-wagon family out on a holiday drive. Somehow, living in my truck a month a year became comfortable, or at least familiar.

And yet, I had a other beekeeping duties. Hives needed paint. Colonies needed medication. Some queens were lost, others were poor. These had to be replaced. And I had to visit my landlords - the folks who let me put bees on their farms. "Could I come back again next year?" I'd plead. None ever turned me down, but I must have been a sight a their door - a greasy, long-haired youth in dirty jeans. Smelling from bee stings and the smoker. Or they'd catch me throwing boxes on my truck, shirtless, and often with loud country music blasting from the truck's speaker. Even then, the farmers and ranchers allowed me to return again and again to set my hives in their fields, groves, and pastures.

I'd Sometimes Work on my Farmer's Tan while Wrestling with my Bee Hives

But it was the time of year to move bees - away from the ever hotter subtropical sun in Florida. North to Wisconsin, Pennsylvania, and Saskatchewan. Moving bees was the project which consumed my time. And consumed me.

Some beekeepers claim that the stress of moving bees from place to place doesn't justify the activity – bees and beekeeper get confused and it takes time for them to recover. In reality, those years of my beekeeping career were my most profitable. Only after I tried to stay in one place with my hives did I start to lose money.

But hauling bees is tough. Off the highway, other problems await the beekeeper. Trucks get stuck. For me, in southern Saskatchewan, it was slick, greasy brown clay, *gumbo*. After a rain, the surface of a country road is as slippery as ice. In Florida, soft white sand, *sugar sand*, can swallow a truck, each turn of the tires tossing more sand into the air, digging a deeper hole, leaving only a small depression in the surface to indicate the spot the Dodge once occupied.

One spring, I was half a mile from the nearest house, isolated in a sandy orange grove on Ralph Ward's farm. Alone, I'd hand-loaded my ten-wheeled behemoth with two hundred colonies of bees bound for the north. After firing up the engine, throwing the unit in low gear, and sipping some cold coffee, I let the clutch engage. I liked getting on the road. By the time the truck was loaded, the hard work was done. Planning, packing, lifting, carrying, stacking hundreds of boxes, moving thousands of pounds. Nothing left to do but sit and steer a path around the other motorists on the highways. In two days, I'd be off-loading bees in a Wisconsin clover field - if I could get my truck out of the soft sand. Before I had gone the first fifty feet of my thirteen-hundred mile trip, I felt the rear wheels sink. I climbed down and walked to the back of the truck.

"Pretty soft sand, son," a farmer said. He watched me looking at my stuck truck. I agreed with him. I had never seen him before, and hadn't heard his tractor approach while I was starting up my truck. His tractor was an old John Deere, the green paint faded by the Florida sun. Behind the tractor were a double set of discs, used to chop weeds growing in the sand between the citrus trees.

"Yea, pretty soft," I said. He climbed back on his tractor and it roared. *Was he leaving?* I should have asked for his help.

He drove in front of my truck, then backed up and stopped. Pulling a chain out from under the tractor seat, he said, "Hook this around your bumper." I did. He looped his end of the chain around the hitch between the last set of discs. "Get in." He looked at me as if he thought I were a slow-witted boy. Hadn't I figured out that he was going to pull me out of the sand?

A week later, with a different collection of bees on the back of a different truck, I slowly slid off a slimy Saskatchewan trail near my Cote beeyard east of Val Marie. I walked around to look at what I had done. My boots were caked in gumbo, becoming heavier and fatter with each step. Mud filled the space between the dual wheels, hid the tread of the tires. A farmer arrived with a tractor, its green paint scarred by Saskatchewan wind. He dragged a chain out from under his tractor seat, pulled me out of the mud.

Bringing Bees Back a Few Miles
Photo From Al Root's 1913 <u>ABC & XYZ of Bee Culture</u>

How to Raise Queen Bees

1) Transfer 3-Day-Old Larvae to Cell

2) Finish Queen Cells in Strong Builder Colonies

3) Put Ripe Queen Cells into Mating Nucs

4) Inspect the New Queen's Brood Pattern

5) Find the Queen

6) Put Queen in Shipping Cage with Attendants

Spring on the Range

In cold climates, bees survive long winters eating honey produced the previous summer. The colony is a furnace, burning honey, producing heat. A tight cluster of thirty thousand bees is organized around the queen, a few eggs and larvae. Outside the nest, on the Saskatchewan prairie, it may be forty below; in the winter cluster it's as warm as a Hawaiian afternoon. On the fringe of the cluster, the exposed posterior of a frigid and motionless bee contributes to the insulating outer circle, protecting the queen and her progeny, keeping them warm. With the approach of spring, the cluster becomes less dense, the brood nest less constricted. The bundle of bees breaks. The insulation bee moves to the center of the cluster, near her queen. A new season of work begins.

I drove twenty-five hundred miles - four thousand kilometres - from Florida to Saskatchewan. I carted two hundred eighty cages of insects. Within my home-made van were enough bees to stock five hundred sixty new hives. The tall wooden van, side windows covered in wire mesh, looked like a hippie's mobile home. Or a garbage collector's truck. A hippie trash wagon. My long hair and shabby face suited the role. The truck may have looked like it was carrying garbage, but the insects drifting in a cloud around my vehicle whenever I stopped for gasoline were bees, not flies.

My truck and I reached Saskatchewan. Alone, quietly, I unloaded the bee cages onto the concrete loading dock in front of my tiny warehouse. A black and white King Bird floated overhead, across the dock and back again. Two hundred and eighty cages of Florida bees stacked in the cool dry prairie air, bees clustered tightly, a muffled hum of contentment barely audible. From Martha Briand, I borrowed hot water, mixed in a few pounds of sugar to feed my caged insects. I used a weed sprayer, not one contaminated with Round-Up, but a clean new one that I had picked up at Edge's in Groveland the week before I had left Florida. I wet the cages with sweet syrup. The bees sucked it up from their side of the wire screens.

The bees were fed, cool, safe - and out of the unwieldy van. I drove to the back of my honey shed and unbolted the awkward box. With a lanky industrial jack, I levitated the van above the flat bed of my six wheeled Chevy. Then I supported it with a set of stilts. Finally I dropped the van down a few inches onto six heavy, sand-filled steel drums. I chained everything together. My truck was free; a simple flat-bed again. The van would stay anchored to its perch until October. Then I'd reverse the process, drop it on the truck, prepare for the drive back to Florida.

From the honey shed I carried one hundred twenty brood chambers – wooden boxes with combs of honey and pollen. I loaded an equal number of lids and bottom boards, then stacked sixty clunky cages of bees – enough bees and queens to start a hundred twenty new hives – onto the tail of the truck's flat deck. I drove half an hour, to a sage-brush pasture on the edge of a hay field at the irrigation flats' west end. I set bottom boards on the ground, then the brood chambers. I pulled four of the nine combs out of each box and leaned them with a hive lid against the brood chamber. Repeated the procedure one hundred nineteen times that evening. Then I distributed the caged bees.

I doused the first package of bees with syrup, slid its cage door open, shook half the sugar-coated bees into a brood chamber, walked a few metres to a different box and released the rest of the bees. I didn't put the two groups of bees into adjacent hives. The bees were so familiar which each other after the long trip north in the same cage that they might abandon one of the boxes and live together as one huge happy family. The bees had to think of themselves as separated Siamese twins – equal but different, now on their own. Along with the bees, queens - liberated from their tiny cages - settled into each box of bees, honey, and pollen. The four combs that had been set alongside the box were dropped back in the hive box. A lid covered the whole thing.

It was dark by the time the last set of packages were in their summer homes. Bees were crawling and stinging urgently. I drove back to my shed in town; loaded more brood chambers, lids and bottoms on the truck for the next morning's work. It had been a long day, one that began at a roadside hotel in the States and ended with over a hundred new colonies settled in Canadian brood chambers. The rest of the packages were installed the next day.

Saskatchewan in April looked much as it did when I had left in the fall. Trees were leafless, barren. Grass was brown. Occasional patches of dirty snow covered the brown grass. Dust was blowing. Everything looked like October – a bit of grimy snow, brown grass. The world had slept for five months. I had missed a few weeks of forty below temperatures while I earned a farmer's tan, raising queens and making orange blossom honey in Florida. But the long cold dark night of winter seemed to have had little effect on the prairie - April looked like October here.

This illusion was shattered when I inspected one of my over-wintered apiaries. I began to respect the season I had missed. Vicious winds had shredded some of the hives' wrapping materials. Skunks had scratched big holes in the grass in front of the hives. There were dried bits of honeybee body parts - carcasses spit from the mouths of the marauding skunks which had sucked the organs and blood from my bees, discarded their wasted bodies on the grass.

But the winter losses were not overwhelmingly bad. Only twenty percent of my colonies had died, and many of the survivors were in good shape. Compared to the tiny clusters shaken from the Florida packages a few days earlier, these hives were powerful. Destined for great things.

Buzz was waiting by his barn. He laughed as my six-wheeled Chevy slid sidewise, off the trail and into the ditch. But it was still moving, and slid just as easily back onto the gumbo and gravel that led to his homestead. I parked in the grass beside the horse barn. Buzz opened the door of my new truck.

"New truck?" he asked.

Spring on the Range

"Yes, I got it in Florida. I'm allowed to bring two new vehicles into the country. And all my personal junk. I've immigrated. I'm legal now."

"Great," said Buzz. "Another white man. There goes the neighbourhood." He grinned at me. " You want to feed some cows?" He motioned towards his truck.

I started to climb into his four-wheel drive.

"No. Get in the back." He dropped the tail gate and told me to sit next to the tub of oats and meal. Buzz fired up the truck. We bounced across the muddy prairie, gliding past tufts of bunch grass and slipping down the side of a butte. Fuzzy red and white cattle turned to look at the truck. Buzz stopped amidst the animals, got out of the truck and walked to the back where I had been hanging on. "Guess I could have let you ride up front with me," he said. Guess he could have; perhaps he was expressing his sense of humour. "I'll show you how to feed cattle," Buzz said.

Buzz scattered a bit of hay from one of the broken bales that were leaning against my perch. He took a plastic pail and dumped a scoop of grain into a wooden trough, dropping it between the wet noses of his property. "Hang on, we've got more to feed," he said. We bounced to the next trough. He slowed down so I could scatter hay and dump more grain, but he didn't stop. Some oats spilled on the ground. "Got to get your timing right," Buzz said.

Before long, we were parked at the last feeding station. Buzz pointed out half a dozen prong horn antelope. They were half way up a nearby butte, their narrow, pointed noses faced us. They watched us put out the feed. "If I put out too much feed for the cows, I'd be feeding a hundred deer and antelope. That's why I only put out a little at a time," Buzz said. As I was about to ask why he didn't fence the beasts out, an antelope shot up into the sky, way above and over the tall barbed wire. Fencing keeps big puffy cows in, it doesn't keep mule deer, antelope, or coyotes out. I pointed to his cattle.

"They look healthy. Fat, I mean," I said. They were immense. Saskatchewan cows are blimps. Fat and muscle drape their large frames; thick hairy hide wraps muscle. Even their faces were broad. In Florida's swamps, where I'd been a few days earlier, the cattle were rangy, ribs and hip bones drew skeletal outlines on taut multi-hued skin. Here, these Saskatchewan cows ate short grass from scant tufts, yet were enormous.

"We'll need to brand calves soon," said Buzz. "You'll help."

The old cows were already branded. Wearing the letters TU on their hips. "Trottier University?" I asked Buzz Trottier.

"Teats Up," he answered.

I unwrapped my overwintered Saskatchewan bees, then stowed the insulation and black wrapping paper in a shed until fall. New hives, from the Florida packages, were gathering pollen. All these Saskatchewan bees could be ignored for a few weeks. I flew back to Florida to move bees to apples, to Wisconsin clover. And to get my second truck, part of my landed immigrant property. I had three months to get everything I wanted into the country. After that, anything I brought north would be subject to tariffs and duty.

So I was in Florida for a week in May. It was hot and sticky. My skin was wet and smelly. The love-bugs had hatched, they flew around in thick masses, coupled together, apparently stuck like that their entire adult lives. The insects hovered around our eyes and drifted in and out of our mouths as Eleanor Dern and I tried to talk. I had a couple of pictures of Val Marie. She was incredulous. "Why on earth would you *choose* to live in a place like that?" she asked. I had selected the best photos to show her.

Later, I showed the same photographs to Sandy's grandmother. She was much more diplomatic.

"Interesting," Grandma Knight said. "This is where you live in the summer? S.B., come look at these pictures. My, look at these cows. Don't see the likes of them here!" Grandma put more collard greens on my plate. I still found the food unfamiliar. I chewed the greens until they became a wad of thick grass in my mouth.

Sandy asked if I had a picture of the house, my little house on the prairie. Fortunately, I did not. I told her again that I'd write. And I'd send some pictures.

A week later, back in Saskatchewan, I drove on a quiet road, sipping cold coffee and listening to Peter Gzowski on the CBC. I heard an odd noise and then I realized the wheels flying past my truck were my own. I had just crossed a ravine on Highway 37, going north towards Eastend. Had the tires left me at the bridge, I may have joined them in the murky water below. But when the lug nuts broke and the rear dual wheels sprang free, I was on a flat and straight road and driving quickly. When the truck sank down on its side, it tilted, with the axle on the ground where the twin wheels had once been. My truck, my tall load of empty honey supers, and I, were all safe. Not really very shaken. But my coffee had spilt.

I got out of the truck, surveyed the damage. I was reminded of the seventeen year old driver who took his father's truck on a three hundred mile trip from the Shenango Valley near Pittsburgh, to upstate New York, near the Finger Lakes. I was the kid, seeking new hive equipment from the Dadant bee supply company. Mid-way on my trek, I stopped in a damp forest atop a high Pennsylvania mountain. I needed to pee. I got back in the truck, began the steep descent. Without brakes. It could have been bad. Lucky for me, I was in a low gear when I realized there was no way to stop the machine.

I tried the parking brake. Useless. I turned off the key, the engine kept running. The steep drop eased into a long low grade - six miles, actually - and by the time the world leveled off, I was moving pretty quickly. There was no other traffic on the road as I swung broad curves. Only me and the singing tires of the big truck I was steering.

That shopping trip from home to upstate New York had marked the beginning of my beekeeping career. I had been taking care of my father's hives – about three hundred colonies – but I'd wanted to have beehives of my own. Dad had allowed me to keep a third of the honey from his three hundred hives - that was my pay. If the bees made no honey, I made no money. My father figured a third of the honey had to go to capital – the truck, the shed, the hives; a third had to go to expenses – feed, new queens, gasoline. He paid those bills. From thirty barrels of honey, twenty thousand pounds, I earned one third - three thousand dollars for my work. Most of my honey money went to purchase my own hive equipment, the boxes I'd gone to New York to get when the brakes went out.

My father's bees weren't the only thing keeping me busy those days. I had a part-time job. I was a teen-aged bee inspector, back in '73, '74, and '75. It was my job, as an agent of the State of Pennsylvania, to insist on entry into every apiary within a three county area. I opened hives, looked for the black, rotten, smelly brood that usually signaled American foulbrood disease. I had to burn hives that were badly infected, much to the disappointment of their owners.

Some beekeepers made me go through a ritual when I inspected their colonies. I had to stand off to the side of the hive. I could understand this. If I stood in front, it would disturb the bees' flights as they entered and left their home. But sometimes the beekeeper would insist that I stand on the side of the hive that cast the least shade on the hive. Such a fussy beekeeper would insist that I not use smoke ("It will kill brood.") and that I only hold a frame for a few seconds ("So the brood wouldn't get chilled."). Some of the demands made it impossible to do an effective inspection job, which required that I control unruly bees with smoke and that I poke at disfigured brood to detect disease.

It took me a while to realize that sometimes this was the beekeeper's real motivation - if he couldn't keep the inspector out of the beeyard, he could at least make the job difficult. Then, perhaps, a diseased hive might be missed and not burned. The burning of the hives was, at the time, mandatory, though I was permitted to use discretion in the execution of the law. For thirty years, effective medications had been available to treat American foulbrood.[60] But the law had not been updated. So, if I felt the beekeeper would try to restore the health of her bees, I would teach her how to conduct a medication program. But if I found abandoned or neglected hives, or suspected that the bees' owner would not be interested in doing the necessary work to keep bees healthy, I killed the bees with government-issued cyanide. I dug a deep, narrow trench in the ground at the apiary, stacked the infected hive equipment over the hole, and lit a fire. Cruel? The alternative was to allow the bees a slow diseased death. Then healthy bees might discover the old honey and wax from the dead colony. Disease would spread; the healthy bees would become infected. Luckily for honey lovers, the spores have no effect on humans, but they are deadly to other bees.

Two brothers, middle-aged bachelors, kept one hundred fifty hives of bees in a sheep pasture, fenced in next to their unpainted house in south-east Mercer County. The lack of care in the dwelling, a truck on cinder blocks, hood up, power lines that sagged and beer cans that formed a small hill exposed these folks as Anglish people living in a mostly Amish country-side. I pulled up to their house in my pale blue, government-issue car. Government license tag. *Pennsylvania Official Use Only.* I was nineteen, a skinny and confused teenager.

Bees, attracted from the nearby colonies by a sweet aroma creeping from the house, hovered about the porch. Yellowed curtains, cut from old sheets, swayed through the front window. I was being watched, but couldn't see the watcher.

I tapped on the door. Then again.

"What you doing here?" said a voice from behind me.

"I've come to inspect your bees," I said.

"We got none."

From the porch, I could see dozens of hives lined up in the pasture. Neat lines, but the boxes were unpainted, like the house.

"Those hives," I said. I pointed towards the hives.

"Don't want them bothered. Don't need no inspectors," said the voice.

Bad Beekeeping

"It'll only take an hour or two. I won't hurt anything," I said.

"You ain't touching nothing."

"Do you want me to come back with the police?" I asked. I wasn't bluffing. I was told to bring in the state police if anyone wouldn't let me look at their bees.

"Suit yourself," said the man.

I returned the next day, leading a Pennsylvania State Patrol car manned by a single disinterested trooper.

"We don't need no police here," a man shouted from the unpainted house. Two men emerged.

"This fellow has to inspect your bees, it's the law," said the policeman.

"Sure, we know. Told him yesterday he could do it," said one of the brothers.

"How much time will you need?" the officer asked me.

"Two-three hours."

"OK. Get started. I'll leave in a few minutes, then I'll be back in two hours. If you finish early, wait in your car. Over there, across the road." He pointed towards a drive into an Amish farm.

The men on the porch followed me to the first hive.

"You gonna open all the hives?" one asked me.

"Depends. Probably not," I said. I knew it would take more than two hours to open all the hives and inspect a few brood combs from each. I had decided that if the first few hives looked good and healthy, I would randomly select a few more hives. This was typical inspection procedure. And I'd look closely at any hives that seemed to be abnormal – hives with no bees flying at the entrance and hives with too many bees flying at the entrance.

I lit a smoker, donned my veil. They handed me a hive tool, asked me to use it. "Never know what diseases you're carrying on your used hive tool." They were right, diseases can spread from apiary to apiary if the inspector is unclean.

I opened the first dozen hives quickly. The bees were strong, good flight at the entrance. The brothers had relaxed a little, but one kept bumping hives, aggravating the bees. "Shit," he'd say, as if he were apologizing. I asked him to close the hives after I'd finished and he quit bumping them.

I parted brood chambers, pulled three combs from the center of each colony, pulled a few extra combs from the outside edge. Everything appeared normal. No rotten brown larvae toppled over in their cells, no crusted black scaly remnants of former larvae with fossil tongues glued to the cell walls. In short, no sign of American Foulbrood disease. I stepped away from the colonies, surveyed the apiary, picked out a few more hives to inspect. I peered into forty hives. Everything was fine. The policeman was back. I filled out a form, indicating that I'd done a partial inspection and no signs of disease were evident. I explained that they couldn't sell any hives - for that I'd have to inspect everything. "Hadn't sold any hives in thirty years, figure we won't begin now," said one of the men. I left, not certain every hive was healthy, but satisfied that the brothers were not harbouring a massive collection of diseased and dying bees.

I learned a lot about beekeeping from the beekeepers I was sent to destroy. And I made a little money from the state job. But civil service was not my first love. I much preferred caring for the bees my father owned. I was not a particularly good beekeeper, but I enjoyed working with bees. I didn't always get honey supers on at exactly the right time, didn't take advantage of the best bee locations. I should have fed the colonies more in the fall; should have replaced more queens in the spring. I was learning.

I thought of these things, five years later, as I inspected the lopsided truck with two missing wheels. If I returned to the family farm, I knew I could produce honey, lots of it. I had learned from beekeepers in Florida and Saskatchewan. But could I apply my new knowledge to the damp acidic soils of western Pennsylvania? Could I learn to make honey from goldenrods and asters that secreted a fickle amount of nectar in September, instead of alfalfa that oozed profusely under Saskatchewan's summer sun?

**Dr. C.C. Miller,
the Nervous Physician who
Found Peace among his Bees.**

Dr. C.C. Miller was a beekeeper who had a lot to say about what we can – and can not – learn from other people. Doctor Miller was a physician a hundred years ago. When many of his med-school buddies were earning a lot of money, poor C.C. was fretting about his patients. Too much. He lived and breathed their problems, sometimes caught their ailments. Or thought he had. Miller grew so ill from stress that he finally gave up his practice, became a beekeeper.[61] Within months, his health returned. He became a skilled beeman, an artist at the craft. Wrote books. Sold thousands of pounds of honey. His business was expanding. Though he was the most successful beekeeper in North America, many beekeepers were offering him gratuitous suggestions and advice.

In 1897, Doctor Miller wrote, "As a beekeeper, I am particularly typical in this way: I am interested enough to learn from another man's habits, but wise enough not to adopt them. When I see another who is more successful than I, it can be credited to their good luck, not their skill or talent. What should one beekeeper learn from another? If they use very different techniques and suddenly exchange ideas, both will probably be poorer for the exchange."[62] There is some truth in Dr. Miller's humour.

Why does it work this way, especially with beekeeping? Probably, the beekeeper has subconsciously absorbed information suited to her own particular situation. In a few years of beekeeping, her habits have been defined by the micro-climate, the pasturage, the breed of her bees. If another beekeeper – from a different environment – helps her consciously unlearn what her bees have subconsciously taught her, she will not be a better beekeeper. Perhaps the beekeeper who can teach another beekeeper something is the one who owned the farm before the new beekeeper came along. And if the new beekeeper kept bees in a different part of the world, she may have a long struggle unlearning and then relearning the art of bee culture.

Bad Beekeeping

I was from another part of the world, a different environment, trying to unlearn old habits, train myself to be a good Saskatchewan beekeeper. I had a lot to learn, but at the moment, I was in a wheat field, retrieving the tires which had snapped off my truck.

Some people are born into a beekeeping family. It's a family business, a trade - like doctoring, lawyering, selling seismic data. At one time, my father had about eight hundred hives of bees. By the time I was a teenager, my mother realized that it was never going to be very profitable. She convinced my father. They cut back to three hundred hives, began growing flowers in a greenhouse. There she built a very successful business.

Is there an advantage growing up among beekeepers? Probably not – it may mean you will end up being a beekeeper yourself. But some of the luckier beekeepers' kids get stung badly enough to avoid bees for the rest of their lives. They move on, get real jobs. They try to forget childhood memories of sunny summer afternoons spent in the hot, dark, sticky honey shop getting stung on their fingertips as they loaded and unloaded heavy combs of honey from the extractors. The smart ones move on.

People who follow the family business are sometimes less innovative than folks who strike out in completely new and different directions. Many second and third generation beekeepers are stuck with grandpa's old honey barn. And they may be stuck with grandpa. Nothing slows innovation like a wise old sage who won't let you cut a window in the wall to let in some light. However, the non-innovative family is realistically grounded in a routine pattern of traditional beekeeping that works - or at least once worked for grandpa.

The person who has never worked around bees probably never will. Unless, of course, she picks up a book like this one and becomes mesmerized by the eccentricity of it all. There is the unfounded - yet widespread - belief that the beekeeper lives a happy, pastoral, independent, nomadic lifestyle. Sounds like fun. The beekeeper, we want to believe, is a kindly, intelligent creature who gently tends some honeybee friends for fun and profit. The beekeeper takes time to smell the clover, taste the nectar. Most people who were not the children of beekeepers have this image somewhere in their minds.

Tragically, these gentle people sometimes give commercial beekeeping a try. They bring along the zeal and energy of the newly converted. Occasionally this is enough to sustain the enterprise until the new beekeeper has learned some practical skills.

It's easier to get started at beekeeping than say, wheat farming. Machinists and teachers have set up a hive or two in the back yard, learned a little, added another hive or two, made some money, built more hives, then some more, and suddenly found themselves running a huge operation.

You can not start that way with wheat farming. You can't start small. You can't experiment with a tiny patch in the corner of your yard, then perhaps plant some wheat in the ditch in front of the house. In a year or two you won't have a thousand acres, all planted and harvested by hand.

But with bees, a person can start a business with very little cash and squeeze the work around free time away from a real job. Some beekeepers have hundreds of hives and still live in the suburbs. The bees are kept out of town, on farms and fields belonging to other people. The beekeeper may handle all the honey in the family garage. Of course, a two car garage would have advantages. Recall my own shop in Saskatchewan – it started without water. Then I dug a shallow trench - by hand - a hundred meters from house to shop and buried a black plastic water pipe in it. Added a sink. A hot water heater. Then another room, making concrete for the new floor with a little mixer, one shovel at a time.

Beekeepers amass a huge assemblage of expensive equipment. They usually build their own warehouses, their own boxes and frames. Beekeepers keep old trucks running by cannibalizing older trucks. A few beekeepers, perhaps better at bartering, may hire people to pour their floors and raise their walls. I had little confidence in my physical skills, so I tended to commission my major chores. But then I found myself dissatisfied with the professional results. Eventually, I learned to mix my own cement and drive some of my own nails. The quality was almost equal to that of the tradesmen who sporadically worked my projects. The cost was always less.

Something strange was happening to my bees that spring. It had been cool and damp, yet the colonies increased in population at an amazing pace. I split eighty of my best over-wintered colonies – the sort of hives that would swarm if not managed dramatically. To prevent swarming, I distributed bees, brood, and honey rather evenly and installed new Florida queens in the queenless divides. The splits rebuilt quickly and the hives did not swarm.

By early June, still a few weeks away from alfalfa bloom, I had seven hundred fifty colonies, each in two brood boxes. Lifting a lid from a hive revealed a wiggling, teaming mass of bees. They danced about the top bars, percolated and boiled over the outside edges of their hives, rolling down to the ground. I had never seen bees with such strength so early in the season. By mid-June I began stacking six and seven shallow supers on each hive – overwintered colonies, splits, Florida packages. They all looked great and they all needed the empty space the new boxes could provide.

I was at the Hutterite Colony. Standing on oily cement near an arc welder. A blue-white flash lit the dim corner where Ben Kleinsasser stood. A steel helmet masked his face. He peered through a purple porthole, sparks scattered around his hair. I liked the way Ben spoke - direct. After he welded a pipe to the bottom of my steel barrel, Ben lifted his hood. "Today's my birthday. Thirty years old. You come up to my house now."

Ben's father was Peter, the older minister at the colony. He also spoke directly, but seemed severe. Reverend Peter tried to maintain discipline at the colony - enforcing rules of conduct, including the mandatory Hutterite dress code - fashion designed in 1535. He had to try to keep the kids on the farm, focused on work, and away from drugs. I never saw drugs – other than alcohol and coffee (and rarely, cigarettes) – on the colony. It was not difficult, at least to an *Anglish* observer, to keep people at the colony dressed in traditional garb. The bigger challenge for the old minister was dealing with the Anglish when they came to visit. The Anglish didn't know the rules, and sometimes showed up in shorts, tank tops, and tiny blouses. A small white sign with black letters was eventually posted in the colony parking lot. "*Visitors welcome when appropriately dressed.*"

I didn't think Reverend Peter would allow his son's birthday party. I was right, up to a point. He tolerated a bit of wine and suggested we enjoy a hymn and some

Bad Beekeeping

conversation to commemorate Ben the Welder's thirtieth birthday. I'm not sure what wildness he expected. The old preacher, partially hidden behind his thick white beard, quietly occupied a chair at our table and peered at us with his deep gray eyes.

We drank too much wine. Told stories of what it was like, reaching thirty. I was not far behind Ben. I was looking for advice on graceful aging. Ben told me the funniest, most embarrassing story he could think of about himself.

"I just couldn't pass my driver's test. The police man, he come down from Swift Current every month, give me my test, and I blow it. Every month."

"The driving part?"

"Yes, the driving part. I'd drive through a stop sign (there were only three stop signs in Val Marie) or I'd forget to use my signals when a turn would come."

"But you drive now?"

"Oh, yes, I drive good now. When I finally pass the test, the RCMP guy he gives me my license. He says to me, 'Ben, this is an important piece of paper. *Keep it somewhere safe.*' Man, I was happy. The next day, we had a load of grain to go to Swift Current, so I told the other boys I was going to drive."

"You mean a big grain truck?"

"Yes, a big grain truck. I drive OK, all the whole hour from the colony to Swift Current. Then, I got going down the wrong road. It was the one-way."

"But, Ben, there are only four one-way roads in Swift Current, and they're all downtown, not out by the grain elevators…"

"Well, I know that. We were going to go - " he glanced over at his father, the minister, "shopping for an air compressor. Anyway, cars are coming at me, flashing their lights and blowing their horns. I didn't know it was the one-way so I couldn't figure out why the cars were driving on my side of the road. One of the cars was the police car."

"The police stopped you?"

"Oh, yes. So, it was the same policeman who gives me my driver's license the day before. 'Ben, Ben, Ben,' he says, 'I wouldn't have given you a driver's license yesterday if I had known you'd get into trouble so fast!' Then he asked to see my driver's license… I told him I didn't have it with me, my mother had it at home, because yesterday he told me to *keep it somewhere safe.*"

White or Dutch Clover.

Dr. Cook Idealized Dutch Clover in 1883; But Alfalfa and Sweet Clover were Better Honey Plants in Saskatchewan

Dad

Perhaps every society – every collection of creatures – requires a segment, a fringe group, which acts, thinks, and lives differently from the masses. While the average bee in a colony scurries about, the drone is a more relaxed animal. Philosophers, these unhurried bees are. But at a price.

The drone, the male bee, begs his sisters for food. Usually unwilling to feed himself, he taps an antenna on the thorax of a passing worker. She pauses. Tongue touches tongue and a droplet of honey flows to the drone.

Drones don't participate in comb-building; don't forage; don't tend the young. Drones drift from hive to hive, always welcome if conditions are good, never welcome if the weather is bleak.

Mating with a queen kills the drone. All drones living in a hive are virgins and most will remain that way. Eventually, the drone's season ends. Workers refuse to feed the pestering male and without a stinger for defense, he is dragged from the hive, exiled to the cold grass where he will starve to death in a few days.

My hives were doing well. It had been a wet spring, rained once a week, an inch each time. The hay meadows were lush beds of thick green alfalfa and clover. I examined my colonies regularly, reversing brood chambers to prevent swarming. Hives were strong; drones were everywhere, another sign of prosperity. Colonies don't normally raise, feed, or otherwise tolerate males if conditions aren't really good. Finally, I stacked five, six, even seven honey supers atop each hive, placing four thousand honey boxes in the field before the end of June.

Dad was in Pennsylvania. I phoned him each week, looking for ways to entice him to come up and look at Saskatchewan.

"I've got ten kids. Can't fly to everyone's place. Too expensive. I'd go broke," he said.

But I wanted to show him the little beekeeping business I'd bought. Show him I knew how to make honey. I knew he'd only visit if I bought his plane ticket. When I drove up to Swift Current later that week, I stopped at a travel agency and placed six hundred dollars cash on the counter, enough for Dad's fare. From the Purolator place in Swift Current, I couriered the ticket to him.

On the day I met Dad at the Saskatoon airport, boxes were stacked high on my strong colonies of bees. I was anticipating a huge honey flow. Dad came during a year and at a time that would make me appear somewhat successful. I wanted him to like the business I was creating, approve of my work.

Bad Beekeeping

The Pennsylvania Farm had Thirty Acres of Potatoes and Tomatoes - Mostly Picked by Children's Hands

Good work meant more than casual praise. I was a kid from a big, old-fashioned farm family. We had acres of tomatoes, potatoes, cucumbers, cabbages. Tons of vegetables, most of it picked by little hands.

Ten kids. It was hard to be noticed. Dad often confused our names. The twins suffered the most, being known collectively as 'the twins'. With so much familial competition for as simple a thing as name recognition, we sought excellence and the acknowledgment it earned – at school, in the tomato patch. We were children, but we learned that work was the yardstick of self-worth. Human dignity measured in the number of tomatoes picked per hour. Slower pickers were less worthy people. I was colour-blind, I picked slowly.

I drove north five hours from Val Marie to Saskatoon in my new Dodge half-ton truck. A simple black vehicle with a manual three-speed transmission and small, slant six engine. Unpretentious. Reverend Peter, of the Hutterite Colony, approved of it, called it plain and simple.

I reached Saskatoon at ten in the morning. Dad was at the Trav-a-leer Hotel, on Twenty-Second Street. His plane had arrived at midnight, he'd caught a three dollar cab to the twenty dollar hotel room. I tapped on a green, windowless door.

"That you, son?" he said. Without waiting for an answer, he swung the door open. He was dressed in his khaki pants and shirt, dirty brown work shoes with long laces. Same clothes he had worn when I'd seen him in Florida. Same clothes he had worn most of his life.

I looked past my father at the unmade bed with a small gray suitcase, zipped shut, sitting on the sheets. To the right, on a round table, were reading glasses and the Star Phoenix. A corn-cob pipe next to a tin of Union pipe tobacco, a bottle of Canadian Mist. The whiskey flask was almost full.

Dad

"Sorry I didn't get here last night," I said.

"You didn't need to. I got in at midnight."

"You ready to go?" We didn't hug, though he had flown two thousand miles to see me. We shook hands, I threw his bag in the back of the truck. While in Saskatoon, I bought terramycin and clover seed at Early Seeds'. The medicine was to prevent foulbrood disease in the bees, I'd treat them in the fall. I'd scatter the clover seed along the road north of Val Marie where it would grow into nectar-secreting plants the next summer. Feed for the bees. We had our own food at the Husky, then drove five hours south from Saskatoon, to my place in Val Marie.

We reached the village late on a sunny, windless afternoon. The western sky was banded red and purple, orange and gold. Not from clouds, but from fine dust in the air that scattered the light. In late June, the sun didn't set until almost midnight. During the summer, it never really became completely dark before the sun was back above the horizon again. I parked the truck along the east side of the house, driving past my front steps and door.

The door to my house was already wide open. I wasn't sure why, I thought I'd pulled it shut before leaving Val Marie earlier that day.

I carried my father's bag. Symbolic gesture, unnecessary. Up four wooden steps and through the door. Had I really left the door open all day? There was a bundle of rhubarb on the table. It hadn't been there when I left the house that morning. There was a note beside the rhubarb.

My father spoke. "In Pennsylvania, someone would probably come in to the house and *take* something. Here they come into your house and *leave* something." This was good, I figured he liked Saskatchewan.

"It's from the Hutterites," I said. "Maybe they think I'll make a pie or something."

"What's the note say?"

I didn't answer right away.

Instead, I led my father down the stairs into the dark musty basement. Past the water pump and furnace. In one corner of the cellar was the only spare room in the house, equipped with a foldable spring cot I'd bought from the new owners of the deconsecrated Sisters of Assumption Convent. Many nuns had slept on this hard little bed. Now it was my father's turn. I dropped his gray suitcase on the cot. Until now, I hadn't noticed the spider webs between the floor joists of the unfinished ceiling overhead. They caught a bit of light from the small high window. Dust outlined the webs, sunlight cast cob-web shadows against the unpainted plasterboard wall like silhouettes of rope. I had washed the sheet and pillow case. Dad wasn't fussy, he told me. I knew that already. Just a place to sleep. That's all he needed.

Up the uncarpeted wooden steps, out of the mouldy basement. I asked my father if he wanted some coffee. And I told him the note with the rhubarb on the table was from David, at the Hutterite Colony. They invited us to supper. Even if we got back from Saskatoon late.

"Maybe tomorrow, I just want some soup and then I'll go to bed," Dad said.

"It's not late."

Bad Beekeeping

"I was up past midnight last night. We just drove god knows how many hours. Do you have any soup?"

I opened a can of Campbell's chicken noodle. My pot was dirty, so I turned on the tap to wash it. There was no water.

"Maybe we should go out to see your Hutterites?" he said. "Do they eat soup?"

David Kleinsasser met us at his door. He must have seen my truck, or the trail of dust behind it, as we spewed up the long gravel road to the colony. He and his family occupied one of the apartments that faced west. A thick blue and red blanket hung like a curtain over the door, shielding it from the evening's hot sunlight. Reverend Kleinsasser was in black boots, white shirt, black top coat, black hat. A broad smile above his black bearded chin greeted us. We followed him into his apartment. Annie and two kids sat at the table. David's father stood by the sink. The kids moved to a bench across the room; we sat with Annie and David at the table.

"Would you like some wine?"

David's father, Peter, made the wine. He was a master of the craft, producing clear white wine from rhubarb, red from pin cherries. "I'll take the rhubarb first," said Dad.

Peter Kleinsasser, the wine-maker, was also the colony's business manager. He paid the bills, made final decisions about purchases and sales. The farm boss, Mike Wurtz, decided which crops would be planted, when harvest would begin, and whether anything would be irrigated, fertilized, or left fallow. A business manager, a farm boss, two preachers, twenty employees. With women and children, almost a hundred souls. Uncles, aunts, cousins, grandfolks, all sharing work, sharing profits. The system wasn't completely autocratic, but it was very well organised. And everyone had some say in how the farm was operated. Even the women had a few words about the farm's management from time to time. Socially, the colony structure was similar to a very large and very traditional family. Chores were mostly gender dependent - the communal kitchen had a chief cook; other women specialized in fabrics, ran the kindergarten, some performed healings. The men taught German school and religion, fixed machinery, planted the crops, wired and plumbed.

Peter the Business Manager and Wine Maker reminded me of my grandfather. Grandpa Miksha spoke quietly and delivered his wisdom in parables. Grandpa Miksha never told me I was acting stupidly or impatiently, he told me little tales about stupid or impatient people he remembered from his childhood in Croatia. When I was seven years old, I ran away from home. I went a mile, to Grandpa's farm, though I planned to go farther. I told my grandfather that I had no need for my father, my mother, or any of my family. So Grandpa told me the story of the bag of cherries. One morning, a lad in Poljana went to neighbouring Gorica. He carried a bag of cherries. He ate all he could, then dumped the bag on the road. He laughed as he peed on them, my grandfather told me. *'Whoever finds these and eats them will never know,'* the boy thought. In the evening, the little boy went home. Hungry. He, of course, saw the cherries. He ate a few around the edge, certain they were clean. Then a couple hidden under the center of the pile, they must have stayed dry. A few more. Eventually, he had eaten them all. This is how my

Dad

grandfather talked to me. But my father would tell the same story in six words or less: "Don't shit in your own nest," he'd tell us.

My friend Peter never told me I sold my honey too cheaply. Instead, he told me about a farmer who was so kind and generous to all his neighbours that he finally went broke. Then his neighbours divided up his property at an auction.

We each held a small clear glass of Peter's wine. "From the rhubarb I left at your house, you also could make wine," said David Kleinsasser. Rhubarb wine, not rhubarb pie. Then he said something in Low German, something that sounded guttural and sloppy. It surprised me when Low German was spoken at the colony. I understood their High German, Church German, as the Hutterites called it. But this Swiss derivation made no sense to my ear, it sounded gruff, crude. When David finished speaking, the seven-year-old girl sitting on the nearby bench jumped up and fled. I was unable to decipher the strange German dialect, but I guessed she was going to the communal kitchen for food.

David Kleinsasser went through an archway, out of the family kitchen, into a dark sitting room. I could see him slide open the narrow drawer of a handmade oak writing table. He returned with a map.

"You left Pennsylvania yesterday?" He asked my father. David unfolded his map. Dad placed his empty wine glass on the table. Annie refilled it.

"Yesterday, about noon."

"Which way did your airplane fly? Did you need in Toronto to stop?"

Dad's wine was almost gone again. "This is really good wine. Who made it?" David slid his map towards us.

"My father makes the wine. He is Peter," said David Kleinsasser.

Dad smiled at Peter the Wine Maker. More Low German was spoken; another child left the bench. Then Peter told us his story about the traveler who was thirsty and lost. Strangers gave him wine but he wasn't told how to find his way home.

Two more Hutterites entered without knocking, older men with gray beards. I hadn't seen them before.

The map. My father needed his reading glasses, which he had left at my house, so I pointed out the path to David. "Dad left Pennsylvania from Pittsburgh - "

"The Aim-ish. You know the Aimish? They live there, in Pennsylvania," a visitor said.

"Yea, they live near us." My father liked a lot of things about the Amish. Frugal, self-reliant. According to Dad, they don't mess with politics or science, so they don't mess up the world. Amish children left school early. Dad was decidedly anti-education. "Too much education messes up the world," he said. My father quit school in Grade Nine; none of his ten children were encouraged to attend university.

In many ways, Dad admired the Amish. But my father also thought that the Amish had inflated opinions about themselves. I was hoping that he wouldn't start telling my friends that the Amish were taking advantage of everyone: selling their homemade trinkets for big prices to sympathetic city people; working on construction jobs for less than minimum wage; paying cash for the best farmland. I wanted my father to reserve his opinions, at least until after the soup had arrived.

Bad Beekeeping

"The Aimish, they have good farms?"

"Really good farms. They've got the best farmland in Mercer County."

Two younger Hutterites men entered, again without knocking. Sam and Paul.

"How did they get the best farmland?"

"Cash. Lots of cash. They don't spend any money. They make everything they need. Grow their own food, raise their own horses. No electricity. No trucks. They never borrow money. Never. They never sell any land. Never. They just keep buying more and more."

"And they work it all by hand and with horses?"

"No, they use a few machines."

Suddenly everyone sat quite still and looked at my father. Until now, the Hutterites had not heard anything they didn't already know, and they knew quite a lot. Some of the folks at the colony wrote long letters to pen pals on Amish farms in Ontario and Pennsylvania. The two groups held very similar beliefs - pacifists who shunned flashy clothing, avoided the military and politics, read German Bibles every day. But there were differences. Hutterites lived in *colonies* - a hundred people sharing the work on one huge farm. And Hutterites used trucks, tractors, electricity. Their computerized chicken barn doled out scientifically formulated mixes of grain while birds bathed in timed artificial light dropped perfect eggs onto rolling rubberized conveyor belts. Meanwhile, Amish chickens ran freely around the yard. One Hutterite tractor could cover two hundred acres a day. An Amish horse might plod over two acres in a day. But the Hutterites were learning, from my father, that the Amish used machines to help them with their work.

"*Machines?*"

"Some of the Amish have tractors..."

Silence.

"Maybe you are thinking about the Mennonite Brethren. They drive black cars and they use tractors," said Paul. He had an Amish pen-pal.

"No, these are straw-hat Amish," said my father. "They don't drive their tractors on the field, but they use them to run hydraulic pumps. Hydraulic pumps are allowed."

"But the tractors, they burn gasoline?"

"Oh yea, the tractors have regular engines. But the rear wheels are pulled off and belts are attached to the axles." The Hutterites gazed at my father a long while.

Soup arrived. Dad's hand froze mid-air before touching his soup spoon – Reverend David was reciting grace. A blur of Platt Deutsch, followed by *in den Namen Jesus Christus*, then a loud plop as Annie Kleinsasser dropped a thick chunk of fried pork into Dad's soup.

We were in the bees the next day, Dad and I. He would only be in Canada for five days, so we opened hives even though the sky was dark and rain was coming. I didn't want to have a heavy rainfall, have the gumbo trails to the beeyards all slicked up and greasy and not be able to show Dad my hives.

The first apiary was charming. The bees were quiet, despite the dark clouds that would normally irritate them. Dad lit his corn cob pipe, an old fashioned devise that was never far from his lips. He puffed blue-gray smoke into the entrance of a hive. I lifted the lid, he blew more smoke. The top boxes were empty, as expected. It was early in the season and the honey flow was not quite on. I set five empty shallow honey boxes on the lid beside the hive, white combs rattling. Bees roiled within the sixth and seventh boxes. By the time I stripped the hive to the upper brood chamber, thousands of bees flowed about the outside surface of the beehive, a dark, fuzzy mass that buzzed softly. I pulled a brood comb from the center of the hive, Dad pointed out the queen before my eyes had even focused on the frame. "Nice," he said about the long golden insect and her smooth, regular patch of emerging brood. "Nice."

I shook the comb, brood cells facing down. A few bees tumbled from the frame. Fresh nectar splashed from uncapped cells and puddled on the top bars of the upper brood chamber, drizzled on the mass of golden and brown honeybees. A serious honey flow had not yet started, I told my father. It would become even more intense in a week or two. "Nice," he said again.

Then my father noticed a poor hive.

I followed him to the colony. He pointed at drones loitering along the entrance. We opened the hive. I had only placed one honey box on it, so I must have recognized its poor strength earlier when I was supering.

Dad lifted a brood frame.

"Look here. Bullet brood," he said.

Pure Nectar Splashing From a Honey Comb, Looking like Water Drizzling Out of the Frame

Bullet brood. When bees try to rear drones in cells reserved for worker larvae, the bigger drone pupae stick out the top of the cells, forcing workers to cap them high. Instead of uniform, flat worker brood, this hive had brood that looked like bullets.

"Laying workers," my father said. I knew this was trouble. Not a disease, but a serious problem for this hive, nevertheless.

Bad Beekeeping

Normally, only queens can lay eggs. But the thousands of worker bees are also females. Immature, under-developed females. If a queen dies, and the bees somehow don't replace her with a new monarch, aggressive worker bees may step forward to fill the void. But workers never mate. Though they may lay a few eggs, the eggs are not fertilized. And here's the amazing part: Unfertilized bee eggs always become males.[63]

There aren't many creatures on earth with no father. But every drone – whether the son of a queen or laying worker – is fatherless. All a drone's DNA is issued by his mother. When a queen elects to lay an egg, she usually fertilizes it at that moment with sperm stored in her spermatheca - the sac she filled in her youth while mating. Fertilized, the egg has a contribution from both father and mother. It always becomes a female. But if the queen chooses, she may lay an unfertilized egg – it becomes a male. Drones are haploids, fully functional animals with a half set of genes. When they mate, their cells don't divide – each sperm cell has identical DNA content, identical to all the other cells in the drone's body.

A hive with laying workers slowly dwindles, no new worker bees to replace the ones that die or drift off to other hives. Tolstoy, in <u>War and Peace</u>, compared the collapse of Moscow to a queenless hive. "Moscow was empty," wrote the beekeeper Tolstoy. "There were still people in the city; a fiftieth part of all the former inhabitants still remained in it, but it was empty. It was deserted as a dying, queenless hive is deserted."[64] And so I had my own miniature Moscow in this hive - a dying, emptying box of bees with an imitation queen - a laying worker.

"You can't requeen it, the laying workers will kill your new queen," Dad said. I knew how to treat a laying worker hive, but I allowed him to teach me anew. We carried the boxes past the edge of the beeyard, shook all the bees onto the grass, stacked the evacuated equipment on other hives. "Laying workers won't fly back to the old spot, but the field bees will," said my father. "This way, you still get use of your bees, your equipment. But the laying workers are stuck over here." I knew.

Shortly after we began the drive back to Val Marie, I swung onto the lane that led to the Kornfeld ranch. We stopped at the house, Norman fixed coffee, I got permission to continue onto his prairie dog colony. This was the largest prairie dog community in Canada, the local tourist attraction, complete with a stone monument and a place to sign your name in a notebook. People had written things like "Awesome!" and "God Awful!" in apparently the same handwriting. We parked amidst the holes, shut the truck off, listened as the fat animals chirped to each other.

"This is the biggest prairie dog colony in Canada," I read. Wind blew dust in our faces, though it had rained here earlier in the morning. There were no trees for perhaps a dozen kilometres, except for some shrubby willows along the Frenchman and a few Walker poplars the Kornfelds had planted near their ranch house. The short prairie grass was green, but sparse.

"God-forsaken country," my father said. "I couldn't live in such an empty place." We drove back to Val Marie and I wondered if he meant the prairie dog colony, the prairie, or Saskatchewan in general.

168

Dad

At my honey shop, which I had painted and scrubbed before his arrival, Dad examined the hot water heater Joe had installed for me. Dad had never had hot running water in his honey shop in Pennsylvania. Instead, he heated water by the tub-full over an open gas flame, sloshed it on the sticky floor at the end of the day.

My first memory of the honey house on the Pennsylvania farm was not pleasant. I was five years old, my mother was toiling in the shop. She did the sticky, difficult extracting – scratching wax from combs, dropping them two at a time into the extractors, wheeling full honey drums, six hundred pounds each, from the settling tank to the storage dock. Normally, she kept my sister Joanne and I perched on empty honey supers that served as desk and chair for our books and pencils. We drew pictures on the soft white paper that came in the boxes of beeswax sheets Dad used as starter combs for new honey frames. We were always in her sight, in our little pre-school in the corner of the extracting room. Unless we had to go pee.

The lavatory was a bush behind the shed. I wanted to leave, went to the door, and started to push it open. Mom yelled at me to stop. I had no idea what she said, why she said it, or even if it was I who should do whatever it was she was saying. I pressed against the door and was immediately covered in a mass of irritated bees which I'd dislodged from the casing overhead. They fell, like warm rain, onto my hair, down my shirt. I got stung and it hurt.

I didn't hate those bees. And I didn't stay away from the extracting shop. Later that fall, when Mr. Silvers came to the farm to buy a hundred twenty pounds of dark honey, I followed him and my mother into the shop. Mr. Silvers came every September, bought dark buckwheat honey. Always paid cash. On the way out, each of them hoisting two thirty pound buckets of honey, Mr. Silvers asked why I wasn't in school.

"I'm five. I start next year," I said.

"Do you know your A-B-C's?" Mr. Silvers asked.

"Yes. And backwards, too."

"Backwards? Are you sure?"

I nodded.

"OK... I'll give you five cents if you can say the alphabet backwards."

"Z-Y-X-..." I rattled it off, non-stop. I don't remember when I'd learned it that way, or if I was reciting the alphabet backwards for the first time. When I reached "...-C-B-A" Mr. Silvers dropped a nickel in my hands, rubbed my fuzzy head, and closed the trunk of his car, smiling, but not saying a word.

Dad was standing in the Saskatchewan field, west side of my honey shop.

"You should put up some black plastic pipe for your water supply. It'll collect the sun's heat, warm the water before it reaches your hot water tank. Save you lots of money... I'll do it for you."

He did. He spent the rest of the day, and part of the next, gluing ABS and PVC joints and pipes, then assembling a wooden jig to hold the contraption in place. It looked weird, attached to the west side of the warehouse, visible to traffic out on Highway 4. But it heated the water as Dad predicted and possibly saved me a hundred dollars in power bills over the next few years.

Bad Beekeeping

While he worked on the pre-heater, Dad noticed a grain swather in my neighbour's farmyard. The strong Saskatchewan winds whirled the long flat plates that would lift wheat and feed it through the blades whenever the machine was pulled behind a tractor through a grain field. At the moment, the apparatus spun idly.

"You know, Ron," Dad said. "People always build tall wind-generators to make electricity. But look at this thing spin. This is a better way to catch wind power. You should buy an old swather, park it behind the shed and make your own electricity. Or maybe just set up some gears and pulleys, run your extractors directly from wind. Save you lots of money."

The next evening, I called Sandy. My father was in the living room. He could hear me, so I talked softly, quickly. Sandy was working at the radio station, WWFL, in Florida. I'd hear her introduce a song, give the weather. "It's 95 degrees in Florida," I said to my father. He was in the next room, reading the old Star Phoenix he'd picked up in Saskatoon. "95?" he said.

Sandy sounded great, her slight southern drawl directed towards me, then her radio audience, then towards someone else. "It's Ron, he's calling me from Canada," she said to someone. I asked her who was in the studio with her. "My friend Eddie, the football player. Remember, I told you about him."

We chatted a bit longer, I ended the call, went to sit on the old overstuffed chair in the living room, close to where my father was reading his paper in near darkness. I thought of talking to him, maybe telling him about the girl I had met in Florida. Maybe asking him things about my mother. All of us thought about Mom a lot, how she worked eighteen hours a day, did all the cooking and cleaning and sewing and gardening and bee work and transplanting in the greenhouses. She died at forty-nine. Cancer. It was hard on all of us; almost impossible for my father. But we didn't talk. When Dad poured Canadian Mist into a glass and asked if I wanted some, I shook my head. Soon after that, I went to bed.

My father's time was nearly finished – we prepared to drive back to Saskatoon, back to the airport. On the way out of Val Marie, I took him past a beeyard north of town. We left the Number 4 and descended into the valley towards the first irrigation reservoir. Dad pointed out the steep, narrow river valley, how the badlands were cut by wind and rain.

"Just like California," he said. My father knew California; he'd worked bees there many years earlier.

"No, it's colder here and we've got fewer trees," I said, though I had only seen photographs of California.

"And the valleys are deeper in California, but just as dry," my father said. "They get some damn awful droughts down there from time to time."

I stopped the truck at the edge of my beeyard, we walked in. We didn't wear veils, it wasn't necessary. The bees were too busy gathering nectar to notice us.

Dad did his hive thumping – he walked around the apiary, striking each hive cover with his fist, listening to the echo. "Good hive. Good hive. Poor hive. Good hive," he said, basing his judgments on the tone of the thump. At a 'good hive' he lit his corn cob pipe, blew gray tobacco smoke through the bottom board entrance and into the small cracks I'd left as ventilation slits between honey supers.

"I put empties on last week, just before you got here," I said. I wasn't expecting much honey yet. The season had barely started.

"These were Florida packages?" my father asked.

"Yea, I put them out the end of April."

Apiary in the West Flats, Partly Protected from the Wind by Buttes and Badlands.

I lifted a dark gneiss rock from its sentry position on the hive's cover. It was heavy - had to be to keep the lid on the hive when it got windy. But it was a calm day, the lid stayed in place until I peeled it off with my hive tool. Dad stepped forward, blew smoke across the frames. Bees ducked into the box. I set the box, and the next three, on the ground atop the hive cover. The upper-most boxes held thousands of bees, but no honey. However, the fifth box, still on the hive, was nearly filled with water-white honey, some of it capped beneath snow-coloured wax. "Twenty pounds, shit that's good," my father said. "Take off this box, too."

I removed the final super, honey dripping out as I swung it into position on the small stack of boxes nearby.

Bad Beekeeping

"In California," my father said, "when I worked for Al Winn, we didn't use as many supers as you're using. We didn't use any supers at all. Hell of a lot cheaper to run bees when you don't need supers."

"Then I wouldn't have any honey," I said.

"Still could," my father said. "See here, look at the honey on the outer combs of the brood chamber. " Dad pointed to the frames that skirted the colony's main cluster. They were old, black frames, full of yellow dandelion honey the bees had gathered much earlier in the season. But each comb held about six pounds of honey.

"What we did in California, thirty years ago, was take four combs out of the brood nest every week. Then shove the other six combs out to the edges, and put empties in the middle. Split the brood nest, so the bees wouldn't swarm. We'd use a brush. We'd brush each comb of honey until all the bees fell off. Put the heavy honey frames on the truck, take them home, extract them, bring empty combs along to the next yard."

"That was better than using supers?"

"In California," my father said. "Jesus Christ. You wouldn't have to own any honey supers. And if the flow lasted a month, you could get eighty pounds from a hive."

"But Dad," I said, "My bees make two hundred pounds. I'd have to come back every day or two and take combs out. And the honey would be darker, coming off the old brood frames."

"I'm just telling you what we did in California. Al Winn made a lot of money," Dad said.

"Al Winn made his money raising queens. We can't raise queens here," I said.

"I'm just telling you what we did in California when I worked for Al Winn, that's all. You wouldn't need supers. You'd save a lot of money, you know."

I didn't answer; I restacked the hive, empty boxes next to the brood chamber, the heavier boxes on top. Then the lid, the mottled rock.

"You know, I always thought you'd be a southern beekeeper. In Florida or California, not up here in Canada," Dad said when we reached the truck. "I would come see you again if you were in California instead of here. I liked California," said my father. He tapped his pipe out, ashes scattered through the back of the truck, some landed on his small grey suitcase.

We continued towards Saskatoon, the airport.

We stopped at a beekeeper's shop south of the city. A woman was cleaning the extracting room and we chatted about the chances for a good honey year.

"Lots of rain, lots of honey, that's how it works here," someone said.

My father examined the storage tank, the huge valve at the bottom that lifted up with a hard pull of the hand. The tank was empty now, but in season, it could hold ten thousand pounds of honey.

"Can fill a barrel in thirty seconds," someone said.

Dad suggested a person would want to keep one hand on the tap, all the time.

"You bet we do. And the left thumb hangs down from the rim of the barrel's lid. That way you get your thumb sticky before the barrel overflows. Except Marvin. Last summer he had his whole hand in honey and didn't wise up until honey was flowing on the cement floor and his boots got sticky. Cost us a thousand dollars, that mistake."

172

Dad

We continued on to Saskatoon, to the prairie airport north of town. It would be his last glimpse of the west, the wide and dry farmland. Dad would never return.

We shook hands, he turned away.

"Remember what I said about the windmill," Dad said as he walked towards the departures gate.

My father was gone. The rains ended. It became hot. A superior honey season was developing. I would make a lot of honey. Seemed likely.

Carniolan Drone. — X2.

(From Department of Agriculture.)

A Drone with Possible Croatian Heritage
from the 1883 <u>Beekeepers Guide</u> by Professor Cook

Florida, 1965:
Dad, Mom,
Judy, Ron,
JoAnn, Fred,
June, Jane,
Joe

1968 on the Pennsylvania Farm: Fred, June, Joe, Jane

Miksha Clan
Pennsylvania
1973:
Joe, Jane,
June, Fred,
JoAnn, Ron,
Judy, Larry,
Don, David,
Dad, Ivan

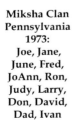

Personal Best?

When the honey flow starts, a blast of electrified excitement transforms the hive from a society of laggards and relaxed souls to a community willing to work its individuals to exhaustion, and death. The worker bee is first aware of impending success when the wild erratic buzzing of a sister returning with a gorged stomach stirs up the nest. A dozen bees taste her nectar and watch her dance, then share the news with another dozen times a dozen bees, everyone dancing and sharing sips of nectar. Within minutes, the entire hive is dancing. Thousands of bees leave the colony, descend on the honey patch, return with gorged stomachs, then fly back for more. Over and over again. Day after day while weather is fair and flowers secrete. Bees waste their youth and spend their health, but combs fill with honey and the colony prospers.

I was twenty-four years old. My ten-year plan included a series of huge honey crops – quite possible in the hay fields surrounded by Saskatchewan's limitless horizon. Ten successful honey seasons, retirement at age thirty-five. Or keep bees forever, but without worrying about money.

Beekeepers use different criteria to gauge their level of success. A lucky few claim they have achieved their life's goals if they have good health, good friends, fair crops; if they enjoy their time working the bees as much as they enjoy any other activity in their life. Some beekeepers like to set production goals or use other tangible markers to celebrate their brilliance. In Sweden, the most successful beekeepers have the fewest winter losses. A very good Swedish beekeeper may only lose two percent of his bees during the course of a winter. A poorly organized, sloppy beekeeper may see half of his colonies dead in April.

Beekeepers with more focus on tangible success often cite production of honey. Total pounds of honey produced or average pounds per hive. Depending on environmental factors, this may range from thirty pounds of honey to several hundred pounds per hive. The average, of course, may be adjusted by discarding the worst colonies from the count. I heard a beekeeper declare he had a four hundred pound average – from one of his hives.

Dr. C.C. Miller, the Illinois medical doctor who became a beekeeper to preserve his failing health, justified a relatively poor average from his bees one year. Writing about his 1897 crop in Fifty Years Among the Bees,[65] Dr. Miller said, "It is not the yield per colony I care about, unless it should be to boast over it; what I care about is the total amount of net money I can get from my bees." I should have spent more time with Dr. Miller's book.

During June, my scale hive had made a lot of honey – 74 pounds. Things looked good during my father's brief visit to Val Marie. But then the spring season turned cool and wet. Heavy rains delayed the honey flow. The morning air was chilly, nearly reaching frost twice during the first week of July. "Summer's over," one farmer said. I hoped not.

The bees consumed the dark willow and dandelion honey they'd gathered in April and May. They replaced honey and pollen laden frames with brown and tan combs of brood. Three thousand new bees on each frame, all the brood emerging in three week cycles. My colonies had sixty, seventy, eighty thousand adult bees. Apiaries had millions of workers, milling about their nests, waiting for hot, dry, sunny weather. It arrived.

The wind stopped, the clouds parted, the sun shone down upon the fields. Alfalfa and sweet clover suddenly began oozing pure white nectar. It smeared against the bumper and sides of the truck as I drove through the hay meadows. It smelled like a great bouquet – fresh, fragrant, tasty. The honey flow was on.

I measured the progress daily. One of my hives, perched on the sort of scale used a hundred years earlier to weigh sacks of potatoes, testified the strength of the honey season. Each day at sunset, I walked ten metres behind my house and slid a weight along the scale's balance beam. Nine pounds. The hive behind the house, not my strongest or best colony, had added nine pounds of new honey. If this was representative of all eight hundred hives, I would have almost five tonnes of new honey to harvest, just for this one day. And the season had just begun. A few days later, the scale tipped at twenty-one pounds. Under intense heat, high humidity, and long sunny summer days, the scale hive gained two hundred sixty-five pounds by August first.[66] I replaced boxes, gave the bees more space. They gave me more honey.

Joe was back from the States, working with me again. Charlie and Merlin wore veils and heavy gloves; pulled and extracted our honey. We worked sixteen hours a day, day after day after day. Joe was noticeably tiring from the routine. Hard work was not the issue.

"I should be back on the farm, in Pennsylvania," said Joe. He shot a forty pound honey super up over his head, landed it smartly on the top of a stack of six others.

I looked at my young brother, his white beekeeper's uniform covered with wax and dirt and streaks of sticky honey. He turned away from me, heading off to fetch another super from another hive at the far end of the apiary. He returned quickly, tossed it to the top of the stack of seven.

"But I thought you were moving to Wisconsin in the fall," I said.

"Yea, that's the plan."

"Well, you're here until then." I wondered if he wanted to leave these bees, this sticky work, or if he missed Pennsylvania. But I knew Wisconsin would be the best place for him. I leveled a super, waited for Joe to return with another box. "Wisconsin is nice, you'll like it there. Sort of like Pennsylvania, but cleaner and not as crowded. It'll work out for you."

"Yea, I know," he said. He was off to lug back still another box of honey.

We were working in our favourite beeyard, almost an hour east and south of Val Marie. It was rugged country, the real badlands. Ranch houses were separated by tens of thousands of acres of blue sagebrush and the sparse scrawny grass upon which Saskatchewan cattle thrived.

Personal Best?

Winter Hibernatorium of Western Rattlesnakes

We Called it the Snake Pit: Thousands of Intertwined Rattlesnakes Spent the Cold Nights of Winter Here, Then Dispersed to Roam the Range for the Summer

Prairie dogs, bob cats, wild flowers. One lone tree ("Look! A tree!" said Charlie.), the rattlesnake pit, a one hundred metre drop down from the butte to the valley floor along a snarly, rutted dirt trail. These were the things we absorbed and it made us glad to be part of the west.

Lise Perrault and her husband Fernand introduced me to parts of the west I would have missed. They were advocates of the Grasslands National Park, a federal preserve which would one day fence off the trail that led to my favourite beeyard.

Lise guided a group of us to the craggy rattlesnake pit and showed us where the creatures hibernated in the winter. It was summer. Most, but not all the residents had slithered off across the prairies, in search of mice and ground squirrels. "Here's a nice one," Lise said, pointing near my feet. She gently pinned the rattler with a forked stick and held the snake to the earth so we could admire its camouflage scales, its long rattle. "This one's about four years old," Lise said. She released her stick and the snake quickly escaped.

"You know about Will James?" Lise asked me. I shook my head. She told me that he was a cowboy who had lived nearby, many years ago. His shack was on the Larson ranch, not far from the rattlesnake pit. We went to the old building and Lise Perrault showed off the Will James cabin as if it were her own.

"You'd like Will James, his novels," Lise Perrault said.

Bad Beekeeping

"I would? What did he write about?" We stood near the homesteader's shack, a small house on the Larson ranch, close to Dixon's where some of my bees were sitting. Three windows faced us. Lots of light would enter the cabin. It was Will James' home. It made sense – Mr. James came to Val Marie to be a cowboy, to enjoy the prairie.

The Will James House, East of Val Marie

Will James wanted to see the cacti, prairies, the badlands, and the sage brush. Lots of windows. Lots of view.

"He wrote about cowboys, and he painted, too," said Lise.

"He was a cowboy. He came here from Quebec, and stayed until he was accused of stealing a horse. But he was no horse thief. I'm sure of that. Anyway, he went down to California, and New Mexico, I think. Wrote lots of books, some of them they made into movies." [67]

I didn't read any of Will James' books. I liked bees, not cows. I wanted to believe beekeepers tamed the west, not cowboys.

"He wrote a lot about the west, how we lived here. How the people settled this country," Lise Perrault said.

Lise Perrault's Prairie Dogs

I considered what the ranch lady was saying. Lise Perrault had been a school teacher. She taught English and French. But she quit teaching when she married Fernand. Soon she had the first of her nine children. They were all born at the hospital in Val Marie – a hospital that opened in time for her first child's birth and closed after the youngest was born.

And Lise Perrault was an artist. Her simple schemes of bold colour captured the badlands. And captured the attention of collectors. She knew about light, shape, form. Her oils on canvas showed the daily lives of the ranchers, and dramatically exhibited the hills and prairie she knew so

178

well. The Perraults lived in Val Marie but had ranch land to the east, not far from the Larson ranch, not far from the valley with its rattlesnakes and cacti, sage brush and prairie dogs, and the shack Will James had lived in fifty years earlier. This was big ranch country.

The biggest ranches were south of Val Marie. The Larson, Kornfeld, Dixon, and Walker ranches covered thirty to sixty square miles of grassland and river valley - each. You had to drive a long time - up and down buttes, through hay meadows, across narrow wooden bridges that spanned the Frenchman River, past prairie dog towns - to get to the next ranch. I kept bees on those ranches, about thirty hives to a spot, separated by five or more miles.

Near the Frenchman Creek on Dixon's ranch, my bees congregated in a small hay meadow. The field erupted in sweet smelling bright flowers by mid-July. But these bees didn't usually do as well as others near Val Marie. In dry years, there was little water for irrigation at the south end of the river. In wet years, bees did well everywhere. I could have kept all my bees near the honey shop in Val Marie, but I liked the scenery and I liked the drive out to the south valley. The badlands held a history, long past, nearly forgotten.

I recalled again how Sitting Bull camped here. In 1876, he led 5000 Lakota Sioux into these badlands from the USA. Over the hill from where we stood, Canadian policemen gave the Indians rifles and ammunition so they could hunt buffalo and feed themselves. When buffalo were scarce, they fed on snakes and gophers, raccoon and mule deer. Questioned about the wisdom of handing out guns and shells to a huge visiting war party, Inspector Walsh of the Royal Canadian Mounted Police said, "My opinion is they will obey the law of the country. War they have had enough of."[68] And they had.

As we drove back to the shop with our load of honey, Merlin pointed out the Indian teepee rings, explained how the circle of rocks once held buffalo skins down at the bottom of each teepee. I hadn't noticed the large rings of stones before. Merlin told me more about the Indians. "Surprising you Americans still like Canadians. We burned your White House to the ground in the War of 1812. We took in and fed Sitting Bull after Little Big Horn. Took in your draft dodgers during the Viet Nam War. We haven't been the nicest neighbours, eh?"

I shrugged, said I really didn't know much about these things. But it made little difference to anything now. I asked Merlin if he knew when the cattle ranchers arrived in the badlands. Where had they come from?

"Americans and Brits came in and set up the really big ranches. The '76 and the Turkey Track. In those days, my grandpa says, they could lease a hundred thousand acres for a thousand dollars. Worked out fine until the winter of '06. Snow piled up and buried all the grass in November, stayed until March. Too deep for the cows to eat through. And no one put up much hay in those days. Half the cows in the valley died. Ranchers went broke. Everything changed."

I looked out the driver's window. Everything changed? Maybe for the American ranchers who were once here. Their dreams, their expectations. But to me, the dry buttes and sage brush could have been harbouring Sioux Indians that very afternoon.

Bad Beekeeping

A few days later, I went north again, alone, and visited Earl and Josephine Emde. My bees were making a lot of honey; I needed empty honey drums, Earl had extras. Joe stayed behind in Val Marie – it was a seven hour drive each way and I'd be gone only one night. I suspected Joe deserved a break from me.

The year before, Earl Emde had sold me some hives and equipment, but he couldn't slow down. He was only seventy-three, so he had built his hive count back up and was once again running three hundred hives. Earl was having a fair season, though it was raining a lot and he thought his bees would do much better if the weather cleared. After loading up my barrels, he suggested I drop by a new beekeeper's shop on my way south from Big River. "He keeps bees with his father. They're not on the ball, you may end up buying them out someday."

I stopped at their little honey farm north of Saskatoon. I met Kenny. He looked pleasant, dressed well, talked calmly. It looked like he practiced good beekeeping.

But Kenny and his father also made a few mistakes, as Earl had suggested. A year earlier, they had gone fishing about twenty miles north of the end of farming country. They were still in the parkland – the shrubs and bush and small trees that farmers eradicate to create fresh canola fields. But no one had yet seen an economical reason to move in with dozers and graders to turn this last bit of far north bush into farmland. The country where they fished was still wild.

Near a jackfish lake, wedged between pines, tamaracks, and quivering aspen, Kenny and his father found meadows of lanky fireweed blooming. Fireweed. The tall perennial colonizes in the wake of forest fires – hence the name – and produces a nice mild light-coloured honey. But unlike the alfalfa and canola found on the western prairies, it is a fickle yielder of nectar. Some years, bees gorge themselves on sweet droplets of fresh fireweed; other years, nothing at all comes out of the flowers. This may be due to moisture, either too much or to little; or temperature, too hot or too cold.[69]

Kenny and his father moved one hundred twelve big, strong hives off the alfalfa fields of central Saskatchewan and trucked them into the distant fireweed meadows. Near the jackfish lake, pines, tamaracks and aspen, their bees starved. Fireweed wasn't secreting nectar that summer. The few hives they left behind in the alfalfa fields made a good crop. Everyone does this from time to time. Things are going along fine. But we decide we can make good enough better. I stayed in touch with Kenny and his family, but one year I stopped at the farm and found they'd sold all their hives. They were growing mint and thyme for the Japanese market.

Perhaps Kenny was a good beekeeper who simply made a few bad mistakes. People have been doing bad beekeeping for a long time. Cave man robbed bees. Civilized man houses bees, then robs them. Archeologists found honey in an ancient tomb. Apparently the pharaoh thought there'd be fine dining on the other side. Kenny told me all about the Egyptians.

"When they opened Tutten-nut-huts' tomb, there was this jar of honey. It was three thousand years old. But the honey tasted as good as when the bees made it," said Kenny.

Personal Best?

I don't usually trust food older than three months unless it's been fortified with dozens of preservative chemicals. I looked up Kenny's story. It was partly true.[70] Honey had been found in an Egyptian tomb. But Kenny said it was as good now as it had been when the bees made it. If true, the ancient Egyptians produced some pretty frightening honey. It was dry, almost as hard as a rock. Black, like tar. But it was three thousand years old. The professional archeologists who found the honey didn't eat it. Eating it probably would have been unprofessional. Instead, they took the unidentified stuff to a lab where carbon testing and chemical analysis verified its age, sugar content, and pollen spores. *Pollen spores?* Proof that it came from flowers - which give off pollen with their nectar. The gooey stuff was most likely honey.

Beekeeping history. A microcosmic glimpse of the progression of human history and culture, from philosophy through warfare. Man's pursuit of a perfect food. Or perhaps man's addiction to sweets - a quick sugar rush. And when fermented, drunkenness. Perhaps part of the power and mystery of honey comes from the ancients who discovered wild bee nests exposed to rain. The wet honey became alcohol - mankind's first intoxicant.

Hieroglyphics tell us that the Egyptians were big on beekeeping. Ancient beekeepers moved their hives on barges at night, following the northerly progression of seasons along the Nile. In return, they gave gifts to the gods - by way of pharaoh. Every spring, Ramses III - Egyptian Pharaoh, King, Deity, and Ruler of Heaven and Earth (but only from 1198-1167 BC) - would have a honey party, sacrificing about ten thousand gallons of honey to the river god.[71]

Egyptians weren't the only ones to think honey was important stuff. Most ancient cultures thought the art of beekeeping was given by the gods to humans. Sort of like fire. Four thousand years ago, in the Indus valley, the first food given to little baby goddess Indra was honey. Other Hindu ancestors taught that eating honey and pollen would lead to a long life. Krishna, the Hindu deity, was often drawn as a fuzzy honeybee. An early hairy Krishna.

Pythagoras - early Greek mathematician, cult founder, beekeeper - had followers who ate only bread and honey.[72] It was probably seven-grain bread with a thick crust, but it still sounds suspiciously spartan. By the time of the ancient Greeks, beekeeping had become common enough for beeswax to be used as money and as glue for astronauts' wings. The Greeks told the story of Icarus, the Inquisitive. Like most of us, he wanted to meet the gods. In his pursuit, Icarus flew too close to the sun and the beeswax holding the feathers to his arms melted - the feathers came loose. Icarus became an asteroid, one we can see with a good set of binoculars on a clear dark night.[73]

Democritus was a famous ancient Greek beekeeper and philosopher. A whole political system is named after him. But not all of his thoughts were inspired. He taught his students that new bees could be made from the flesh of a rotting oxen. The King Bee, he figured out, came from decaying bull brains.[74] I remind myself that Democritus was the greatest scientific mind of his time. If I had been in his entomology class, I would have been taking copious notes and probably would have had no cause to doubt his wisdom. And so I must wonder about the things I am taught today - are they the modern equivalent of rotting bulls' brains?

Bad Beekeeping

There were other Greek beekeepers. The scientist Aristotle used a beehive with removable combs. Hippocrates recommended bee products as medicine: *"Honey and pollen cause warmth, clean sores and ulcers, soften hard ulcers of lips, heal carbuncles and running sores."* [75] Great suggestions from the father of medicine for those of us who are oozing and leaking.

Also among the early Europeans writing about bees was Virgil. According to Virgil, two thousand years ago, lazy drones were being driven from their homes. A beekeeper and a poet, he wrote this (and much more) about honey bees in the Aeneid:

> *"Such is their toil and such their pain;*
> *As is the bees' in their flowery plain...*
> *All with united force combine to drive,*
> *The lazy drones from the laborious hive...."* [76]

In the Middle Ages, there was Olga, the Slavic warrior princess, saint, and beekeeper. She invited her enemies to her son's funeral, and gave them her most potent honey wine – mead containing five times as much alcohol as regular wine. The guests became drunk. Then, revenging her son's death, she had her soldiers hack five thousand guests to death.[77] Olga remains the patron saint of not getting drunk in an enemy's home.

Scientists enjoyed bees as raw material for the interpretation of nature. The Italian Prince Cesi, in 1625, was the first person to sketch a microscopic anatomy of a cadaver honeybee.[78] Gregor Mendel, who started the genetic revolution, minded the monastery bees and peas. He figured out the peas, but could never explain the genetically inherited traits of the bees.[79]

Ground-breaking work in the field of bee behavior was conducted in the early 1900s by Charles Henry Turner, an African-American biologist from Ohio. He was the first black person to earn a Ph.D. from the University of Chicago. Dr. Turner published over 30 papers, but due to his complexion, wasn't able to land a research job or professorship. He settled on teaching high school biology in a black community in Missouri. In 1908, in a city park, Turner trained bees to arrive for feeding at fixed times of the day, to land on pre-selected colours for feed, and to communicate feeder locations to other bees in the hive.[80] After building on Dr. Turner's research and translating the honeybee waltz into German, Professor Karl von Frisch was awarded the 1973 Nobel Prize in Medicine and Physiology.[81]

American presidents George Washington and Thomas Jefferson poked their hands into bees' nests more than a few times in their careers.[82] The Englishman, Lord Baden Powell - founder of the Boy Scouts - proudly produced honey for a public showing. He accidentally overheated it, the honey burnt. In a hurry, he had to show the dark honey anyway. Due to Lord Baden's prestige, this created a fashion for dark honey in England for years. Other Englishmen also enjoyed beekeeping. According to Sir Arthur Conan Doyle, when Sherlock Holmes retired, he took to beekeeping along the British south coast.[83]

One of the most intriguing individuals to poke his nose into a beehive was a Yale College graduate (Class of 1808) and former minister and educator from Philadelphia.

Personal Best?

Reverend Lorenzo Lorraine Langstroth ultimately had the greatest impact on beekeeping as an industry and on how bees are kept. The tongue-tied, self-effacing minister who was too shy to approach a congregation with a sermon, invented modern beekeeping. Until Langstroth, most beehives were made of logs, straw skeps, or clay jars. He built the modern hive after his discovery of "bee space." He took advantage of the fact that bees seldom glue their combs one to another. Instead, they keep a fixed spacing (a bee space) between each comb so the bees can maneuver between the combs. From his observation, Langstroth created removable frames - wooden racks holding bits of honey comb.

Rev. L.L. Langstroth,
The Inventor of the Modern Bee Hive, 1853

Langstroth discovered bee-space in the fall of 1851 and adapted the distance (three-eighths of an inch) as the fixed distance between his wooden racks so that bees could be worked by humans without ripping the fixed combs apart. He noted his discovery in his diary:

"Pondering, as I had so often done before, how I could get rid of the disagreeable necessity of cutting the attachments of the combs from the walls of the hives... the almost self-evident idea of using the bee space... came into my mind, and in a moment the suspended movable frames, kept a suitable distance from each other and the case [hive body] containing them, came into being. Seeing by intuition, as it were, the end from the beginning, I could scarcely refrain from shouting out my "Eureka!" in the open streets."[84]

Langstroth's idea was so simple that no patent could sufficiently hold it. He was also an extremely poor business manager and suffered for sixty of his ninety years from a severe manic-depression which would at times see him working twenty-four hours a day with ecstatic energy, trying to solve mysteries of the hive. (He wrote <u>The Hive and the Honey Bee</u> in a single energy-charged winter, 350 pages, brilliantly composed.) But he would lapse into severe depression, so deep that he spent months in a darkened bedroom, dreading his life and his bees. "I would see the letter 'B' and it would push me deeper into darkness," he wrote.[85]

183

Bad Beekeeping

His health and his generosity prevented him from capitalizing on his discovery. Much to his chagrin, he never made much money from his discovery and died rather poor. He is buried in Dayton, Ohio, in the Woodland Cemetery where a large monument marks the resting place of "The Father of Modern Beekeeping."[86]

Langstroth was a famous beekeeper – famous, that is, to other beekeepers. But there were also other people who attained a degree of fame and also kept bees. Sir Edmund Hillary experienced perseverance, hard-work, and self-reliance on his family's honey farm early in his life. He led the first party up Mount Everest. Much of his character was shaped tending sixteen hundred hives of bees in New Zealand. Sir Hillary wrote "my father took up commercial bee-keeping full time. This meant my brother and I were even busier, carrying 80 lb boxes of honey for extracting and even 120 lb crates holding two four-gallon tins of honey. By the time I was sixteen years old I was as strong as a man and worked harder than most."[87]

Bill Dennison, mayor of Toronto, kept bees. When someone would call city hall complaining about a problem swarm, Bill would light up his bee smoker, don his veil and capture the renegades. He could have sent in Henry Fonda. When Fonda wasn't busy starring in one of his ninety-six films, he quietly gave away his production in jars labeled *Hank's Bel-Air Honey.*[88]

General Le Quy Quynh was the military strategist who led the defense of Viet Nam against the French and, later, the Americans. He was also a beekeeper for fifty years. Today he's a healer and lives in Ho Chi Minh City. He treated victims of the wars with all sorts of bee products developed in his laboratories.[89] And, of course, Martha Stewart has been a beekeeper for over twenty-five years. Beekeeping is a good thing.

How did so many different sorts of people in so many different parts of the world become smitten by the little honeybee? A stinger at one end; a mouth full of honey at the other. Rather than being an obscure and quaint pastime, bee culture seems to have occupied an almost mystical place in the minds of some of the earth's finest poets, scholars, and philosophers.

Joe, Charlie, Merlin, and I removed all the honey from our bees' hives. Extracted a hundred and fifty barrels. Placed all those emptied boxes back on the hives. The bees filled them again. Another hundred and fifty barrels. It was getting late in the season, we put half the supers back on the bees. They filled them again. Seventy-five barrels. From less than eight hundred hives. The bees had produced three-hundred ten pounds of honey per hive. It was an incredible honey crop.

A series of semi-trucks arrived at my shop, each taking sixty-four barrels. The young men and I loaded the drums of honey by hand, pushing the barrels up the ramp and deep into the hired trucks. Each time the driver would sign a copy of the cargo list and then he'd ease his truck through its gears. The tractor-trailer lurched a few times, but soon would be heading north on Highway 4 towards Swift Current, then east towards central Canada. I always walked around the west side of the shop and watched the highway until my honey disappeared.

Personal Best?

The season was ending; honey was harvested, shipped. Merlin was in school, Charlie took a job in Swift Current. Joe left Saskatchewan. We parted without much conversation, exhausted by the long busy summer. I left him at the Saskatoon airport. He would arrive in Milwaukee within hours.

Late in the fall, I still had twenty barrels of honey left in the shop. I would leave for Florida in a week. I decided to haul those last drums south into the States. I made arrangements with a beekeeper in Malta, Montana, and I filled out export papers. The trip was quick, down to the States and back in four hours, including a stop for a hamburger, shake, and fries which I ate on the drive home.

I stopped in Loring, Montana, to toss out the burger wrapper and plastic milkshake cup before reaching Canada. Better off leaving American garbage in America, I figured. Loring was deserted. A tiny town - bar, post office, grain elevators at an uncontrolled railroad crossing. No people. I wondered where they might be. I thought there were no other vehicles anywhere on the eighty miles of highway between Malta and Val Marie. Just me, the prairies, the wind. I was wrong. A pickup with Colorado plates pulled up, swung around, parked in front of me.

"Ever been to Canada?" someone in the truck asked me. Either he didn't notice my Saskatchewan license plates or he thought Saskatchewan was one of the sixty or so U.S. states. I told him I lived there. "How much further is it?"

It was about twenty miles. Then they asked if it was true about the guns. "We can't come into Canada if we're carrying guns?"

"It depends," I said, "on what kind you're carrying. But if you lie about the guns, they'll keep you out and take away your guns. If you tell them what you've got, maybe they'll let you in. Or maybe you leave the guns at the border, I don't really know." I looked at the four kids crammed into the rusty Chevy pick up. *They were carrying guns.* Hopefully, the guys working at the border would send this group back to Colorado.

"You folks don't have guns, do you?" someone else asked me.

"Oh, yea, we do. Most Canadians carry guns. Mine is under my shirt." I thumped the sunglasses bulging in my pocket. "I have a license to use it on my job. But Americans can't come in with guns. We figure you're too violent already, eh?" I'd realized that my pushy way of talking made me sound suspiciously American, so I quickly ended the sentence with an artificial "eh?" The kids in the truck believed me. Probably heard that Canadians never lie. They returned to their truck, turned it around, headed back south.

I wondered what their plan had been. A series of armed robberies against defenseless Canadians? Or maybe they hoped

Canadian Border Guard Shows her Tongue.
Canada was Disarmingly Protected by a Cute Solitary Girl.

185

to get the mule and forty acres of free land they thought the Canadian government was giving away to homesteaders? At the border, I reported the truck I'd seen and it's Colorado plate. The girl working the crossing radioed the American side and gave the agent a description. The kids never showed up in Canada.

Instead of a few hefty well-armed guys, there was just one young lady working the border crossing. Younger than me. Long black hair. Big, round, brown eyes that seemed to notice everything. She looked good in her uniform. She was unarmed.

"So, Debbie, what do you do if four guys in a rusty pickup truck show up at the border and you find drugs and guns under the seat of their truck?" I asked.

"*Do?* I don't *do* anything."

"You... don't... do anything? You let them into the country?" Canada is being protected by a pretty girl in a cute uniform. The guys working the American side of the border, a hundred metres south, wear guns to keep bad Canadians out. The arrangement didn't seem quite right.

"Of course I'm not supposed to do anything," she answered. "If I spot drugs or guns, I pretend I don't notice anything. I'm not supposed to get *killed* working here. I tell them to have a nice day. Then I go back in the office and phone the RCMP. There's only one road north from here. I get the description, the plate number, how many people, what they're wearing, what they're driving. The RCMP block the road. They're the ones carrying the guns."

Waltzing Bees in a Skep, photo by Professor Zander,
Appearing in The Dancing Bees by Karl von Frisch

The Florida Farm

The lone bee drifted from flower to flower, stuffing pollen of various sorts onto her hairy legs. Her sisters always returned to the hive with a solidly packed wad of uniformly colored pollen. This was normal. A honeybee likes to stay with one type of flower. This may be easier for the collector – the bee gets used to a certain petal type, shape, form, color. The bee learns the flower, gains experience, becomes efficient at what she does. This system, in turn, helps the flower. Pollen from peaches is not mixed on the stamen with pollen from dandelions. Peaches are pollinated, fruit grows, seeds develop.

But the occasional lone bee isn't satisfied with monotonous speed and efficiency; she mixes pollens from a variety of flowers and tastes the nectar of many buds. And returns to her hive with a haphazardly prepared mass of pollens.

Saskatchewan was good. I made a lot of honey that summer, some sort of record, I suppose. My barrels were sealed, labeled and delivered to the honey packers in eastern Canada. I drove back to Florida, Saskatchewan license plates on my Florida Dodge pick-up. In Florida, I received the bees that my brother Don had been running for me in Wisconsin, set those hives of bees among the citrus trees. I became a Florida beekeeper again - feeding my hives a bit, grafting cells, caging queens, producing orange blossom honey.

In the spring, I'd blow packages from the honey producing hives, carry the colonies to apple pollination in Pennsylvania, then on to Wisconsin. I hauled a big truck filled with packages and new queens to Saskatchewan. In Saskatchewan, I'd install the Florida packages, check through wintered hives and within a few months, harvest more honey. Then fall would arrive. I'd wrap the Canadian bees, head back to Florida and start the winter season again. It was hard work. The charm was wearing off.

The labor, the physical exertion, was tiring. I still lived in poverty. Almost every dollar went to buy more beehives, new trucks to move the new beehives, gasoline for the new trucks, and wages for the people I hired to drive those trucks. I took no vacations – no leisurely trips to Mexico, Europe, or the strand of islands off Florida's east coast. I didn't play golf, didn't go to the clubs or bars on weekends. I worked weekends. I ate well – ketchup with spaghetti; butter with boiled potatoes. I wore the same clothes until my knees and elbows were exposed, but that was somehow stylish among my small group of friends, most of whom lived and worked as I did. The overwork and poverty continued for three more years. The charm was really wearing off.

Apple pollination was the first project I killed. The logistics were complicated. The hours on the road were making me sick. It was impossible to deliver five hundred hives to eastern Pennsylvania the same week I needed to haul seven hundred packages of bees to

Bad Beekeeping

Saskatchewan. Adapting Schroedinger, one can't really observe oneself and be oneself at the same time. I wasn't yet thirty years old, too young to realize that the dead cat in Schroedinger's box might be me. For a while, I thought I could be everywhere, do everything. I was gaining life skills and now knew I'd have to cut back. No more apple pollination.

Without the apple pollination contracts, I had three thousand dollars less money, but I drove two thousand fewer miles each spring. The long truck drives with live honeybee freight were fatiguing. Accidents happen to weary beekeepers every season. I never caused a serious problem on the road; no one was injured as a result of my highway antics. I was lucky. But I knew I should spend less time on the highway.

I hired Jerry Berg to transport my big heavy hives on pallets each fall the 1300 miles from Florida and then back to Wisconsin again in the spring. Ray Myers, Joel Vetter, and Stan Kanter took turns using their forklifts to heft my bees onto the rented semi-trailer. My only bee haul was with a smaller truck, carrying a few hundred packages (the light-weight screen-covered boxes with 6000 bees and a queen in each cage) from Florida to Saskatchewan every spring.

Friends Drove the Forklift that Hefted Pallets of my Hives High onto a Semi-Trailer. Wisconsin Bound!

In Florida, I spent time and some of my money developing my Bay Lake acreage. A new sand trail, topped with clay, led past the neighbor's grapefruit grove, the shared lake, and into my swamp. I decided to build a small warehouse, a place to keep my beehive equipment and graft my queen cells. I phoned my father, told him my plan.

"Go way back into your cypress swamp, cut a few tall trees, straight, smooth trees, use them as studs and rafters," my father said. When he was sixty years old, Dad had built a sawmill on his Pennsylvania farm. Cut the trees in his own woods and turned them into benches for his greenhouse.

I told him that I could buy twenty-foot long, pressure-treated two-by-eight's for six dollars each. With two hundred dollars, I could buy enough lumber for the roof and they'd be straight and even, plus I wouldn't get bitten by a water moccasin.

The Florida Farm

"Yea," he said, "but then you wouldn't have your two hundred dollars anymore. Someone else would have it." My father. This was the man who told us, when we were small children, to "use one small square of toilet paper, poke your finger through it, wipe your ass, then wash your hands." To save money. He described what he called 'the toothpaste tube phenomenon'. When the tube is fat and puffy, we squeeze a big plump wad of toothpaste on our brush. When the tube is almost empty, we squeeze a tiny dab out and use it – our teeth get just as clean. "Learn to live your life like the tube is almost empty," he said.

I built the workshed my way, pressure-treated rafters supported a tin roof. Sheets of plywood encased the one inch by four inch grid nailed to huge posts which I ripped evenly with my chain saw. I did all the work myself, and was inordinately proud of the simple structure.

**I Built a Simple Wooden Shed on my Florida Farm.
I was Inordinately Proud of my Accomplishment.**

**Johnny Stiefel Let Me Use One of His Trailers in Mascotte.
Mine was the Third from the Right.**

The Florida farm and the small workshed comprised my operations base. I parked my trucks and hundreds of bee boxes on my forty acres of sand, swamp, cypress, and oak hammocks. But I continued to live in a two-bedroom mobile home at Johnny Stiefel's trailer park. Johnny charged me two hundred dollars a month for the tin box I called home. An unfair price. Too cheap. Had he charged me more, I would have been

189

motivated to move on, build a shack on my farm, live there. But I would need electricity, running water, a phone. Power would have to come from transformers out on Bay Lake Road – a mile away. The farm lacked a well for water and there was no telephone; Johnny Stiefel provided running water and the phone was plugged in for twenty dollars. And I was still announcing at the radio station - it was closer to drive from Stiefel's Trailer Court than from the farm. I had a lot of excuses, but mostly I was too tired and too poor to build a cottage on the farm. Perhaps next year.

The Florida Bee Farm, Shortly after I Bought it from Tom Booth

Nevertheless, I invested quit a bit of time and energy on the forty acres I'd purchased from Tom Booth. About half the land was unusable as farmland or building sites - it was too low, too wet, too swampy. But there were beautiful areas of small knolls with enormous live oak trees draped in Spanish moss. I cleared walking trails and beat down brush and shrub, making places to set out queen mating hives. The property was isolated, a mile from the nearest road. I liked that, but I had to spend three thousand dollars to get a buried electric cable rolled out to a transformer near the building I had erected. I couldn't get phone service.

I hired brothers from Stuckey to come to the farm with an ancient backhoe. They dredged the sides of my sandy trail through the muckiest areas, topped the path with clay. The work was slow, partly because their equipment required constant maintenance, partly because they had to quit early each afternoon. It was winter, grew dark by about five, and as William told me, "Us negro-folks shouldn't be in Bay Lake after dark." But they finished my road in two weeks. It cost me a thousand dollars and served my trucks well.

The Florida Farm

**Ron, Jim Edwards –
Picking at a Park**

It would be untrue to suggest I was working every moment of every day. I was learning to socialize a bit. I picked guitar occasionally with a tunesmith named Jim Edwards, and I sat in with his Bay Lake Boys. Jim taught me more about picking guitar in two months than I'd learned from assorted teachers in ten years. Jim was good.

And I visited Sandy; learned to relish Grandma Knight's grits and greens. Her family welcomed me, made me comfortable. Gave me advice.

"You can't have a farm without a gun," her step-father advised me. He sold me his twelve-gauge shotgun.

"You might enjoy our church before you come over for Sunday dinner," said Sandy's Uncle. So, I started spending Sunday mornings at the Bay Lake Missionary Baptist Church - as an observer, not a member.

Sandy sometimes helped with the bees. She'd ride out to the beeyards, smoke the hives, carry empty boxes, look for queen bees. Then one day, she got stung.

Her eyes swelled, puffed out huge until she could barely see through tiny slits. Red blotches mottled her arms and neck. Her throat was swelling shut. We raced to the clinic in Clermont. "I can't breathe," she said. "We're almost there," I said when we were almost there. I pushed her into the office. The doctor shot epinephrine into her arm. She survived. "Thirty-five dollars, please," said the doctor's assistant, handing me some anti-histamine tablets. "The next bee sting may kill her, keep her away from bees," said the doctor.

Keep her away from bees, they may kill her. If I had taken the physician's advice, he may have been right. But allergic reactions are strange and unpredictable. Sandy visited the bees the next day. We were caging queens on the farm and a bee stung her wrist. *God, I've killed her.* Her wrist swelled, red blotches appeared. We hurried to the truck. I thrust two anti-histamine tablets at her. "The doctor said I should only take one," she said. But we were half an hour from the hospital, I figured I needed twice as much time to get to the physician. I started the truck. "Wait," she said. "I'm O.K." She was. I shut off the truck. Her swelling receded. The blotches cleared. Within the next few months, she was stung twenty-seven times. Each sting was less severe than the one before. They hurt, they welted her skin. But there were no swollen eyes. No near death experiences.

"Shouldn't she be dead?" I asked the doctor later.

Bad Beekeeping

"Apparently not," he said. "Allergies are strange and unpredictable. Maybe getting another sting the next day kept her body from developing antigens in its immune system. Maybe she was lucky?"

My brother David and I went to a beekeepers' meeting for Sioux Honey members in Dade City, Florida. Sioux Honey is a co-operative. Hundreds of beekeepers are members and they supply the organization with fifty million pounds of honey every year. Most of the profits from sales are paid back to the beekeeper-members. Meetings are held in different regions of the USA once a year and at the company headquarters in Sioux City, Iowa. Hence the name, Sioux Honey Association.

Meetings usually dealt with sales and production figures and the one thing all beekeepers wanted to know – how much money they could expect to earn from the honey they sent to the co-op. Occasionally other business, of local interest, was introduced. At the Dade City meeting, a beekeeper from Umatilla wanted to lodge a complaint against nearly all the other beekeepers in the state of Florida.

"I've kept bees in Florida for thirty years," he said. "It's getting harder and harder." I studied the small, aging beekeeper's frame. Someday I would be him, the work getting harder and harder, the body getting smaller and smaller. "The problem is," he continued, "there are way again too many foreign beekeepers around here these days." For a moment I thought he meant Hungarian or Swedish beekeepers. But he meant foreigners from Pennsylvania, New York, North Dakota.

"We used to have only a hundred thousand colonies in Florida. Now we've got three hundred thousand. Local people, like myself, kept bees in the same yards for years and years. Now I've got all kinds of bees in my neighborhood, some from Ohio, some from Wisconsin. My production's gone way down."

My brother David leaned towards me. "I've seen his bees, his production is down because his bees are crap. I've tried to help him. He doesn't know how to keep bees," my brother whispered.

The man continued. "There just isn't enough honey with all the bees, coming in these days from foreign parts of the country... I resolve that we hereby send a recommendation to the state of Florida, on behalf of the members of Sioux Honey Association, to close the border to these interlopers."

I doubt that the man who spoke expected a positive reaction. Almost every member of the honey co-op migrated bees down from the north. And likewise, many of the Florida beekeepers had started huge honey farms on the northern plains, in the Dakotas and Minnesota. Instead of spirited debate, the chairman suggested a committee be formed to study the issue and report back in one year. The man with the complaint was assigned to the committee with four other beekeepers. Foreigners.

The complaint, though doomed to failure, made me think. Perhaps Saskatchewan beekeepers would feel the same. Would they try to close the border, keep American beekeepers out? After all, Americans really are foreigners in Canada. I decided to research the argument. What if the old beekeeper was right? What if my bees really do decrease the nectar supply? What if the old fellow was making less honey because of people like me?

The Florida Farm

I phoned several bee scientists the next day. The results were unanimous. There can seldom be too many bees. In places like Florida, each acre of orange trees can secrete enough nectar for three hives of bees and some honey would still drip to the ground for lack of bees to collect it.[90] With a million acres of orange trees, three million hives could be placed in Florida's groves. There aren't that many hives in all the United States. Up in Saskatchewan, an acre of canola, alfalfa, or sweet clover typically furnish at least five hundred pounds of honey – enough for two hives.[91] Saskatchewan had four million acres of these hay plants and canola seed.[92] With more bees, at least a billion pounds of honey would be produced in Saskatchewan - a billion dollar's worth of honey. That would really stimulate the province's economy. In 1984, the honey crop only added about ten million dollars to the pockets of Saskatchewan farmers. Increasing production fifty times is certainly conceivable – the hive density would only start to rival that of some parts of Florida and California.[93]

I knew these figures were stretching the imagination a little. There were times of the year – say January in Florida – when only a few oak and willow trees furnished pollen and nectar. Those trees could be over-grazed by bees if hive counts are too high. However, early sources like oak, maple, and willow are never very dependable. Good Florida beekeepers – and good Saskatchewan beekeepers – feed their insects protein and carbohydrates all through the cool and unpredictable early spring season.

But in the end, over-stocking doesn't seem to be the beekeeper's greatest problem. The statistics show that as colony counts increased in Florida (and citrus groves were replaced by parking lots and trailer courts), the average production per hive had nevertheless increased. Florida went from an average of 45 pounds per hive in the decade of the 1940's to 80 pounds in the 1970's, and a hundred pounds per hive in the past few years.[94]

I decided to gather the information from the research scientists, create a story from the data, and mold it into a little magazine article. I sent it to the *American Bee Journal*. They printed it.[95] I got a few phone calls, irate messages from beekeepers who disagreed with me. But I was applauded when the president of the Central Florida Beekeepers' Association pointed me out in the audience at the next meeting.

In Florida, there were monthly beekeepers' meetings. This gave me a chance to meet people, even if they were just beekeepers. But I had other things on my social agenda, too. I occasionally bounced down the sand trail across from Gallows Lake and visited the retired school teacher who was chums with the President. I visited Eleanor Dern and her dogs. We played scrabble - Eleanor and I. The dogs watched. I sometimes invited a friend, but few returned for a second visit.

I went because I enjoyed the trips, not because of any sense of duty to the grey-headed lady. I learned a lot from her. Eleanor had been a teacher; she suggested I go back to school. She thought I should be a lawyer.

We discussed the history and settlement of Florida, the changing political ideals of her friend, Ronald Reagan, and we talked about some of Mrs. Dern's favorite poets, especially Burns and Frost. "Fire and Ice,"[96] she called them. She gave me Milton's *Paradise Lost*, a marker set to his description of the bee-like creatures - rebellious angels

Bad Beekeeping

- who tirelessly, persistently, stoically build hell.[97] I read Milton, but my mind was on the load of bees to be driven from Florida to Saskatchewan, the hives to be assembled, the honey to be extracted. I didn't see myself the way Eleanor Dern did.

"I wanted to be a missionary when I was about your age," Mrs. Dern told me. "I know this sounds silly, but at the time, I didn't think I could touch a Negro person. Doesn't bother me today, but back then, it seemed impossible. Wish I'd done it, traveled to Africa, taught school in Africa." I studied Eleanor's dry, wrinkled face. I wasn't shocked by her words. This was a woman who contributed to the Negro College Fund, donated books to her Presbyterian Church's overseas ministry. *Couldn't touch a Negro when she was young, doesn't bother her now.* The words seemed strange, but not shocking from a woman of her age, her generation.

We were outside her house, in the warm sunshine. I was leaving.

Eleanor handed several ears of sweet corn to me, fresh corn on the cob from Webster's Farmers' Market.

"You know how to cook corn?"

"Sure," I said. I took the corn, fumbling with it. She told me how to cook it.

"It's easy. Get the water boiling first. Drop in the corn. But pull off the husks first, you know. Then take out the corn exactly the minute the water starts to boil a second time. That's all. Don't overcook it, Ron."

I was still standing there near my truck, holding the five ears of corn, but now I was cradling them like a baby.

"What about chicken?" Eleanor asked me.

"What about chicken?" I said.

"You know how to bake a chicken?"

"I guess so," I said. The truth was, I usually ate salami and lunch meat from the Winn Dixie. I was nervous about baking raw meats, figured I'd end up diseased.

"It's so easy," she said. "Buy a whole chicken at Winn Dixie. Put it on a pan. Stick it in the oven for one hour. 350 degrees. Take it out. Eat it."

"That's all? That's all I need to know?"

She nodded, waved me into my truck. I headed over to Carter Island to see what Sandy's Grandma Knight was cooking for supper.

Scenes of Industry, 1827

One Country

A colony of bees needs stability. A strong, erect tree, aging yet firm, may have a deep crevice, a decaying hole. The oak is virile and dying at the same moment. The fracture in the tree opens into a dark, warm, protected place where autumn drizzle, summer heat, and the cold winds of winter never reach. The bees do no great favor for the tree. They reside within its trunk, much as birds reside on the oak's branches in their nests. But the tree provides a great service to the honeybees dwelling within. They will abide there many seasons.

Sandy and I married in May, as soon as she finished her high school exams. Our wedding cost six hundred dollars. I remember the amount - we paid for it ourselves. Her family helped with most of the arrangements and with decorating the Bay Lake Missionary Baptist Church. My father didn't attend the wedding - spring was the busy season in his Pennsylvania greenhouse, we were getting married in far-away Florida, and, he explained, he had ten kids so he couldn't be expected to attend ten weddings!

A week after the ceremony, we drove north in my black Dodge truck, wedding gifts hidden under an orange tarp flopping in the wind. In four days, we arrived at North Portal, where North Dakota ends and Saskatchewan begins. I parked the truck, grabbed the sheath of visa documents, asked Sandy to follow me into the office. "I have no idea how much trouble they'll give us," I said. "You never know with these people. All the papers can be perfect, but they still find a problem." I turned around. Sandy was gone.

I walked back to where the Dodge was parked. She was bent over, examining stones, heisting a few red and black shards into her pocket.

"What on earth are you doing? If they're watching us out the window, they'll think you're weird and won't let you in!"

"We don't have stones like these in Florida," she said. She was erect now, following me to the big steel door labeled "Canada Customs Excise and Immigration".

The immigration officer hadn't seen my wife on hands and knees, picking up rocks. Or perhaps he had. He smiled, stamped the documents, wished us a good trip. Sandy was a landed immigrant. We were on our way.

It was five hours from North Portal, through Estevan, across south Saskatchewan, heading west, to Val Marie. Sandy liked the tiny house and as soon as I was able to get the water running, she began washing walls and windows. With discarded railroad ties, we fenced the front yard to keep me and visitors from parking on our sod. I chopped up the tough, packed gumbo in front of the cabin and Sandy seeded Kentucky bluegrass.

Three years passed; it seemed longer. Summers were spent in Saskatchewan; winters in Florida. Each winter, Sandy saw her grandparents. I kept raising queens and packages and trucked them north each spring. But Florida wasn't easy. The farm was

195

Bad Beekeeping

remote, dangerous. I bought my brother David's mobile home and dragged it out to the swamp, but we couldn't get a phone line put in. I had spent three thousand dollars bringing in electricity from Bay Lake Road, a mile away. I pounded a plastic pipe into the ground, barely deep enough to suck surface water. We used the cloudy water to wash clothes and dishes. We brought drinking water from Grandma Knight's.

Three years. Florida and Saskatchewan. In 1983, we had twenty-two inches of rain during February and the swamp invaded my new clay-capped road and turned it into a mucky mess. Snakes slithered up to the house, sharing the highest bit of property we had – the hammock of oaks where I'd positioned the trailer home. For a while, we parked the truck a half mile away from the house, hiked in barefooted through the mire. It stayed like that until we loaded bees and drove back to Saskatchewan.

The next fall, when we arrived back from Saskatchewan, the swamp was gone but so were a few of the things I'd stored in the old cypress barn on my property. Nothing particularly valuable was stolen, and the gate with seven strands of barbed wire was still nailed in place across the trail that led up to the house. But I felt the property had been violated and I was more careful with my things after that.

I continued to work bees in Florida, caring for the hives which yielded my packages and queens for Saskatchewan. The people at the shop on the Little Brown Church Road still extracted the bit of orange blossom honey I harvested each March.

One day, I hauled a load of honey supers from the farm and headed north, still only three miles from my farm, driving past orange groves and cattle pastures. I stopped when I saw police cars lined up in the ditch. A young officer I knew as Swampy – Bob Swanson – came over to my truck.

"You phone this one in, Ron?" Swampy asked me.

"Phone what?" I stabbed a finger near my eye, dislodged a beetle.

"Oh, you don't know. That," Swampy pointed to a lump under some sheets. "Knifing. We know the guy. Bad news. Was in a drug fight, looks like he got it in the neck and was dumped here. He used to be a local."

I was thirty. We were expecting Erika. I decided to stay in one place. The people in Canada were friendly. There were no drug wars, no swamps, no snakes invading the house. Saskatchewan seemed nicer. I was making lots of honey in Saskatchewan. In Saskatchewan we'd stay.

A Protected Beekeeper, 1883

Dust Clouds

The weather is hot and dry. A persistent bee faces the sun at the hive entrance, her legs folded under her thorax. Her sisters crouch beside her on the hive's landing board. Bees are fanning their wings, moving hot dry air through the hive, up into the box, between the combs hanging from the ceiling. But one bee spreads her wings and becomes airborne.

She circles the hive in a small loop, expands the circle, then again, a wider circle. Farther and farther from the colony. The dry air crackles with static and the bee is slightly disoriented. Purple-headed alfalfa blossoms had secreted thick sparkling orbs of nectar a week earlier, but today they are dry. Blasted by sun and wind and drought. The flowers, struggling to survive, can not spend their scarce energy and water producing sugary luxuries for bees. The persistent bee returns to this patch of alfalfa each day, searching among the blossoms for food. Each day she flies back to the hive. Empty.

I sold the Florida farm, sold my American bees. I would live in Saskatchewan, become a full-time Canadian beekeeper. Crops had been good. Val Marie - remote, rural - was pleasant. I could relax a bit during the winter, perhaps package honey for a few stores. Perhaps take correspondence classes, learn about business and science and language.

Saskatchewan was dry. I enjoyed the crisp air. Florida had been too wet, too humid. I had been sweating constantly, my oily skin dripped. In Florida, my hair was thick, greasy, twisted in kinky strands. In Saskatchewan, my skin was dry; my hair flattened nicely.

When I lived in the east, I had a runny nose. All the time. In the arid western climate, my nose was dry and often ached and burned. Buzz told me it was the difference between easterners and western folks. He said that the people in the east are wet-nosed; westerners are hard-nosed.

We were becoming more hard-nosed. It grew ever drier in Val Marie. Florida got fifty inches of rain a year; in southern Saskatchewan, ten inches is normal.[98] By 1985, we were getting even less.

It was dry, but I was confident there would never be a honey crop failure in Val Marie. The government irrigated ten thousand acres of alfalfa in our valley. Two huge lakes quenched the hay meadows. We could never lack water.

I told my banker I would always make two hundred pounds of honey per hive per year. He encouraged me as I borrowed money to expand and take advantage of the boundless opportunities southern Saskatchewan presented to her farmers. In the summer, it was always hot and sunny, so I wouldn't expect cold rainy weather to interfere as the bees sipped nectar from flowers. Many crops in the east were lost because of too much rain - this had been the bane of Pennsylvania beekeepers. But summertime in southern Saskatchewan was always hot, dry, and sunny. Good honey weather. I would thrive.

Local folks assured me, "It never gets that dry here - well, maybe in the '30s but that was fifty years ago. The government won't let that happen again." They were as unprepared as I when the drought arrived.

Late in the winter of '83, farmers were optimistic. There was a heavy snowfall west of us, up in the Cypress Hills. "No drought this year," farmers told me. However, only a light dusting of snow lit on the fields around Val Marie. No rain fell in our valley. The snow in the distant hills melted. The ground - dry and baked hard - couldn't soak up the water streaming from the hills into the Frenchman River. Run-off, the farmers called it. From the Frenchman River, the run-off flowed up against the dams west of Val Marie. The reservoirs filled. Water kept coming.

Thus it was, on the first week of March during a drought in a land with little moisture, there was a great flood. To prevent bursting, the steel gates at the earthen reservoirs were opened wide - the narrow valley below was soaked. The main bridge across the Frenchman had a fast moving current lapping at its base. We expected the bridge to rip lose, severing our route to Swift Current. But the bridge held. The low flat farmland along the valley was flooded with three feet of green, murky, ice-cold water. A few cows were trapped on islands of grass. Few died in the flash flood, but some of my hives were soaked. An entire beeyard that I had wintered on the river bank floated away. White hives, insulation, and wrapping paper were bopping in the river, flowing southeast towards Montana.

The rush of flood water was gone. In a week, drenched alfalfa fields and feed-lots became greasy mud. A warm south wind blew. The mud dried and hardened. Farmers talked about drought and mourned the loss of all the water that had flooded their fields and then swept past their village. Gone.

**It was the Worst Drought in Thirty Years,
Yet a Flood Swept Away some Hives.**

Dust Clouds

Mrs. Moine, Buzz Trottier's aunt, had seen this all before.

"It's a circle, God's circle," she said. "You get good times, then bad times, then good times again. It's the way things will always be."

Mrs. Moine made rose hip tea for us. She had saved last fall's red bulbs from the wild roses that cluttered the roadside east of town. Mrs. Moine boiled and strained the tea, served it on china. We sipped the tea in her house, two doors west of our own tiny home.

Buzz Trottier and his Aunt Louise Moine at a Campfire

Louise Moine handed me her book, a story that told of her arrival from Manitoba, part of a group that fled the British Canadians when they seized her parents' land near Winnipeg. I opened her book. *Remembering Will Have to Do.*[99] Half the words were in English, but every second column was printed in the blocky Cree alphabet, where triangles, squares, and circles caught my eye.

"You can read this?" I asked her.

"Oh, yes," she said. "English and Cree. It's my story." She dripped more honey into her tea, stirred it again. "It's going to be dry this year, Ron. And windy."

I objected. Surely it would rain during the summer. And we had had a flood.

But the prairies dried up; the circle never ends.

f Indian, French and Scots ancestry,
less guided by a mixture of these
ce my parents were both Metis, it
t my Indian blood predominated.
s a mixture of Cree and French. We
tsteps of our ancestors, adopting
customs suited our way of life. We
ly, with no anxiety for tomorrow.
he white settlers started moving in
a free and happy people. Not only
infringe on our liberties but their

ᴠᵘᐃᑲ ᐁᐧᒣᑐᑯᖮ
ᓂᒍᑲ ᓂᒍᒥ ᑲᴠᑈᔭ
ᐅᒡᵘᐃᐧ ᒣ ᓂᑲᵘᐃᐧ <
ᔨᒫᔭ ᒪ ᐅᑏᒍ ᓂᑲ
ᓂᑭᑈᓂ ᐊᐳ ᓂᐊᑭᔭᐃᐧ
ᴠᵘᐊᐸᐧᐃᐧ ᒣ ᴠᒥ
ᓂᐱᑎᔭᐧ ᑲᵔ ᔄᐸ
ᴠᑭᑐᑭᐧ ᒣ ᒍᑭ ᴠᑭ
ᴠᑯᑕ ᴠᐊᐧᑯ ᐃᒥᵘᐃ ᴠ
ᓂᐊᑎᓂᑭᐃᐧᓂᔭᐧ ᴠᑯᵔᑭ ᶜ

From the Louise Moine Book, <u>Remembering Will Have to Do</u>

Six years earlier, when I had moved into the dark green valley, I had expected to be excused from any crop failures. Alfalfa thrived. Drought seemed a very remote probability. An impossibility.

I had been enthusiastic, confident. Young, inexperienced. Thick meadows of clover and alfalfa surrounded my apiaries. The PFRA-operated reservoirs contained twenty thousand acre-feet of water - enough water to flood ten thousand irrigated acres knee-deep in water. Enough to give every alfalfa stem twenty-four inches of moisture. Perfect. I believed that if it were hot and dry, each hot dry day would be a nice, cloudless, rainless honey day - the bees wouldn't be needlessly delayed in their nests by days of drizzle; they wouldn't be bothered by rainy weather. Life would be good. All the time.

We didn't get our twenty thousand acre-feet of water. Much drained down the Frenchman River, through Val Marie, south to Montana. Half the Canadian water, by international treaty, had to be sent south to quench the parched American prairies. Part of a deal between Ottawa and Washington. We were told by our government that, yes, it was too bad, but we had to look at the big picture. If we kept all our water, the Frenchman River, south of Val Marie, would dry up. With a dry Frenchman, the Milk River would start to go dry, then the Missouri. Finally, big barges of Canadian wheat would be stuck on sand banks next to an empty Mississippi River near New Orleans.

So, we gave the Americans half our water. We grumbled, but we knew that before Canadian ranchers started diverting the Frenchman River for irrigation, the Americans got all the water. By treaty, we were disrupting the natural flow of things. In a normal year, this left our people twenty-thousand acre-feet to flood onto the hay fields. In a normal year, plants would flourish, my bees would make honey.

Weeks passed. It didn't rain.

One evening, gray clouds gathered on the western horizon. We stood on the dusty road that led past our tiny square house. We wanted to feel rain droplets, taste moisture on our dry lips. Grass rustled, leaves began to quake, then shake. Thick dust blew in our eyes. The grey clouds were clouds of soil, not clouds of rain. The sky darkened. The taste of dust was upon our dry lips.

Dust Clouds

Hot strong winds continued from the south. The air felt like the steel smelting furnace my grandfather worked alongside in Pennsylvania. He'd described a searing heat that could ignite the hair on a man's arms, peel skin from the bone. Saskatchewan was becoming a hot, dry furnace. I felt my own hair might ignite, my skin peel.

Wheat, oats, alfalfa, withered. The river that had flooded our valley stopped flowing, turned into patches of murky water broken by bare river bed. The irrigation lakes dried into cracked, parched spans of hardening earth. The first year of the drought, 1984, my bees made a little honey. The spring flood had left enough moisture deep in the ground for the alfalfa to blossom and secrete a bit of nectar. I harvested fifty pounds per hive. A quarter of a normal crop.

The second year of the big drought, I made only seventeen pounds per hive. My bees and I earned a gross income of ten thousand dollars. Expenses were forty thousand. I was in trouble. This land of glorious honey crops failed me.

In 1985, the hot dry winds had begun early. Easter Sunday. In church, a little lady with a sun-dried face said, "If it's windy on Easter Sunday, it'll be windy for forty days - says so in the Bible." I touched her mottled hand and told her it was certainly a nice story. Immediately, angry gods sent a gust of wind which shook the tiny church. Dust blew in from beyond the hay meadows; blackened the sun. It stayed dark and windy for forty days.

I tried to do my normal work during the six week dust storm - putting extra boxes on the bees, anticipating that they would stretch their brood nests; they would need space for the honey crop. I cleaned and polished my little shop, thinking it would be only a few weeks before the first honey would pour from the combs into the barrels.

A bit of irrigation water spread through the network of canals and onto the fields. Half of it disappeared down deep cracks in the earth and much of the rest evaporated out of the canals and off the surface of the fields, vanishing into the dry thin air. The water that should have remained in the lakes for the second irrigation also disappeared - transpiring into the cloudless sky.

The Val Marie Reservoir was Dry.
We Scouted the Lake Bottom for Cans and Coins.

Bad Beekeeping

Newton Lake, the biggest reservoir, was shrinking from its shore ten meters every day until July, when it could shrink no more. The water was gone. Village people drove out to the reservoir and walked across the dry hard floor of the lake, finding watches, billfolds, and broken beer bottles lost from the pleasure boats of their grandparents.

Meanwhile, I was trying to grow a garden. With a shovel and much effort, I had flopped over all the sod in a small patch behind the house. It was black soil, once part of a small corral where horses fed and subsequently enriched the earth. I soaked the small garden patch daily, laying a hose on the ground and letting the water flow in trenches between rows of potatoes and zucchini – not directly on the plants; not wastefully sprayed into the air. We had a drought, but wells in Val Marie ran freely, unabated. There seemed to be plenty of moisture in the sands under the village - our home and garden had water, even if the alfalfa fields outside town did not.

Erika was two years old. My daughter stumbled through the short brown grass in the bit of yard between our house and garden. She screamed.

"Grass alive! Grass alive!"

Grasshoppers - green animals as large as her hands - bounded from the ground, landed on her white cape, tangled in her blonde hair. The dry grass – dead though it was - seemed alive to her. It was crawling, hopping, wiggling with huge green locusts. I lifted Erika and we continued towards the garden, each step liberating more locusts, each step producing a crunch as brown grass broke beneath my hiking shoes; each step producing a dull hiss and rattle as the grasshoppers jumped up, spread their wings, then descended on us and on tufts of dying grass along our path.

Grasshoppers ate the lawn. Devoured our little patch of garden. I stood there, Erika in arms, looking at the skeletal outlines of cabbage heads. Only the tough core and some thick white veins remained, the fleshy parts of the heads had fed the locusts. All the leaves of our potatoes were gone. The beans. God, they had even eaten the zucchini!

A Plague of Locusts Ate our Food

A beekeeper's life is governed by climate. When the weather is gorgeous - warm and sunny with a light breeze, the beekeeper isn't on a golf course or poolside - even on a

202

Dust Clouds

Sunday afternoon. Every day with pleasant weather is a day for the commercial beekeeper to exercise his hive tool and smoker. Not a day for play. In fair weather, the beekeeper is cloaked in an almost sting-proof white uniform, complete with canvas gloves and wire mesh veil. An astronaut-farmer. The armoured knight of the hayfield.

Beekeepers hate bad weather - any weather that isn't good for the bees. A beekeeper doesn't mind an occasional rainy day in July - a chance to work on equipment in the warehouse, catch up on extracting, slow down a bit without feeling too guilty - as long as the rainy day is followed by six days of bright, clear, sunny skies. Sufficient rain followed by bright sunshine sets off a flower's photosynthesis process and ultimately allows nectar to ooze. Beekeepers like sunny weather. And they have other demands. No frost. No wind. Not too hot. But beekeepers don't always get what they want.

Bitter, howling winter winds tore insulation from my hives in December. Cold drizzle kept the bees eating honey in their hives for weeks in the spring. Snow in May and frost in August sometimes created short summers with little honey. Other beekeepers had similar tragedies. In the San Fernando forest fire of 1906, in Los Angeles County, 16,000 colonies were destroyed.[100] Hives have been swept down the Mississippi, have been shattered by lightning, and have been buried under sand dunes.

A strong wind peeled lids from hundreds of small colonies of bees Murray Hannigan once wintered in a warm British Columbia valley. An ice storm followed the winds. His small hives filled with ice, some bees died. Earl told me about the afternoon he drove home to his farm in South Dakota and parked in the spot where his warehouse had stood that morning. The gray metal building had been plucked away by a tornado. Beekeepers have had hives washed out to sea, ravaged by bears, melted by scorching heat waves. Strange that anyone bothers with a business at which the gods have such great sport.

We usually associate bad weather on the prairies with winter. Rightly so. Forty-five percent of Canada is permanently frozen. Permafrost. And while one hundred and eight people are killed each winter in Canada by extreme cold (that's an average, not a requirement), only eleven are killed by the effects of extreme heat. Particularly pesky, though, are the persistent prairie winds. In my part of Saskatchewan, gale-force gusts appeared on calm days in mid-summer. Then things settled down again. For a few hours.

Sometimes there would be no change in temperature, no storm clouds, simply a gratuitous blast that would topple tall beehives - as a child might upset a stack of blocks with her toes. This would often happen in late June, shortly after I'd stacked six or eight empty honey boxes on top of the colonies' brood chambers.

With a strong wind, boxes would tilt and sway. Sitting on uneven ground, some of the hives were already leaning. The wind was sometimes a gentle hand, a finger that slightly shifted the center of balance, selecting a direction that made an unsteady hive fall against its neighbour. The neighbour would invite a third colony to participate. The bees may have been aware of the consequences. Perhaps they rushed to the opposite side of the hive. In despair, one bee would scream out "We're going over!" and they'd all hug each other and wait for the jolt and the crash of beehive against hard prairie earth.

Bad Beekeeping

What do bees do in a drought? Dry weather is not a problem for bees. Some of the world's finest honey crops are produced in desert areas – if irrigation or sub-surface moisture are available. But if it is both extremely hot and dry, the bees' efforts are diverted away from flowers and engaged in gathering water to cool the hive. Wax combs begin to sag and melt at temperatures of about 140 Fahrenheit, 60 Celsius.[101] Bees can lower the temperature in their hive by collecting droplets of honey and strategically exuding these in the hive. The bees fan their tiny wings above the water drops; evaporation removes heat, cools the hive, saves the combs.

As the hive temperature increases, the fanning becomes furious, with wing-beat frequencies of nearly 200 per second and a forward thrust one-third greater than the bee's own weight - if she doesn't cling to the hive's bottom board, the bee would go shooting off into the air.[102] Flapping their wings to move air and cool the hive, bees can survive desert-conditions in domestic hives.

But extended dry periods become droughts; droughts kill plants. Without plants, there's no nectar; without nectar, there's no honey. Bees starve in a prolonged drought.

Alfalfa and sweet clover – both indigenous to semi-desert climates[103] – can survive with little water. Twelve inches a year will keep these plants alive and allow ranchers to cut a modest hay crop. More water yields lush growth - two, three, or more cuttings of hay a year. The Frenchman River Valley averaged ten inches of precipitation. Enough for one hay harvest. But the farmers baled twice a year because the reservoirs – the huge man-made lakes constructed by the federal government during the thirties – permitted two irrigations. One in the spring, the second in mid-summer. Two irrigations every year. Until the mid-eighties. Alfalfa and sweet clover were lush in the valley until the summer of 1984.

It was becoming really dry.

I called Earl Emde.

"Ron! How are the bees?" Earl asked.

"Well, it's getting pretty dry down here," I said.

"It might rain," said Earl. "You know bees can do really well in a desert. I kept bees in the California desert when I was about your age."

I knew.

"Ron," Earl continued. "You could move all your bees up here, but it doesn't pay to chase rain clouds. You never know what can happen. When I had bees in Loma Linda, we had a miserable·flood, right at the end of a drought."

I knew about his flood. Earl lost five hundred hives that night, just about put him out of business. Earl spent the night in a tree, clutching a small lost boy – a stranger – who would have been swept downstream.

"Earl," I said, "what would you do?"

"Well, Ron, I'd put supers on the bees. It might rain. And bees never fill the boxes stacked in the honey shed."

I put empty honey boxes on my hives. I watched for the heavy rain shower that would soon settle the dust, end the drought. I expected the bees would fill the boxes. I waited in vain.

204

Dust Clouds

South of Val Marie, a kilometre west of a grid road, was the Chandler Ranch. Visits to my friends John and Sidney provided lessons in survival. Any problems I may have felt from the pressures of drought and over-work eased a great deal when Sidney, at age 94, would race out of his ranch-house to greet my truck, his face beaming with the inner light of his savior, Jesus Christ. Sidney would boom, "Isn't it a GLORIOUS DAY!"

Sidney Chandler arrived in the badlands in about 1913 - he was perhaps the first of the

Sidney Chandler, Riding and Mending Fences at 94

non-French, non-native settlers. He, his wife, their six children, built a ranch. Within a few years he was possibly the wealthiest man in the district, with several dozen horses and three hundred cows. But, as he readily told me, he mis-read the Bible and had convinced himself that Jesus was coming to collect him and his family. So, in the summer of 1927, after giving the horses and cattle to neighbours, he led the Chandler family to the top of a butte and sat and waited. Quite a long while later, he recognized his enthusiastic misinterpretation of his scriptures, and led the family back to the house. He had to start ranching all over again, though most of the neighbours returned the horses and cattle to Sidney. Later, when the drought of the thirties seared his rangeland and starved his cattle, he survived this, too. "Adversity makes us strong, Ron. Builds our faith," Sidney said.

We stood in his south lawn among huge poplars and a sea of flowers. I complained about the small honey crop, the drought, and I joked that the ten pounds of honey I had brought as a gift for the Chandlers was most of the year's honey crop. Perhaps I sounded a bit bitter. Sparrows mocked me from the poplars. But Sidney said, "Listen to that beautiful music!" Isn't it a GLORIOUS DAY!" And we went into his house to eat supper.

There was a small roasted chicken, which Sidney wouldn't eat. ("Don't eat much meat, haven't for years.") Lots of vegetables, mostly steamed. Broccoli, cauliflower, turnips. Boiled potatoes with parsley and butter. Water to drink, and a small glass of green tea. "No, no, not green tea," one of Sidney's daughters said to me. "You might not like this, but it's very healthy. We chop grass from the lawn and mush it up with a bit of water. Try it. It's very healthy." It was sour and bitter at the same time. I swallowed a tiny sip, put the glass back on the table and agreed that it was probably very healthy.

Bad Beekeeping

Ron, Sidney, John - at the Chandler Ranch

Sidney had something to tell me. He had been listening to my complaints about the drought.

"Ron, God's got a reason for what He tells us and how He tells us. It's your job to figure it out, but the drought might be His lesson for you."

I had no idea of what he was talking about. But the potatoes were good, and I nodded my head towards Mr. Chandler.

During the fall of the driest year, with little honey to harvest, package, or market, I caught up with some of the pesky jobs around the farm.

Over the years, I'd gathered a small assortment of ugly steel drums crammed with bits of wax. I rigged up electric heat belts - tight wire mesh that girded the outside of the wax barrels.

Electricity flowed through these belts. The belts grew hot against the steel wall of the drum. Wax inside the barrel melted. As soon as the contents became liquid, I'd unplug the belts and ladle out hot wax, pour it into plastic moulds, twenty pounds to the mould. The liquid wax would cool, turn yellow and hard.

A barrel might hold a hundred fifty pounds of wax, giving me much more than a fair wage for the time and effort involved. At the bottom of the barrel would be an assortment of caramelized honey and some black ugly stuff called slum gum - a mixture of dirt, bee cocoon shells and burnt wax. I shipped the gunk to someone in Ontario who apparently had use for such stuff.

It was messy work, dealing with hot wax and sticky by-products. But it wasn't particularly hard. I could leave the thermostatically controlled belts on the drum, walk away for a few hours, return to ladle out the wax.

The thermostat, if functioning correctly, keeps the belt from getting too hot. A too hot belt can ignite the wax, which would then combust like a huge ferocious candle.

This primitive system worked fine for the first few barrels. Then the thermostat, the simple piece of electronics that kept the heat belt from getting too hot, failed. It happened after I left the drum alone in the warehouse and walked the hundred metres to my house. Supper was good. Sandy had made spaghetti with a hot sauce. Broccoli on the side. An hour later, I glanced out a window towards the honey shed and it looked like I had left a light on. Except the light flickering in the shed's window would die down, then grow bright, die again, then become brighter.

Dust Clouds

I had a fire. I needed help. Did the village of Val Marie have a fire department? I didn't know. I remembered the fire truck from the parade a few years earlier. I found a listing on the one-page phone book for the town. In big, bold letters: FIRE DEPT. I dialed quickly.

"Hello, yeh?" someone was saying.

"I have a fire!" I shouted.

"Oh?"

"Is this the fire department?"

"This is Barney's Garage."

"Barney's? 298-5555? Is that what I dialed?"

"Yea, but we're not the fire department. This is the garage."

"But this is the fire number in the phone book," I said. I had to be right. I'd dialed the right number. "Does Val Marie have a fire department?"

The young man working for Barney was silent for a while. I was afraid he may have gone out to pump gas, but then he answered, "I don't know. Maybe you should call the Hutterite Colony."

I hung up and raced out into the dark, guided to the building by the light of the fire inside. Five minutes had passed from the moment the flames caught my attention to the time I reached my honey shed. The burning barrel had filled my building with thick, dirty smoke, but the flames that searched for something new to ignite had barely licked the ceiling of the shed.

Rafters were blackened, scorched, but not on fire. I didn't have a burning warehouse - just a huge, hissing candle, confined within an old steel drum. I found a lid for the barrel and let the flames sear the hairs on my arms and eye lashes as I dropped the cover over the drum. Starved for air, the fire died. I had a mess in the shop. It would take days of scraping and washing and painting to get the tar and smoke smudges off the walls. But I still had my shed.

Hot Liquid Beeswax Cooled into Yellow Wax Cakes

Beekeepers can't survive on the proceeds from a few pounds of old wax. I needed a big honey crop, but I didn't get one. Luckily, I had taken most of the money from my good years and paid off the mortgage on my Saskatchewan honey farm. I was thirty years old, and had no debt on my two hundred thousand dollars worth of bees, warehouse, home, and trucks.

Other beekeepers, older, wiser, but with more debt than I, were also feeling the effects of the drought. The government set up a complicated system of crop insurance for beekeepers. After a fixed deductible, it paid farmers part of the money they would get from an average crop. Premiums were based on gross income each year.[104]

Crop insurance had long existed for wheat and canola producers. Beekeepers thought it would be a good idea to get similar coverage; some had been talking to the province about a honey crop insurance program for years. I lived in Val Marie, a place with big irrigation reservoirs and much sunshine, so I didn't believe I would need the crop insurance other beekeepers were soliciting. When it was first discussed, I rejected the idea of buying insurance on a crop. I could self-insure for the bad years. But lucky for me, disaster struck before the program began. I was able to sign on. Crop insurance paid me thirty thousand dollars the worst year of the drought. Like many farmers, I discovered the money wasn't enough. I had bought package bees from Australia to replace my winter losses. I needed sugar to feed my bees and gasoline to feed my trucks. It cost thousands of dollars to run my little honey farm.

As the drought worsened, some farmers left Val Marie. But most stayed - they'd been through hard times before, they would see good crops again, then perhaps another drought. The circle that never ends. They borrowed money, mortgaged their land. Gambled their future. But the drought sent others on their way. Arid fields cracked and splintered families.

Some farmers moved on, but I was determined to stay. I would find ways to produce more honey and to earn more money from the honey I made. I had to get innovative - figure out a way to turn a small amount of honey into a big profit. I needed a new product. Something like Honey Fudge.

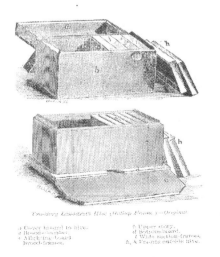

**Langstroth's Inventions were Better than Mine .
This is his Original 1853 Bee Hive.**

Honey Fudge

A bee gathers honey for energy; pollen for protein. Mixed together in the hive, she creates bee-bread. It's a fortified food. Preserved. Nutritious. She rubs honey into cells, stirring with head, tongue, forelegs. Bee-bread, a colourful blend that soothes the hungry.

But the bee has another product, more difficult to procure and more potent as a life-saving balm. Propolis is the sticky resin secreted from the buds of trees. Bees tug tiny pieces, tote the specks of brown resin back to the nest. As an antibiotic, it keeps infectious diseases at bay. As a sealant, it plugs drafty holes and gaping cracks in the nest. Propolis glues up sources of waste, preserves scarce heat. A minor product, but a resource bees discovered to improve their chance of survival when conditions become bad.

The drought was a disaster. But the Val Marie farmers told me droughts only last three or four years. It could rain any day.

As long as prices were good, I figured I could still make a living producing honey. Even if it were only a small amount. Honey prices had been high through the early eighties – I'd sold one semi-load to a honey packer in Orangeville, Ontario, for seventy-five cents a pound. The Hutterites paid eighty-five; ranchers and farmers a dollar. I might survive with small crops for a few years, as long as I got a good price for the bit of honey I could produce. I needed high prices, but the market crashed.

Wholesale honey was worth seventy cents a pound in 1984; forty cents in 1986. A small-time commercial beekeeper producing a hundred thousand pounds of honey would earn thirty thousand dollars less in 1986 than in 1984.

Honey prices fell largely because of a new law put in place to protect American beekeepers from foreign honey production. It became more lucrative for packers and brokers to buy American. At about the same time, Chinese beekeeping came of age.

Thirty years earlier, there were few honeybees in China. In a single generation, colony count went from a handful of hives to eight million. Five hundred thousand new beekeepers. Many Chinese beekeepers produced only a hundred kilograms of honey, but there were a lot of beekeepers. China became the largest exporter of honey in the world.[105] These new Chinese beekeepers sold their crop to government-operated co-operatives. Chinese beekeepers received twenty cents per pound; however, with a typical production of one hundred kilos, it earned them forty or fifty dollars. A nice supplement to a family's welfare. Government-regulated processors in China bought it for twenty cents; they graded, cleaned, filtered, and repackaged the honey. It looked good and sold well on the world market for about thirty-five cents a pound, delivered to Japan, Germany, and the USA - traditional customers for Canadian surplus honey.

I couldn't compete with thirty-five cent a pound Chinese honey. I needed twice as much to pay my bills. I looked for new markets for my honey, hoping that someone, somewhere, would be able to offer more money. Derek Alen extended help. Derek had

209

started a new honey farm two hundred kilometers away, in Maple Creek. He and Ben Broderick, an ex-cop, operated two thousand hives. They produced honey similar to mine – white, mild honey from the nectar of alfalfa and clover. Derek had an offer from a Toronto exporter who would pay sixty-five cents a pound for nice white Canadian honey. This was a lot of money. She could offer this much because her German clients wanted pure legume honey – clover and alfalfa. They wouldn't buy the honey if it was from canola blossoms. Lucky for me, canola wasn't grown in Val Marie in 1984. It was too hot, too dry, and the soil was considered too poor for the crop. Val Marie honey was as pure a clover-alfalfa honey you could find on earth. Until 1985, when canola arrived.

I didn't have new honey yet, so I sent a sample of the previous year's crop to the lady in Toronto. She analyzed the honey's pollen to determine floral source. The buyers didn't want canola-tainted honey. Had to be 95% pure clover. In a few days, the exporter phoned from Ontario. She sounded like Reverend David: "This is the best honey I've ever seen. I'll take all you produce this year!"

In the summer of 1985, a few Val Marie farmers were experimenting with canola. Canola seed was fetching a nice price, better than wheat, so five hundred acres were planted in small irrigated patches around the valley. When my new honey crop was in, I hauled fifteen drums of Val Marie honey west to Maple Creek. The trip took two hours, Erika sat in her car seat. Together, we counted cows and grain elevators, driving on and on along south Saskatchewan's grid roads. When we reached Derek's shop, I backed my truck to his concrete dock. We stacked the barrels in his warehouse. A month later, samples were drawn. My load was rejected, it had 12% canola pollen mixed in with the clover and alfalfa. I lost the sale, drove back to Maple Creek, reloaded the honey, hauled it back to Val Marie, sold it to a less discerning customer - for much less money - in eastern Canada.

**Selling Honey a Pound at a Time from the Tail Gate
of a Truck in Swift Current, Saskatchewan**

Honey Fudge

It was obvious I wasn't having much success selling my honey in big steel drums for top dollar. I needed to find a better way to get a good price.

I decided to fill more of the small retail containers, and expand my delivery route. I began driving hundreds of kilometres to peddle honey at stores in exotic places. Gravelbourg. Mankota. Frontier. Shaunavon. Grocers in a dozen towns proudly stocked my honey. And it sold. But how much honey can you sell in McCord, Saskatchewan, population forty? One hundred twenty pounds a year.

Driving hundreds of kilometres a month on the honey route kept a steady, but small, supply of cash flowing through the house. All the McCords and Shaunavons added up to twelve thousand pounds of honey a year, sold at a price which was twice what I could get directly from a packer. This was an extra six thousand dollars - well, actually, about three thousand dollars after I paid for the expensive little jars and their labels. And paid for the gasoline I needed to drive out to all those towns, villages, hamlets. I donated my labour - the honey route tied me up four days every month.

We sold some honey by the side of the road, set up at the parking lot of Canadian Tire in Swift Current. It was arduous, marginally rewarding work. Wind would blow dirt in our eyes and dirt onto plastic honey containers. Often a pail would tip over on the hundred twenty kilometre trek from Val Marie to the city and it would take half an hour to clean the sticky mess. But nothing was ever completely clean and honey bears and money would cling to our fingers, working themselves free with effort. However, the honey sometimes sold well and we could occasionally make reasonable wages.

With Reverend David's help, my sales to the Hutterite colonies also expanded. Hutterites in North Dakota, Manitoba, and Alberta had Val Marie honey on their tables. A few of the colonies had their own bees, but bought my honey for their kitchens while selling their own production at the local markets. Sales to the Hutterites reached twenty thousand pounds. By filtering the honey and pouring it into plastic containers that the Hutterites supplied, I was able to charge more than when the honey was put into big steel drums and sent by the semi-load to bottlers in eastern Canada.

I saw a nice display of favourably priced (if you are the producer) honey at a big health food store in Saskatoon. It got me thinking. If I could sell a hundred thousand pounds of honey at two hundred dollars a pound, I'd have twenty million dollars. So, I went home and started to pour honey into tiny 100 gram crystal clear glass jars. The crystal, the designer labels,[106] and the ribbons tied neatly around the lids cost a bundle, but once this stuff started to sell at the Val Marie grocery store, I was going to be rich.

The first problem, of course, was getting the honey into the little jars. Pouring honey into huge barrels is pretty easy. Open a tap, fill it up. There was little cleaning, grading, or fussing involved.

In the years before I participated in beekeeping, some beekeepers started by dumping a gallon or two of water in the bottom of the honey barrel. This was not done to clean dust out of the drum. Water is pretty cheap. When honey is mixed in with water, the beekeeper can sell the barrel of honey to a packer who will pay the same price as he would for undiluted honey. Sometimes, selling a few thousand pounds of water to honey packers for fifty cents a pound was the only profit a beekeeper earned. Beekeepers can't do this any more. The packers caught on to the trick and bought optical refraction gadgets that told them how much water was in the honey. They started rejecting products that were watered down. And they paid a premium for low-moisture honey.[107]

Sandy Fills a Barrel with 662 Pounds of Honey.
This Takes about Three Minutes.

These days, to fill a barrel with honey, we start with a clean empty drum. No water on the bottom. Open a valve. Honey streams from the bottom of a huge tank.

In about three minutes, the barrel is full. The 660 pound drum gets a lid, the lid gets a label, the beekeeper gets a cheque.

But it works differently when you try to fill teeny little crystal jars. First, you need to buy a forty-thousand dollar packing system. This still didn't seem expensive, because I knew if I could produce a really big crop and pack my entire production in little jars, I'd make twenty million dollars.

But I didn't have forty thousand dollars to invest in a modern packing system. I didn't buy the shiny new machinery. I designed something much cheaper myself, but it filled jars more slowly than I expected. It took me days to get it running correctly. Sometime the following week, I had my first case of 24 jars filled with honey. I priced it at $15 per bottle - I'd still be making $60 a pound and could still be a millionaire within a few months. A friend, though, said no one would pay $30 for a jar of honey. She said the store might sell some for $9.99, but not for thirty bucks.

"No, no," I corrected her. "I want fifteen dollars, not thirty dollars, a bottle."

Anne took a moment to explain how stores make their money. A slow selling novelty item like my gimmicky honey jars would be priced at about ten dollars. I'd get five. The grocery guy had to make something. Stunned by the use of words like slow-selling-novelty-gimmick, I missed what she was telling me. Anne repeated, "Nine, ten

Honey Fudge

dollars. Tops. Probably less. That means you might get five." She was almost certainly correct. But at five dollars a pound, a hundred thousand pounds of honey would still give me half a million dollars. So, I'd be a millionaire in two years - if the drought ended and I had normal crops again. And I wasn't including expenses in my calculations.

I realized that Anne was right about the grocery store markup. Every store owner in the small towns of western Canada has a gorgeous, luxurious mansion high on a hill somewhere. And a winter home in Arizona. The money obviously comes from the profit they make selling honey.

It surprised me when the local store owner refused to buy the entire case of 24 jars. "We'll try three," he said. I was utterly bewildered at his incomprehensible lack of business acumen.

"Three cases?"

"Three jars."

"OK." I found myself agreeing, "I'll write up an invoice." "No," replied the storekeeper, "Why don't we do this on consignment? I'll pay you, eh, if the stuff sells." I decided not to pack all my honey in tiny crystal jars. Standard barrels, honey jars, and pails would have to do.

Sandy Making Honey Fudge

I didn't sell many tiny fancy jars, but grocery stores in south Saskatchewan were marketing my honey for three dollars a pound and giving me over half of what they collected. I had a steady route, twenty-three little stores in hamlets and villages scattered around southwest Saskatchewan. I was learning a lesson about value-added products. Put something into a small jar, add a cute label, and it's worth five times as much as the same product in a big gray steel barrel, but it takes much more effort to sell.

I figured if I went a step further – made something even more exotic from the honey – I'd make enough money to stay in business. Even if foreign competition brought low prices and the drought gave me a small crop. I thought about a honey product that would be popular and easy to make and market. Easier than honey.

I bought an abandoned restaurant and converted it into a honey fudge factory. The diner's tables and chairs – long unused in a town with a shrinking population –

were replaced by shipping cartons and bags of carob, sunflower seeds, almonds.

The kitchen was still a kitchen – a place to melt the carob and honey and mix in seeds and nuts. We poured the candy onto a slab where it cooled. We cut it and weighed it into plastic trays. I interviewed with CKSW and we had photos in the newspaper.[108] The wonder food of the future. Carob instead of chocolate. Honey instead of sugar. Everyone wanted some. All the health food stores in Swift Current – both of them – took twenty pounds of Honey Fudge. It sold out. We replaced it. But then the newspapers and radio stations went away, pursuing some other exciting new technological break-through. The candy began to sell more slowly. A few pounds a month. At great expense, I extended my delivery route to Regina and Saskatoon, hundreds of kilometers away. Again, I was busy for a few days, but then the product sold more slowly. The plastic trays that held the fudge collected dust on the store shelves. I had my fifteen minutes of fame. It was someone else's turn. I continued to make and sell a few hundred pounds of candy a year, but it wasn't a wildly successful venture.

There were other problems trying to run the honey business. The mid-1980s were a time of great inflation. Prices were out of control on everything except farm products. Grain and farm produce prices went down. Honey fell in half. Oil and gas doubled in price. Wax went down thirty per cent. Vehicles went up thirty per cent. The cost of beehives, nails, straining screens, and extractors rose so quickly that equipment dealers quit publishing prices in their catalogs. They stuffed little sheets of paper with the month's latest prices into their brochures. Banks charged more, too. With high inflation, they had to raise interest rates weekly so they could keep making money.

With the drought-stricken honey crop and low prices, I was beginning to worry about feeding the family. Literally. The Hutterites took some extra honey, gave us vegetables and milk. Often they wouldn't take any honey. They'd hide a few bags of corn and potatoes and cabbage in the truck and we'd find this when we got home. There was no meat in the freezer and Erika complained. "I like meat." We bought cheap cuts from a farmer. Then, on a cold October morning, Buzz Trottier called. I hadn't seen him in weeks.

Six in the morning. "You sleeping?"
I hadn't been asleep. I was nervous, worried, awake at four.
"You want to go hunting?" Buzz asked.
"I don't have a rifle, just a 12 gauge."
"I'll loan you my 30-30."
"I don't have a license."
"We'll wake up Kermie. He'll sell you one."
"I've never hunted before. Besides, it's too cold."
"I'll show you how... And it's never too cold to hunt."
"But Buzz, it's twenty below."
". . . I know, but it'll be OK," Buzz said.

Honey Fudge

I had run out of excuses. Besides, the honey crop had been poor and we needed the food that a deer might provide. Buzz was offering to teach me, loan me his gun, take me to a place where I could shoot a deer.

At 6:30, I paid five dollars for a hunting license. At 7, Buzz dropped me out of his truck at the end of a ravine on his ranch.

There I stood. Loaded gun. Safety off. Tripping along a trail at the bottom of a deep coulee. It was quiet, except for my steps crunching stiff snow. My bare fingers were freezing, but my head and shoulders, sheltered by a toque and hood were getting warm.

I walked less than ten minutes. I glanced up at the canyon ridge, now eighty feet above me. An enormous white tail deer looked down. I pointed. Fired. The deer fell. Buzz heard the shot, drove back to where he had left me. He prepared the dead warm animal for hauling and together we pulled it into his truck box. 7:30.

Buzz Dropped me from his Truck, not Far from Seventy-Mile Butte.
In a Few Minutes, a Deer was Dead.

Buzz showed me how to prepare the meat, slicing hunks of venison off the carcass while it dangled from exposed rafters in a shed. I spent two hours alone, butchering. A hundred twenty pounds of food. We ate it all by early summer. I'm not sure what I learned from the episode. The hunt was too easy - I never hunted again. Did I learn that a clever human with a gun can drop an old animal? Only later did I think about it in this way. At the time, my thoughts were far away from the hunt and the dead animal. As I cut and wrapped the meat I thought of what Erika had said ("I like meat.") and I knew I was doing the right thing.

215

Bad Beekeeping

And I thought about the few words Buzz had spoken to me while we rode together in his truck, carrying the food back to my shed.

"People like you don't stay here," he said, "They move on. But they take part of this country with them."

I had no plans to move on. Somehow I was surviving in this rough beautiful country. The wind, the dust, the grasshoppers. Low prices, small crops. I knew I could survive anything man and nature threw at me.

I was wrong.

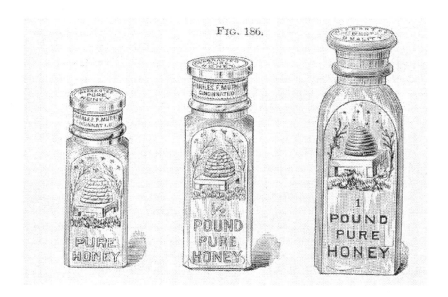

Fancy Crystal Honey Jar Display
from Professor Cook's 1883 Beekeeper's Guide Book

Mites

Two hives. A strong hive; a weak one. They sit side-by-side, oblivious to the other's presence until times get tough. One hot day nectar is unexpectedly scarce in the field, the weak colony is vulnerable, open to attacks. The war begins slowly, with a few robber bees snooping and sniffing at the entrance of the weak hive. Finding the doorway poorly guarded, they sneak in, steal a bit of honey, slip back to their home colony. Soon dozens, then hundreds, of robbers from the strong hive attack the weak and poorly defended. The vicious attack results in the death of the small colony, but all the spent energy and stolen goods produce little gain for the powerful thief. The strong hive also suffers - its robber bees become lazy, unwilling to work the fields again. Many of the victorious bees, worn and tattered from their frenzied attack, age quickly and perish.

There were about a dozen of us. Young American immigrant beekeepers, scattered from Val Marie to Nipawin, and up into the Peace River district of northern British Columbia. Some Canadian beekeepers saw the noisy newcomers as stiff competition. Others, of course, took the arrival of Americans as an interesting learning opportunity.

But in the early 1980s, people started to talk about closing the border.[109]

"Canadian bees and Canadian beekeepers should be making Canadian honey," a young lady told me as her husband served up another portion of pasta. Both were very bright, very nice folks. Young Canadian beekeepers. We talked about Americans.

"But I'm Canadian," I said.

"Canadian? I thought you were born in the States... but we don't mean *you*," the young woman said. Pointing at me with her fork.

"Just other Americans, the pushy ones," said her husband. It was confusing, and probably difficult, for them to be so nice and so thoughtless at the same time.

Beekeepers in British Columbia and Ontario seemed most keen to stop bees entering Canada from the States. A border closure offered these folks two advantages: sales of bees and queens to beekeepers on the prairies, and higher honey prices.

Most American packages were purchased by prairie beekeepers. Border closure would cut the number of hives kept in Manitoba, Saskatchewan, and Alberta. Fewer bees on the prairies mean less honey production. A scarcity could result in higher honey prices across Canada.

Bees wintered well in the milder parts of southern Ontario and coastal British Columbia. Spring arrived earlier than on the prairies. It was possible, in theory, to economically produce and sell queens and packages to western beekeepers – replacing the American source of bees. The political environment was ripe, but a compelling excuse to keep American packages out was lacking until the summer of 1984.

Bad Beekeeping

Meanwhile, I'd sold my American farm and hives. But I was still bringing bees north from Florida. I had made an arrangement with the new owner of my southern hives - Clifton would give me packages and queens every year instead of money. He had little cash, but he was likeable, genuinely honest, and I assumed I could always get bees from him – a few hundred packages every year for the next ten years. I had made a deal with a poor beekeeper which I knew he could fulfill. I assumed I'd always be able to drive to Florida, load up my bees, return home. I never expected that my biggest beekeeping troubles would be with the Canadian government.

Bees have a lot of enemies. Bears crush their hives, eat their young. Skunks, opossums, and raccoons sneak around the hives and eat a few bees, gobble a bit of honey. Smaller vermin, like mice and wasps invade the nests and kill and plunder. Microscopic pests also take their toll.

The tiniest of the pests include foulbrood. Foulbrood diseases are caused by spores that sprout and mature in developing bee larvae and kill them. But there are other tiny creatures, too. Fungi cause stone or chalk brood and mummify developing bees. Another organism - nosema - grows in the adult bees' stomachs, spreading indigestion and deadly dysentery.

In addition to trouble with bears, skunks, mice, wasps, spores, fungi, and viruses, bees may host several types of mites. Most are harmless. Hitch-hikers on the bees' backs, using *apis mellifera* as aircraft. Other mites cause varying degrees of destruction. The worst mite pest is *Varroa destructor*, but something called the honeybee tracheal mite is often blamed for bee deaths. The tracheal mite is smaller, lives in bees' breathing tubes and usually causes little damage to bees.[110] Honey bee tracheal mite has been known for a century in England and northern Germany, and is not considered a major pest there.[111] But multiplied a hundred times under a microscope, tracheal mite is very scary. The varroa mite doesn't need to be magnified a hundred times by a lens. It is huge, easily seen by the naked eye. It clings to the outer surface of a bee, sucking out its life. Varroa is a major problem for beekeepers. Tracheal mite is not. Neither existed in North America when I began my beekeeping career.

The mostly benign tracheal mite appeared in the USA, in Texas, July 1984.[112] It incited apparent panic among many government regulators and bee scientists. Beekeepers were less concerned. But bureaucrats – and this includes many research scientists – survive on government funding. A good case was made that the tracheal mite could devastate beekeeping. It needed to be studied, regulated. Civil servants require regulations to justify their employment. Beekeepers dread regulation. Regulations mean quarantines, destruction of hives, and plenty of government interference. A serious battle ensued.

After its discovery in Texas, the mite was found within months in New York, North Dakota, and then Florida. It may have been in the United States - and possibly Canada - for several years before it was found in Texas, considering its widespread occurrence once people started looking for it. [113] Looking for tracheal mite is tedious and destructive. The mite lives inside the breathing tubes of bees and you only find it if you collect bees, kill them, dissect them, and study their stained slices with a microscope.

Mites

Europeans have the most experience with the honey bee tracheal mite. Some people assumed the mite killed bees in England's south, starting out from the Isle of Wight, in 1905. But other researchers doubted the mite killed many bees, they implicated a variety of factors.

Dr. Leslie Bailey, a British scientist and expert apiculture pathologist, suggested tracheal mites were usually a minor pest. In particular, he disagreed with the widespread notion that the honey bee tracheal mite had once decimated the bee population of England, and pointed to documents printed at the time which showed beekeepers were producing large honey crops and not having significant colony losses during the early part of the past century.[114]

Dr. Bailey visited a North American beekeepers' meeting where he was snubbed by some boisterous Canadians (in Tampa, Florida, of all places), but even worse, ignored by many North American research scientists. He was the world's leading expert on the honeybee tracheal mite – Bailey had studied the pest for twenty years and used hundreds of test hives. His words of advice were rejected in favour of a study conducted one summer by a young Canadian scientist using just a few hives of bees.[115] Some of the hives did poorly. This was blamed on mites. It was the sort of data required for urging border closure.[116]

It took only a few years before tracheal mites were "relegated to relatively minor notoriety," in the words of one Canadian researcher. (Dr. Winston, in his book From Where I Sit, writes, "tracheal mites have been relegated to relatively minor notoriety, if not in their impact, then certainly in the attention they are receiving from beekeepers and researchers.")[117]

Twenty years after their arrival, few states test for the presence of tracheal mites. Beekeepers use cheap and wholesome treatments (menthol, vegetable and natural essential oils) to control mite populations; or, don't bother to treat for tracheal mites at all. But in 1984, when they were first discovered in North America, the regulatory efforts to confine and eliminate this mite were draconian.

Our society has evolved far from the ancient Babylonian codes of Hammurabi. Four thousand years ago, the wise leader wanted to create a charter - a set of laws - that would assist the administration of his vast empire. Hammurabi's legal experts, drawing up a set of rules for governing the people, tried to make the law simple. Instead of publishing reams of clay tablets describing how a contractor should build a house, there was only a single, but very effective, rule: "If a builder builds a house and if the house collapses and kills someone, the builder shall be executed."[118] That's incentive. It wasn't necessary to have building inspectors looking over the contractor's shoulders, checking the amount of sand, gravel, straw, and mud used to make the blocks that built the house. No one tested the tensile strength of the roof. No one had to. That's how Hammurabi conducted the business of government thirty-seven hundred years ago. And that's how most beekeepers want their government regulators to conduct affairs today.

Interference only when necessary to save someone's life. Otherwise, beekeepers really don't want to see or hear from anyone who works for the government. Most beekeepers would like Hammurabi's code. Government simplified and out of people's lives and affairs.

No one has a greater interest in the health of a business than the person who owns the business. If a pest – a bear or a mite – can cost a beekeeper money, the beekeeper will take care of it, or go out of business. And they will certainly do this without the interference of petty civil servants. Many beekeepers asked the government to stand down. But others argued that if the majority of beekeepers wanted the border closed (not necessarily because of the mite), then the wishes of a majority in a democracy must be followed. Science by popular vote. It leads to disaster - the perpetuation of antiquated traditions, ineffective techniques, and expensive mistakes long after basic truths are exposed.

Governments inaugurated a containment policy. Counties in New York and Florida were quarantined. In other states, hundreds of colonies of bees were poisoned by government agents; several beekeepers were bankrupted. In Canada, a young Manitoba beekeeper was among the first found with tracheal mites in his bees - they probably arrived in packages he purchased from Texas. Packages which were inspected in Texas and declared "apparently mite free." His 852 hives of bees were destroyed by Manitoba government employees - bureaucrats thinking they could arrest the flow of mites. The farmer threatened legal action. He argued that the mites were widespread, that he wasn't the only beekeeper with tracheal mites. He may have been right, but it was a sample from *his* colonies that tested positive and there was pressure to do something about it. The government of Manitoba poisoned his bees and offered him a cash settlement, on condition that he quit beekeeping.[119]

Jim Powers, the respected and talented American beekeeper with 30,000 hives, wrote a letter to me – and many others in the honey business. Jim urged the immediate cessation of all efforts to control the spread of the tracheal mite. As he said in his brief missive, regulation had already resulted in one death [a suicide], at least five bankruptcies, and extermination [by government regulators] of 25,000 colonies.[120]

Some beekeepers reasonably argued that it might be worth destroying other people's bees if it were known that the mite causes serious problems, if it were an untreatable syndrome, and if it could be stopped by mass extermination. But facts seemed to indicate the mite wasn't so serious,[121] was easily treatable, and was destined to spread regardless of quarantines and bee poisonings.[122] In England, the place the mite was first discovered, I found beekeepers are much more concerned with honey prices, wax moths, and genetically altered pollen grains.[123] Those Europeans who treat against tracheal mites usually apply menthol, which reduces tracheal mite populations to nearly zero.[124] Or they don't bother to treat their bees at all. This information was readily available to the people making decisions to exterminate bees with tracheal mites.[125]

In North America, in 1984 and 1985, the treatment against honeybee tracheal mites was the massive killing of bees. Honey bees and bee equipment were smothered under tarps, poisonous gases were introduced. It soon became apparent - even to the regulating people - that a wholesale slaughter of honeybees wouldn't stop the spread of the mites. However, as late as 1987, the chief apiary inspector for Saskatchewan, Mr.

John Gruszka, still felt massive killing of bees was the way to go. He urged at the Manitoba beekeepers' annual meeting that "although the province must do a better job of locating the infected hives, he believed the eradication program is working."[126]

One problem was the testing and examination system. Inspectors - underpaid and overworked - could only select small random samples of bees for dissection. The subject bees were killed, sliced into thin wafers, their trachea examined through stereo-microscopes. Not every bee in a colony can be checked, unless every bee in the hive is killed for examination. A single hive has fifty thousand bees, only a dozen might be selected by inspectors for dissection. In an apiary of fifty hives, perhaps five colonies were sampled. As a result, the chances of finding a mite at initial stages of infestation was about one in ten thousand.[127]

Often, beekeepers whose bees were without finds were allowed to move their hives, even if other people's hives in the pasture next door had tracheal mites. Bees with tracheal mites may be healthy most of their life, even while carrying the parasite in their breathing tubes. Affected bees fly, visit other bees at little honey bee parties on flower pods or at neighbouring hives. The mites continued to move from hive to hive, area to area. More states reported finds. The mite spread rapidly, covering twenty-eight states in three years and most of the continent soon after.[128]

As if slicing and dicing bees for viewing under a microscope wasn't tragic enough, a secondary issue with regulation was the irregular and arbitrary legal jurisdictions to which quarantines were applied. A county or state was declared 'mite-free' on the basis of low-level sampling while a neighbouring state was declared 'mite-infested' when a single positive find was discovered. Some states, beekeepers claimed, were not vigorously looking for mites and those states were therefore *apparently* mite-free, while other states pursued the mite carefully, and consequently beekeepers in those jurisdictions had the stigma (and tribulations) of keeping bees in known mite-infested areas.[129]

The entire honeybee tracheal mite mess was one of the biggest boondoggles in the history of agricultural science and regulation. It seemed that anything that could be done wrong, was.

With tracheal mites appearing in more and more places in the USA, Canada banned more and more states from shipping bees north.[130] For me, it meant I would spend lots of money on packages from New Zealand and Australia. Somehow it made more sense to Canadian regulators to have beekeepers cart bees in by air freight from the other side of the globe. It was impossible to thoroughly search those countries to be sure bees were not carrying any *new* pests from the southern hemisphere into North America.[131]

Who were we protecting when the border was closed? Not the consumer – the market place benefits from competition and high levels of production. More bees. More honey. More pollination. More food. Cheaper food. A few retroactive souls would have us turn back the clock, to 1491, say. But we have to feed six billion people. We can't do it using fifteenth century technology.

Bad Beekeeping

I called my brother, he was raising queens in Florida, making honey in Wisconsin.

"What's the answer? What should the Canadian government do?" I asked.

"Well, if they close the border, beekeeping will go downhill in Canada. Maybe honey prices will rise for American producers," David said.

"Should they close the border?" I asked.

"That would be fine with most of us down here," David said. "But I guess it'll be a big problem for you and the other beekeepers in Saskatchewan."

I pressed my brother for more. "What would be best for Canada?"

"Well," David paused. "you know the smartest thing they could do up there would be to let you guys truck your hives down to California for the winter. Haul the full hives down. It's pretty stupid to let bees winter in Canada – it's cold, they die of starvation. I mean, you could take five hundred hives south, one semi-load, get paid twenty-five thousand dollars for almond pollination, split the hives into a thousand, all with new queens. That's what your neighbors in Montana and North Dakota are doing right now. They make a lot of money and have strong hives with new queens every year. If the people running the show up your way were on the ball, they'd throw the border wide open and let you guys winter all your bees in California."

"We'd be over-run with American beekeepers coming up from California,' I said.

"Over-run? Hardly." David said. "You've got enough room for millions of hives. Canada could use more bees and more beekeepers."

It's been suggested that if Canada allow American bees, then Mexican beekeepers should be allowed to move their hives into the USA. Dr. Roger Morse, of Cornell University in New York, would agree. Writing in Bee Culture, February, 1998, he says, "A fear of spreading bee diseases has been the excuse to keep borders closed in the past, but that thought has no validity today since we all have the same problems. I can envision a time when bees are trucked into the Yucatan and other parts of Mexico in the fall, requeened or split three for one, and moved to California for almond pollination in February. They might then be used to pollinate another crop in northern California, Oregon or Washington before being hauled to the Peace River District of northern Alberta for honey production... I expect there will be resistance to moving colonies across borders, but change is in the works!"[132]

Canada has eight million acres of canola. Ten million acres of clovers and alfalfa.[133] Each year these flowers yield enough nectar to furnish ten million hives of bees two hundred pounds of honey each. China, a crowded country smaller in area than Canada, has eight million hives of bees. Ten million hives could be kept in Canada, but we keep scarcely over half a million.[134] Canada could produce a billion pounds of honey a year, but it produces sixty million pounds[135] - a second-rate country in terms of volume, somewhat behind Mexico and Argentina. Canada is a huge and potentially viable agricultural country - yet Hungary and France frequently out-produce our beekeepers.[136]

We have a pathetic little industry, generating a few million dollars in terms of honey sales. Is it any wonder there is so little money available to support research scientists in Guelph and Simon Fraser University? Is it any wonder we can get so little enthusiasm to find protection for bees from pesticide applicators? One chemical company's research budget for better bug sprays (and other initiatives in improved agriculture) is four times the gross receipts of all the beekeepers in Canada.[137]

So we should open the doors. Canadian beekeepers could move hives south to pollinate almonds and citrus trees and come home for the summer to make big crops of honey on the prairies. For fifty years, beekeepers have been doing exactly this in the Dakotas, Minnesota and Montana. They have mites and other creatures in their hives, but they still make enormous honey crops. They still keep a lot of bees.

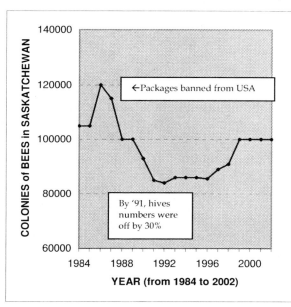

Colony Count in Saskatchewan Crashed from its Peak in 1986, the Year Before Packages from the USA were Banned   - Source: Statistics Canada

From 1984 to 2003, Canadian decisions have blocked the free exchange of American hives. Saskatchewan suffered seriously. Its honey bee industry was virtually moribund, stagnant.[138]

Bureaucratic bungling helped the number of colonies drop over 30% in Saskatchewan, from 120,000 in 1986 to 84,000 three years later.[139] Clearly, the Saskatchewan model (a tightly sealed border to keep American hives out) is a dismal failure.

Across the invisible line to the south, North Dakota beekeepers increased twenty percent from 280,000 in 1986 to 348,000 hives today.[140] North Dakota farmers, the ones growing alfalfa, clovers, canola, and sunflowers, had extra pollination for their crops. Beekeepers also did well – their receipts from honey production went from 10 to 50 million dollars a year.[141]

The smart consensus is to open the border. What's the worst thing that could happen? American beekeepers may start trucking thousands of hives of bees into Canada. But Canadians could move their bees south for the winter. Free competition and movement would encourage better beekeeping, the exchange of ideas, and a stronger and bigger honey industry. It would be nice to see Canada producing as much honey as Mexico, Argentina, and perhaps even China!

In Val Marie, we still had the drought. And low honey prices. I didn't hire my summer crew - Charlie and Merlin were out of work. My brother Joe would phone occasionally from Wisconsin. He had begun a fresh life, growing flowers and trees which he sold to folks around his new place in New Holstein. I told him he was doing the right thing, prospects were bleak in Canada.

Bad Beekeeping

Drought. Low prices. Now it looked like our American source of cheap packages to replace winter losses would disappear. I thought that if I attended some of the important bee meetings, explained the issues, beekeepers would understand and keep their supply of bees open. My main argument centered on the idea that since tracheal mites existed elsewhere in the world and weren't a big issue, the cost of the problem was less than the cost of the solution – government interference, regulations, border closures.

However, it was apparent that beekeepers at the big meeting in Saskatoon weren't very sympathetic.

"Don't forget," Steve told me. "A lot of these beekeepers don't get all the facts. They don't subscribe to bee journals. The only material they get about beekeeping comes from the chief inspector, John Gruszka. He mails his *Bee Lines* to them every few weeks.[142] You can't fight much of a battle when the government has a monopoly on information."

"The *Bee Lines*? I've heard it called the *Bee Lies*," I said.

"Don't go that far, but you're definitely fighting against a well-oiled machine when you take on the government here," said Steve. "Any beekeeper who needs money or wants to expand goes to the bank or the federal government – the Farm Credit Corporation. The bankers may call Gruszka to ask if the loan applicant is a good beekeeper. Sure, he'll be honest and fair, but if you're a beekeeper, you don't want to do anything to bug John Gruszka. And he wants the border closed."

I realized beekeepers at this meeting weren't going to let me continue bringing my bees in from the USA. I knew that without my American packages, I would need to buy bees from Australia and New Zealand and it would cost me thousands of dollars a year. And since it was autumn in the south Pacific when it was spring in North America, the offshore queens were likely to be less virile than continental ones – the best queens are reared in the spring, not fall. I wasn't the only one thinking this way. Within the biggest honey producing district in the country - along the Peace River Valley and into the northern agriculture districts of Alberta - the majority of beekeepers supported keeping the US border open.[143] They knew that without cheap, high-quality American packages, many of them would go bankrupt. And this group had elected the federal government's agriculture minister. He was on their side.[144] But too many beekeepers – in the east, in Saskatchewan, in B.C., were being told that a border closure would be in their interest.

At the beekeeping convention, I read aloud a letter I'd received from a French research scientist working in Texas. The letter that said the tracheal mite was not a serious problem.[145] I quoted from Bailey and from the USDA news releases.[146] But there was a well-planned and well-presented counter-argument and it made beekeepers nervous. "What if Mr. Miksha is wrong, and the mite kills all our bees?"

It wasn't just Canadians who debated at the meeting. A select group of American queen breeders also spoke. A commercial queen breeder from Texas suggested that since his bees had no mites, people should buy from him and demand that all states not eradicating mites should be banned from Canada. He raced back and forth across the stage, swinging his arms about, and shouting like a preacher raving about the approach of doomsday. His bottom line: Buy my bees and you'll be safe.

224

Mites

A commercial queen breeder from California said that his state was working hard to kill all the bees found with mites and that the Saskatchewan Beekeepers' Association should write a letter of thanks to the California government.

When someone from the audience asked him, "How many colonies actually have died because of tracheal mite disease?" Steve Parks smiled and said, "In California, all hives with tracheal mites end up dead." [147] It was a joke, referring to how effectively his state was exterminating hives with mites, putting beekeepers out of business in California. Later the same year, California changed its strategy, defining 'mite-free' zones around individual queen producers, first by county, then as more and more mites were found, in smaller and smaller circles. Before any of the major queen breeders had their own hives exterminated, the state decided that the mite was not such a serious threat after all and dropped the quarantines and eradications.[148]

Brother Adam in 1966 with his Friend,
Prof. Dr. O. Morgenthaler, first General Secretary of Apimondia
- from Adam's Book, In Search of the Best Strains of Bees

At the bee meeting, we heard from California queen breeders and Canadian bee inspectors, but neither group had much first-hand knowledge of the honey bee tracheal mite or its treatment.

Brother Adam, a monk who bred queens in England, had such knowledge. But he didn't make it to Saskatoon.

Brother Adam was an amazing man. He was a Benedictine monk who helped rebuild the Buckfast Abbey in Devon, England. But he is remembered as the monastery beekeeper. Possibly no one has ever kept bees with such vigor and determination nor for so many years – 80! – as the man originally named Karl Kehrle. He left his home in Bavaria, Germany, and joined the Order at age 12. Karl's name was changed to Adam, Brother Adam. He was educated in religion and the classics, but was also required to learn a vocation and contribute to the financial success of the monastery. His day job was beekeeping and queen breeding.

Brother Adam felt that the honey bee tracheal mite killed bees and was responsible for a plague of sorts that had struck England many years ago. During the winter of 1915-1916, about two-thirds of the hives at Buckfast died. Adam noticed that the surviving bees were mostly Italian – the native black bee suffered greater losses. His conclusion was that certain types of bees were more resistant to mites and disease than other types of bees.

Bad Beekeeping

Brother Adam at Buckfast Abbey,
from *American Bee Journal,* **1985**

Brother Adam exploited this idea, developed the Buckfast Bee, licensed it to queen breeders in England, Israel, and Texas. It was Brother Adam's claim that "infected colonies can be saved by the simple expedient of requeening them with queens of proven resistant stock."[149]

Some of us tried to put this claim forward: if the tracheal mite were a serious problem, then at least it would be a simple one to solve. But few beekeepers were listening.

It became obvious that beekeepers in Saskatchewan were going to side with their bee inspector - and the guests from the USA who wanted to close all sources of bees to Canada except their own. Monks and scientists held less appealing opinions. At the Saskatchewan bee meeting, I presented a motion.

"If tracheal mite is so serious, I move we resolve to have all Canadian bees removed from within ten kilometres of the US border so the natural spread of mites would be slowed," I said into the microphone.

A young research scientist from Guelph jumped up to respond to my proposal. "We could never get our beekeepers to agree to this! We aren't the ones with mites in our bees. I have a better proposal. Why don't the Americans remove all their bees from within six miles of the Canadian border?" He was serious and there was considerable support for this idea.

Apparently some Saskatchewan beekeepers thought they could go to the Americans and say, "Excuse me, but we'll catch your bee disease if you don't scoot back from the border, eh?" And the Americans would say, "Oops! Sorry, man." This exchange highlighted a fundamental difference between Canadians and Americans. Canadians are nice. They often expect a sick person, or a problem, or a mistake, to make an effort to correct itself. Americans can also be nice, but they temper niceness with pragmatism. They expect you to be at least a little bit interested in your own self-preservation. In the end, it was my proposal, not the professor's, that was voted on.

I had one yard of bees near the States, my beautiful Dixon Yard, the one with the prairie dogs and rattlesnakes. But I could easily load up those thirty hives and move them to Val Marie. I assumed other beekeepers whose hives were within site of the assumed mite menace from the south would move as easily. This would stop the co-mingling of fifty thousand American hives with perhaps ten thousand Canadian hives that shared common fodder in the berry bogs of New Brunswick/Maine, the clover fields of North Dakota/Saskatchewan, and the apple orchards of B.C./Washington.

Mites

At this same raucous February beekeepers' convention held on the coldest day of 1986, I proposed that the Saskatchewan Beekeepers' Association give me support with a petition to allow me to bring my packages in from Florida. My Florida bees had been inspected, no mites were found. I would place my bees in an isolated part of Saskatchewan - Val Marie. My nearest neighbour beekeeper was a hundred and twenty kilometres away. There were places in New Brunswick and British Columbia where American and Canadian bees sat antennae to antennae across the border, within easy buzzing distance of each other. I was much more isolated. I claimed that the bees I would bring in probably had no mites. But if they did, it would give us all a chance to see how tracheal mite infested hives affect real, live, commercial beekeeping. Someone quickly seconded my resolution.[150]

Then the discussion began. Some worthy points, some heated moments. Finally, a simple, humble, elderly farmer strolled up to the microphone. He removed his John Deere cap and held it nervously in his hands. The room grew quiet. "This is not a bad idea," he began. "But I have a big problem with a beekeeper doing this sort of research, eh? Ron's just a beekeeper. Just a beekeeper. I move that we support having the government look into this. We need a committee, and some government people, like Mr. Gruszka - the bee inspector - and some trained government bee scientists. They should bring some tracheal mite bees into Saskatchewan to study. Not some beekeeper, eh?"

Mr. John Gruszka, Chief Apiary Inspector, Province of Saskatchewan, Editor of *Beelines* Photo from *Beelines*

And that was that. Canadians tend to set up committees.[151] Then we entrust a god – some government person – to carry out our work. The old farmer's resolution passed. The Saskatchewan Beekeepers' Association would fund and sponsor the experiment. John Gruszka, chief government guy for bees in Saskatchewan, brought a few packages with tracheal mites from Florida,[152] put them into equipment donated by Saskatchewan beekeepers. The infested bees were placed in one of the worst beekeeping areas in Saskatchewan - far north on the Canadian shield, near La Ronge. A place so bad for beekeeping – because of early frosts, acidic soil, and lack of agriculture (no canola, no harvested clover, no alfalfa) – big commercial honey farms never operated there.

The mite-infested bees performed more poorly than the control hives. The problem was blamed on mites. Toward the end of the second year of the project, Lawrence Cutts, the chief apiary inspector in Florida, advised the fellows running the experiment to look at their bees a little more carefully. They may find more than the tiny tracheal mites. They may find a pest a hundred times worse and a thousand times bigger. A new exotic pest had arrived in North America - *varroa* mites.[153]

Remember, there are two different mites that hurt bees. The small honeybee tracheal mite that Bailey in the U.K. tried to convince us was a minor problem. It arrived in North America some years before the varroa mite.[154] Varroa was - and still is - a real killer.

Hundreds of varroa mites were found in the experimental Saskatchewan colonies. The people handling those bees week after week somehow missed noticing the big red blood-sucking mites clinging to the bees' bodies. As a result, the first people to bring the wicked varroa mite into Canada were not beekeepers whose livelihood depended on their ability to keep healthy bees. Varroa was first imported into Canada by Canadian bureaucrats. Government guys. They quickly destroyed the bees. And we are told that no other beekeepers' hives were accidentally infected by the big ugly varroa mite from this embarrassing incident.[155]

When I left the Saskatchewan Beekeepers' Meeting in Saskatoon, few people talked to me. Some looked away, at their shoes, at the Jones and Sons Bee Supplies wall poster. Anywhere. But before I departed, the chief bee inspector – Mr. John Gruszka – promised he'd call me if in fact the Florida border were closed. I would need this information. I didn't want to drive all the way to Florida, load up bees, drive four thousand kilometres back to the port of Monchy and have a customs agent tell me I couldn't enter Canada with Florida bees. Within weeks, the border was closed, but only to bees from Florida. Gruszka didn't call.

Back in Val Marie, isolated from the other beekeepers in Canada, I continued to hope reason would prevail. I thought I would be able to get my packages from Florida. I certainly wanted to believe I would soon be heading south to pick up my Florida packages.

I needed packages urgently. It was spring, I was checking my over-wintered colonies, and results were not very good. My hives had not wintered well. It had been much too dry the past summer. Although I had fed tonnes of sugar syrup to my eight hundred colonies, many hives had died of starvation. There simply had not been enough reserves in the hives. I would need more bees from Florida to stay in business.

I told Buzz Trottier about the mites and the border closure.

"Well, Ron," said Buzz. "What if your friend Mr. Gruszka is right? What if these mites in the States kill all the bees here in Canada?"

I thought about this for a moment. Mr. Gruszka hadn't said the mites would kill all the bees. But what if they did? What if all the literature I'd been reading was wrong? Maybe I was simply· hoping the tracheal mite wasn't serious because I needed to bring in my bees from Florida.

"Buzz, these mites haven't caused much trouble anywhere else, except maybe in England, when they first started out. Since then, hardly anyone even gives them a second glance. Except here in Canada."

"You know," Buzz said, "when the white man came to America – we didn't call it America back then – there were millions of us Indians here." I was expecting Buzz to finish with a joke and a wink. He didn't. "The Indians died from disease. Like smallpox. Almost wiped them out. But white people were immune. Maybe these mites work that way. Wipe almost everything out, then the ones that are left are strong and survive."

Mites

Buzz might be right. I knew he could be, it was similar to what Brother Adam had claimed. And now one of my best friends was telling me the same thing. But what did that mean for beekeepers? The mite was moving across the continent. It was coming - open borders or closed borders - it was coming.

There was still no word of a Florida border closure. It had, in fact, already become law, but I was busy cleaning and repairing my empty package cages, and preparing my truck for the trip to Florida. I still had not heard anything from Mr. John Gruszka.

At this time, in March of 1985, we had a slight problem with Erika. Our year-old baby had a blocked tear duct. It became infected. We headed up to Swift Current – a hundred kilometres away – to take Erika to the nearest doctor, our closest source of antibiotics. I parked on the street, carried Erika to the office. Sandy waited with Erika. I went back outside to move the truck to a parking lot a few blocks away. It was noon, the radio played the CBC news. John Gruszka was being interviewed.

"No," John Gruszka said from the truck's speaker, "Closing the border to bees from Florida won't have any harmful effect on my beekeepers. There are only one or two beekeepers bringing bees in from Florida. They can easily purchase bees from somewhere else."[156]

So I learned my fate. I would need to buy bees from *somewhere else*. But I didn't have much money. The drought and low prices had taken a heavy toll. Three years earlier, I had cash in the bank – I'd paid off the entire farm mortgage. I had no debts. But with small crops and low prices, I had re-mortgaged the farm and had no spare cash. I kept telling my banker that things would improve, I'd be making big crops again; prices would recover. They had to.

I returned to the clinic where Erika sat with Sandy. Sandy realized something was wrong. I told her. Erika would soon be fine, she was given antibiotics and her tear duct began to drain. But as we drove back to Val Marie from Swift Current, sick baby strapped in the back seat, I knew I'd have to talk to my banker again. My thoughts were on my finances.

Al Anderson was manager of the Val Marie Credit Union.

"I need to borrow eight thousand dollars to buy packages," I said.

Al whistled, a long slow mournful tone. "Gees, Ron, that's a lot of money."

"How 'bout six, can you do six thousand?" I asked.

"Awful short notice, Ron. Didn't you anticipate this expense? I thought you were running down to Florida to get your own bees for free."

I told him I had just heard that I couldn't. I told Al that the chief bee inspector for the province of Saskatchewan had promised to call me, let me know ahead of time, but he hadn't. Al turned to his telephone, called Prince Albert, got John Gruszka on the phone. They talked a few minutes. Al hung up, turned to me.

"Well, Mr. Gruszka says he's sorry, but he says that he's too busy to call every beekeeper in the province. But it's true, he says you can't bring any bees in from Florida."

Bad Beekeeping

Al Anderson approved a loan – eight thousand dollars. I had the money to buy packages. I made arrangements with W.C. Berry in Montgomery, Alabama. W.C.'s had been raising and selling bee packages since 1914, but I had only now heard about them. I selected their company as my source for bees because all the other package producers in the USA were sold out for the year. Berry's thought they could shake a few hundred packages for me. Business was brisk for producers in Georgia and Alabama as they raced to fill Canadian orders that their neighbours in Florida were not allowed to ship.

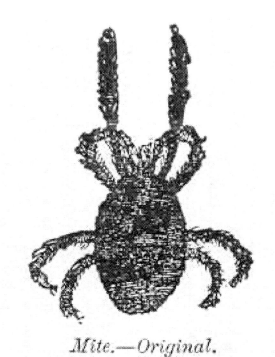

Mite.—Original.

Bee Mites are Nothing New.
Professor Cook Created this Drawing of an
External Mite Observed on a Honey Bee in California in 1883.

Departure

Bright summer afternoon. Alfalfa and wild clover blooming. An excited young bee lands at the entrance of a hive. The bee's tummy is full of nectar, its small pollen baskets dusted with yellow powder. Confused, a novice, the young bee has landed at a wrong hive. It happens. Bees get lost. But the guard bees of this hive, overwhelmed by the sweet scent of fresh nectar becoming honey within the walls of their nest, ignore the mistake. Besides, the lost bee is bringing pollen and nectar. The new bee becomes a member of the hive. From now on, it will build new combs and store honey and pollen to profit the adopted colony. Life goes on for the bee and for the hive.

The same guard bees, on a windy day in late autumn, would not be so tolerant. With winter coming, they would drag old drones from the hive to their deaths. On a bad day, guards would reject a young lost bee as a thieving opportunist. They would grab the innocent insect, shred its wings and legs. And discard the mutilated body.

Revenue Canada is the same as the IRS in the States, except it's Canadian and therefore even more polite. During my eighth year of beekeeping in Val Marie, things were not going very well. This drew the attention of federal auditors. They were wondering how I was able to eat while continually posting a negative income. They sent someone down from Regina to investigate.

"See you next week, Sincerely, Ashri Rashani," said the letter. It arrived at a bad time - busy season. But I doubt there is a good time to get a letter like that from Revenue Canada. It was summer. I was working fourteen hours a day. I didn't know if I could find the shoe boxes labeled "1983" and "1984." I knew I wouldn't have time to look at the papers - even if I found them.

In those days, in rural Canada, the auditor would drive out to the village or farm house. This gave the poor guy stuck in the office a chance to meet his people and to run up a tab on his expense account. Most auditors sent to investigate farms were new on the job, usually accountants in training. Not a pleasant job.

I told a neighbour that the tax man was coming. Soon I had calls from people all over Val Marie, offering me advice on what to say, what not to say; what to hide, and how to hide it. The recurring wisdom of my neighbours manifested an urgent suggestion that I not let the tax man take any papers away from my house. "They take your papers, they lose your papers, then they give you a re-assessment and a big tax bill. And you can't prove anything because they took your papers and they lost your papers. It happened to Eric Neusonne." According to various versions of this local legend, Eric, a south Saskatchewan farmer, let the tax man take his papers away for audit in Regina. They were accidentally shredded. Then Eric was told that he owed three million dollars in back taxes. He had to sell his farm and move away. Now he lives under a bridge in Calgary, I was told.

I didn't want to end up under a bridge in Calgary. But I didn't want to be uncooperative, either. I wasn't sure what to expect from Agent Rashani when he tapped on my door. I told Ashri the story about Eric who lives under the bridge and he agreed that it happens all the time, but he said he'd be very careful with my papers. I told him he could live in my house as long as he wanted, or at least until he got the audit done, but he really wanted to take my bills, receipts, and bank statements and go away. Finally, we compromised. He could take my papers for two days but he wouldn't travel any farther than a hundred kilometers. That put him in Gravelbourg where he booked a room and set up a temporary office.

When Ashri returned (with my papers) two days later, I was sticky from honey. I had been using my bee smoker and I smelled like a burning hay stack. He was polite anyway. He asked me if there was any reasonable explanation as to why I would claim ninety per cent of my truck expenses one year, and a hundred per cent the next.

"Didn't you sometimes use the truck for personal use?" he asked.

"Oops." I said.

"Well, then, you owe us two hundred and fifty dollars for 1983, but then I noticed that you forgot to use a tax credit for two hundred twenty dollars in 1984, so the two mistakes cancel each other out. We won't be changing your tax bill."

Then, he wanted to leave. But at this point, I felt like I had established a rapport with Agent Rashani. He was my friend, perhaps. I asked him if he had any advice - after all, I didn't have a balanced, double entry accounting system. I had shoe boxes. I expected he would want to tell me how to keep better books.

"No, no, your papers were all together. No problem. I see this sort of mess all the time. But if you would like some advice, Mr. Ron Miksha, I have gone through two years of your incomes and expenses and I would advise you to consider a better way of making a living than keeping bees. You should quit this beekeeping as soon as possible."

**It Took Ten Years, but the Little Beekeeper's Shack
in Val Marie Finally Looked Like a Real Home**

Quitting beekeeping was on my mind a lot. It was another dry year and not much honey was in the hives. It was the second year without my own Florida raised queens and packages.

The bees I bought from Australia were expensive. Honey prices were still low – around forty cents a pound. And 1985 was the year that ended with a violent car crash.

The car wreck began a day earlier, in

Departure

Wymark. At Lisa and Erwin's home.

We had met Lisa and Erwin Reimer at the Swift Current Farmers' Market. Sandy and I sold a few hundred pounds of honey to the Swifties, as Swift Currentians were sometimes called. We filled plastic honey pails that held one kilogram, three kilograms, seven kilos. Lisa and Erwin walked past, picked up a honey bear.

Erwin held the clear plastic bear towards a light. "Look, Lisa. This is fine honey," said Erwin. "You make this yourself, down in Val Marie?" he asked me.

"It's our own honey," Sandy said.

"You've got a southern accent," said Lisa. "I miss that. I'm from the south." She took the clear honey bear in her hands. "Where are you from?"

"Florida," said Sandy.

"Florida? And you're living in Val Marie?"

The Reimers bought a kilo of honey. Three dollars. They said they might be back. I watched the young couple walk to a table where Hutterites from Hodgeville sold corn and tomatoes, then I was distracted by another honey customer. I forgot about the Reimers.

The next week, Lisa and Erwin were back. "That was the best honey I've ever tasted," said Erwin. He thrust his hand out to me. "We should be friends," he said. So we became friends. They visited us in Val Marie with their children – Esther, Eric, Larissa, Lyle. We toured the Hutterite Colony together. Hiked the badlands, looked for fossilized wood and bones. When my son David was born, two-year old Erika stayed at the Reimer home in Wymark, ten minutes south of Swift Current. We shared children's births and birthdays and we ate holiday suppers together.

Friends, the Reimer Family, Hiking the Badlands...
Children are on the Distant Butte,
Shadows in Foreground are (from the left) Erwin, Ron, Lisa.

Bad Beekeeping

Christmas dinner, 1985, at the Reimer's home in Wymark was a treat. Delicious food and lots of it. But now it was becoming late, dark, and we were an hour from Val Marie. I pushed towards the door, towards home. I hadn't heard the weather forecast, but earlier in the day, Erwin had pointed out sundogs – the glare in the sky that meant a storm was coming. It began to snow. We needed to reach Val Marie before it got too late.

We drove south on the Number Four. Within minutes, winds shook our little car, snow blew across the road from west to east, blinding my sight of the highway. A blizzard. The road was gone, enveloped in white. Indistinguishable from fields and ditch. I stopped, realized I was edging off the road. Straightened out, crept along even more slowly. It took two hours to reach the village of Cadillac. We still had fifty kilometres of blizzard between us and our home in Val Marie. The winds slid the car, I felt it lift slightly. I pulled up to a shed, out of the gale. Snow swirled past.

I looked for a place to sleep. A stranger in the pub gave us the keys to a cabin – two rooms and a small gas heater. The cottage was in the town of Cadillac. "You can't go on, you'll get stranded in the storm," said the stranger as he pushed on the door of the little house. It was empty.

"Does someone live here?" Sandy asked.

"Yea, an old farmer... He's visiting his daughter up in Moose Jaw."

The shack was cold, damp. No clean sheets. We slept in our clothes. But the generosity of the fellow who owned the keys to the cabin was enormous. He had never seen us before, wouldn't take any money, and despite the blizzard, he sent his wife by with tea and cookies later in the evening.

The storm ended at day break. The sky was cloudless, baby blue. The fresh snow which made us storm-stayed in the evening had settled. It covered the earth like a clean and pure conscience. A fresh start.

Boxing Day, the December 26 holiday. I knew the café would be closed. No breakfast. We left the cottage unlocked, put the key on the table as instructed. We climbed into the car, strapped Erika into her baby seat behind me. We drove without eating, without coffee. But I was wide awake. It would only take half an hour to reach our home in Val Marie.

Except for a few patches where trees sheltered the road from the blizzard, the wind had wiped the snow completely off the highway. Driving was easy. The speed limit was ninety. We'd be in Val Marie in thirty minutes. Perhaps less.

We were ten kilometres south of Cadillac, barely started on our journey home. A cluster of caragana blocked my view, I didn't see the truck darting across the highway until an instant before it hit us.

I didn't see the impact; didn't hear the crush of steel. I was numb. It took time to understand we'd been hit. Our car was upright. My stomach and chest hurt. God, they hurt. I gasped for breath. Sandy's head had smashed the windshield, broke glass. But she wasn't bleeding; she was breathing fine. Her door was crushed, but her leg hadn't gotten caught in the twisted metal.

Erika was snug in her car seat. She looked at us. She seemed fine.

Departure

I could see the truck that had hit us, now lying on its side. A woman was screaming. She was the passenger. Her husband had been driving. He was partially flung through his open driver's window. I walked to their truck, a few metres from our car. He breathed, slowly. Very Slowly. I pulled off my heavy coat, covered the man with my parka. I helped his wife as she squeezed out of the truck window.

I talked to the man in the snow. Blood came from his nose and mouth.

"Did you have breakfast this morning?" I asked.

His eyes opened. Closed. Still labouring for breath. "What the hell you need to know that for?" he said.

"Did you have breakfast?"

"Yea, bacon, toast, eggs."

"Coffee?"

"Where are we?"

"Did you have coffee?"

"Yea, I had coffee."

I told his wife to keep him awake, ask him questions. Stupid questions. Anything. Keep him awake.

The accident happened at seven in the morning. There were no cars on the highway. I knew it would be a long time before anyone came along early on a holiday morning. To the west, I saw lights in a building. I walked to the farm house, a thousand feet away.

I rapped on the door. The woman inside was shocked to see me, she thought the sound came from her husband who had gone out to milk cows. She called an ambulance and the police. Her husband came in from the barn, carrying a pail of milk. He drove me back to the accident. The man in the snow was still alive.

I sat with Sandy and Erika in our smashed car, went back out to see the man in the snow. It was my turn to talk to him. Still no traffic on the highway. Half an hour later the ambulance arrived from Pontiex. A police car pulled up behind it.

"You guys all OK?" someone asked us. I pointed to the man in the snow.

"Just him, he's hurt pretty bad," I said.

"You should all come to the hospital," the paramedic said. "All of you." We rode in the police car, the woman rode with her husband in the ambulance. He was still breathing.

At the tiny community hospital, the lone doctor glanced at us. He was worried about his badly injured patient. The doctor stabilized the man, got him ready for the four hour ambulance ride to Regina Plains Hospital. The man's wife looked at Sandy. "Oh no, you're pregnant, aren't you?" Sandy told the woman that she was fine. The doctor suggested we go home, but he said that if we weren't feeling well for the next day or two, we should consider going to a physician in Swift Current. The doctor didn't examine us.

One of the policemen gave us a ride back to Val Marie. There I undressed and discovered that I was bleeding at the hips, where the seatbelt had anchored me in place.

Bad Beekeeping

My chest had a purple bruise, either from the shoulder seat strap or from the steering column. My neck, back, stomach hurt.

Friends came to see us. Colin MacDonald, minister of the United Church, brought lunch and books. I showed him my bruises.

"The doctor sent you home?" Colin asked.

He shook his head, told us to get in his car. He took us all up to Swift Current to see a doctor. It was an hour away, my muscles hurt so miserably that I walked slowly. My neck and back were stiffening up. We were examined at the Swift Current Hospital. Erika, Sandy and the unborn baby were apparently well enough. Sore and bruised, but healing already. X-rays showed I had crushed vertebrae. The doctor gave me pain killers and a neck brace. I wore the brace for the next three months. The man in the snow was kept in Regina. In a few weeks he was able to return to his farm.

In 1986, the summer following the accident, I went through the routine of keeping bees. I was often sore, tired, my back and neck ached. The drought continued, the honey crop was small, I couldn't import my Florida bees, honey prices had not recovered. I needed to borrow more money.

By fall, I had re-financed my honey farm for the third time. The Val Marie Credit Union had been amalgamated with a bigger credit union in Shaunavon. Al Anderson had left Val Marie and the new bank managers were nervous. The drought had forced several farmers out of business. My prospects appeared grim to the people who had to approve loans. But they gave me more operating cash and held their collective breaths.

Other beekeepers were similarly desperate. Beekeepers in northern Saskatchewan didn't have a drought, but the low prices and lack of American packages drove many of them out of business. Three of the biggest and most prolific Nipawin operations, north of Tisdale's rape and honey, went bankrupt. Other beekeepers simply quit, got jobs in town, or moved away.

I knew I needed to make a move. During the winter, neck in a brace, I began taking correspondence classes. French, Statistics, English Composition. I was trying to discover if I could still learn school material, still pass exams. A year after the car accident, two years into the border closure, after three years of drought, I applied to the university in Saskatoon. I thought I could be a high school science teacher, keep bees as a summer hobby. I was thirty-two years old. Not too old to start over again. But first, I needed to sell my honey farm.

When I felt certain of my decision, I called my father. It was gray and wet in Pennsylvania, he said. It was thirty below in Canada, I told him.

"I'm selling out, Dad," I said.

"Can't take it?" he asked.

I explained about the small crops, the low prices, my bees stranded in Florida.

"Can't you tighten your belt a bit? You can't stay in business if you waste your money. Did you build the wind-mill we talked about?"

I told him I had no money to waste, didn't build the wind-mill. I told my father I'd try university, become a teacher, keep bees in the summer.

Departure

"Well, not everyone gives up when things get a little tough," said my father.

I realized that I could not explain the drought or the poverty to someone who had lived through the depression and dustbowl years. He was right, I was tired and I couldn't take it any more. I tried to consol myself, knowing that my father had given up beekeeping when he was forty-five. In those days, crops were small in Pennsylvania and the honey price had been stuck at ten cents a pound for twenty years. He, himself, had changed careers.

"You gone bankrupt?" he asked me.

"No," I said. "But I'm pretty close." I never went bankrupt, but it got pretty close.

I needed to find a buyer for the Val Marie honey farm. I had a copy of the membership roster for the American Beekeepers' Association. Five hundred members. I used the names and addresses and sent one hundred direct mail advertisements to beekeepers in the United States. I knew that Canadian beekeepers were too broke to buy my business. I sent information about my hives, the little shop. My honey production averages since 1978. I didn't get any responses. No one was interested. Until late May.

The evening the Fox brothers called, I was coming in the door from the Hutterite Colony. The Fox brothers were in Montana, an hour away. They had received my advertisement, had driven up from California. They asked if they could drop by the next morning to see the honey farm I was selling. I told them that would be fine with me.

At ten o'clock that night, I went up to the honey shop and swept the floor. I restacked a few boxes, but realized that there was little I could do to make the place look more attractive.

The Fox brothers arrived the next morning. They liked what they saw.

"Reminds us of California twenty years ago. No neighbor beekeepers. Nice small town. You got a nice little honey farm here," said Lloyd.

They liked it. I showed them the bees. "Not bad. We'll gas them all off in the fall, start with our own breed next spring," said Lloyd.

They liked the town, the shop, the house, the hives. They bought everything except my trucks and a few hives and supers I'd moved up north, near Saskatoon. I told them I'd like some bees to fuss over while I was going to university.

I held back tears when the papers were signed, and when I heard Erika – three years old – tell a visitor that she liked Daddy's honey house more than she liked the house she slept in. Everything would be changing. The kids would not grow up watching me from the window of a truck while I supered bees or caged queens. They'd become city kids and I'd see them only in the evenings and weekends, after my work day was over.

A letter arrived from the University of Saskatchewan. My application to enroll in the College of Education had been rejected, but I was offered a place in the College of Arts and Sciences. I was satisfied. I could always switch my curricula later, get into education after I'd done a science degree. I prepared to move the family to Saskatoon. I had no job, no income. I had sold the Val Marie business to the Fox brothers for a hundred thousand dollars. Unfortunately, I owed the Credit Union one hundred twelve thousand dollars.

Bad Beekeeping

Twelve thousand dollars short, I signed a low-interest loan with the bank. We started packing.

I was going to leave Val Marie. I wasn't being run out of town - accused of horse theft like Will James. Nor was I leaving for glory and fame - as Bryan Trottier did when he headed to New York, hockey stick in hand.

I was simply leaving. Some of the folks in town gave us a farewell party. It was well attended, but it was sobering and sad. No one celebrated our departure. I think a lot of people felt it may be themselves – their family – packing up and heading off to a big city the following year. And some of the farmers and ranchers did leave shortly after us. But others stayed on.

On our last week in Val Marie, we drove to Climax. Dale and Dora Bennet had been my friends since I'd first arrived in south Saskatchewan, ten years earlier. On the Sunday before we left for Saskatoon, we met Dale and Dora at the United Church, then went to their farm. While Dora worked on Sunday supper, Dale offered to take us on a tour. A south Saskatchewan loop tour. Erika and David played in the living room, in sight of Dora. Sandy, Dale, and I climbed into Dale's old farm truck and headed south on a grid road.

A trail of July dust followed us. Dale slowed and stopped his truck. We hopped out. "There," he said pointing to a marshy slough, "that's where I learned how to swim. It had a beach, with sand, forty years ago. Farmers dug the slough out, it was a pretty big lake then. Everyone brought a picnic lunch, we'd spend the whole day. There'd be a hundred people splashing about. Right there." Dale was still pointing. Pointing at a mass of weeds, alkali grass, willow.

"Where'd those hundred people come from? Bracken? Climax?" I asked.

"Oh, some of them. Mostly it was folks who lived right around here." He spread his arms out, pointing towards big wheat fields and small patches of poplar trees. "No one lives on this road anymore, but it used to have hundreds of people. Hundreds. Every quarter mile, there was another farm house, another big family. No one lives here at all anymore."

No one lives here anymore. Once, farmers worked small patches of land, kept hogs and cows and bees and chickens. Tractors were simple enough to repair with chicken fence wire and a screw driver. Not a Phillip's or a Robertson's or a plastic handled metric screw driver. Just a simple slotted one. That and some chicken wire, a half-inch open-ended wrench and in twenty minutes, seeding could continue. Women canned vegetables, made jam from rhubarb and the wild pin cherries that lined their yards. Families splashed in the lake - now a marsh - on weekends.

Back in the truck, we drove past abandoned farm houses, mason jars and pickling urns long since removed. Dale stopped at the Montana border. We looked across a single strand of barbed wire at American farmland. "Durum," Dale said. "That's what people grow now." We looked out towards the horizon, followed the line where sky met Montana wheat fields. It stretched, uninterrupted, miles and miles. "We had a lot of friends across the line. They're mostly gone, too," said Dale.

Departure

At the border, we rode east for a few miles, then took the grid road back north. We passed the place a school had stood twenty years earlier. A small plaque, cemented to a concrete post, marked the spot. Past old wooden barns, boards loose, but still standing up against the wicked prairie winds. Our journey into Saskatchewan's past, present, and future lasted two hours. We had traveled forty miles. A loop through history.

Dale Bennet found no fault with his passengers, two young people joining all the other farmers who had already moved on. "Well, I can't blame any of the folks for leaving. There's lots better ways to make a living than farming."

Erika, Entertaining the Young Men of Sand Lake Colony

Back in Val Marie. We were getting ready to leave. The Reverend David Kleinsasser came with a group of little boys from the colony. While the Hutterite children played with Erika in the dust, David told me again that ours was the best honey anyone had ever made. I told David it wasn't me, it was the bees, and the bees were staying. He said he'd miss us anyway. He handed us a box stuffed with food Annie had packed for our journey. Sausage, bread, cheese, cookies. Joe Kleinsasser had added a bottle of Peter's wine.

As David's van pulled out to return to the colony, Buzz came by with his youngest son, Rocky.

A year earlier, Buzz, Rocky, and Monty had done some carpentry work for me, adding on to my house. "Too bad you won't get to enjoy this a bit longer. Or maybe you've enjoyed this too long already?" His eyes twinkled. He wasn't worried about us moving to the big city.

"A lot of people come and go from this valley. It changes them all," he had once told me. I told him to come see us in Saskatoon. He said he might.

Bad Beekeeping

My three ton truck, outfitted with the clumsy homemade van I once used to carry packages from Florida to Saskatchewan, was now loaded with the household possessions of a poor country family. Tools – wrenches and hammers. Books, an ironing board, the ancient fold-out coach, cardboard boxes stuffed with clothes and food. Children's toys. My bee veil stuffed behind the seat.

Four of us sat in the front of the big truck. I shifted from low gear as I turned the corner off River Road, heading north on the Number Four. We left Val Marie, headed towards Saskatoon. I was going to become a student.

Someone is Always Left Behind to Tend the Bees…
From a Johann Gruninger Woodcut, 1502

Fifteen Years Later

The swarm moved on. No tree offered enough shelter from the wind. Neither cave, earthen hollow, nor abandoned nest were deemed sufficient against the elements. The bees moved into unknown places, not with bravery, but with necessity, driven by desperation.

Shortly after the border closure and the drop in honey prices, about a third of the beekeepers in Saskatchewan quit. Some sold trucks and honey tanks and hive equipment to beekeepers in the States, dissolved their holdings. Some went broke, foreclosed by their banks. During the early and mid-eighties, there were dozens of auctions of beekeeping businesses. Many of the most vigorous buyers were American. Not all the beekeepers saw these foreign bidders as vultures, though some did. The reality was that Canadian beekeepers didn't have money to buy more hives from the folks going broke - they could barely keep their own colonies alive. The Americans brought cash - the beekeepers who had to quit ended up with more money than if only Canadians were bidding on their bees. Hundreds of hives were sold and carried south, across the border, into the United States.

Many of the beekeepers who remained in business had real jobs. They were teachers, storekeepers, oil rig workers. For them, beekeeping degraded to a part-time project. They cut expenses, reduced hive counts,[157] waited for the economy to change.

It didn't help if the honey farm had been in business fifty years. Excellent family enterprises, operated by third-generation beekeepers, were terminated. In 1987, most of Canada's honey sold for forty cents a pound. A typical beekeeper, with a thousand hives, would have earned only sixty thousand dollars - gross receipts. Then, the beekeeper needed replacement bees from Australia, sugar for wintering the hives, cash for hired help, gasoline and tires for trucks. Perhaps groceries for the family. If the beekeeper had any debts at all, there was a nervous banker looking for interest and at least some tiny amount of principal on the debts. A small honey farm cost two hundred thousand dollars to set up - interest on risky loans was up to twenty per cent - forty thousand dollars on that size of an investment. A beekeeper who owed money on his farm in 1987 was in trouble.

I moved on. Attended the University of Saskatchewan. We settled into a tiny rental house in the northwest corner of Saskatoon. I never entered the Education College, I took the Arts and Sciences curriculum. My first class was *Wave and Particle Motion Physics*. When mid-term exams were returned to us, I was shocked. I had a perfect mark, one hundred per cent. Class average was fifty-two. A classmate noticed my score and asked for my life story. I told him I'd come to the university to become a science teacher.

Bad Beekeeping

"Ronnie, Ronnie, Ronnie," Wayne said. "Forget teaching. With marks like these, you should be a geophysicist." This is what my friend Wayne was doing – becoming a geophysicist. He had already earned his geology degree and had some industry experience.

At the time, I didn't know what a geophysicist did. Maybe they photographed the earth from airplanes, somehow analyzed the pictures. I had no idea. I went to the head of the Earth Sciences Department. Dr. Hendry, and later Dr. Merriam, explained it all to me. A geophysicist uses physics to study the earth. In Canada, most geophysicists end up in the oil patch. They interpret seismic and magnetic data and make decisions on where oil and gas wells should be drilled. I was also told the pay was very good. And while studying, I might be able to get a scholarship. They were right about the bursaries. Over the next three years, I earned seventeen scholarships of various sorts. The money helped feed my family and I completed an honours geophysics degree.

With Jim Merriam's help, I'd also landed the National Sciences and Engineering Research Council grant. The NSERC grant allowed me to study the affect of atmospheric pressure on a super-conducting gravimeter with Dr. Merriam. The sophisticated gravity meter could detect motions of plumes and resonations deep within the earth's mantle. Writing 3-dimensional calculus programs was a broad step from washing honey extractors, but somehow I survived that, too.

There was a graduate degree in my pursuit of these solutions, but Exxon phoned my house just as I finished my Bachelor of Science degree. Their exploration manager called from Calgary, offered me a nice salary, a permanent job. His company would move me and my family to the big city by the mountains. Erika was seven, David, five. I decided it was time to have a real job. We all changed with the years.

Eleanor Dern, the Florida orange grove owner who loved scrabble, died peacefully in her sleep. Her dogs went to live with Eleanor's neighbours.

Earl and Josephine Emde both passed away in Florida – Josephine first. Earl followed a few years later. His son found Earl – Earl was pulling on his boots, heading out to the beeyard to cage queens one last time. He was past eighty.

I lost touch with most of the people who had helped me in Val Marie. I got a call one morning that Buzz Trottier, the Indian rancher who was my sagacious advisor, had also died. So had David Kleinsasser, the Hutterite minister who loved Val Marie honey so much. And Dale Bennet, the farmer who took me on my last tour of the south country, passed away late in 2001.

The Fox brothers, the gentlemen from California who had bought my Val Marie honey farm, moved back to the States. Merlin, my employee, had a business partner and together they operated two thousand hives of bees in northern Saskatchewan – but they quit after three years.

The beekeepers in Florida did much better. My brother David produces more queens than he did in the 1980s – he sells a hundred thousand queen cells a year and ten thousand caged queens. Most of the other beekeepers from my honey flow party still operate one, two, three thousand hives each. Beekeeping was not destroyed in the United

States, even with the arrival of the *varroa* mite, Africanized bees, and other exotic pests. Beekeepers continue to migrate with their bees from the orange groves of Florida to the North Dakota alfalfa fields bordering Saskatchewan. Those states - Florida, North Dakota, along with California and South Dakota – continue to lead their nation in honey production.

But there are reasons for optimism in Canada. In February, 2002, members of the Canadian Honey Council, meeting in Banff, Alberta, discussed a recommendation that Alberta beekeepers be allowed to bring packages of bees in from the United States. The first steps at reversing damage that began twenty years ago. And some beekeepers have started a movement to allow full migration of beehives – not only packages of caged bees, but entire hives. They could be moved to California for almond pollination in the winter and back to Alberta for honey production in the summer.

The other exciting change for beekeepers is the sudden and unexpected rise in honey prices. In March, 2002, wholesale honey prices in the USA rose from sixty cents a pound to ninety. By August, a dollar. And it continued to rise. With the high exchange rate, beekeepers in Canada are receiving a dollar sixty for a pound of honey, four times the 1985 rate. This huge price spike arose from the disappearance of Chinese honey on the world market. Unfortunately for the Asian producers, low levels of antibiotics were discovered in many of their food products. This led to wariness, and finally rejection, of five hundred million pounds of Chinese honey offered on the world market. A huge shortage suddenly occurred; prices rose dramatically. Just as dramatically, when the crisis is solved, honey prices will tumble, but the unexpected brief windfall will help.

Despite the recent good news for Canadian honey producers, the beekeeping industry in Canada has stagnated for years while many American producers did very well. Why were the Americans able to succeed while the Canadians failed? Many reasons, of course. For me it was the closed border, the drought, the low honey prices. But a key factor is systemic to Canadian culture. People who are innovative and energetic – the doers and builders and achievers – have little patience for systems that challenge their potential and retard their progress. Canada regulates and controls business much more than the United States does. Entrepreneurs gravitate out of over-regulated businesses.

A Canadian, Brad Clawsie, living in California and working in the Silicon Valley, has said, "Canadian culture is more concerned with reducing losses than promoting gains. ...accessibility and excellence rarely occupy the same space. Canada as a nation appears more focused on the former than the latter. Risk-takers typically flock to systems that have low barriers to entry – this means low taxes and low bureaucracy. Such a system will inherently create both losers and winners. Until Canada is more willing to allow people to lose, those capable of winning will go elsewhere."[158]

My older brother, Don, the one who operated my American bees each summer, stayed with his greenhouse and nursery business in Wisconsin. He and his wife are still building larger and more dispersed home garden shops.

From Joe's fifteenth birthday, he never spent more than three consecutive months on the family farm in Pennsylvania. In his senior year, he had eighty-nine unexcused absences - he'd been harvesting honey in Saskatchewan, transplanting

Bad Beekeeping

petunias in Wisconsin, painting beehives in Florida. Yet he finished high school in Sharpsville, Pennsylvania, with good marks. Today, Joe owns a huge greenhouse business north of Milwaukee. He loves what he does and does his work with great enthusiasm and skill. Joe married; he has four children. His kids work evenings, weekends, and summers on his Wisconsin farm; Joe works about eighteen hours a day, everyday.

Sandy and I didn't stay together. Sandy continues to live in Calgary, the place we landed after Saskatoon. She studied computer networking, became a systems' analyst. She lives in a nice bungalow with a wall-screen television and a hot tub and she sings with the Calgary Opera; big changes from the isolated life in the tiny dusty house on Saskatchewan's windy prairie. She's not far from my dwelling and the kids spend time at each of our homes.

I talked to my father occasionally, but after I quit commercial beekeeping, I didn't see him for six years. He never came back to Saskatchewan. He told me that if I had stayed with the bees in Val Marie a little longer, things might have gotten better. And if I'd stayed a beekeeper, my father suggested, Sandy and I would not have divorced. But he followed my career in the oil patch with interest and encouragement and was glad to see me when I finally ventured back to Pennsylvania for a visit at the family farm.

My profession as a geophysicist has been rewarding, but not as challenging nor interesting as my life as a beekeeper was. I stayed with Exxon for five years. They treated me well, but I quit. I wanted to work for a smaller company, somewhere I felt more in control. I took over as vice-president of a seismic processing company, then bought the little geophysics company.

And I stayed in Canada. Canadian culture has been evolving. Taxes are lower, regulations are easing. People are adjusting to life outside a welfare state where benevolent and malevolent bureaucrats nurture and abuse their constituents. Despite the move towards fiscal conservatism and the renewed expectation in self-reliance, Canada has remained socially a very progressive country. The United Nations described it as the most livable country on earth in terms of health, education, crime rate, and civil liberties. It is clean, safe, comfortable. I like it here.

About thirty kilometres from my home in Calgary, nestled on the edge of a rolling alfalfa field near snow-capped mountains, I keep a dozen hives of bees. Erika, now nineteen, and David, seventeen, help me check for queens and super the bees from time to time. But my best assistant is a physician from Hungary who hoists honey boxes without complaining and helps with all the beekeeping chores of our little hobby. I married Eszter fourteen years after I left the honey farm in Val Marie. And a new adventure begins.

Notes

These end notes are not a scholarly treatise of research, but they are intended to give the reader a more detailed understanding of some of the things incidentally introduced in this book, and to substantiate and verify some statements made in the body of this book which some readers may have difficulty believing.

I am not the sort of student whom the Hungarian poet, George Faludy, once described: his friend Eric Johnson "would walk farther for a footnote than most of us would drive for a book." My research is not as exhaustive, but nevertheless encompasses a life-time of study and the review of hundreds of books and articles. A small part of those resources are quoted in the end notes which follow.

This book can be enjoyed without reading these notes, or conversely, you may wish to read these notes and skip the rest of the book. And for the incurably curious, other excellent resources exist, some of which are listed in this book's bibliography.

[1] I hope not to frighten the reader, but I frequently use the metric system to describe distances, temperatures, and weights in this book. Canada joined the "civilized" world with the introduction of *le Systeme Internationale* in 1978. Therefore, most - but not all - of the units of measurement in Canada are metric. Passages and chapters of this book relating to the U.S.A. generally use the old Imperial system of feet, miles, pounds, and degrees Fahrenheit.

Systems of measurement can seem arbitrary but are typically stewed in the traditions and customs of a people. The French, not willing to accept a British king's over-sized twelve-inch foot as a basic measurement of length, divided the distance from the equator to the North Pole by 10,000,000 and called the result a metre. The founder of modern beekeeping, Reverend Lorenzo Lorraine Langstroth, in his 1853 Hive and the Honey-Bee, (page 70) suggests that the six-sided honey-comb cell should be a universal standard of measurement for volume. It didn't catch on. But, in a sense, beekeepers have developed their own standards for length (one deep super), weight (one frame of honey) and time (a honey season).

The sole advantage in using the US measurement system is its familiarity. Beyond that, it can be baffling to people born in nearly all other parts of the world. For example, in the metric system, water freezes at zero, boils at one hundred. We are chilly at 10, comfortable at 20, hot at 30. It takes exactly one hour to drive a hundred kilometres; the average adult man weighs a bit under one hundred kilograms.

Having said all this, one is most at ease in one's mother-tongue, most comfortable being weighed in the same system the nurse used on one's day of birth. I occasionally bracket the metric or Imperial equivalent within the text of the book, but I remind American readers that the new generation of Canadians really don't know Fahrenheit nor miles; likewise, Canadians should be aware that their American neighbours have heard that Canada is a very cold country where the summertime high rarely exceeds 30!

[2] Macdonald and Mackenzie were likely *not* the names of the customs and immigration officers working the border the day I arrived in Canada. Typically, a lone agent would man the gate and his name was as apt to be Carlowitz, Spitutio, or Jones. Most of the detail in this book is derived from my diaries, journals, notes, and calendar entries; but I did not write down the names of the guards who were manning the station when I first arrived in 1978. The fact that these two people now bear their given nomenclatures is not meant as a slight upon either of Canada's first two Prime Ministers.

[3] The standard industrial container for honey is the barrel. Steel drums hold 660 lbs. (300 kg) of honey - 55 US gallons, 45 Canadian. When honey is purchased from a commercial beekeeper by a North American packer, broker, or distributor, the barrels are weighed and the producer (beekeeper)

is paid a pre-negotiated price listed in dollars per pound. International distributors usually trade in terms of dollars per metric tonne (2202 pounds).

[4] Folk culture suggests that the term 'badlands' was assigned by railway men, doling out parcels to homesteaders. The agent would point at a map and declare, "This here is good-lands, eh? But stay out of there, them's badlands." But the agents were often poorly informed - this according to Sidney Chandler, who at age ninety-four, told me he selected a parcel from an agent's map in Swift Current, rode his horse 150 kilometres south to the hills beyond Val Marie, and three times returned to the agent to trade his badlands for good lands. In the end, he acquired several sections of semi-desert along the edge of the badlands south of the village of Val Marie.

[5] Beekeepers frequently use small classified advertisements in beekeeping journals when searching for assistants. My father responded to the January, 1944, Gleanings in Bee Culture offer:
WANTED - Experienced man, married or single in queen, package, and honey production. Year around work. Give full particulars when replying. Al Winn, Rt. 1, Petaluma, Calif.

[6] John Lovell's classic (among beekeepers) Honey Plants of North America, 1926, cited migratory commercial beekeeping in California extending back to the nineteenth century. Lovell's list of northern California honey plants (pp 387-397) reads like a botany encyclopedia:

"The chief source of surplus honey in the Central Valley is alfalfa... The first pollen and nectar in some sections are from Eucalyptus groves... Willows may yield a surplus.. and in mid-summer and autumn a dark honey-dew is often gathered from the foliage." As honey plants, Lovell goes on to name almonds, plums, carpet grass ("blooming from May until frost"), spike weed, tarweed, star thistle, mustard, bur clover, alfileria, white clover, horehound, wild radish, manzanita. And quoting Lovell directly again: "A great variety of garden truck, such as asparagus, celery, and parsnips is grown in the southern part of the Sacramento Valley; and 'celery and parsnip,' says E. R. Root, who made a journey up the river in 1919, 'is stored in five and six story hives'."

[7] Honey gatherers had long used smoke to confuse the bees' sense of odour detection and to invoke the bees' natural gorging instinct. When bees smell smoke, the nasty human stench is cleverly disguised as burning straw, burlap, pine needles, or even dried manure - which apparently create a more pleasant odour than the human underarm, at least from a bee's perspective. Quinby's contraption works by confining a smoldering fire within a metal canister, drafting air through it, out a spout which can be directed at the bees' nest. Intensity of smoke is manipulated by a set of leather bellows attached to the smoker.

Moses Quinby invented the modern beekeeping smoker with a bellows and firepot in 1875. He made no effort to patent his work. A Mr. Bingham used Quinby's model, got a patent, manufactured the tool, and sold it for $2. Refinements have not substantially changed the smoker in one hundred thirty years. The Illustrated Encyclopedia of Beekeeping, edited by Roger Morse and Ted Hooper, E. P. Dutton, Inc., New York, 1985, p 352.

Paul Jackson, in his book Smoking Allowed, writes, "Prior to 1875, no practical method of using smoke efficiently had been found. Tobacco smoke blown from the mouth was about the best thing available at the time. Moses Quinby is credited with the invention of the first practical bee smoker. This bellows-driven smoker was a great step over previous methods of applying smoke to the bees."

[8] The Canadian dollar goes up and down against the American. But very slowly. The looney has traded at sixty-five to eighty percent of the US dollar for so long that we have forgotten that for a while, it took more American money to buy Canadian dollars. When I arrived in Canada in 1978, the American and Canadian dollars were approximately at par. Since then, the Canadian dollar lost one-third its value compared to the American. That sounds like brutally poor fiscal management, but a cheap Canadian dollar encourages the export of resource-based products, and may be partly responsible for Canada's high standard of living.

Notes

[9] The PFRA, Prairie Farm Rehabilitation Administration, was originally inaugurated by an Act of Parliament in 1935 in response to widespread drought, farm abandonment and land degradation of the 1930s. It led to soil, water, and land conservation methods and improved farming and ranching practices. The original mandate stated the purpose of the program:

"...to secure the rehabilitation of the drought and soil drifting areas in the Provinces of Manitoba, Saskatchewan and Alberta, and to develop and promote within those areas, systems of farm practice, tree culture, water supply, land utilization and land settlement that will afford greater economic security..."

By 1939, the reservoirs in Val Marie were built, and the PFRA was working with Ducks Unlimited to establish wildlife conservation areas throughout the prairies.
More on the history of the PFRA is available at: http://www.agr.gc.ca/pfra/pfhist_e.htm

[10] Bryan Trottier was the New York Islanders' second choice in the 1974 NHL draft. He set the National Hockey League's rookie record with 95 points and won the Calder Trophy as the NHL's top rookie in 1976. Trottier scored at least 100 points per season six times and scored 50 goals during 1981-82 as an Islander. As center, he helped the Islanders win four Stanley Cup Trophies, and for the Pittsburgh Penguins, two. During his 18-year career he earned the Art Ross and Hart Trophies in 1979, the Conn Smythe Trophy in 1980, and the King Clancy Trophy in 1989.

Bryan Trottier credited his father with much of his success. In his 1984 interview with *Goal* magazine, Bryan says, "My dad gave us opportunities in everything. If it wasn't hockey, it was baseball. If it wasn't baseball, it was rodeo. Then there was schooling, too. We had to do our homework along with our other activities." In describing their home in Val Marie, the article's author (Bob Glauber) says, "[Bryan lived in] Val Marie, the rolling ranchlands of southwestern Saskatchewan, where the winds howled by day and the coyotes by night. ...the main attraction became the ice on Frenchmen's creek, a spring-fed water supply that served the cattle well. When Bryan's father decided a new rink was needed he would chop a hole in a beaver dam, releasing just enough water for a glistening surface." (*Goal: The National Hockey League Magazine*, Volume XII, December, 1984)

[11] The CBC, Canadian Broadcasting Corporation, operated radio and television stations throughout Canada when I arrived in the country in the late 1970s. Before moving to Canada, I had heard that the government of Canada owned and controlled the airwaves - operating it like a sort of propaganda factory, a Canadian *Pravda*. Quite the contrary. I was surprised to hear a skewed balance of unfriendly remarks about the way the government was running its affairs. Certainly not the party line espoused by a crackly voice in far-off Ottawa that I'd been conditioned to expect. So why a nationally owned broadcasting corporation? The CBC was created as a Crown Corporation in 1936 by an Act of Parliament, following a Royal Commission that was concerned about the growing American influence in radio. It is partially funded by the government to ensure Canadians hear and see something other than CNN and NBC. As it turns out, The Canadian Broadcasting Corporation may have arisen without federal help and money, as its principal private sector competitor, the CTV (Canadian Television Network) has been able to present a separate, equally independent voice for Canadians. Nevertheless, CBC radio - thanks to public funding, continues to offer erudite and diverse programming, commercial-free.

[12] Jim Powers writes about his formula for good beekeeping in the Dadant publication, *The Hive and the Honey Bee*, fourth revision, 1978, *Section C: Management for Commercial Honey Production*, pp 410-412.

"Beekeeping for honey is three things: good locations, young queens with good breeding, and adequate stores. A good location is a site where one can place an economic number of bees (Powers Apiaries, a minimum of 40 colonies) and get a profitable surplus of honey. It should have a windbreak; it should have spring pollen and nectar; it should be out of the way of people and animals. Many times all these conditions cannot be met. The important thing is that it be profitable. If it isn't, move it.

"If a beekeeper does not have a systematic requeening program to keep young queens in his colonies, 20% of the colonies he is running for honey will be non-productive during the honeyflow. They will be going through supersedure or be queenless or have a just-mated young queen without a large enough bee population to store a surplus of honey. It costs a beekeeper just as much to operate these non-productive colonies as it does the honey producers.

"Perhaps 20% of the total number of colonies of bees starve to death each year. They starve during the winter either because they don't have enough honey to winter on, or if they do, they can't reach it. Many colonies starve to death in the spring, when the colony is expanding rapidly and has short stores for an extended cold spell. A colony needs from 40 to 100 pounds of honey to get through the winter and early spring, depending on geographical location..."

"One thought: A bad beekeeper will make a living with good locations; a good beekeeper will go broke with poor locations." - Jim Powers, 1974

[13] Hutterian Brethren: 1528-1931, by John Horsch.

"The Hutterian Brotherhood is named after Jacob Hutter who suffered martyrdom by being burned alive at the stake on February 26, 1536, at Innsbruck, in the Tyrol. This Brotherhood descends from the Swiss Brethren who constitute the oldest of the Anabaptist bodies."

[14] [To fully appreciate the following passage, keep in mind that the Hutterites are a religious sect whose adherents must profess non-violence and who must dress simply, in plain black clothing. Also remember that when the U.S. Government asked the Hutterites to settle the Dakota plains in the 1880s, the United States government agreed that Hutterites would 'be forever exempt from military service'.]

"The Selective Services Act, passed in 1917, allowed the [United States] Government to call all men between the ages of 21 and 31 to join the military service. The Hutterites agreed among themselves that their young men would register and report for their physical examination, but that they would not wear the uniform or obey any military work orders. The military officers, on the other hand, were determined to pressure the Hutterite men into service in any way they could.

"At Camp Funston, Hutterite men who refused to co-operate with the military were bayonetted, beaten and tortured. Some were dragged along the ground by their hair, while others were hung by their feet above tanks of water until they almost choked to death. Still others were chased across fields by guards on motorcycles until they dropped from exhaustion. Hutterite ministers went to Washington, but could do nothing to improve the lot of their young men.

"Of the many cases of brutal torture, the incident that did most to convince the Hutterites to move to Canada involved Jacob Wipf and the three Hofer brothers. These men were summoned to the military camp at Fort Lewis. When they refused to wear the army uniforms or perform their work orders, they were put into the guardhouse. After two months in the guardhouse, the men were sentenced to 37 years in prison at Alcatraz. Here they were handcuffed during the day and chained to each other by the ankles at night. When they still refused to put on their army uniforms the men were put in solitary confinement. They had to sleep on the wet concrete floors and received one-half glass of water every 24 hours, but no food. At times they were tied to the ceiling and beaten with clubs.

"After four months at Alcatraz, the four men were transferred to Fort Leavenworth. From the railway station they were forced to march on foot through the streets, while being prodded with bayonets. The weather was cold and they were given very little clothing so they were soon chilled to the bone. Joseph and Michael Hofer collapsed and were taken to the hospital. Jacob Wipf and David Hofer were sent to solitary confinement and placed on a starvation diet. Each day they were made to stand nine hours with their hands tied and feet barely touching the floor. Joseph and Michael Hofer later died in the hospital and their bodies were dressed in the uniforms they had refused to wear while alive." The boys were placed in simple wooden coffins and shipped back to their parents' colonies. When the boxes were opened, the families found their sons dressed in the uniforms they'd refused to wear while they were alive.

"Meanwhile, Hutterite colonies were raided by patriotic neighbours who stole their cattle and sheep, sold the animals at auction, and contributed the proceeds to the U.S. War Loan

Committee. The Hutterites then negotiated with the Canadian government and settled in fifteen colonies in Alberta and Manitoba in 1918."

From John Hofer, The History of the Hutterites, published with assistance of the Multicultural Program of the Government of Canada, 1978, pp 62-63. Other reports of this story have been published in The Hutterian Brethren in Military-Prison (J. G. Ewert) and Coming of the Russian Mennonites (C. Henry Smith). The book, Hutterian Brethren: 1528-1931, by John Horsch, pp115-116, describes the Hofer brothers as martyrs and, "the only conscientious objectors to die as a result of persecution" in the United States during World War I.

[15] The amount of canola grown in western Canada varies widely with seasonal seeding conditions (moisture, late frosts) and world market prices. Reuters, April 2000, reported twelve million acres, while in 2002, the amount had dropped to ten million. Statistics Canada states the acreage of canola seeded in western Canada ranges from 8.7 to 12.2 million acres. Assuming an over-all average of ten million acres (four million hectares), and a typical yield of 100 kilograms of honey per hectare, optimal honey yield from canola could be four hundred million kilograms – about a billion pounds.

StatsCanada reports recent alfalfa crop holdings as varying from 3.6 million hectares (1996) to 4.5 million in 2001. With potential yields of 200 kilograms of honey per hectare, 800 million kilograms of honey could be available from this source.

Not every season yields optimal quantities of nectar from canola or alfalfa, but in a normal year, these two sources secrete enough nectar in western Canada to produce over a billion pounds of honey. Western Canada produces about fifty million pounds per year. The potential to expand is enormous; with more bees, honey production in Canada could be a multi-billion dollar business.

[16] In the 1970's, Canadian research scientists genetically altered *rapus* in two ways - reducing the levels of glucosinolates (which contribute to the sharp taste in mustard) and licosenic and erucic acids (two fatty acids not essential for human growth). They named the stuff "Canadian Oil" - *canola*. But the rapeseed from which it originated has a long and honourable history. "Ancient civilizations in Asia and along the Mediterranean recorded the use of rapeseed oil for illumination and later it was used in foods and as a cooking oil. Although the crop was grown in Europe in the 13th century, its use was not extensive until the development of steam power when it was found that rapeseed oil would cling to water and steam-washed surfaces better than any other lubricant." (*Canola: Canada's Rapeseed Crop*, prepared by the Canola Council of Canada by Dale Adolphe, 1974.) Hence, rapeseed oil was largely an industrial grease until its genetic alteration resulted in a viable food product. That food product is now a billion dollar industry in Canada with about ten million acres sewn annually. Roughly fifty percent of all farmland in a hundred kilometre wide swath from the Peace river country to the American border south of Winnipeg is planted in rapeseed.

[17] Bland wrote extensively about honey-house cleanliness and championed the cause for adequate hygiene. He reviewed this theme continually in public forums and helped raise the standard for proper honey handling techniques. His presentation to the Manitoba Beekeepers' Association, February 13, 1979, was reprinted in the Spring 1979 issue of Manitoba Beekeeper, then picked up by *American Bee Journal*, July 1979, and published as "Honey House Hygiene and Sanitation." Ed Bland deserves great credit for his crusade on a very necessary work which did not usually receive much attention, funding, nor thanks. He helped raise the level of awareness and reformed some primitive honey processing techniques, improving the quality and wholesomeness of the Canadian honey product.

But his tactics - suggesting that women have a natural disposition towards dustpans; and publicly flashing slides of poor beekeepers' honey shops at meetings - were not universally appreciated. In his 1979 speech and subsequent magazine article, Ed Bland illustrated one of his suggestions to improve the hygiene standards of the honey house:

"I maintain that women have a penchant or inclination towards tidyness and cleanliness. It is both part of their nature and part of their training. I think this is quite understandable. A woman's day, especially if she is also a housewife, entails a multitude of tasks and much of her day involves cleaning: clothes, dishes, floors, etc. Without some order and an acceptance of the concept of hygiene, the potential for disaster is much greater than in a man's world. One of the prime

answers to an untidy, unsanitary honey extracting set-up would be to get the man out of the extracting plant and into the field and put a tidy, neat and authoritative woman in charge of the extracting, for where cleanliness has become a habit it has ceased to be a chore."
- Ed Bland, "Honey House Hygiene and Sanitation" July, 1979, *American Bee Journal*.

[18] Ed Bland, assistant provincial apiary inspector for Saskatchewan, co-authored <u>Beekeeping in Saskatchewan</u> with J.H. Arnott, in 1954, and acknowledged that packages are the best way to start beekeeping and to expand an operation. On page 26, they write, "Package bees are imported in large numbers from the United States each spring to replace colonies gassed in the fall and those which have died during the winter. This is the best source of bees for the beginner and for the beekeeper who is expanding the business." The next eight pages of their publication delineate proper package bee care and management.

[19] Mr. Emde describes queen production, the necessity of abundant drones, care in caging, and holding queens for shipment and he laments the often casual way these precious queens are treated in transit: "I would like to stress the care of both package bees and queens, as it can be most discouraging to a queen breeder when, after all possible care is taken, the product of this work is damaged by improper handling."
- Earl Emde, "Care of Package Bees and Queens," May 1978, *American Bee Journal*.

[20] In the book, <u>Following the Bloom</u>, Tom Emde (Earl's youngest son) is interviewed by author Douglas Whynott. Tom describes his parents' early days this way:
"My father, Earl Emde, started in California in the early thirties. By the time he finished high school he had several hundred colonies of bees and a truck. He began migratory beekeeping, on very poor roads, going up to Oregon, and going into southern California. He'd go out into the desert, and move into the higher elevations in the mountains for different crops. He'd go up to Oregon and back, up and down the West Coast.
"He started with a Model T, loading by hand. It was quite an ordeal. Little trails over the mountains. It was an all-night procedure just to get over one little range.
"In the forties he drove out to Iowa and Nebraska. He heard that there was good country back in the Midwest. He just took his truck and put a couple hundred hives of bees on it and headed east, not knowing anything about where he was going.
"His plan was to go to Iowa. He drove to Sioux City, and around Council Bluffs. He went all the way around Iowa in a big circle, with the bees on the truck....
"He remembered that there was an area back in Nebraska along the Missouri River Valley with lots of yellow sweet clover, a big, tall bushy plant. So he went back to Sioux City and located there, and along the eastern border of Nebraska he found places to put bees. They did so good he went tearing back to California to get another load and came back. That was the beginning of long-range beekeeping in California.
"...All through the forties and fifties he moved bees from California back to Nebraska... In the 1950s, he had enough of traveling and we stayed in Nebraska for about five years. And then he heard that Florida was good. He was always looking for new territory. He bought an outfit there, and we started moving from Nebraska to Florida in 1956."
- from <u>Following the Bloom: Across America with the Migratory Beekeepers</u>, Douglas Whynott, Beacon Press, Boston, 1991.

[21] Earl Emde reluctantly adopted the forklift and pallet beekeeping system which his son David pioneered during the early sixties. Earl was concerned that the bees wouldn't do as well with four hives per pallet - he believed colonies needed space between their neighbours. Earl was right, but the ease of management and the labour saved in moving tall strong colonies made the transition to palletized beekeeping inevitable for large commercial operators. Years later, David Emde - Earl's eldest son – received a recognition award from the American Beekeepers' Federation for this innovation.

Notes

[22] Herbert W. Armstrong founded the Radio Church of God, using radio to reach millions of folks who seldom attended church. Armstrong dispensed homespun wisdom based on healthy dietary habits and a successful, positive lifestyle. But Mr. Armstrong held some deep convictions which became apparent to his followers only after they delved deeply into his writings. Further promulgated by his eloquent son and successor, Garnet Ted Armstrong, the family built a multi-million dollar empire based on Armstrong's received divine revelations. God told Herbert, his prophet, that the 'Ten Lost Tribes of Israel' are not lost – they somehow migrated to the United States, Great Britain, Australia... Hence, the Anglo-Saxons are the true Israelites, God's Chosen People, and members of Armstrong's faith (re-named The World-Wide Church of God when Garner Ted took the message from radio to television) keep a Saturday Sabbath, abstain from pork, and selectively follow several other Old Testament commands.

The cornerstone of Herbert W. Armstrong's church is his book, "The United States and British Commonwealth in Prophesy," published in 1967 by Armstrong's Ambassador College. Some adherents believe the book is divinely inspired scripture. Among the delicious tidbits in this treatise, Armstrong describes "Race, Not Grace" (page 34) as critical to salvation and he bemoans the British Empire's loss of India, Barbados, Uganda, and thirty other countries no longer ruled by God's chosen race - the English. Armstrong offers proof that the Anglo-Saxons are *"descended from Isaac, and therefore are Isaac's sons. Drop the "I" from Isaac (vowels are not used in Hebrew spelling), and we have the modern name "SAAC'S SON'S", or as we spell it in shorter manner, "Saxons!"* – according to Herbert W. Armstrong, page 116, Commonwealth in Prophesy.

[23] The Palliser Expedition (1857-1859), supported by the Royal Geographical Society and the British Government, was led by John Palliser, a wealthy Irish landowner, accompanied by geologist James Hector, and various cartographers and botanists. They studied the natural resources and agricultural potential of the area - which Palliser reported as dismal. His dismissive conclusions slowed settlement in the area for decades.

[24] Single colonies of bees occasionally produce some spectacular crops. Mr. Ormand Aebi held a Guinness World record in verified honey production, 404 pounds, from a hive. Ormand wrote two excellent books about honey getting which relate his wisdom. He passed away on Christmas Eve, 1985, at the age of 94.

I had several colonies produce over six hundred pounds each during the summer of 1980, though Guinness was never employed to substantiate my production. Many other beekeepers in Canada, Australia, North Dakota, Florida, and the mid-west have seen similar results on rare occasions. However, Mr. Rob Smith surely holds the world's most astounding result for an apiary. I received this note from Bill Winner, Beekeeper Services Manager, capilano.com.au:
"We can confirm the average production of 346 kilograms (762 lbs) per hive from 460 hives. The beekeeper's name was Bob Smith from Manjimup, Western Australia. The honey was Karri. The year was 1954." Mr. Winner adds: "This figure is confirmed by R. Manning Land Management Journal Vol1 (5) P24-26, in a table provided as Fig 1. in "Honey production from the Karri with Redgum & Jarrah." Stating that commercial beekeeping commenced in 1936 with reference to Smith's crop in a box titled "World Record".

[25] It is not unusual for bees to collect ten pounds of honey per day. In fact, hives occasionally produce over thirty pounds in a single day - though the weather seldom allows a colony to keep this pace for very long. In Val Marie, I kept detailed records of hive production, jotting down the daily gain registered on the scale hive behind my house. The best single day's gain for the scale hive was 33 pounds, on July 14, 1978 (In four consecutive days, July 13-16, 1978, the scale hive collected 102 pounds of honey!). Further north, in Big River, Earl Emde recorded a 38 pound gain on July 28, 1982, part of a week's gain on his scale hive of 164 pounds of honey. Conversely, cool rainy days would keep the bees confined and no increase was noted – in fact, the hive often lost one or two pounds on such days, either through consumption by the bees, or from the reduction of moisture from the nectar as it became honey.

Bad Beekeeping

The appendix of this book includes several years of daily production records from the scale hive kept by the author in Val Marie. Also included are the set of weights recorded in Big River, by Earl Emde, for the years 1971 through 1990. Mr. Emde's records are among the most complete sequence of scale hive recording ever collected in western Canada.

26 "For many years, beekeepers had been using chemicals to remove their honey crops. The first chemical that was used was carbolic acid or phenol. This was reliable, but had several drawbacks. Most important was the fact that it was poisonous and could cause severe burns... During the early sixties, propionic anhydride was used briefly as a bee repellant with varying results. About the same time, two new chemicals were introduced: butyric anhydride and benzaldehyde... Both are used as food additives and approved by the E.P.A. for honey removal. Butyric acid is used in artificial butter flavorings and benzaldehyde, "artificial oil of almonds" is used as a food flavoring in bakery products."
- Al Reich, A Brief History on Removing the Honey Crop with Chemicals, American Bee Journal, September, 1978, page 621.

27 I wrote a short essay for the Canadian Honey Council regarding removing honey from hives:

New beekeepers sometimes ask me if bees get mad when you steal their honey. Bees don't really know you are taking their honey. But they certainly know that you are causing trouble, or creating a stink, as we used to call it back in Saskatchewan when we used smelly chemicals to chase the bees from supers. So take off your honey with the least amount of disturbance you can and the bees will be the gentlest. Always use a little smoke, but don't blast your bellows non-stop at the comb honey boxes. The combs will absorb the smoke odour and then you'll have to sell the honey at Safeway's cured meats counter. You can use stink boards, bee blowers, or Porter bee escapes. Or you can brush the bees off, one at a time. A Manitoba beekeeper tells me he thumps his combs on the ground until all the bees fall off. I've used all these techniques at one time or another. Each has some advantages, and serious disadvantages. Thumping is hard on the equipment, and like brushing, it requires extra smoke and irritates the bees. The chemicals and blowers are expensive environmental nuisances. Porter bee escapes require some special equipment and an extra trip or two out to the beeyard. And don't always work.

There's another method, which also has its hidden hazards, and may be illegal where you live. I read about it on the Internet, the place where you can learn how to build bombs, speak Croatian, and remove honey from bees. My son and I arrived at the apiary at two in the afternoon. My son, who is fourteen, doesn't like bees, and therefore, hopefully, will never have to suffer through being a beekeeper. He goes to the beeyard with me only to practice his driving skills. I digress. With minimal smoke and almost no jarring of the hives, we lifted off every box of comb honey, stacked them end-on-end (so the sun shone into all the frames) at the edge of the beeyard. Those honey boxes were full of bees. Then we went for a drive, coffee in Bragg Creek, a short hike up Elbow Falls. Got back to the apiary two hours later. Every bee had drifted out of the boxes and gone home. Every single bee! We simply stacked the liberated comb honey supers in the van and drove away.

Why doesn't everyone take honey this way? When I pulled this trick on my bees, there was a very light honey flow on. But during a dearth, the bees would not be distracted. They'd find the supers and rob like crazy. Everyone within four kilometres would know what you were doing because everyone would be getting stung by angry, frantic honey bees. And, returning to the apiary two hours later, there would be more bees in the supers than when you'd pulled them. I would never do this with the hive behind my house, preferring to brush those combs free of bees. Just in case.
- "Honey Combing", _Hivelights Magazine_, Canadian Honey Council, Ron Miksha, November 2000.

28 "Humans react to stings on three levels: local, systemic, and anaphylactic. In a local reaction, the initial localized swelling is followed by more extensive swelling a few hours later, and the affected area may be red, itchy, and tender for two or three days. Systemic reaction generally occurs within a few minutes of stinging, and may involve a whole-body rash, wheezing, nausea, vomiting, abdominal pain, and fainting. Symptoms of an anaphylactic reaction can occur within seconds and include difficulty in breathing, confusion, vomiting, and falling blood pressure, which can lead to loss of consciousness and death from circulatory and respiratory collapse."
- Mark L. Winston, _From Where I Sit_, Comstock Publishing, Ithaca and London, 1998, pp 24-25.

252

Notes

[29] Harvard Medical School states, "About 100 people a year die from allergic reactions to bee stings." It is not clear if Harvard Medical school assumes the world ends at the US border, or if this is a world-wide figure.

However, eMedicine's web-site, http://www.emedicine.com/emerg/topic55.htm, claims between 30 and 120 deaths per year in the United States from all types of bees. eMedicine.com estimates over a million bee stings each year in the USA, indicating the chance of death due to a bees' sting as less than one in ten thousand stings.

From the University of California, http://www.ipm.ucdavis.edu/PMG/PESTNOTES/pn7449.html: "Nearly everyone has been stung by an insect at one time or another. It is an unpleasant experience that people hope not to repeat, but for most people the damage inflicted is only temporary pain. Only a very limited portion of the population (one to two people out of 1,000) is allergic or hypersensitive to bee or wasp stings ...

"With honey bees, the toxic dose (LD_{50}) of the venom is estimated to be 8.6 stings per pound of body weight. Obviously, children are at a greater risk than adults. In fact, an otherwise healthy adult would have to be stung over 1,000 times to be in risk of death. Most deaths caused by multiple stings occur in men in their 70s or 80s who were known to have poor cardiopulmonary functioning."

[30] According to CNN, five people were killed by Africanized Honey Bees in the United States from the time of the bees' arrival (1990) through 1999. This implies an average of one death every second year. If the average number of fatalities due to all types of bees is fifty per year in the United States, the additional count due to the Africanized variant does little to impact the final tally.

[31] The dry short-grass prairie southwest of Val Marie, Saskatchewan is the only place in Canada where prairie dogs are found. The black-tailed 'prairie dog' is not a dog, but a relative of the ground squirrel. It was originally called a dog because of the bark-like sounds it would make. Prairie dogs live underground in massive burrows and form large social units called colonies. Their diet of roots and leaves was adopted from their home range – the arid grasslands and short-grass prairie.

[32] It is not accidental that Jacob Hutter's followers live in 'colonies'. The similarities between the bees' colony and this sects' are many: shared wealth, disciplined behaviour, ultimately swarming when the old colony becomes too crowded. By 'swarming' (the Hutterites call the event 'splitting-off') Hutterite colonies expanded from three in North America to about 500 in a bit over a hundred years.

[33] I wasn't the only commercial beekeeper to notice the potential in the Maple Creek area. By 1983, Derek Alen and his business partner, Ben Broderick, established 2000 colonies among the irrigated alfalfa flats. Derek brought his bees and experience from the town of Lashburn, in west central Saskatchewan, where he had produced mostly canola-tinged honey. The honey of southern Saskatchewan is considerably milder, lighter, and denser. His friend, Ben Broderick, was recently retired from the Royal Canadian Mounted Police. They operated their farm for about ten years.

In his book, Welcome Home, Stuart McLean describes encountering Ben Broderick in 1991:
"I meet Ben Broderick on one of my last days in town [Maple Creek]. Broderick is an ex-Mountie and now, like many other people in many small towns, he has cobbled together a collection of pastimes to help pay the bills.
"He is the deputy sheriff for the area out of Swift Current, the coroner, a part-time brand inspector and a sometimes justice of the peace. He ran a honey-bee operation for a while but now works on the pipeline in the autumn and as a security guard in the provincial park in the summer.
"...He has a big basset-hound face. He has big ear lobes and a bigger laugh. Mostly he likes to laugh at himself. When he is not working at something, he likes to get out into the prairie with his metal detector. He has an extensive collection of old coins, buttons, and rings."

Bad Beekeeping

[34] "An estimated 258,696 honey bee colonies were managed in Florida in 1999. Twenty-seven percent of beekeepers reported managing migratory beekeeping operations for approximately six months annually outside of Florida. Sixty-two percent of honey bee colonies (160,000) were migratory."
  – Economic Impact of the Florida Apiculture Industry, by Alan Hodges, David Mulkey, Effie Philippakos, Gary Fairchild, and Malcolm Sanford, University of Florida Cooperative Extension Service, EDIS document FE 273, a publication of the Department of Food and Resource Economics, Florida Cooperative Extension Service, Institute of Food and Agricultural Sciences, University of Florida, Gainesville, FL. Published January 2001

With roughly 500 hives per average truck load, about 200 semi-tractors loaded with bees arrive in Florida each autumn.

[35] From Root's 1913 edition of ABC and XYZ of Bee Culture (page 392):
  "Some beekeepers practice what is known as migratory beekeeping. For example, in one yard it is evident that bees are not getting any honey, and there is no flora of any sort that gives promise of any. On the other hand, there is another yard that is doing well, and there are still other locations without bees where there are immense quantities of alsike or red clover, or of buckwheat. Evidently it is a part of wisdom and business sense to move the yard that is yielding no returns to the location in which the honey can be secured.
  "While migratory beekeeping is not practiced to any considerable extent in this country [in 1913], largely because of the expense of moving, yet there are sections in the country that make the practice exceedingly profitable. In Germany migratory beekeeping is carried on somewhat more extensively than in this country, and occasionally we hear reports of a whole beeyard being put on an immense raft on a river. This raft is secured near the shore, and when the honey crop is taken the raft is let loose, when the raft, bees and all, are towed to pastures new. These floating apiaries have never been much of a success. Too many bees appear to drop in the water and drown. Mr. C. O. Perrine, many years ago, tried out this experiment on the Mississippi River, but the experiment was a financial failure."

[36] I am not, of course, the first person to comment upon the effect monoculture chemical farming has on the ecosystem. In the April, 1935, issue of *The National Geographic Magazine*, James Hambleton, Senior Apiculturist, U.S. Department of Agriculture's Bureau of Entomology and Plant Quarantine, had similar comments in his feature article, "Man's Winged Ally, The Busy Bee." Remember, Mr. Hambleton was writing in 1935:
  "In the pioneer stages of American agriculture, bumblebees and other native pollinating insects that fed upon nectar and pollen were plentiful everywhere. But the planting of vast areas which were once forests, prairies, and swamps with fields of grains, orchards, and gardens upset the delicate balance of Nature.
  "Wide-spread cultivation of single plants in huge acreages brought about an abnormal condition of insect population. Injurious species, afforded an enormous food supply, prospered and multiplied until now serious insect pests menace almost every important crop.
  "Insecticides must be used to protect farm crops, particularly fruits. Unfortunately, these materials kill not only harmful but beneficial insects. The toll includes honeybees and other wild bees, as well as the efficient bumblebees - all the insects that carry pollen from one blossom to another... the result that more and more dependence has been placed upon the honeybee, the only pollinating insect that can be propagated and controlled." -Hambleton, *The National Geographic Magazine*, April, 1935, pp 401-402.

[37] Statistics Canada census figures for 1995 show that an average Canadian family (2.57 people) spent $86.24 per week on non-restaurant food (restaurant spending was an additional $37.52). This is $33.56 per person per week for groceries, of which honey is about eight cents per week. Our cars and other modes of transportation cost us $56.84 per person per week. The average person's sports and recreation budget is $29.90 per week, roughly the same as the groceries.

Notes

[38] The severe freezes in 1894-95 hurt the citrus industry, and this area of Lake County turned to turpentine production. T.M. and C.C. Taylor sold their turpentine-production still in the southern portion of the county and went to Mascotte, planning to start tapping pine trees with a crew of black laborers. However, since Mascotte had never had a black resident, town leader Theodore Ruff refused to let the Taylor brothers set up shop. The Taylors then followed the railroad eastward to a place they named Taylorville, and erected their distillery on the lot where L. Day Edge later built his home. His father, Elliott E. Edge, bought out the Taylors in 1899 and laid out the foundation of a town. In about 1911, the community was renamed Groveland because of the citrus groves to the east and south of the town. The elder Edge was the town's first mayor and a founder of the Lake County Historical Society.
   - History of Lake County, Florida, by William T. Kennedy (Lake County Historical Society 1988)

[39] This peculiar story of the unusual beekeepers' meeting is correct – though Grossbomb was not the speaker's name.

[40] Originally from the *Australasian Beekeeper*, reprinted in the *American Bee Journal*, August 1973, then picked up as a 'filler' bit of news and distributed rather widely. The story in part says that the production of wild honey and beeswax fell fifty per cent in Bengal, India, due to a ban on hunting tigers. The ban resulted in some bold behaviour on the part of the tigers as they began attacking people working in the forests. In the words of India's Minister of Forests, "So far, twenty-nine honey collectors have been eaten by tigers and this has rather discouraged enthusiasm and diligence [in the pursuit of wild swarms]."

[41] From the Chicago Record, August 1, 1898, three hundred head of short-horned cattle belonging to Mr. J. McKeegan were totally lost when several swarms of wild bees attacked the cattle which were grazing on a high bluff overlooking the Missouri River. The cattle stampeded, raced over the embankment and were killed by their fall or drowned in the river.

[42] "The earliest direct evidence of honey hunting comes from rock paintings. There has been a suggestion of bee-connected paintings in the palaeolithic art of Altamira in northern Spain, dating possibly from the last major glaciation of the Ice Age (30,000-9000 B.C.). But mesolithic paintings in eastern Spain certainly show honey-hunting scenes. They have been dated provisionally to the period 8000-2000 B.C."
   A rock painting from 4500 B.C. found in a cave at Barranc Fondo, shows an organized group of five people on a ladder - a woman, second from the top, is apparently falling off the rope and stick ladder used to reach the bee nest.
   - Eva Crane, The Archeology of Beekeeping, Cornell University Press, Ithaca, 1983, pp 20-21.

[43] It is rare for more than one excellent source of nectar to occupy nearby locations and bloom in succession. The northern Canadian prairies has this advantage with legumes (alfalfa and sweetclover) blossoming in July, canola blooming as the hay is harvested, then a second blossoming of the legumes as they recover from the baling. Other areas may receive good nectar flows very early in the season - before the bees can store much of the nectar as honey. These areas typically have enormous dandelion and fruit tree sources, but weather is often cool and rainy - resulting in colonies that don't yet have the population necessary to make crops from these early bloomers.
   Along Florida's coast, citrus, gallberry, mangrove, and pepper bush are sometimes found in close proximity and in enough quantity to each supply a crop of honey. In theory, using Lovell, Howe, Pellett, and Florida state research reports, crops may exceed 200 pounds for each of these floral sources. It would be rare to find a year when the perfect combination of colony strength and weather conditions combined to allow such enormous production.

[44] The big, poisonous non-native Florida buffo toad occasionally delights in honey bee treats. This creature belongs to a distinguished list of vermin which enjoy colonial insects in North America – including the skunk, bear, and occasional human.

Bad Beekeeping

⁴⁵ Charles Butler was appointed vicar of a small rural parish in England in 1600. He used his spare time to observe and write extensively about the honey bee. He was among the first to give a reasonable description of the metamorphic development of the bee from egg through larva and pupa to adult. And, against common reasoning of his time, he recognized and publicized the fact that the queen bee is a female. Until his time (and for a century afterwards) most people believed that the largest bee in the hive was the 'king bee' and ruled over the other members of the colony as an iron-fisted royal despot. In his book <u>The Feminine Monarchie</u>, Butler clearly demonstrates the sex of the queen and her egg laying. He also offers much practical advise, including several pages of musical score, the tones of which identified the pitch of the buzzing within the hive at the time the bees were about to swarm. It was his expectation that the reader would identify the tone and its rhythm and be ready to nab the issuing swarm before it escaped the farmer's property.

⁴⁶ Jan Swammerdam researched the honey bee in the 1660s and 1670s, but it was not until 1737 that *Biblia natura* was printed and another twenty years before it was translated into English. Swammerdam lived a short, extremely productive life - five years of which were devoted entirely to the study of the bee. His daily work schedule found him in his laboratory each morning by six and he continued his sketches and observations far into the evening. He pioneered the use of alcohol and balsam as preservation agents for his thousands of specimens. His drawings of the bee's anatomy – including stinger and intestines – were nearly perfect and were used in classrooms for two centuries.

⁴⁷ It was long believed that Huber, perhaps the most brilliant beekeeper of the late eighteenth century, figured out the details of the queen's mating in about 1795. But in 1951, Dr. Fraser published a synopsis of the work of a peasant beekeeper from Slovenia. Anton Jansha was given a grant to the Vienna school of engraving, where he was befriended by Queen Maria of the Habsburg Empire. She persuaded him to engage in beekeeping for the royal gardens, as that was his family's trade in Slovenia. Twenty years before Huber began investigating the mechanics of how queens mate (high in the air with drones, away from the confines of the hive), Jansha had written two books in which he accurately described the mating process.

⁴⁸ E.B. White, *New Yorker Magazine*, 1945:

When the air is wine and the wind is free
and the morning sits on the lovely lea
and sunlight ripples on every tree
Then love-in-air is the thing for me
I'm a bee,
I'm a ravishing, rollicking, young queen bee,
That's me.
I wish to state that I think it's great,
Oh, it's simply rare in the upper air,
It's the place to pair
With a bee.

Let old geneticists plot and plan,
They're stuffy people, to a man;
Let gossips whisper behind their fan.
(Oh, she does?
Buzz, buzz, buzz!)
My nuptial flight is sheer delight;
I'm a giddy girl who likes to swirl,
To fly and soar
And fly some more,
I'm a bee.
And I wish to state that I'll always mate
With whatever drone I encounter.

Notes

[49] Harry H. Laidlaw, Jr. was a brilliant honey bee geneticist and research scientist at the University of California, Davis. He streamlined, commercialized, and promoted artificial insemination of the queen bee to assure parentage and maintenance of genetic stock. But he wasn't the first to attempt controlled mating of the queen.

In the early eighteenth century, it was generally believed that the queen mated inside the hive. De Reaumur tried a series of experiments (1734-1742) to control honey bee mating by placing a virgin queen in a glass box with several drones. Though unsuccessful, this probably represents the first attempt to control bee mating. The Slovene scientist, Anton Janscha in 1771 discovered that the queen mates away from the hive. Huber repeated the observations and his publication led to Huber's attempt to paint semen onto the queen in the first effort at artificial instrumental honey bee insemination. It was unsuccessful.

In 1885, the United States Department of Agriculture hired Nelson W. McLain to develop a syringe to inject drone semen into the queen bee – presumably building on successful work among bovine herds but using somewhat smaller tools. McLain was not successful, but the ground-work and theory were established. It wasn't until 1926 that a partially successful insemination using a microscope, syringe, and lamp was completed. Lloyd Watson was the first to use the term "instrumental insemination" but he neglected to observe nor work around an anatomic obstruction called the valvefold. Harry Laidlaw, in 1934, made the correct observations and developed a workable methodology which is used today to inseminate queen bees.

Why all this work to secure what could happen quite easily and naturally? When a queen bee mates, she copulates in the air with several drones who have traveled a long distance from diverse colonies carrying a mixture of genetic stock. The result is usually a hardy blend of honey bee attributes, but a blend, nevertheless. Controlled mating is used primarily in research situations when particular traits are being developed – notably disease resistance. These traits would be quickly diluted and tests of their efficacy in developing a superior bee would not be as clearly accomplished.

[50] Li Jianke and Cheng Shenglu, researchers from Zhejiang University (Hangzhou, China) briefly trace the beginning of royal jelly use (citing early studies from the 1940s) and the phenomenal growth in its production – from a few hundred pounds to several million pounds per year today.

"People have been familiar with Royal Jelly (RJ) for more than half a century. It has been a commercial product in many countries for more than 30 years, especially used in dietetics and cosmetics. Research was initiated in the 1950s. In the beginning, for example in China, RJ production was as low as 10g per colony in a three day period, thus making the price exceedingly high. At that time RJ was used for study purposes only. With the improvement of the producing technology, particularly in the last decade, RJ is undergoing a spectacular revolution in production. The 1990s have seen a successful cultivation of high yield RJ. RJ yield is as much as 20-30 times higher than before in China, where around 2000 tons is produced each year, accounting for 90 per cent of the world's total output."
  - "Royal Jelly and Human Health" by Li Jianke and Cheng Shenglu, *American Bee Journal*, May 2003, pp 398-401.

[51] In Taiwan, beekeepers earn the biggest part of their income with royal jelly production. Incredibly, beekeeping products rank as the second largest agricultural commodity to be exported, following tea but ahead of silk-worm-breeding and citrus fruits. The average Taiwanese bee farm has about 200 – 250 hives. These tend to be family operations, with the very labour-intensive grafting and jelly harvest limiting the potential numbers of hives. An average harvest of 600 to 1000 kilograms per farm yields more than the average income for a family in this part of Asia, but the nine hour days, seven days a week, nine months a year is quite a tough grind. Most hives are kept on three or four apiaries within a few kilometres of the farm home. Hives are tended with small trucks which double as laboratories containing grafting tools, lights, tables for production, and suction equipment for harvest.
  – *Beekeeping in Taiwan*, by Gilles Fert, http://www.apicultura.com/articles/us/taiwan.htm

Bad Beekeeping

In Japan, modern systems for royal jelly production were developed during the 1940s. Consumption is high, Japan imports over 400 metric tonnes a year. Japan once produced quite a lot of royal jelly, but labour costs are high, so commercial operators have relocated in other countries. Japan has a long history of beekeeping, the art arriving with Christianity, chickens, and goats, all on the boat leased by the missionary, Saint Francisco Xavier, in 1549. But royal jelly production didn't begin commercially until 1954 when the father of Toshio Morikawa found a way to mass-produce the jelly. At that time, royal jelly cost $500/gram, so there was a lot of motivation to streamline systems and produce large quantities. Distribution was a problem. Royal jelly must be kept cool, but refrigeration was uncommon in Japan in the 1950s. Morikawa solved distribution problems by drying the royal jelly to a powdered form and selling it in capsules in 1957.
   – personal communication with Mr. Toshio Morikawa, 2002.

China leads the world in royal jelly production and consumption. Li Jianke, writing in the *American Bee Journal*, May, 2003, states that the world's production of royal jelly is about 2250 tons, ninety per cent coming from China, and half consumed there.

In Thailand, a new commercial royal jelly production business began when Mr. Chen, of Taiwan, air lifted 600 colonies to the north of that country. He created a 2000 colony royal jelly factory-farm in an area where floral sources, temperate weather, and low wages all combine to make the enterprise profitable.
   - *Beekeeping in Taiwan*, by Gilles Fert, http://www.apicultura.com/articles/us/taiwan.htm

[52] Along with proteins (especially albumin and globulin) and various fats and ashes, royal jelly contains from 2.84% to 3% of an unidentified mystery material which Li and Cheng call substance 'R'. They demonstrate that royal jelly has 20 kinds of amino acids, at least 26 types of fatty acids, and one gram of royal jelly contains about 4 mg of RNA and 200 mg of DNA. There is also one unique free fatty acid, 10-hydroxy-2-decenoic acid, which is found only in royal jelly – nowhere else in nature. We can not know which of these substances is the precise material which triggers the transformation from worker to queen during the bee's early development. All worker bees are given some royal jelly, but the queen is nearly drowned in pools of the stuff and she is fed royal jelly for a much longer period.

"Queen bees are made, not born, and their feeding with royal jelly is the key to this process," says Li in the *American Bee Journal*, 2203. With royal jelly supplement, the queen averages 42 per cent larger and 60 per cent heavier than a worker bee. They live 40 times as long. They lay 2000 to 3000 eggs a day, equal to two and a half times the queen's weight.

Li continues his article claiming and documenting the potential human health benefits of royal jelly, including "pharmacological functions such as hypotensive activity, antitumor activity, insulin-like action, disinfectant action, and so on." - Li Jianke and Cheng Shenglu, "Royal Jelly and Human Health", May, 2003, *American Bee Journal* (pp 398-402).

[53] Humans have long consumed nutritious insect snacks. Primitive man sometimes survived by plucking termites and ants from nests and eating them raw. With bees and wasps, it is usually the brood – larvae or pupae – that are eaten. However, in certain circumstances, adult bees and wasps are also enjoyed. Canned wasps (wings, stinger, legs, and body) are sold in Japan. Emperor Hirohito enjoyed wasps served on a bed of rice. In some cultures, even today, wild bee nests are attacked by humans as much for the bee brood as the honey that the hives may contain. Similarly with bears, the real attraction is the protein rich grubs, not the honey.

On a Bee Biology users-net, September, 1994, Dave Pehling states:
"I have eaten bee brood several times and find it delicious! Very much like very tiny, sweet shrimp! By the way, shrimp and crabs would think nothing of feeding on a rotting corpse, while baby bees are fed only the finest honey and pollen. I find it interesting to explore various food sources that are all around us and wonder if world hunger would be less of a problem if more people would have more of an adventurous spirit about new foods. I prefer my bee brood lightly fried in oil and mixed with vegetables. One dish I've made is "Peas & Bees" - very tasty.

"The biggest problem with bee brood as a food source is removing the tasty morsels from their snug little cells. I have seen a video of someone removing drone larvae from a comb with a fine jet of water but have not tried it myself. I usually pick my own "brood-for-food" out of burr comb I scrape off while working my hives."

Kevin Johnson, Big Johnson Beekeeping, Lillington North Carolina, February, 1999, writes: "The practice of consuming bee brood as well as other high protein natural foods is common practice in many jungle areas. And is included in many wilderness survival training programs. The brood can be consumed raw, as many of the native amazon tribes consume it (whole in the comb) or can be shaken out into deep fat for a crispy treat, lightly seasoned, salt to taste. *Crunchy like pork skins.*"

In Asia, bee larvae are a traditional treat. Connoisseurs usually eat the two-or three-day-old larvae simply mixed in an omelet. Alternatively, they may be cooked with wine. In Taiwan, in particular, where a thousand commercial beekeepers efficiently keep 300,000 hives of bees, plump queen larvae from royal jelly producers are frequent menu items on finer, traditional menus.

[54] Queen quality varies greatly. The best gauge of value is egg-laying ability, which can vary from a few hundred per day from aging or malnourished queens to 3000 eggs a day. J.E. Eckert (Journal of Economic Entomology, Volume 27(3) pp 629-635) identified that the total number of ovarioles (tubules that comprise a queen's two ovaries) varies from 260 to 373 among a study of 280 queen bees. The number varied by queen size and weight and this was also directly proportional to the nutrition of the developing queen larvae and to the number of eggs the adult queen bee could produce.

[55] Among the honey bees kept in most of the world, laying workers are underdeveloped female honey bees which lay eggs. Unfortunately for the hive, this female has never mated and all her offspring are drones, so the colony eventually dies out. An exceptional case exists among the Apis mellifera capensis, a south African race of honey bee commonly called the Cape bee. In queenless colonies of the Cape honey bee, workers soon begin laying eggs which frequently develop into females - without fertilization. From these budding young females, the bees can raise a new, fully developed, replacement queen bee.

[56] "It was A.I. Root who first conceived the possibility of shipping bees without combs. We find in the original edition of his ABC of Bee Culture, published in 1879, an account of his experiments in shipping bees in wire screen cages without combs, very similar to those now made. His original idea was not to eliminate the possibility of transmitting disease [which might inadvertently occur in wax combs] but to reduce express charges. A heavy, bulky hive complete with combs necessarily made the express charges very high. A.I. Root early saw the possibilities of shipping a half-pound, a pound, or two or three pounds of bees in a light wire-screen cage. Two or three pounds of bees, enough to make up what would be equivalent to an ordinary colony wintered over, would weigh not over six pounds, cage and all, as against 45 or 50 pounds for a whole hive and colony. There might be no more bees in the full colony than would be in the wire cage, and one would gather just as much honey as the other, provided it was released upon combs of honey in a hive already prepared...
"At first, Mr. Root met with many difficulties. His early experiments, while often successful, sometimes met with failure. He was not able to make the candy just right, and the bees starved to death. He therefore used metal containers for syrup or water. With the water bottle and candy he finally succeeded in making good deliveries even over long distances. But there were so many failures in shipping bees on candy alone without combs that for a time the idea was abandoned."
    - ABC and XYZ of Bee Culture, published by A.I. Root Company, edited in 1972, page 499.

[57] "The first to make successful shipments of package bees from the South to the North, in 1912, was W.D. Achord, then of Fitzpatrick, Alabama, near Montgomery. For a year or two he was the only one who could make a candy, not too hard nor too soft, to carry bees through to destination. He was willing to show his neighbors how to make the candy, and the result was that in a few years thousands of packages of bees were sent from the vicinity of Montgomery alone to the northern beekeepers and orchard growers."
    - ABC and XYZ of Bee Culture, published by A.I. Root Company, edited in 1972, page 500.

[58] One beekeepers' guide book describes three ways to collect packages. The Illustrated Encyclopedia of Beekeeping, edited by Roger Morse and Ted Hooper, explains:

"Three basic techniques are in common use. One method is for a "queen finder" to work ahead of the shaking crew. This individual finds the queen, places the comb on which she is found back into the brood chamber, and places all the remaining combs on which there are bees outside the hive. Shakers shake these bees into the funnel and packages, and replace the combs and close the hive. A second method is to remove the hive cover, place an excluder over the brood nest, place an empty, covered super on top of the excluder, and drum the bees from the supers below into the empty box. The excluder keeps the queen and drones in the brood nest super while workers crawl upward. The bees are shaken from the super into a large funnel and into the package. A third method is to shake bees from frames, without finding the queen, into a funnel with an excluder at the bottom. As the bees are shaken, they are smoked heavily, which encourages them to move through the excluder. When the queen is seen on top of the excluder she is picked up and placed back in the hive."

[59] If rhythmic tapping is done to the side of a beehive, "it appears to exert an hypnotic effect, causing a peaceful, upward movement of bees, and a beekeeper can use this to his advantage...as a means of removing bees from comb...to drum, or drive, bees...

"How driving was discovered is not clear: it is not mentioned in any of the Roman or Greek writings that have survived. It has been used, however, for hundreds of years to remove bees from fixed-comb colonies in early or mid-season, so that the honey and wax might be harvested..

- The Illustrated Encyclopedia of Beekeeping, edited by Roger Morse and Ted Hooper, 105.

Unfortunately, uneven or erratic tapping may excite the bees to attack. Experience teaches the beekeeper to use the proper method of drumming. If performed correctly, smoking the bees is not required during drumming exercises. Smoke is essential, however, when drumming to shake packages.

[60] Sulfathiozole was shown effective in the treatment of American foulbrood in 1944. Sulfa drugs were used effectively to suppress manifestations of this ravenous disease for forty years, but were banned when it was shown that trace elements of the drug could survive in honey - hence reaching the consumer - months after its application to treat the bees. Today, oxytetracycline is used - it has a shorter life-span, breaks down quickly and doesn't enter the food chain, but treats foulbrood diseases effectively.

[61] C.C. Miller was born in 1831. Dr. Miller's father died when C.C. was ten years old, leaving a family of six and little money. Young C.C. Miller worked his way through grammar school (taking three years off to help support the family) and eventually moved from his native Pennsylvania to Schenectady, New York, where he worked his way through college.

He writes, "This last undertaking was a bit reckless, for when I arrived at Schenectady I had only about thirty dollars, with nothing to rely on except what I might pick up by the way to help me in college. I had a horror of being in debt, and so was on the alert for any work, no matter what its nature, so it was honest, by which I could earn something to help carry me through.

"I had learned just enough of ornamental penmanship to be able to write German text [Dr. Miller's mother was from Germany, he likely spoke German from childhood.], and so got $4.00 for filling in the names of 88 diplomas at two commencements. I taught singing school; I worked at Prof. Jackson's garden at seven and a half cents an hour; raised a crop of potatoes; clerked at a town election; peddled maps; I got $100.00 for teaching a term at an academy. Neither were my studies slighted during my course, which was shown by my taking the highest honor attainable, Phi Beta Kappa, which, however, was equally taken by a number of my class."

With such sacrifice, hard-work, and dedication to become a physician, one assumes Dr. Miller would have easily made a career of medicine. Unfortunately, his disposition did not allow him to follow through with a practice:

"It did not take more than a year for me to find out that I had not a sufficient stock of health myself to take care of that of others, especially as I was morbidly anxious lest some lack of judgment on my part should prove a serious matter with some one under my care. So with much regret I gave up my chosen profession."

Soon Miller was married, was teaching voice and instrumental music, and had become principal of a public school. He needed something extra to stimulate his vast intellect, to allow a bit of challenge, and to improve his health with "robust work and fresh air." A swarm stumbled onto his porch. He became a beekeeper.

[62] "As a beekeeper, I am particularly typical in this way: I am interested enough to learn from another man's habits, but wise enough not to adopt them," Dr. Miller from <u>Fifty Years Among the Bees</u>, Dr. C.C. Miller, 1915, Marengo, Illinois

[63] Although unfertilized eggs of the common honeybee always develop into males, there is one uncommon type of honey bee which forms an exceptional class. In her book, <u>Bees and Beekeeping</u> by Dr. Eva Crane, *A. m. capensis* is described in detail (especially see pages 10 and 109). The Cape honeybee's natural zone is within fifty kilometres of the Cape of south Africa. The bee is described as similar to the common races of honeybee, but with two divergent features in its reproductive history - it develops much more quickly from egg to adult and if the queen should lay an unfertilized egg, it can develop into a fully-functional female, capable of laying eggs. Hence, Cape honeybees never have the problem of colony collapse in event of a poor, 'drone-layer' queen.

[64] Leo Nikolayevich Tolstoy, 1828-1910, beekeeper, pacificist, writer, and philosopher, enjoyed beekeeping to such an extent that his wife sometimes worried about his sanity. She should have realized that he was engaged in research for a book.

<u>War and Peace</u>: Chapter 20

Meanwhile, Moscow was empty. There were still people in it, perhaps a fiftieth part of its former inhabitants had remained, but it was empty. It was empty in the sense that a dying queenless hive is empty.

In a queenless hive no life is left, though to a superficial glance it seems as much alive as other hives.

The bees circle round a queenless hive in the hot beams of the midday sun as gaily as around the living hives; from a distance it smells of honey like the others, and bees fly in and out in the same way. But one has only to observe that hive to realize that there is no longer any life in it. The bees do not fly in the same way, the smell and the sound that meet the beekeeper are not the same.

To the beekeeper's tap on the wall of the sick hive, instead of the former instant unanimous humming of tens of thousands of bees with their abdomens threateningly compressed, and producing by the rapid vibration of their wings an aerial living sound, the only reply is a disconnected buzzing from different parts of the deserted hive. From the alighting board, instead of the former spirituous fragrant smell of honey and venom, and the warm whiffs of crowded life, comes an odor of emptiness and decay mingling with the smell of honey. There are no longer sentinels sounding the alarm with their abdomens raised, and ready to die in defense of the hive.

There is no longer the measured quiet sound of throbbing activity, like the sound of boiling water, but diverse discordant sounds of disorder. In and out of the hive long black robber bees smeared with honey fly timidly and shiftily. They do not sting, but crawl away from danger. Formerly only bees laden with honey flew into the hive, and they flew out empty; now they fly out laden. The beekeeper opens the lower part of the hive and peers in.

Instead of black, glossy bees- tamed by toil, clinging to one another's legs and drawing out the wax, with a ceaseless hum of labor - that used to hang in long clusters down to the floor of the hive, drowsy shriveled bees crawl about separately in various directions on the floor and walls of the hive. Instead of a neatly glued floor, swept by the bees with the fanning of their wings, there is a floor littered with bits of wax, excrement, dying bees scarcely moving their legs, and dead ones that have not been cleared away.

The beekeeper opens the upper part of the hive and examines the super. Instead of serried rows of bees sealing up every gap in the combs and keeping the brood warm, he sees the skillful complex structures of the combs, but no longer in their former state of purity. All is neglected and foul. Black robber bees are swiftly and stealthily prowling about the combs, and the short home bees, shriveled and listless as if hey were old, creep slowly about without trying to hinder the robbers, having lost all motive and all sense of life.

Drones, bumblebees, wasps, and butterflies knock awkwardly against the walls of the hive in their flight. Here and there among the cells containing dead brood and honey an angry buzzing can sometimes be heard. Here and there a couple of bees, by force of habit and custom cleaning out the brood cells, with efforts beyond their strength laboriously drag away a dead bee or bumblebee without knowing why they do it. In another corner two old bees are languidly fighting, or cleaning themselves, or feeding one another, without themselves knowing whether they do it with friendly or hostile intent. In a third place a crowd of bees, crushing one another, attack some victim and fight and smother it, and the victim, enfeebled or killed, drops from above slowly and lightly as a feather, among the heap of corpses.

The keeper opens the two center partitions to examine the brood cells. In place of the former close dark circles formed by thousands of bees sitting back to back and guarding the high mystery of generation, he sees hundreds of dull, listless, and sleepy shells of bees. They have almost all died unawares, sitting in the sanctuary they had guarded and which is now no more. They reek of decay and death. Only a few of them still move, rise, and feebly fly to settle on the enemy's hand, lacking the spirit to die stinging him; the rest are dead and fall as lightly as fish scales. The beekeeper closes the hive, chalks a mark on it, and when he has time tears out its contents and burns it clean.

So in the same way Moscow was empty when Napoleon, weary, uneasy, and morose, paced up and down in front of the Kammer-Kollezski rampart, awaiting what to his mind was a necessary, if but formal, observance of the proprieties - a deputation.

[65] Dr. Miller said, "It is not the yield per colony I care about, unless it should be to boast over it; what I care about is the total amount of net money I can get from my bees." - Fifty Years Among the Bees, Dr. C.C. Miller, 1915, Marengo, Illinois, Page 42.   Considered a classic in Apiculture literature, the book exudes good humour, good sense, good beekeeping.

[66] Please see this book's Appendix for scale hive results.

[67] Originally from Quebec and originally named Ernest Dufault, at age fifteen Will James arrived in the lower Frenchman River Valley in 1907 - about ten years before the village of Val Marie was founded. He worked for the big ranches as a cowboy, and filed for a homestead in 1911. He left a few years later and ended up in California. He began a career as an artist and writer - and was rather successful at it. His books have been translated into thirty-seven languages and several were produced as major motion pictures. The best private collection of Will James materials in Canada is at the Perrault Museum in Val Marie.

[68] Perhaps the biggest difference between how the Canadian west was settled contrasted with the American settlement involves the national police forces and their stated goals. The Americans sent the army – most notably General Custer and his kind, to pacify the Indians, moving them to reserves, keeping them from lands which were awarded to white settlers. Canada also gave native lands to white settlers and eventually moved its aboriginal peoples to squalid internment camps which we call 'Reservations'. But originally, a non-military police force (not an army) was sent west. And their mandated job was to protect the native Indians from whiskey traders and thieves.

The Canadian patrolman in charge, Inspector Walsh of the Royal Canadian Mounted Police said, "My opinion is they will obey the law of the country. War they have had enough of." Inspector James Walsh estimated 2900 American Sioux crossed into Canada in November 1876. Bringing 3500 horses and 30 United States Army mules. Over the next few years, the number of Sioux would rise to 5000 and a large number of Tetons also entered along the Frenchman River Valley, seeking political asylum from the United States. R.C. Macleod noted, "It is sufficient to note that fair treatment of the Indians by the Canadian police controlled the Sioux... thereby avoiding even a single violent incident."

- From Wood Mountain to the Whitemud: A Historical Survey of the Grasslands National Park Area, D.M. Loveridge and Barry Potyondi, Parks Canada, 1983, pp 73-80.

Notes

[69] Lovell calls *fireweed* by the name willow-herb (*Epilobium angustifolium*). "It is a perennial herb, 2 to 8 feet tall, with long lance-shaped leaves and red-purple flowers in long spike-like groupings. After forest and brush fires it springs up in great abundance, and flourishes for about three years, when other plants crowd it out.... [However] on the Canadian Pacific Railway in British Columbia, there are localities where fireweed blooms year after year without diminishing." It can be found throughout north Europe, Asia, and North America and Lovell adds in italics of his own that "*Willow-herb has a more northern range than any other honey plant of first rank.*" The honey is reported as the "whitest and sweetest honey I have ever tasted," according to Lovell. But "...unfortunately the best areas for fireweed honey production are difficult to reach and are, consequently, seldom utilized by beekeepers."
   - Honey Plants of North America, John H. Lovell, 1926, A.I. Root Company, pp 241-243.

[70] Dr. Eva Crane, author of numerous books on the history and archeology of bees and beekeeping, says properly stored honey has a shelf-life of at least 20 - 25 years. She writes, "The oldest honey I have seen is in the Agricultural Museum of Dokki in Egypt, where two honey pots from New Kingdom tombs still have their contents in them.". Dr. Crane also notes that the earliest known record of keeping bees in hives and harvesting honey from them dates from 2400 BC, in Egypt.
   - A Book of Honey, Crane, pp 42 and 109.

[71] In Ancient Egypt, honey was regularly sacrificed to the gods, by dumping into the river Nile, and by feeding to sacred animals. Breasted's *Ancient Records of Egypt* (1962) mentions honey in 21 entries of offerings made by Ramesses III (1198-1166 BC), totaling thousands of jars.
   - The World History of Beekeeping and Honey Hunting, Eva Crane, Gerald Duckworth and Company, Ltd., 1999, page 595.

[72] Pythagoras lived in the fifth century BC and he attributed his long life to a regular use of honey. A century later, the Pythagorean Brotherhood still ate honey as a principal food, according to Athenaeus, who wrote (in 350 BC) "Bread and honey were the chief food of the Pythagoreans."

[73] Icarus made wings by gluing bird feathers to his arms with beeswax. He ignored the advice of his father Daedalus, and flew too close to the sun, the wax melted. The asteroid Icarus has an unbalanced orbit around the sun, coming very near it, then swinging quite far away. As it passes through the earth's orbit, it could theoretically bump into our planet, causing the end of all life on earth. Russian scientists have announced that possibility for the year 2015, when Icarus will be close (in astronomical terms) but probably not close enough to kill us all.

[74] Democritus, a leading Greek philosopher and scientist, was not the only person of his time to believe bees can arise from rotting flesh. Indeed, the concept of 'spontaneous generation' was current through the middle ages. Proof seemed to exist simply by viewing dead stuff on the side of the road. Within a few days, it would be teeming with worms, flies, sometimes hornets (which it was believed were a type of bee). A seventeenth century recipe for the spontaneous production of mice involved dirty underwear and wheat seeds, placed in an open jug. Within 21 days, the mess would transform into mice.

   In 1668, Francesco Redi, an Italian physician, believed that maggots developed from eggs laid by flies. To test his hypothesis, he set out meat in a variety of flasks, some open to the air, some sealed completely, and others covered with gauze. As he had expected, maggots appeared only in the open flasks in which the flies could reach the meat and lay their eggs. But not everyone was convinced. Debate continued. John Needham performed experiments in England in the 1740s that supported Francesco Redi, but Father Lazzaro Spallanzani suggested that micro-organisms could exist in all inanimate material and give rise to life under ideal conditions. The theory of spontaneous generation was finally and completely dispelled in 1859 by Louis Pasteur, then a young chemist, who contrived elaborate methodology to decisively disprove the theory.

   It is not hard to understand how early philosophers could believe honeybees arise from carrion. Bees are bugs, much like wasps and flies, which seem to spontaneously generate from dead animals. Why not bees? And if honeybees arise from dead carcasses, why not from the noble bull?

Bad Beekeeping

The earliest mention of bees from bulls comes from Antigonos of Karystos dated at around 250 B.C.. Virgil gave poetic life to the notion in his Georgics, telling the legend of Aristæus, the son of the god Apollo:

"Aristæus had a beehive. He tried to seduce Eurydice, Orpheus' wife, but she died from a snake bite because she refused Aristæus' advances. In revenge, Orpheus destroyed Aristæus' hive. To appease the wrath of the gods, Aristæus sacrificed four bulls and four heifers. From their entrails, new swarms suddenly appeared, so Aristæus was able to rebuild his hive and teach beekeeping to men."

[75] Hippocrates of Cos (Greece, 400 B.C.) wrote quite a lot about the healing powers of honey, particularly as a balm or salve for open sores. In Francis Adams' translation "On Ulcers", which clearly describes the medical treatment of open blisters and sores, Hippocrates describes several methods for creating a healing salve:

"Having pounded the white unripe grape in a mortar of red bronze, and passed it through the strainer, expose it to the sun during the day, but remove it during the night, that it may not suffer from the dew; rub it constantly during the day, so that it may dry equally, and may contract as much virtue as possible from the bronze: let it be exposed to the sun for as great a length of time as till it acquire the thickness of honey; then put it into a bronze pot with fresh honey and sweet wine, in which turpentine resin has been previously boiled, boil the resin in the wine until it become hard like boiled honey; then take out the resin and pour off the wine: there should be the greatest proportion of the juice of unripe grape, next of the wine, and third of the honey and myrrh, either the liquid (stacte) or otherwise. The finest kind is [by] stirring it in the wine; and when it appears to have attained the proper degree of thickness, it is to be poured into the juice of the unripe grape; and the finest natron is to be toasted, and gently added to the medicine, along with a smaller quantity of the flowers of copper (flos aeris) than of the natron. When you have mixed these things, boil for not less than three days, on a gentle fire made with fuel of the fig-tree or with coals, lest it catch fire. The applications should all be free from moisture, and the sores should not be wetted when this medicine is applied in the form of liniment. This medicine is to be used for old ulcers, and also for recent wounds of the glans penis, and ulcers on the head and ears.

"Another medicine for the same ulcers:-The dried gall of an ox, the finest honey, white wine, in which the shavings of the lotus have been boiled, frankincense, of myrrh an equal part, of saffron an equal part, the flowers of copper, in like manner of liquids, the greatest proportion of wine, next of honey, and least of the gall. Another:-Wine, a little cedar honey, of dried things, the flowers of copper, myrrh, dried pomegranate rind. Another:-Of the roasted flower of copper half a drachm, of myrrh two half-drachms, of saffron three drachms, of honey a small quantity, to be boiled with wine."

[76] Virgil's Aeneid, on bees:

For ornaments of scenes, and future view.
Such is their toil, and such their busy pains,
As exercise the bees in flow'ry plains,
When winter past, and summer scarce begun,
Invites them forth to labor in the sun;

Some lead their youth abroad, while some condense
Their liquid store, and some in cells dispense;
Some at the gate stand ready to receive
The golden burthen, and their friends relieve;

All with united force, combine to drive
The lazy drones from the laborious hive:
With envy stung, they view each other's deeds;
The fragrant work with diligence proceeds.

Notes

Virgil uses the image of the hive in an almost Orwellian description of the builders of Carthage, Rome's enemy - the invisible Aeneas looks down on the workers of Carthage building their city:

They are like bees
In early summer over the country flowers
When the sun is warm, and the young of the hive emerge,
And they pack the molten honey, bulge the cells
With the sweet nectar, add new loads, and harry
The drones away from the hive, and the work glows,
And the air is sweet with bergamot and clover.
"Happy the men whose walls already rise!"
Exclaims Aeneas, gazing on the city,
And enters there, still veiled in cloud--a marvel!--
And walks among the people, and no one sees him.
        (Translation by Rolfe Humphries, *Aeneid*, Book I.447-57)

Virgil also wrote at length about bees in the <u>Fourth Book of The Georgics</u>, describing the best beekeeping wisdom of his time. Virgil believed the queen was a king; bees were thought to go to war against other bees high in the air above us; larvae were gathered from dew-covered leaves; wax and glue were collected from trees and shrubs; and entire swarms were spontaneously generated from rotting bull's carcasses.

An excellent interpretation of Virgil's <u>Georgics IV</u> is found at http://clarksville.org/cd/MONARCH/dp/0219/02195.txt, (no credits are given):

(The Georgics: Book IV, Lines 1-87.)

The first thing the bee-keeper must do is find a safe home for the hive out of the reach of the wind. It should be located as far from where sheep and goats are apt to go as possible. They will trample all over the flowers, or knock the dew off the blades of grass. Birds and lizards are the enemies of bees too. A shady spot near springs or a pool is the best place. Then when the kings lead out the swarms of young in the spring-time they will find pleasant shade from the heat. Plant cassia (an herb of the pea family) and thyme with its pervasive fragrance, and savory, and "let violets drink from the overflowing spring."

Having settled the location of the hive, the next step is its construction. It can be made of either hollow bark, or woven of osiers, but it is important to make its entrances small. Otherwise the cold will freeze the honey in winter, and in summer the heat melt it. Either event would be a dreadful calamity for the bees, as they work so hard filling up the crannies with wax or gluey substance made from the pollen of flowers. And don't let yew trees grow near the hive, or roast crabs where the smoke can reach the bees. And never place the hive in a muddy location or in a spot that echoes. Bees are extraordinarily sensitive creatures. When summer comes they will take to the woods and gather pollen from the purple flowers. If the keeper wants them to return, he must spread about perfumes which the bees like, and make a clanging sound by clashing the cymbols of the Great Mother, Cybele. Then they will come back of their own accord.

(Lines 88-228.)

Jupiter, the king of the gods, has given marvelous qualities to the bees because they fed him when he was hiding from his father Saturn on the island of Crete. The bees practice a communism that truly works: they have children in common, common dwellings, and live according to great laws. They work hard together all summer in preparation for the coming winter, gathering everything into a common store. Some look after the finding of food, some work in the fields, some work in the hive, some bring up the young, and some pack the honey. Their perfect division of labor produces the liquid nectar, sweet with the fragrance of thyme. The aged build the hives while the young carry home the pollen. They all rest at the same time and work at the same time - in the morning they swarm out of the hive together, in the evening they all return. For a while they buzz around the entrance, but soon all is quiet for the night. If it looks like rain, they stay close to home and only make short forays out to the nearby fields. If it is very windy they pick up tiny stones as ballast to keep them from being buffeted around.

Bad Beekeeping

Their method of propagation is nothing short of miraculous. They do not have intercourse or waste their strength in love-making, or endure the pains of child-birth. Instead they find the young on the leaves of herbs and carry them to the hive in their mouths. But as easily as they come into the world, just as easily do they leave it, dying willingly out in the fields under their loads. They obey the king bee as if he were a monarch more absolute than an eastern potentate. If they loose him, they give up the hive altogether.

It is because of these wonderful characteristics that some people believe that the bees partake of a share of the divine spirit which permeates the universe. For these philosophers hold that "God goes through everything, the lands, the paths of the sea, and the heavens. From him flocks, herds, men, and every kind of wild beast summon their tenuous lives as they are born. And doubtless to him they all return; nor is there a place for death but, still living, they fly among the number of the stars and mount to the depths of heaven."

(Lines 229-566.)

To get the honey without being stung, carry a smoking torch in front of you to stun them or drive them away, for when maddened, their stings are poisonous. Honey can be collected twice a year, at the times when the constellation of the Pleiades rises (in May) and when the constellation sets (in November). Even if you think the winter will be severe, and that some honey should be left for the bees themselves, you should still gather it. Otherwise pests, such as salamanders, beetles, or hornets will get what you leave. The more you take of the bees' honey, the harder they will work to restore it.

[77] Mead, an intoxicating drink made from a honey base has also been used to gain tactical military advantage. In 946, the Slavic St. Olga, on the occasion of her son's funeral, provided limitless quantities of mead. She invited her enemies only, who, presumably, had somehow been instrumental in the death of her child. Five thousand inebriated 'mourners' were slain in their stupor by Olga's allies. Similarly, in 1489, 10,000 Tatars were thwarted by Russians whom the Turkish invaders had been pursuing. The Russians left mead behind in their flight and returned after sufficient time for the Tatars to drink themselves into a daze.
 - Gould, J.L. and C.G. Gould. 1988. *The Honey Bee*. Scientific American Library, New York. pp. 2-3

[78] A friend of Galileo, Prince Cesi was a scientist, astrologer, and alchemist. In 1625, he published the first drawings of the anatomy of the honeybee, based on his own observations using the newly invented microscope. He also coined the word 'telescope' and used the instrument to support Galileo's findings.

[79] At a celebration at the University Club commemorating the opening of UCLA's *Harry H. Laidlaw. Jr. Honey Bee Research Facility,* the 93 year-old professor and scientist and his audience were told by Robert Page, chair of the University of California (Davis) Department of Entomology that "breeding of bees had eluded scientists and beekeepers for 200 years. For example, Gregor Mendel, who discovered the fundamental laws of genetics in pea plants, spent the rest of his life trying to breed bees, without success." Laidlaw was able to control the mating of queens, the mastery of a technique which eluded Mendel.

Brother Adam, the Buckfast Abbey monk and beekeeper, describes his own efforts in pursuing Gregor Mendel's unfinished business in <u>Breeding the Honey Bee</u>. He describes some of the reasons for Mendel's failures.

"Mendel's own experiments in this sphere (honey bee genetics) foundered because he had no control over the drones. Presumably he did not appreciate the influence of parthenogenesis and he had no inkling of multiple mating...
"We know that Mendel was a very keen beekeeper, but as we have just mentioned, his attempts at cross-mating with his bees were doomed to failure from the outset. On the other hand his careful experiments with peas combined with his natural mathematical genius enabled him to establish the general laws of heredity."
 - http://www.fundp.ac.be/~jvandyck/homage/books/FrAdam/breeding/partI85en.html

266

Notes

[80] "One of the best examples of Turner's behavior work is his studies of color and pattern vision in the honey bee. Turner's honey bee work is all but forgotten in the honey bee literature. For both papers, elaborate apparatus was constructed and controls were implemented that conclusively show that honey bees can perceive both color and pattern.

"The rationale behind the color vision paper (1910, Experiments on color-vision of the honey bee, Biological Bulletin, 19, 257-279) was to provide data under controlled conditions on the ability of bees to see color... To investigate the problem, he studied honey bees in O'Fallon Park in St. Louis. He designed various colored disks, colored boxes, and 'cornucopias' into which the bees were trained to fly. Thirty-two experiments were designed, and controls for the influence of odor and brightness were instituted. The results of his experiments showed that bees can see colors and can discriminate among them."

- *Charles Henry Turner: Contributions of a Forgotten African American to Honey Bee Research*, by Charles Abramson, *American Bee Journal*, page 643-644, August 2003.

Dr. Turner's honey bee papers were published in 1910 and 1911, a decade before the first von Frisch publications. Turner describes in great detail a methodology adopted by von Frisch for von Frisch's studies in Germany. It is almost impossible that Karl von Frisch was unaware of Turner's writings - which appeared in North American and European journals - though von Frisch never cites Dr. Turner's work. Von Frisch won the Nobel Prize for these and other innovations; Turner became a footnote in a beekeeping memoir.

[81] Karl von Frisch's research on the honey bee included studies on the insect's memory, time measurement skills, color perception, and ultimately, the bee's ability to convey information - through a physical language we observe as a 'dance'. Von Frisch divided the dances into the 'round' and 'wiggle-tale'; the former for conveying the fact that food was nearby, but the latter for more complex statements relating to distance and direction of food sources which were a bit further from the hive. For his ingenuity, decades of observation and lucid writing, Karl von Frisch shared the 1973 Nobel Prize in Medicine and Physiology.

To see an action demonstration of the honey bee dance, and learn more, log on the internet at http://ourworld.compuserve.com/homepages/Beekeeping/beedance.htm

[82] Visitors to Washington's Mount Vernon and Jefferson's Montebello Estates will find that these American presidents kept bees, a common practice on the bigger progressive farms of their time. Exhibits hold 'nail keg' box hives and show early beekeeping tools.

[83] *The Lion's Mane*, by Sir Arthur Conan Doyle, describes Sherlock Holmes' retirement cottage:
"My villa is situated upon the southern slope of the downs, commanding a great view of the Channel. At this point the coast-line is entirely of chalk cliffs, which can only be descended by a single, long, tortuous path, which is steep and slippery. At the bottom of the path lie a hundred yards of pebbles and shingle, even when the tide is at full. Here and there, however, there are curves and hollows which make splendid swimming-pools filled afresh with each flow. This admirable beach extends for some miles in each direction, save only at one point where the little cove and village of Fulworth break the line. My house is lonely. **I, my old housekeeper, and my bees** have the estate all to ourselves."

It has become a matter of curiousity and interest among the keenest of Holmes enthusiasts to try to determine the exact location of the retirement cottage. Using clues from The Lion's Mane – a great view of the Channel, chalk cliffs, a long path to the beach – several have tried to find the spot Doyle had in mind when he retired his famous detective. A critical piece of evidence is the necessity of an adequate apiary location, implying shelter from the ocean breezes. This, in turn, has ruled out many potential cottage sites.

In 1967, the Chairman of the Sherlock Holmes Society of London, Charles O. Merriman, was rather certain he had located Holmes' retirement farm. Mr. Merriman wrote in *The Game Is Afoot,* "The land attached to the farm rises to an eminence eastwards known as Michel Dean, which gives a commanding view of the Channel. When I was informed in the course of conversation with some of the downsfold that Cornish Farm produced acres of which clover each year and that the bees from

Bad Beekeeping

Birling Manor Farm, the only farm [nearby] which keeps bees by reason of its sheltered position, feasted on the white clover after and early-in-the-season diet of wild raspberry, which is prevalent on the Downs in this area, I felt my researches had at last borne fruit. I have not pursued the matter further but I should imagine that Mr. Stackhurst's school, *The Gables*, must lie at East Dean or Friston or its environs up to a mile north of Birling Manor Farm."

[84] Until Langstroth hit upon the idea of fixing individual combs into wooden frames, a variety of semi-removable comb hives were employed. The Greeks, as early as Aristotle, fixed honey combs to wooden strips (top bars) which hanged from the top of a box. The combs were removeable until the bees glued the edges of the comb to the inside of the box. Langstroth observed that bees always leave enough space between each comb so they can crawl about from place to place within the hive, but given the chance, the bees will anchor the edges of the comb to anything available – the inside walls of a box, skep, or tree, for example. He quite intuitively hit upon the idea of sticking the combs into frames and spacing the frames so that the frames' edges, tops, and bottoms always came close to the walls of the receptacle, but never touched it. The appropriate spacing for 'closeness' Langstroth discovered, was three-eighths of an inch. His observation and his creation of frames revolutionized beekeeping. It allowed easy observation of the hive for scientific study, for control of swarming, artificial division of hives, control of pests and diseases. It was a brilliant practical discovery.

In his column, Reminiscences, published in *Gleanings in Bee Culture*, xxi, pp 116-118, he recalls:
"Returning late in the afternoon [of October 30, 1851] from the apiary which I had established some two miles from my city home, and pondering, as I had so often done before, how I could get rid of the disagreeable necessity of cutting the attachments of the combs from the walls of the hives...the almost self-evident idea of using the same bee space [which Langstroth had noticed could keep a lid from sticking to the combs of the top of a hive box] came into my mind, and in a moment the suspended movable frames, kept at suitable distances from each other and the case [hive box] came into being. Seeing by intuition, as it were, the end from the beginning, I could scarcely refrain from shouting out my "Eureka!" in the open streets."

[85] "For many years I have suffered from what I have been wont to call my 'head trouble,' which not only unfits me for mental exertion, but also disqualifies me for enjoying almost anything personal to myself. While under its full power, the things in which I usually take the greatest pleasure are the very ones which distress me most. I not only lose all interest in bees, but prefer to sit on that side of the house where I can neither see nor hear them. Gladly, if at all convenient, would I have my library of bee books hidden from my sight; and often I have been so morbid that even the sight of a big letter B would painfully affect me. At such times, fearful of losing my reason if I allowed my mind to prey upon itself, I have resorted to almost constant reading to divert my thoughts."
- America's Master of Bee Culture: The Life of L.L. Langstroth, Florence Naile, 1942, page 144, quoting Langstroth's *Reminiscences*, originally printed in *Bee Culture*'s 21st volume.

[86] L.L. Langstroth, the minister-turned-scientist who invented the modern beehive, ended up in Dayton, Ohio, at the end of his life. He is buried at Woodlands, next to the remains of aviators (the Wright brothers), authors (including Erma Bombeck), the creator of the *Yellow Pages* (L.M. Berry), the inventor of the step-ladder (John Balsley), actress Leslie Carter, the inventor of cellophane (William Church), a Republican candidate for president of the United States (James Cox), a renowned African-American poet (Paul Dunbar), a famous bordello operator (Elizabeth Richter, who is buried with three of her working girls), two Civil War generals (Robert Schenck and Robert Cumming Schenck), and three Gypsy Kings (from the Owen Stanley family of the English *Roma*).

[87] Sir Edmund Hillary's autobiography, <u>View from the Summit</u>, describes a bit of his life as a young man in the family honey business in New Zealand. In his chapter, *From Bees to Flying Boats*, one gets a sense that he learned much about hard work and discipline from the grueling chores of honey harvest and extracting on the commercial honey farm where he grew up.

from Hillary's Chapter FROM BEES TO FLYING BOATS:
For a long time, my father had been involved in keeping bees, initially as a hobby and then as a profitable sideline. My mother, my brother and I all worked hard in the business. Every weekend, all

through the school holidays, and even on long summer evenings, I was fully involved with the bees. I received no pay of even pocket money, which wasn't all that unusual for farming families in those days, and I really enjoyed the challenge of it. Finally, my father had a disagreement on principle with the directors of his small newspaper [where Sir Hillary's father was a reporter and editor] and he resigned and took up commercial bee-keeping full time. This meant my brother and I were even busier, carrying 80 lb boxes of honey for extracting and even 120 lb crates holding two four-gallon tins of honey. By the time I was sixteen years old I was as strong as a man and worked harder than most. (page 42)

[After attempting university and doing poorly at it,] I returned to beekeeping. My father had quite a big operation with 1,600 hives of bees and, apart from our food and lodging, it didn't cost him anything - it was certainly cheap labour. I was too big now to be taken to the woodshed any more but arguments we had in plenty. Although I enjoyed much of the work, particularly when the honey-gathering season was in full swing, I became rather tired of the relentless drive to work seven days a week for no financial return... (page 44)

from Hillary's chapter: SOUTH OF EVEREST WITH SHIPTON:
My brother Rex was a year younger than me and he, too, was part of our family bee-keeping business. Rex and I worked well together as a team. He was smaller than me but very strong and vigorous. In the friendliest fashion we competed energetically with each other, often running side by side with heavy loads of honey to pile them on our truck. Why did we persist in working with a father who paid us so little and whose views varied so often from our own? The main reason I believe was because we actually enjoyed the bee-keeping. Our thirty-five apiaries were spread out on fertile dairy farms up to forty miles away, so we were always on the move. The spring and summer, when the bees were gathering nectar, was a time of great excitement. The weather made bee-keeping a tremendous gamble, of course. Each apiary we visited could have a substantial crop of honey in its hives or almost nothing. Rex and I revelled in the hard work and increasingly the field activity fell into our hands. Our father was a hard and somewhat ruthless man but I never lost my well concealed respect for his tremendous work ethic. But finally even he had reluctantly to concede that he would need to pay us just enough to live on - but no more! (page 58)

from Hillary's Chapter YETIS IN THIN AIR:
[Hillary had conquered Everest in 1953 and had returned from his Antarctica expeditions in 1959, the last year he was a commercial beekeeper.]
I worked on the bees, for the last year, as it happened, and wrote a book on the Antarctic and Louise had our third child, Belinda, who was to prove a joy to us all. After Everest people kept telling me that I would never have to work again, dozens of companies would want me as a public relations director and money would just keep flowing in. I would be a rich man in no time at all. It didn't turn out quite that way. Certainly I was invited to be a director and patron of many worthy causes but none of them paid any money. I had to raise my finances in a quite different manner. (page 190)

- View From The Summit, Sir Edmund Hillary, Doubleday, 1999, pp 42; 44; 58; 190.

[88] There are at least two references to Henry Fonda's beekeeping in *American Bee Journal*:
"Fonda Busy as a Bee in Backyard" reprinted from the Associated Press and published in the August 1980 ABJ notes in part: "There's not a honey on the market like mine," Fonda said in an interview beside his backyard hives. "It has nothing to do with me. It's the variety of forage on my back 40."
   Fonda referred to the lush vegetation at his Bel-Air estate. At 75, Fonda took up beekeeping when a swarm landed in the walls of his house. A beekeeper, John Manke, arrived to give a hand, gave Fonda a hive and an eight-page pamphlet on bees which led to an extensive beekeeping library. Fonda gave away jars of "Hanks' Bel-Air" to co-workers and dinner guests. "Waiting in line [for my honey] are my daughter Jane, my son Peter, my sister in Omaha, a cousin in Denver, nieces all over the place, friends all over town..."

[89] A military strategist and medical healer, Le Quy Quynh resides in Ho Chi Minh City (Saigon), Vietnam. He is well known and respected in Vietnam as a "Hero of the Revolution" for leading forces from the North first against the French, then against the US. He served as Adjutant to General Giiap, and as *defense minister* in Ho Chi Minh's first post-war cabinet. However, his real claim to fame is

his 50 years as a beekeeper and his research, cultivation and medical treatment using bees and bee products. He is famous in Vietnam for his healing techniques – many of his patients are victims of severe war related injuries – and he has worked wonders on their wounds.
 – personal correspondence with Quynh's American grandson, who lives in California.

[90] S. E. McGregor, Insect Pollination of Cultivated Crops, USDA, 1976, shows that the number of blossoms per tree range from 50,000 (Valencia) to 100,000 (Washington Navel). McGregor says blossoms hold a prodigious amount of nectar (20 microliters, or about 1.5 bee-loads) The flowers refill themselves quickly. With each blossom open for 2-3 days, and the entire flow lasting three weeks (Frank Pellet, American Honey Plants), an acre of orange would have 200,000 flowers open, each with over a load of nectar, at any moment during the flow. With (optimistically) 50,000 foragers in a hive, there would be enough nectar for four colonies. In practice, not all hives have 50,000 foragers and not all trees have a healthy bloom. Pellett, Lovell, and a variety of anecdotal sources in the beekeeping literature describe situations where several hundred colonies have been kept near modest-sized groves and large surpluses were secured.

[91] It is difficult to estimate the total amount of honey which can be produced from a single acre of any monocultured plant. The year-to-year variation is great, largely dependent on weather, but the area-to-area variation may also be enormous. Canola, sweet clover, and alfalfa yield much more per acre in Saskatchewan than in Pennsylvania, for example, largely due to the alkaline soil in the west, the longer days, and the much sunnier skies. Nevertheless, some researchers have attempted to estimate the amount of honey yielded per acre for a variety of plant types. Girnik (1969) in Russia, states about 320 pounds per acre may be exuded from sweetclover, while McGregor (1952) claims about 150 pounds per acre each day from alfalfa.

[92] In a 1986 letter to this author, Statistics Canada (courtesy of Crop Analyst Lynda Magahay) data shows that Saskatchewan had an average of 2.5 million acres of canola and 2.0 acres of hay crops for the ten year period 1976 to 1986.

[93] The two US states with the most colonies of bees have historically been Florida and California. Bees are usually kept on farmland, though swamps, mountain ranges, and cities may offer some foraging opportunities. However, hive densities may be described in terms of farmland available per colony. Florida has 10 million acres described as 'farmland' but only third is actually cultivated, the other 65% are pasture and 'woodlands'. Florida has about one bee hive for each fifteen cultivated acres. In California, with 30 million acres described as 'farmland' (two-thirds of which are designated range land and includes desert) the hive density is one hive per 20 cultivated acres. Saskatchewan has 67 million acres of farmland. If we only consider Saskatchewan's ten million acres of tame hay (clovers and alfalfa) and canola - superb nectar sources - the Saskatchewan hive density is one hive per hundred acres. North Dakota, Saskatchewan's neighbour, has about 5 million acres of nectar yielding crops and over 300,000 colonies- hive density is roughly one hive per 20 acres. At comparable concentrations, Saskatchewan would be home to half a million colonies of bees.

[94] In his description of orange honey production in Florida in 1926, John Lovell writes that "the average surplus in a good year is about 40 pounds." At that time, Lovell also writes that there were one and a half million citrus trees in central Florida. (Honey Plants of North America, Root Publishing, 1926, page 176)

My records of production per hive ranged from a few pounds to over a hundred pound average, depending mostly on the timing of winter frosts and on soil moisture conditions. The Florida per hive average in 1974 was 58 pounds per hive, with a three year average of 77 pounds. Today, in the aftermath of such exotic pests as varroa destructor and the small hive beetle, the average Florida beekeeper produced 98 pounds in 1998, 102 pounds in 1999, and 105 pounds in 2000. Sources include American Bee Journal, November 1976 and April 1998; and the USDA at http://www.nass.usda.gov/fl/lvstk/honey/honey01.txt.

Notes

[95] From: "Is it Overstocking... Or is it Jealousy?" *Gleanings in Bee Culture*, 1979:

"It seems that the old question of overstocking bee locations has still not been answered in Polk County, Wisconsin. A couple of years of poor honey seasons – caused by changing agricultural practices, unfavorable weather conditions, and possibly beekeeping ineptitude – has aroused screams that the "outside beekeeper is stealing all our honey". I refer, of course, to the actions of the Polk-Burnett County Beekeepers Association and the December *Gleanings* article Beekeeping Ordinances in North-western Wisconsin.

"The idea that there must be two miles between every yard of bees is absolutely absurd legislation. It seems remarkable that anyone with even the most rudimentary knowledge of bees could have had any hand in enacting such a law as that now afflicting Polk County.

"In the late 1950's when my father first started placing his bees near Groveland, Florida there were three other beekeepers there. Two of those have since ceased their operations. But today, twenty years later, there are seventeen commercial beekeepers within the same area. During citrus bloom we have a density of nearly 200 colonies per square mile. Production seems unhampered. Well-managed colonies in the spring of 1978 averaged 80 pounds. In 1926, when John H. Lovell compiled his tome Honey Plants of North America the concentration of bees per acre of citrus was far below today's number. Yet, Lovell (page 176) says, "The average surplus in a good year is about forty pounds". That was 1926. Of course, the 1978 crop with its 80 pound crop was unusual – sometimes we have springs with poor weather and little orange honey is produced. Nevertheless, the huge number of bees didn't hurt our production.

"Polk County, Wisconsin is far from the "dumping grounds" that local beekeepers apparently imagine it to be. I wonder if the author of that article ever heard of Dr. C.L. Farrar, the most brilliant bee culture scientist in modern times. In many of Farrar's USDA publications he states that "fully 90% of the available nectar is lost because there are not enough bees to gather it". Dr. Farrar should know. He spent his acclaimed lifetime researching the subject in Madison, Wisconsin – and he retired in Balsam Lake, Wisconsin. Balsam Lake...county seat of Polk County!

"Perhaps the father of beekeeping, Rev. Langstroth, can help illuminate the subject. Quoting directly from the original copy of the Hive and Honeybee we find Langstroth telling us, "I confess that I find it difficult to repress a smile when the owner of a few hives, in a district where as many hundreds might be made to prosper, gravely imputes his ill-success to the fact that too many bees are kept in his vicinity". He thought the question had been settled over a hundred years ago – obviously, there are still those beekeepers around who are over a hundred years behind times. How unfortunate that they should find themselves in positions of legislative authority.

"Does anyone have the right to regulate the number of bees which can be located in a specific area when it is absolutely impossible to know how many bees that area can support? The Polk County ordinance says there must be two miles between bees. That gives each yard of bees a mile radius in which to work. Will the local government fine bees which fly beyond their mile limit? What about the millions of wild bees and butterflies and moths and wasps and other nectar gathering insects and birds that already thrive on those eighty-seven and a half million square feet of land that lies within one mile of every beehive? If there were a fixed, immutable amount of nectar available then common sense declares that through a balanced environment and many centuries of time, nature would have allowed the number of nectar seeking creatures to balance the amount of nectar available. Most of us know it doesn't work that way. When the chemistry and physics of weather, soil, moisture, sunlight, plant nutrition, all decide to combine properly, everyone gets fed. If the combination doesn't arrive – move your bees!

"The same opportunities are available to everyone of us. The beekeepers in Polk County, Wisconsin, are free to move their bees to Florida, California, Texas, or Mississippi for the winter. The regulation and legislation problem is in no way unique to the Wisconsin situation. In every corner of this great nation, and in every phase of life and business, people are inviting and encouraging laws which will "protect" them from the opportunity to learn, work, think, and live peacefully in what was a free world. If anyone chooses stagnation instead of growth, ignorance instead of knowledge, poverty instead of prosperity, please...don't ask the government to help you.

"Are there too many bees? No. Not according to every major apicultural scientist in the world. Why the poor crops in certain areas? The fact is, in some parts of the continent the honey crops have never been better. Instead of fretting, worrying and complaining about the successful neighboring beekeeper, perhaps his habits should be imitated. His efficiency, skill and knowledge are available to anyone willing to apply effort and make sacrifices. No, apparently overcrowding is not the problem – the problems are ignorance and jealousy."

[96] Robert Frost, 1923:
Some say the world will end in fire,
Some say ice.

[97]   "As bees in spring time, when the sun with Taurus rides,
    Pour forth their populous youth about the hive
    In clusters; they among fresh dews and flowers
    Fly to and fro, or on the smoothed plank,
    The suburb of their straw-built citadel,
    New rubbed with balm, expatiate and confer
    Their state affairs. So thick the airy crowd
    Swarmed and were straitened; till the signal given,
    Behold a wonder! They but now who seemed
    In bigness to surpass Earth's giant sons,
    Now less than smallest dwarfs, in narrow room
    Throng numberless . . ."
                    (Milton, *Paradise Lost*, I.768-80)

[98] For many years, the Andre Dumont family diligently recorded daily maximum and minimum temperatures, plus rainfall accumulation, for Val Marie. Under contract with Environment Canada, their data covered about twenty years. I copied their observations into my own notebooks. For the period of 1970 through 1981, the weather station located in Val Marie received about eight inches of rain and about three of melted snow per year.   The driest summer was 1971, just three inches of rain in five months. Farmers had a tough time that year. The temperature range was equally extreme. During the period, Val Marie recorded a high of 41.1C (about 106 F) and a low of minus 49.4, roughly minus 50 Fahrenheit. Frosts killed spring flowers as late as June 11 in 1973 and arrived as early as August 26 in 1980. Most summers had 90 days without frost, but when summer arrived – swiftly following a brief spring, most years had many days with temperatures exceeding 30C (86F) and a few over 40C (104F). Val Marie is a brutal place.

The Climate of Canada, published by the Meteorological Branch, Air Services, Department of Transport, Toronto, Canada, offers climatic tables for 45 cities and towns across Canada, including Swift Current, the closest centre listed to Val Marie. Swift Current, according to these figures, has 14.89 inches of precipitation (rain and snow) per year. June is the wettest month (nearly three inches), with July and August typically getting two inches of rain each.

Transpiration is a serious problem on the southern prairies. Although ten inches of rain may fall in a year, the strong winds and extremely arid air have the ability to evaporate about fifteen inches per year. This results in dried lake beds, crusted in white salts which are sucked up from within the soil by a capillary effect - as the bits of intermittent rainfall evaporate, they draw mineral-saturated water from deep within the soil up to the surface.

[99] Remembering Will Have To Do, Louise Moine, 1979. This book, a Native Writers Contest Winning Manuscript, was prepared with the help of the Saskatchewan Indian Cultural College Federation of Saskatchewan Indians. Mrs. Moine describes her early childhood in southwest Saskatchewan:
    "As a descendant of Indian, French, and Scots ancestry, my life was more or less guided by a mixture of these three nationalities. Since my parents were both Metis, it is only natural that my Indian blood predominated. Our first language was a mixture of Cree and French. We followed in the footsteps of our ancestors, adopting whichever ways and customs suited our way of life. We lived from day to day, with no anxiety for tomorrow. Until the time when the white settlers started moving closer to us, we were a free and happy people. Not only did their way of life infringe on our liberties but their discrimination against us was not easy to accept, as we were a proud race. In time we learnt that we couldn't fight them, so we had to join them. Whether this was for better or worse, it's hard to say. I know we learnt a lot from them but they could also have learnt from us."

Notes

[100] The fire in California and other aspects of California beekeeping during the early part of the last century are described by John H. Lovell, <u>Honey Plants of North America</u>, Page 393. Published by the A.I. Root Company, Medina, Ohio. 1926.

[101] "Normal beeswax is a solid of variable yellow or orange color, has an agreeable odor or aroma, is plastic when warmed to about 90F (32C) and melts at about 143 to 151F (62 to 66C)." – William L. Coggshall and Roger A. Morse, <u>Beeswax: Production, Harvesting, Processing, and Products</u>, Wicwas Press, 1984, page 17. Although beeswax melts at about 65 degrees Celsius, hives are in big trouble if they can't cool their nest below 32C, the point where cell structure integrity begins to break down. Under the weight of the bees and honey, the combs can begin to collapse, smothering bees and oozing honey out of the hive.

[102] Elbert Jaycox' Beekeeping Tips and Topics, Modern Press, Albuquerque, New Mexico, 1982. Jaycox reports the finding from an insect flight symposium, reported by researcher Werner Nachtigall that the bee's fanning frequency is from 180 to 195 beats per second, generating a forward thrust one-third greater than the bee's weight. If a bee, fanning fresh air into her hive, doesn't cling on to the floorboard, she would be suddenly airborne.

[103]   "Alfalfa is probably of Asiatic origin... The plant was brought into Greece at the time of the Persian war, 470 B.C., from Media, whence the generic name Medicago. [Alfalfa is *Medicago sativa.*.]

   "It was also very early introduced into northern Africa, where it was called alfalfa, a word of Arabic origin signifying 'the best fodder'. During the Moorish invasion, it was carried into Spain, and later was brought by the Spaniards to Mexico and South America, and finally in 1854, was carried from Chile to California.

   "A most important character of alfalfa is the taproot, which may extend downward to a depth of fifteen feet, enabling the plant to obtain food materials and water accessible to few other food crops." [Hence, its ability to survive prolonged drought and semi-desert conditions.]
   - John H. Lovell, <u>Honey Plants of North America</u>, 1926, A.I. Root Company, pp 56-60.

[104] Val Marie was in the province's highest premium rate area for honey crop insurance. To receive 60% coverage (i.e., to be paid the difference on a poor year for 60% of a running-average crop, we had to pay a 4.33 percent premium. To get 80% coverage, annual premiums were 6.77%. In real money terms, if a beekeeper normally produced $100,000 worth of honey, premiums were $6777 per year. In a disastrous year with no production, the beekeeper would receive $80,000. In the part of Saskatchewan around Nipawin and Prince Albert, crop failures were deemed less likely and insurance rates were about one-third less.

[105] "Chinese planners were predicting a twenty per cent growth in colony count and production between 1986 and the year 1990, when hive numbers were expected to reach eight million."
   -*American Bee Journal*, December 1986, page 787.

China accounts for about a fourth of world honey output. In 2002, China's production increased to a record 257,758 tonnes (almost 600 million pounds). In ten years (1992 to 2002) China's honey production expanded 40 per cent, part of a decades' long trend in growth. – John Parker, "World Honey Prices", *American Bee Journal*, July, 2003.

For decades, the USSR was the world's most prolific honey producing nation. With the collapse of socialism, many producers went bankrupt, cutting Russia's honey production by at least 30 per cent, and dropping its rank to third in the world. Meanwhile, as part of a managed transition to a free-market system, the regime in China began to tolerate limited capitalist initiative among citizens and beekeeping developed tremendously. It is possible that China may one day be the world's first billion pound honey-producing country.

[106] One of the most effective methods for a small honey producer to sell a crop is to promote its regional uniqueness and familiarity. I did this with the small jars of Val Marie honey – writing a tiny, four-page booklet which cost about a penny to produce. Beekeepers in almost any part of the world, regardless of how uninspiring the setting, could similarly promote their product. The label said in part:

SASKATCHEWAN'S FAVOURITE HONEY

You have in your possession one of the world's finest natural products – pure and delicious Canadian Honey. This honey was produced in Canada's foremost agricultural province. . . Saskatchewan! Saskatchewan is a thinly populated, beautifully scenic prairie area situated over a thousand miles from any ocean. From the dusty cattle ranches and wheat fields of south Saskatchewan to the dense aspen and spruce forests dotted with homesteads in the far north, Saskatchewan contains over one-third of all the fertile farmland in Canada.

Val Marie honey is especially unique because it is produced in the most arid part of Saskatchewan. In the extremely dry conditions of the southern grasslands very few trees, shrubs, or flowers are found; but those which do survive the desert-like conditions provide a unique nectar which honey bees convert into a flavorful honey sought by gourmets who respect its thick, delicious bouquet.

The Miksha's honey farm is dedicated to producing a quality food product. This honey is strained to remove wax and pollen, but not excessively heated nor pasteurized. Federal food inspectors have graded it "Canada Number One White Honey."

[107] Water is a natural component of honey. Dr. Eva Crane (A Book of Honey, 1980) indicates the water content of nectar arriving in a hive may be 55 percent, but within an hour reduces to 40 percent by the manipulation of the nectar by receiving bees as they concentrate the nectar and add enzymes to it. Bees continue to evaporate the rest of the surplus water from the liquid as it lies in the wax cells until the sugar concentration is over 80 percent. Crane describes the method by which bees remove excess water from nectar to concentrate it into honey as involving "the bees in much work" - drier climates, warmer temperatures, and nectar that is initially high in sugar content and low in moisture results in more efficient honey production. All these elements worked together to make Val Marie an optimal honey producing area.

[108] The Swift Current, Saskatchewan, newspaper – *The City Sun* – printed a full-page article about our honey fudge business. They described the product as a revolutionary sweet - a healthy candy. Folks at CKSW radio interviewed me for ten minutes. The exposure resulted in a flurry of sales which peaked three days after the publicity, and then quickly faded. The honey fudge sold well for the next few weeks.

[109]   There were two reasons to support a border closure with the USA. A few years before the border was closed, Mark Winston offered a clear and excellent explanation in the December 1983 *American Bee Journal*, in his article "Trends in Canadian Beekeeping" pages 837-840. He did not directly advocate that the border be closed, but he writes "First, there is a growing concern that bee importations could be curtailed or even eliminated due to the presence of Africanized bees and/or Acarine and Varroa mites in packages [from the USA]. Second, the economics of package importation vs. overwintering have shifted so that wintering colonies is now commercially viable."
    The border was eventually closed on the basis of the former criteria. No provision was made to automatically re-open the border when the diseases and pests became wide-spread in Canada through natural migration; nor have allowances been made for those operators who would find migration of colonies (to California during winter) more profitable than letting hives sit idle under prairie snow-banks for half of the year.
    Winston ends his article with the statement "eventually, Canada could become an exporting country for bees and queens, particularly if we maintain freedom from mites and undesirable stock." Unfortunately, Dr. Winston's presage was not fulfilled - Canada has neither become an exporter of queens and bees nor has the nation remained free of mites.

Notes

[110] Dr. Leslie Bailey, author of <u>Infectious Diseases of the Honey-Bee,</u> was the world's leading authority on the tracheal mite. In his book (page 57) Bailey writes, "The life of overwintered [tracheal-mite] infested bees in colonies is shortened, but that result, established statistically, is only slight.... It is conceivable that even this slight pathogenicity of A. woodi is indirect. Infested bees have more bacterial infection, particularly in their haemolymph, than uninfested bees, and it is probable that this causes more disease than the mites alone." In his February, 1985, article "Reflections on the Discovery of *Acarapis woodi* in the United States," Bailey writes in the American Bee Journal: "My concern is less for the harm that the mite will do than about the damage that could be done by man in his attempts to eradicate infestation."

Personal correspondence from Dr. Elbert Jaycox, who had been Supervisor of Apiary Inspection for California, to me in January 1986: "The mites do not appear to be a serious problem. Mite populations in Florida have not been high enough and persistent enough to provide good subjects for research on their control. Mites are quite rare in northern Germany where they have been known for more than 50 years, and losses from mite infestations in that country are far lower than those from starvation, winter losses, and other management and environmental problems."

Dr. Steve Taber, writing in the *American Bee Journal*, March 1985, says, "I have a feeling that if A. woodi [the honey bee tracheal mite] were a major problem in Europe, there would have been many more scientific studies."

[111] In a letter to the editor of *American Bee Journal*, May 1985, page 325, the English beekeeper A.C.E. Ferris writes: "When tracheal mite hit the UK just before the 1914/1918 War, most of the bees were native British black which quickly succumbed. But the Italians, which were imported to rebuild the stocks, were much more resistant and, over the years, we have learned to live with acarine and regard it as a nuisance that can be treated. It does not justify destroying colonies and a small or hobby beekeeper can easily cope with it and get a good crop of honey." As the correspondent correctly points out, Italian bees are much more resistant to any potential problems from the tracheal mite. Ninety percent of North American beekeepers used Italian bees in 1984, when the mite crossed the border from Mexico.

Elbert Jaycox, in January, 1986, wrote "Tracheal Mites, Honey Bees, and California Beekeeping," a short newsletter about his experiences and thoughts on the tracheal mite. Jaycox had been Supervisor of Apiary Inspection for the California Department of Agriculture. He described the situation in other parts of the world where tracheal mites had been found on bees for over fifty years: "Tracheal mites were not even mentioned in a recent review of the reasons for the heavy losses of bees in Germany during the winter of 1984-85." In the same newsletter, Jaycox also predicted that "Infestations will probably be found during 1986 in Canada in colonies established from package bees with mite-free certification from the United States." He was right.

[112] "A significant infestation of honey bee tracheal mite, Acarapis woodi, was first detected on July 6, 1984, in Texas." – A *Method for the Detection and Study of Live Honey Bee Tracheal Mites* by Alan W. Smith, Glen R. Needham, and Robert E. Page, Jr., Acraology Laboratory, Department of Entomology, Ohio State University. Published in *American Bee Journal*, June 1987, page 433.

[113] The honey bee tracheal mite was first discovered in Texas in the summer of 1984, but within three years, it was "identified in 28 of the 48 continental states." – A *Method for the Detection and Study of Live Honey Bee Tracheal Mites* by Alan W. Smith, Glen R. Needham, and Robert E. Page, Jr., Acraology Laboratory, Department of Entomology, Ohio State University. Published in *American Bee Journal*, June 1987, page 433.

[114] Dr. Leslie Bailey was possibly the world's leading honeybee pathologist during the 1960s, 70s and 80s. The British bee scientist wrote several definitive books on bee diseases, including <u>Infectious Diseases of the Honey-Bee</u>. In 1985, Dr. Bailey penned an article for The Speedy Bee. He entitled it: *The Mitey Myth Continues to Confuse Beekeepers*. He built a case that the tracheal mite was confused with other maladies which afflicted bees during the early 1900s in England. Part of his reasoning was the logical conclusion that the mite does little damage today, so it probably was not

responsible for massive bee deaths in the early part of the last century. There were tales that claimed nearly all the bees in England died from tracheal mite; Bailey uses references (actual printed articles from bee journals of the time) that show this isn't true – in fact many beekeepers of the era were reporting huge honey crops and very healthy bees.

Dr Bailey writes in the article: "Belief in the Isle of Wight disease [also called honey bee tracheal mite disease] was nourished by misguided publicity."

It is interesting that the Canadian Association of Professional Apiculturists (C.A.P.A.) apparently considered Dr. Bailey the world's leading expert on bee diseases. Their colourful publication <u>Honey Bee Diseases and Pests</u> has a "Suggested Reading List" in which six publications are cited: one by Dr. Roger Morse (who saw the tracheal mite as a minor pest), one by Dadant and Sons; and the other four suggested reads are all written by Dr. Leslie Bailey. Ironically, many vocal members of the C.A.P.A. ignored Dr. Bailey's cautions about over-reacting to the honey bee tracheal mite and discredited his advice.

[115] Originally, 39 hives were in the test apiary, but twelve colonies were sampled "to determine whether the mites continued to reproduce throughout the winter." This experiment was conducted in New York state by a Canadian entomology researcher, Gard Otis. His results were widely circulated, particularly to Saskatchewan beekeepers in the government mouth-piece, *Beelines*. There were a few problems with Dr. Otis' study. Hives in his study with **no** apparent mite population overwintered the most poorly - with 33% of those hives dying. Those hives with a few mites had only a 26% mortality. This would indicate that low levels of mites actually help wintering. The conclusion, as presented by Gard Otis in *Beelines*, "Clearly mite infestations increase colony mortality" was not the correct conclusion based on all data, though hives with high levels of mites did winter poorly. This, and the fact that the study involved a statistically meaningless sample size (39 hives) did not prevent its inclusion in Mr. Gruszka's government-funded *Beelines*. In fairness to Gard Otis, he does write, "I recognize that these data are from only 39 hives in one location during one winter." Gard Otis is presently professor of Environmental Biology, University of Guelph.

[116] The government-funded newsletter, *Beelines*, for June, 1986, was sent to Saskatchewan beekeepers just before their important summer beekeepers' meeting. That particular issue, "compiled and published by The Provincial Apiculturist, Saskatchewan Department of Agriculture," had results of sampling of 35,000 packages brought into the province in 1986. Mr. John Gruszka writes, "I am confident that the analysis [of those packages for mites] is correct and that the packages which entered Saskatchewan in 1986 were mite-free." He was wrong. Mites were later discovered in Saskatchewan in many of those packages.

In the same *Beelines* newsletter, Mr. Gruszka also writes, "During the summer of 1985 the honey bee tracheal mite has spread in the United States from the original two infected states of Florida and Texas to approximately 22 states." Mr. Gruszka was again wrong. The mite was first found in Texas, then New York. There was only one "original" state and that was Texas - the mites entered the United States from Texas, which shares a border with Mexico. Florida does not share a border with Mexico. Mites did not "originally" occur in Florida, as erroneous reported by Gruszka in *Beelines*.

Beelines was sent to all beekeepers in the province at taxpayers' expense. Studies which showed the tracheal mite was a minor pest and that the cost of quarantines and eradications (not to mention payrolls for government employees to enforce quarantines and to perform eradications) was greater than the cost of any potential damage due to the tracheal mite were not generally included in the document disseminated at taxpayer expense. Nor was it clearly noted that this relatively minor pest was impossible to stop with eradications and quarantines.

[117] "...treatments such as menthol, formic acid, and various vegetable oil patties were developed to combat the tracheal mites, and *Varroa* and Africanized bees appeared. Today, tracheal mites have been relegated to relatively minor notoriety, if not in their impact, then certainly in the attention they are receiving from beekeepers and researchers." Dr. Mark Winston is not implying that the tracheal mite is not a problem for beekeepers.   - Mark Winston, <u>From Where I Sit</u>, page 81.

Notes

[118] The Code of Hammurabi, proclaimed in 1780 B.C.E. by the Emperor of Babylon is the first known codified set laws. It was successfully upheld for 1500 years and was a precursor of Jewish (Talmud) and Islamic law. Laws deal with fair trade, matrimony, adoption, human rights, and even the duties of construction engineers.

Each of Hammurabi's codes is succinct, unambiguous, and stated in a brief paragraph, such as Paragraph 229: *"If a builder builds a house for some one, and does not construct it properly, and the house which he built should fall in and kill its owner, then that builder shall be put to death."*

Hammurabi focused on results, not petty regulations. If his set of laws were adapted to today's world, we would have much more freedom. There would be no building inspectors, simply executions for collapsed houses that resulted in fatalities. And beekeepers would be left alone to figure out how best to maximize their income – no kindly big brother governments would regulate hive distributions, hive movements, and cross-border migrations. The philosophy of *laissez-faire* would prevail. The person most intimate with the details of their enterprise will do the best for his business, not the bureaucrat who receives a large salary and generous pension – regardless of the mistakes he makes.

[119] From <u>The Western Producer</u>, March 16, 1989: *Manitoba bee mite victim demands gov't help*, by Laura Rance:

A Manitoba beekeeper who says he has been driven out of business by the government has won a commitment from officials to reevaluate his case.
Frank Case left his wife and son at home and hitchhiked to Winnipeg from southwestern Manitoba last week, the day after the bank took over what remained of his bee operation.
He said his family has applied for welfare and they can no longer afford to license their car.
He was removed from the Manitoba legislature by security guards and taken to a crisis centre.
Provincial employees destroyed 852 hives belonging to Case a year ago because they were contaminated with the tracheal mite.
The province offered him compensation, but Case refused to accept it because it did not fully cover his losses.
"They made an offer of about 25 percent," Case said. "I'm holding out for enough to get going again."
In a second option, the province offered to buy his operation on the condition he not reinvest in the bee business for five years. Case refused that offer because he said beekeeping is the only way he knows to earn a living.
Case said he opposed the decision to have the border closed or to use the eradication program as a measure to control the mite. The proximity of bee operations just across the Canada-U.S. border made it impossible to keep the mite out, he said.
-       *Western Producer*, March 16, 1989.

    Ultimately, Mr. Case's assessment of the situation was absolutely correct, but ironically, *he* was the one led away to a crisis centre, not the people who made or enforced these irrational rules and regulations. Mr. Case's bees were destroyed by the government because they were found with honey bee tracheal mites, yet experienced scientists around the world advised against killing bees with this mite. It took a few years before Canada's inspectors and regulators realized they had made some grievous errors, though public admissions are rare or non-existent. I haven't heard if Mr. Case ever received a formal apology.

[120] Jim Powers was the most productive beekeeper in the world during the 60s, 70s, and 80s. His 30,000 hives of bees were operated from Hawaii to Florida, and included locations in Idaho, California, and the Dakotas. His letter to commercial beekeepers, dated May 25, 1987, and sent from his home office in Clemson, South Carolina, is printed here in full:

Dear Beekeeper:
There have been, in the last four years, 25,000 colonies killed by honeybee regulators fighting the tracheal mite. There has been one human death, damaged health, enormous anxiety, five bankruptcies, and at least $5,000,000 in lost income [these refer to the USA only].

Bad Beekeeping

The mite, at its very worst, would never do the damage the Scientists, the regulators, and let's face it, the Beekeepers themselves have done to beekeeping in the United States.

The African bee will [also] not be a problem in the United States. The Scientists, the Regulators, and some Beekeepers will be.
Enough!

To stop this, Beekeepers must work together. There is going to be a meeting of Beekeepers interested in developing ideas to counter the imposing quarantines and the killing of bees as solutions to our problems.
This meeting will take place during the Minnesota Summer Meeting at Fergus Falls the 16th, 17th, and 18th of July.
Please come. Please help.
Yours truly,
Jim Powers

Shortly after Jim Powers' letter was distributed and various meetings held, the US stopped killing bees and lifted interstate quarantines. And Mr. Powers was right about the impact of the honeybee tracheal mite and the Africanized bees. Neither has been much more than a minor nuisance on the North American continent. Certainly they have led to much less loss of honey production and crop pollination than regulators and petty bureaucrats.

[121] In a letter to this author from Dr. Roger Morse, Dr. Morse cites some of his experience with the tracheal mite. Among his many expeditions, he traveled to Argentina, a temperate-climate country where tracheal mite had been discovered in the 1940s. "I talked to people about tracheal mite disease. Several had seen mites but no one felt the problem was serious or worthy of concern." - Dr. Roger Morse, research scientist and Professor of Apiculture, Cornell University, April 11, 1985.

[122] Dr. Elbert Jaycox, at the California State Beekeepers Association emergency session on January 6, 1986, called for a quick repeal of the California quarantines and eradications saying, "we should dispense with controls because the tracheal mite will soon be widespread throughout the United States and Canada due to the shipment of bees with undetectable low infestation levels." Dr. Jaycox explained that sampling methods were inadequate and the cost and labour involved to continue mite surveys were prohibitive.
   - Cobey and Lawrence, *American Bee Journal*, February, 1986, page 89.

[123] In 2003, I had conversations with some beekeepers in the Hampshire district of south England, not far from the place where the "Isle of Wight" syndrome was first noted. Beekeepers whom I spoke with were aware of tracheal mite, but did not consider it a nuisance to their particular beekeeping enterprises.

[124] Menthol is a cheap, natural, and readily available remedy for honey bee tracheal mites. Mixed with food-grade vegetable oils, menthol oils was killing tracheal mites in commercial bee operations within months of the discovery of HTM in the USA. It is also used to control varroa, an external parasitic honey bee mite.

In the mid-1990s, the University of West Virginia used the internet to publish their results of the use of 'essential oils' to control mites. Their findings were at first greeted with some skepticism (it was one of the first web pages with practical control information on the mite; and the U of W. Va. had not previously published a lot on bee diseases) but Jim Amrine, Bob Noel, Harry Mallow, Terry Stasny, and Robert Skidmore pointed out a cheap, effective, and environmentally responsible mite treatment.

In 1996, they claimed two modes by which oils reduce varroa mite populations: toxicity by direct contact and impaired reproduction via feeding syrups containing essential oils. They write: "When varroa mites contact essential oils such as wintergreen, patchouli, tea tree oil, et al., mixed into oil or grease, they are killed on contact--usually within a few minutes."
   - http://www.wvu.edu/~agexten/varroa/varroa2.htm

278

Notes

[125] In the *Western Producer*, in 1986, Mr. John Gruszka tells the interviewer that "not enough is known about the tracheal mite and more research is needed." This comment comes long after the publication of books (and dozens of articles) in Europe which indicated very clearly that tracheal mite is a minor pest, not one requiring border closures, quarantines, and slaughter of honeybees by government regulators.

Even years later, it seems possible that Mr. Gruszka confuses bee losses due to other causes (starvation, nosema, dampness, improper wrapping, queen failure, poor locations within the apiary, viral infections, etc.) with bee losses due to the tracheal mite. Evidence of this is presented in the book <u>Mites of the Honey Bee</u>, published in 2001.

Eric Mussen includes several pages of tables displaying results of a survey he conducted with chief apiary inspectors across North America. Mussen is looking for the economic impact of the tracheal mite in 1995. In Saskatchewan, Mr. Gruszka claimed that the mite was causing a peak annual loss of 18,000 colonies. In Alberta, the loss due to tracheal mites was indicated by that province's chief apiary inspector as 50 hives per year.

In all of Canada, the total loss due to tracheal mites (from 1984 to 1995) is reported as 2.3 million dollars - but 85% of that figure (2 million dollars) is given as the dollar value loss due to tracheal mites in Saskatchewan. This dollar value, as reported by Mr. Gruszka, is ten times the loss reported in Manitoba or British Columbia and one hundred times the loss reported in Alberta. It seems very unlikely that losses due to tracheal mites are so much worse in the only province that "has the mite under control." If indeed it were "under control" one would expect the economic impact due to the mite would be very slight - not much, much greater than that reported in neighbouring provinces. One can only conclude that the province of Saskatchewan greatly inflated the damage due to tracheal mite, or inspectors there were confusing the causes of colony mortality.

[126] From the *Western Producer*, 1987, reporting from Winnipeg, Manitoba, Ms. Laura Rance writes:
"Government officials in the three prairie provinces have been carrying out an inspection and eradication program since the mite was first discovered in Canada. Imports of bees from the U.S. were banned in 1987 after a certification program failed to keep infected bees out.

"John Gruszka, apiarist for the Saskatchewan government, said although the province must do a better job of locating the infected hives, he believes the eradication program is working. "It is still our assumption that the infestation we are dealing with is a result of packages imported from Texas," he told the Manitoba Beekeepers' Association annual meeting. "I'd still like to think we're finding an early infestation, and staying on top of it." Saskatchewan destroyed 3500 colonies belonging to seven beekeepers in 1987 and another 900 colonies last year."

[127] *American Bee Journal* published my single page article in March, 1987. I hoped to convince beekeepers and researchers alike that it takes an incredibly huge sample of bees (all killed, dissected, and examined) to reach any level of assurance that a 'mite-free' certificate in valid. The publishers led off the story with the line:

What if 10 bees full of pregnant tracheal mites are in an apiary of 50 colonies? If we sample 1000 bees, there is a .9933 probability that we will miss the mites.

Probability and statistics are tricky subjects. They tend to confuse common sense, and when misapplied, they can cost millions. We are presently relying on surveys and probabilities to police the movement of honey bees in North America.

A short summary of our special application of the science of numbers may be helpful for beekeeper and inspector alike. A probability is a mathematical proportion. It compares the number of times something can happen to the total number of events which are possible. Confusing? Some simple examples will help: The probability of flipping a fair coin and getting "heads" is exactly .50, because the number of times "heads" can show up is ONE and the number of possible events are TWO (the coin can be either heads or tails). The probability of rolling a "five" on a fair die is one (result) divided by six (events), or approximately .17. All probabilities range between 0 (something is impossible) and 1.00 (something which is always expected). Probabilities, then, are numbers like .80 or .65, but not .80% or .65%, both of which in the strict sense are less than one percent, and are not used by scientists.

Bad Beekeeping

Serious problems arise from the validity of samples and sample sets. Many beekeepers (and a few inspectors) seem to think that if 100 samples of 100 bees each are checked for honey-bee tracheal mites and no mites are found. We can be 100% certain that no mites are present in the population that the samples were taken from.

It is tempting to think along such lines because it sounds so logical. But consider this. A family has a 50-50 chance (.50 probability) that a new-born will be a girl. If they have two children, this does not mean they have a 100% chance (1.00 probability) that at least one is a girl. Mathematicians would handle this little problem as follows. The chance of getting a girl in one birth is .50. The chance of not getting a girl is 1.00 minus .50, or .50. If there are two children, the probability of not getting at least one girl is .50 times .50, or .50 squared. This works out to .25, hence 1.00 minus .25 (.75, or 75%) of families with two children have at least one girl, on average. For families with three children, the probability of NO girls is .50 times .50 times .50 - or .50 to the third power, hence .125. In other words, in one of eight families with three children there are no girls, on average. Similarly, if you have three children, there is. a .875 probability that at least one is a girl.

These same laws of mathematics apply to the chances of finding tracheal mites for any given number of bees (sample) taken from a hive or yard (population). Let us imagine a situation where a hive of bees (with at least 20,000 bees) has a one percent incidence of honey bee tracheal mite (HTM). Out of every hundred bees, one has at least one tracheal mite. If we select any bee at random, there is a .99 probability that it has no mites. If we take two bees, there is a .99 times .99 probability that both are "clean." With three bees, the factors are .99 times .99 times .99. If we choose to take 50 bees from the colony, the chances that none have mites is .99 to the 50th power, or .605 probability that you will see no mites and you will certify the colony as "mite free." *[Taking 50 bees from a colony with a one per cent level of mites means you will see no mites over half the time in your sample!]*

What if 10 bees full of pregnant tracheal mites are in an apiary of 50 colonies? This would be 10 bees out of about 1.5 million. If we sample 1,000 bees, there is a .9933 probability that we will miss the mites. If we sample 10,000 bees, there is a .9355 probability we miss the mites. If we choose, kill, slice, and study 100,000 bees, we have less than a 50-50 chance that one bee with a mite will be among them. Only if we are willing to destroy 690,000 bees (the equivalent of the total populations of 23 of the 50 colonies) will we be 99% sure of finding one mite infested bee. Based on these sorts of probability figures, about 25,000 colonies of bees have been "depopulated."
- *Mite Mathematics,* Ron Miksha, American Bee Journal, March, 1987.

[128] United States Department of Agriculture researchers found the honey bee tracheal mite in South America (Colombia) in 1980 and northern Mexico, near the US border, in 1982. It was found in southern Texas in July 1984.

Within three years, it was "identified in 28 of the 48 continental states." – A Method for the Detection and Study of Live Honey Bee Tracheal Mites by Alan W. Smith, Glen R. Needham, and Robert E. Page, Jr., Acraology Laboratory, Department of Entomology, Ohio State University. Published in The American Bee Journal, June 1987, page 433.

Honey bee tracheal mite was found throughout North America within five years (1989).

[129] Florida's chief apiary inspector, Ralph E. Brown, writing in the May, 1985, issue of *The Speedy Bee* explained the difference between his state's level of inspection and that conducted in other parts of the country: "Florida's collection procedure was to collect a composite sample of approximately 100 bees per colony from 100% of the colonies in an apiary and every apiary of a beekeeper...The national survey consisted of sampling 10% of the apiaries owned by a beekeeper at the ratio of 10% of the colonies in the apiary, sampled at a rate of 10 bees per hive, the minimum sample consisting of 500 bees, from which 10% were sampled." The result was that Florida was sampling at a rate 100 times greater than Texas or California and this greatly increased the chances of finding mites in apiaries in Florida. Ironically, colonies which were found mite-free in Florida after such rigorous inspections were not allowed entry into Canada (because non-eradicated mites occurred elsewhere in the state) but bees which had much less thorough inspections in Texas and California were accepted. Ultimately, of course, mites came into Canada on packages given 'mite-free' certificates from both California and Texas.

It also made a difference as to where the bees were taken from a hive. No guidelines were in place, but diligent inspectors grabbed older bees, one at a time, while inspectors hoping not to find tracheal mites shook young bees from brood frames.

[130] Kenn Tuckey, former chief apiarian for Alberta reminded this writer that the border was originally closed from Manitoba/Ontario east only, but the rest of the Canadian border closed in 1987 because of Varroa. Mr. Tuckey instructs this author, "Don't mislead people." Of course he is correct. However, it was not possible for me to bring bees from Florida into Saskatchewan since 1985 - because of the tracheal mite's occurrence in Florida and the decision in Florida not to quarantine nor eradicate bees with this mostly benign malady. The western border of Canada was open to importation of bees only from approved 'mite-free' areas, particularly parts of California and Texas, which fought for easier certification of bees for export. It was these two states which rejected calls from the US Apiary Inspectors to increase sampling levels before 'mite-free' certification would be awarded.

Meanwhile, Florida was shut out right away on the 'clean-zone' policies because diligent inspection work by Florida inspectors found mites in several counties, leading to the state's decision to simply lift internal quarantines and to halt eradication programs. Any jurisdiction which did not aggressively search for the mite obviously did not find it. It is interesting and quite sad that the one state in the USA to offer full disclosure and to move ahead with its policies (Florida) was punished by Canada, while states which tried to ease certification requirements and which punished its beekeepers on the random occurrences of mites (particularly Texas and California) were awarded by being allowed to send bees into Canada. The result was continued sales for those states - but the inevitable introduction of the tracheal mite into Canada from Texas and California. Many observers saw this entire fiasco as the height of bureaucratic bungling, hypocrisy, and just plain poor science.

[131] There are few regulations limiting the free movement of honey bees *from* Canada into the United States (though Canada refuses to reciprocate and allow American bees into Canada). Consequently, any exotic pests accidentally imported into Canada may quickly find their way south into the USA. Therefore, the American Agriculture Department has been studying the pests and diseases in New Zealand and Australia. The 'good' news is that almost all pests presently found in the south Pacific are already in North America. The one notable exception, a syndrome known as half-moon disease, which occurs widely in New Zealand, but according to a March 2002 report by the USDA, half moon does not exist in the USA (Risk Assessment: Importation of Adult Queens, Package Bees, and Germplasm of Honey Bees from New Zealand, by Dr. Wayne Wehling, USDA APHIS, page 19).

From *The Speedy Bee*, March, 1985, page 17, "Washington Sate Apiarist James Bach had attended a meeting with Canadian inspectors, and reported back on a little-heard-of disease called "Half-moon" disease. This is described as a disease like European foulbrood with sacbrood-like characteristics. One colony with apparent EFB did not clear up with routine terramycin treatment. The apparent source for this disease, found in Canada, may have been New Zealand or Australia, from where Canadians brought stocks for queens and packages."

[132] In February, 1998, Dr. Roger Morse, made a strong case for free trade throughout North America by opening the Mexican and Canadian borders to the free movement of honey bees. He envisaged the migration of bees from the Yucatan all the way to the Peace River Valley in northern British Columbia. The Cornell University professor of entomology wrote his article long after the Africanized bee stock commonly found in Mexico were considered to be much of a menace and fifteen years after the border between Canada and the U.S.A. was closed to the free movement of honey bees.
   - Dr. Roger Morse, "Moving Bees from the Yucatan to Canada will Soon be a Reality," Research Review, *Bee Culture*, February, 1998.

[133] In Canada, the average annual acres of canola ranges from 8.7 to 12.2 million; alfalfa and clovers from 9.7 to 12.1 million acres.

The amount of canola grown in western Canada varies widely with seasonal seeding conditions (moisture, late frosts) and world market prices. Reuters, April 2000, reported twelve million acres expected, while in 2002, the amount had dropped to ten million. Statistics Canada states the acreage of canola seeded in western Canada ranges from 8.7 to 12.2 million acres. Assuming an over-all average of ten million acres (four million hectares), and a typical yield of 100 kilograms of honey per hectare, optimal honey yield from canola could be four hundred million kilograms.

StatsCanada reports recent alfalfa crop holdings as varying from 3.6 million hectares (1996) to 4.5 million in 2001. With potential yields of 200 kilograms of honey per hectare, 800 million kilograms of honey could be available from this source.

Total honey production in Canada could – and should – be over a billion pounds a year, if there were enough bees to gather all the nectar canola and clovers secrete.

[134] StatsCanada figures for recent colony count in Canada indicate an average of 556,000 hives were held during the five year period of 1996 through 2000.
http://www.agr.gc.ca/misb/hort/2001_2002/honey_e.html#TABLE%201C

[135] StatsCanada reveals interesting figures about the collapse of Canadian honey production following the ban of importation of bees from the United States. Before the ban, beekeepers were producing as much as 43,300 tonnes of honey (over 95 million pounds) in 1984. Two years after the closure, with inexpensive packages no longer available and many beekeepers operating poor-quality hives with aging queens, honey production fell dramatically to just 27,800 tonnes in 1989. Beekeeping in Canada has never recovered to its package-production glory days. The purpose of the embargo was to protect the Canadian honey industry, but of course, it had just the opposite affect.
 For more details, please see:
http://www.agric.gov.ab.ca/economic/marketing_manual/sp_commodities/spcom_m6.html

[136] Although it is a great and diverse agricultural country with enormous potential for vastly expanding production of high quality honey, Canada does not yet hold a particularly esteemed position in terms of total production. While the annual world crop is 1263,000 metric tonnes (2.8 billion pounds), Canada is supplying only about two per cent of the world's honey supply.

According to European-based Apiservice Ltd., the colony count and annual production for several representative countries is:

```
Canada     13,000 beekeepers,  500,000 hives,        60 million pounds
Hungary    16,000 beekeepers,  600,000 hives,        55 million pounds
Australia   6,300 beekeepers,  673,000 hives,        65 million pounds
France     85,000 beekeepers,  1.4 million hives,    70 million pounds
Brazil    300,000 beekeepers,  2 million hives,     100 million pounds
Mexico     45,000 beekeepers,  2 million hives,     110 million pounds
Argentina  18,000 beekeepers,  2 million hives,     150 million pounds
USA       220,000 beekeepers,  3 million hives,     200 million pounds
China     500,000 beekeepers,  7 million hives,     560 million pounds
```

[137] Monsanto, a major force in food science engineering and chemical and biological controls on pests, had a research and development budget in 1985 of 7% of their gross receipts of nearly seven billion (U.S.) dollars. Monsanto's apparent research budget of $470 million dollars is greater than four times the wholesale value of all the honey produced by all American and Canadian beekeepers combined for that year (roughly one hundred ten million dollars). Sources include Monsanto, and the United Nations University Press, which published Technology and Innovation in the International Economy, edited by Charles Cooper, Director, United Nations University Institute for New Technologies Maastricht, The Netherlands, 1994.
Further information is on the United Nations University web site:
http://www.unu.edu/unupress/unupbooks/uu31te/uu31te08.htm

Notes

[138] Honey production has been stagnant in Saskatchewan: For the past twenty years, honey production in Saskatchewan has been about twenty million pounds annually. Rather than expanding to take advantage of the vast acreages of canola and alfalfa, colony count has dwindled. Presently, there are about 100,000 hives in Saskatchewan, according to StatsCanada. In 1986, the year before the border closed, there were 120,000 hives of bees in Saskatchewan – indicating a drop of 20%. With stagnant production levels, dropping hive counts, and beekeepers leaving the business, something is clearly wrong with the way the Saskatchewan bureaucrats are 'growing' their industry.

For Canada as a whole, the figures are equally sad - in 1984, according to StatsCanada, the five-year average colony count was close to 700,000 hives, but by 2002 it had steadily fallen to about 580,000. The number of beekeepers in Canada has cratered - from 21,000 to 9,000 (down by 60 percent!).

[139] Four years after the border closure, five hundred beekeepers gave up the practice, reducing the ranks of Saskatchewan apiarists by a third. The drop in hive count in Saskatchewan has not recovered to pre-border closure numbers, even twenty years later. Recent census numbers indicate colony count at 100,000 hives. (StatsCanada)

[140] For the year 2003, the North Dakota Department of Agriculture lists 188 licensed beekeepers holding 348,061 colonies. The list includes several small (hobby) beekeepers (24 had less than 100 hives), but 94 beekeepers kept over a thousand hives each in North Dakota, with one individual keeping 10,000 hives in the state that summer. Nearly all the commercial operators moved their hives to winter locations in Florida, Texas, or California where they could earn additional profits with pollination services, winter honey production, and queen and hive sales. The number of hives in North Dakota did not drop by 20% as it did in Saskatchewan between 1985 and 2002, but actually increased by twenty percent. This is an example of doing things the right way. Although North Dakota at first attempted to eradicate and quarantine hives with tracheal mites, the government quickly reversed its decision and allowed free movement of bees. Judy Carlson, Chief Apiary Inspector for the state of North Dakota, sent this author the colony counts which her state tallies each year. I was surprised by the detail and accuracy of information provided. While Saskatchewan officials estimate their beekeeper's colony counts to the nearest tens of thousands, Ms. Carlson's inspectors actually count each hive.

[141] North Dakota has seen a tremendous increase in colony numbers without a change in average production per hive. In 1970, the crop average was 103 pounds from 58,000 hives; in 2002, a 112 pound average came from an astounding 304,190 hives. The following year, the state hive count was over 348,000. It is interesting and important to note that the number of hives in North Dakota increased five-fold, but honey production per hive did not fall (no real issues about 'over-stocking' the range).

Colony count has fluctuated tremendously world-wide over the recorded centuries. Inevitably, it is economics and government regulation which makes the numbers of beekeepers swell or decline, though changing agricultural habits have a role to play in these dynamics. In 1650, there were probably fewer than a hundred hives of bees in the United States. From a 1641 New England obituary: "Nathaniel Tilden died in Sirtuate, Mass and left 10 stockes of bees, appraised at 10 pounds." His were the first hives documented in the colonies.

The first US census to count bees was in June, 1900, when colony count was 4.1 million and average production 15 pounds per hive. In 1900, 80% of Americans were farmers or lived in rural communities. From the January, 1904, *American Bee Journal*: "From the last United States census is given for each state the number of colonies of bees June 1, 1900, and the pounds of honey for 1899. For the whole United States the number of colonies was 4,109,626, valued at $10,186,573, honey 61,196,160 pounds, value of honey and wax being $6,664,904." Hence, an average of 14.9 pounds/hive, $1.62/hive in revenues.

In 1910, according to Beekeeping in the South by Kenneth Hawkins (1920), 297,511 farms in the south and 288,444 farms in the northern USA had bees. These apiarists were rarely professional beekeepers but tended to keep bees in primitive boxes, hoping to gather a few pounds of honey each year. Colony counts and the numbers of beekeepers fell with the urbanization of America. But during World War II, sugar was rationed, except for those people who kept bees and needed sugar to feed their hives. Suddenly, everyone was a beekeeper. Since then, colony counts have rather steadily dwindled in the U.S. up to the present day. But more efficient management has resulted in a relatively steady production level (about 200 million pounds per year).

Colony count peaked in 1946 at 5,787,000 hives. Between 1946 and 1970, over a million hives of bees disappeared in the USA and 200,000 people gave up beekeeping. The gradual drop in hive counts largely reflect changes in society and labour and are not related to any introduction of exotic pests. In fact, it was during this period that a cure was found for the scourge of the time – American Foulbrood – which had been killing hundreds of thousands of hives a year.

142 It was true that few Saskatchewan beekeepers subscribed to bee magazines. I knew of no one receiving the A.I. Root publication, *Gleanings in Bee Culture*, two of my acquaintances subscribed to *The American Bee Journal*. The *Canadian Bee Journal* was slightly more in vogue, probably received by two hundred of Saskatchewan's sixteen hundred beekeepers. Today, with the internet permeating Saskatchewan's countryside, it is easier for ordinary citizens to receive contrary opinions on extremely controversial subjects - such as beekeeping. But in 1985, the most common source of bee information was the official government organ, *Beelines*.

The cover of *Beelines* had the official government emblem of the crossed wheat shaft and the words, "Saskatchewan Agriculture, Apiary Administration Office." The inside cover stated, "Beelines is compiled and published by The Provincial Apiculturist, Saskatchewan Department of Agriculture, edited by John Gruszka", and included a 2 by 3 inch (wallet-size) photograph of Mr. Gruszka.

143 Kenn Tuckey, former Chief Apiary Inspector for Alberta, November 2002, in a personal communication to the author wrote, "a majority of beekeepers [in the Peace River area] supported keeping the border open."

144 Canada's Agriculture Minister, Albertan Don Mazankowski was sympathetic to his constituency of the Vegreville district of Alberta. This probably led to some confusion for regulators. As Dr. Winston says in his book, From Where I Sit, page 104: "Even within Canada there was some dissent, and the federal government had difficulty determining whether the federal-level Canadian Honey Council or local organizations from the same district as the minister of agriculture were the proper representatives of the beekeeping industry."

145 I received a long letter dated January 25, 1986, from Bernard Vaissiere, a research scientist then working at Texas A&M University. He writes, "I am French and have acquired my prior education and knowledge of bees by working with professional beekeepers at the bee laboratory in France." Dr. Vaissiere continues, "My experience in France is that I have yet to meet a beekeeper who has treated against Acarapis woodi [honey bee tracheal mite]."

146 The USDA news release bulletin sent as a Western Union Mailgram from the United States Department of Agriculture dated April, 1985, admitted that eradication of the mite is not possible and *continued disruption of the industry produces negative rather than positive results*:
"On February 20, the proposal to rescind the Honey Bee Tracheal Mite Quarantine published in the Federal Register provided for a 30-day comment period. After taking into consideration (1) comments from interested parties and groups, (2) a determination that 11 states are now known to be infested, (3) beekeepers with infested colonies have shipped bees to many other states, (4) migratory beekeepers have moved infested hives throughout many states, (5) mites are believed to be widely spread, (6) experts advise eradication is not possible, and (7) no practical or effective method of certifying bees to be absolutely free of mites exists, and *continued disruption of the industry produces negative rather than positive results*, therefore, the Animal and Plant Health Inspection Service has decided to revoke the Honey Bee Tracheal Mite Quarantine effective April 16, 1985."
- Bert W. Hawkins, Administrator, Animal and Plant Health Inspection Service.

California proved as early as the fall of 1985 that inspection for tracheal mites wasn't very meaningful. When 400 colonies arrived from South Dakota, they were inspected in California and found 'apparently mite-free" by the California certifiers. However, a few weeks earlier, before leaving South Dakota for the winter, the same hives had been sampled. The South Dakota samples indicated that the bees had the tracheal mite. The California inspectors took fresh samples and realized they had issued a mite-free certificate to bees that actually had mites. Nevertheless, Canada continued to have faith in the California certification system.

I introduced a resolution to the (February) 1986 Saskatchewan Beekeepers Convention that "all beekeepers should be aware that a mite-free certification does not guarantee that bees are absolutely free of mites because the sampling and analysis used for certification can not find mites at low levels." My resolution was voted down – at that time, the preferred view was that a mite-free certificate meant bees were free of mites. My intention was to alert the beekeeping community that they could not trust the inspection of bees for mites. However, the official position was reversed in July 1987, when Mr. John Gruszka sent a memo to Saskatchewan beekeepers which said: "Beekeepers should be aware that there is a substantial risk that this [inadvertent mite importations] could occur in the future with further imports in spite of the certification process since the sampling and analysis used for certification appears not to be adequate to detect low levels of infestation."

As late as June, 1986, Mr. John Gruszka, chief apiary inspector for Saskatchewan, wrote in Beelines, "I am confident the analysis [for tracheal mites] is correct and that the packages which entered Saskatchewan in 1986 were *mite-free*. This is gratifying and reinforces my faith in the good job that various states and the USDA-APHIS has performed in its certification program." Mr. Gruszka was prematurely gratified. By 1987, he was writing: "it was learned that the supplier of some packages from Texas which entered Saskatchewan in the spring of 1986 was found to be infected with the honey bee tracheal mite." Mites were found among the one thousand three hundred packages involved. Queens were also separately sent to Saskatchewan. A year later, Mr. Gruszka was writing: "information has been received from Texas regarding the distribution of queens during the spring of 1986 and these colonies are *now* being traced." The word 'now' in the July 1987 memo from Mr. Gruszka's office meant that a year and three months had passed after those bees had arrived in Saskatchewan. It is unfortunate that a more thorough and accurate job of monitoring and investigating tracheal mite incidences was not in place – either that, or the entire effort should have been acknowledged as unworkable and scrapped.

[147] Andy Nachbaur, a commercial beekeeper from Los Banos, California, wrote in the March, 1985, *Speedy Bee*, "U.S. Mite Quarantines Have No Scientific Basis:"
"Science based on politics is poor science; quarantines based on politics are even poorer.
"My dog has fleas, and if his health fails, he will have an increase in the number of fleas. Some day he will die, and it may be said by some who do not have dogs, or fleas, that surely he died of fleas. Some will believe for all time that my dog died of fleas and fleas kill dogs, and on and on we go."

An excerpt from *The Trouble with Mites*, May, 1986, *American Bee Journal*, page 311:
"The honey bee tracheal mite is here to stay. It has already cost many of us thousands of dollars. . . not in terms of weakened bees and lost honey crops, but rather because of interstate and international regulations, quarantines, and government depopulation programs.
"When Mr. Steve Park visited our Saskatchewan Beekeeper's Convention in February of 1986, the question was posed to him from the floor, "How many beehive colonies have died from tracheal mite infestations?"
"He laughed and replied, 'In California, all colonies with mites end up dead.'
"His flippant remark was meant to indicate the "fine job" that his state has been doing in eradicating bees. He went on to suggest that the Saskatchewan beekeepers pass a resolution to send written words of thanks to California stating that Canadian beekeepers are pleased with the programs being carried out in regards to eradication of acarine and African genetic stock. I must wonder how California beekeepers, who lost thousands of colonies so that California can continue to appear mite-free and remain eligible to ship bees into Canada, feel about this joke. I guess the biggest problem in trying to regulate the tracheal mite is the intrusion of politics into what should be a purely scientific subject."

[148] Eric Mussen, in <u>Mites of the Honey Bee</u>, 2001, indicates 43,367 colonies of bees were destroyed to try to stop the spread of the honey bee tracheal mite in North America - 6,881 were killed in California alone. He writes, "California beekeepers became divided into two opposing camps concerning the mite. One side, including the northern California bee breeders, wished to have mite-infested colonies quarantined and eradicated. This was especially important to protect their sales of more than 250,000 packages of bees annually to Canadian provinces." (page 51) And, "The protection of northern interests lasted only two years. The discovery of tracheal mites in bee breeder territory in late 1987, coinciding with discovery of *Varroa jacobsoni* in the USA, marked the end of shipping bees to Canada and the end of California's tracheal mite regulations." (page 52)

In the *American Bee Journal* article, "More Tracheal Mites Found in California", by Susan Cobey and Timothy Lawrence, of Vaca Valley Apiaries, in Vacaville, California (February 1986, pages 87-88), the authors list some of the known eradication and quarantine actions taken that winter against bees with tracheal mites in California:
- 849 colonies owned by Bates and Gray, to be depopulated November 28, 1985;
- 1900 colonies operated by Marvin Smith, eradication order appealed and stay issued by Superior Court;
- 650 colonies owned by Mark Emde, certified as mite-free, re-examined and found with tracheal mites December 20, 1985 - ordered to remove the bees from the state;
- 576 colonies in one apiary, 192 in another owned by Duane Johnson, given 48 hours to leave state or face eradication;
- 264 colonies owned by Donald McNary, found with tracheal mites in Amador County

With such massive findings in scattered locations, it was becoming obvious that the tracheal mite was wide-spread, even in California. Tom Emde, writing in *The Speedy Bee*, March, 1986, page 3, "Mites Too Widespread to Stop" describes the situation:
"It is amazing that California and Texas are calling so many of the shots in our industry when these two states have a constant source of mites from the south. They share a 1,500 mile common border with Mexico where there is absolutely no hope of eradication of the tracheal mite.
"Any state officials who are reasonable should admit that the more they look for tracheal mites the more they find tracheal mites.
"Interestingly enough, California keeps changing the rules as they discover more mites. First, the label was "mite-free" or "mite-infested" states, then counties, and finally small circles.
"When tracheal mites were discovered in bees that were already located in almond locations in close proximity to many other colonies, the California approach changed again. At that time someone should have put an end to the nonsense of regulation and depopulation. It is long overdue."

[149] Brother Adam was appreciated by beekeepers around the world as a queen breeder who specialised in hybrid crossings of races of bees. In Brother Adam's book, <u>In Search of the Best Strains of Bees</u>, he describes arduous treks into remote parts of North Africa, Israel, Turkey, Yugoslavia, and the Iberian peninsula - looking for bees which were isolated and therefore mostly pure representatives of Italian, Carniolan, Tellian (from Libya), Anatolian, and the 'native' dark bees which were the original races in north Europe, Spain and Portugal. He did this mostly in the 1950s and 1960s, carrying representative live queens back to his thousand hive apiary at Buckfast Abbey in Devon, England, where he experimented with cross-breeding these various types, hoping to produce a superior bee. He developed a patented cross, commonly called the Buckfast Bee which he licensed to queen breeders around the world. His energy, business acumen, skills of observation, and techniques of queen breeding were inspirational for all beekeepers.

Brother Adam, born Karl Kehrle in Bavaria, was sent to the Buckfast Abbey in 1910, at the age of 12. The abandoned monastery in Devon was being rebuilt by Catholic Benedictines, the order which Brother Adam served for eighty-six years. Upon arrival, he was assigned chores with the beemaster and he witnessed the loss of about sixty percent of the monastery's colonies during the winter of 1915-1916. The heavy winter kill was attributed to the presence of acarine disease. Brother Adam noticed that those hives (16 out of 45) which survived were mostly of Italian stock. He assumed the survival was largely due to genetics. This prompted his search for obscure races and sub-races of bees in Europe, Africa, and the Near East - hunting for gentle, economically advantageous, mite resistant bees. He felt very strongly that tracheal mites cause colony death, which can be controlled by requeening bees with his select stock.

Notes

Here is Brother Adam's view on the honey bee tracheal mite:

The Acarine Disease Menace - Short-term and Long-term Countermeasures, by Brother Adam, Buckfast Abbey, England; *American Bee Journal,* March 1985, pages 163-164.

"We managed to establish beyond question that susceptibility and resistance to this disease were subject to hereditary and genetic dispositions.

"Acarine [also known as honey bee tracheal mite] has one redeeming feature: Infected colonies can be saved by the simple expedient of requeening them with queens of proven resistant stock...The loss of colonies can thus be prevented without fail and with a minimal outlay. Indeed, this is the most effective way of eliminating and keeping one's colonies free of acarine.

"The transmission of acarine via Mexico [into the USA and Canada] demonstrates that this disease does not respect political frontiers and that virtually no barriers will hold up its relentless and inexorable progress. Nor can the wholesale destruction of colonies eliminate every case of infection. The European findings, extending over a period of 70 years, have clearly shown that from the severely practical aspect, genetically based resistant stock presents the only short- and long-term solution to the acarine menace."

[150] Chris Wariner, a north Saskatchewan beekeeper who later became president of the Saskatchewan Beekeepers' Association, seconded my failed resolution to allow the Florida bees into Val Marie as a test project in 1985. Thanks, Chris.

[151] "In August, 1985, Agriculture Canada issued a special permit to the Saskatchewan Beekeepers Association to conduct experiments in isolation in La Ronge, Saskatchewan, to study the impact, control and biology of the honey bee tracheal mite in honey bee colonies."
- From *Beelines*, March 1987, #81, by Don Peer and Alan Tremblay.

[152] Laurence Cutts, personal telephone conversation, November 18, 2002. Mr. Cutts, Chief Apiary Inspector for the state of Florida had arranged the procurement of bees with tracheal mites for the researchers in Saskatchewan. Cutts says 60 3-pound packages were drawn from a commercial operator in the Orlando area.

[153] Laurence Cutts, personal telephone conversation, November 18, 2002. When varroa mite was discovered in Florida, Cutts alerted the group in Canada. Gruszka and his team killed the bees, sifted through the carcasses and varroa was discovered. It is disappointing that *varroa* was missed for so long by the people running the tracheal mite experiment in La Ronge. When colonies were sampled using the ether method in October, 1987, it was estimated that 700 *varroa* mites were present in the experimental colonies. (Gruszka, *Beelines*, May 1988)

[154] There is quite a lot of debate about the timing of the arrival of varroa in North America. Clearly, the discovery in a Wisconsin apiary in September, 1987 changed beekeeping in North America. But a previous discovery of the varroa mite was made with a single mite identification by the Animal and Plant Health Inspection Service (APHIS) in Maryland in 1979. This prompted H.L. Comroy, University of Florida, to inspect Florida bees in 1984, but no varroa mites were found.

[155] A retired bee inspector, in personal communication to this author (August, 2002), writes "the find of Varroa was a big joke to the rest of us!" and "They [Gruszka, et.al.] missed the boat by killing those bees so quickly." This latter sentiment was echoed by many who felt that an opportunity to study varroa was passed up. And the opportunity to be the first to discover the mite in North America was missed by Gruszka and his team. They would have looked brilliant if they had seen the mite first and reported the find to Florida, rather than have events occur the other way around.

[156] Mr. John Gruszka was interviewed by CBC Saskatchewan radio's *Farm Report* at noon on Thursday, March 14, 1985.

[157] The "quarantine has had adverse effects on some Canadian beekeepers. Beekeepers in northern beekeeping regions of Alberta were the most seriously affected, because almost all of them depended on package bee importations. A number of beekeepers throughout Canada went out of business in the late 1980s, primarily due to low honey prices, although the sudden embargo on package importations was a contributing factor in reducing the number of Canadian colonies from about 700,000 to 520,000 by 1992."
- Mark Winston, <u>From Where I Sit</u>, Comstock Publishing, 1999, pages 112-113.

[158] Brad Clawsie, in a letter to the editor of *Maclean's Magazine*, p 4, February 7, 2000, explains why Canada is falling behind in the technology race. A Canadian, Mr. Clawsie, living in California and working in the Silicon Valley, wrote, "Canadian culture is more concerned with reducing losses than promoting gains. One of the unfortunate realities I have found is that accessibility and excellence rarely occupy the same space. Canada as a nation appears more focused on the former than the latter. Risk-takers typically flock to systems that have low barriers to entry – this means low taxes and low bureaucracy. Such a system will inherently create both losers and winners. Until Canada is more willing to allow people to lose, those capable of winning will go elsewhere."

****

You will find more notes and facts on this book's web page, www.badbeekeeping.com.

Some Notes on
People, Chronology, and Events

This book is a memoir. The events that occurred are true and are rendered as accurately as memory (and diaries, journals, personal calendars, and printed news stories) can allow. However, there are a few allowances exercised in the construction of this story.

The episodes described occurred over a period of ten years, from 1978 through 1987. It would have been very tedious for the reader if every activity were depicted in precise chronological order. For example, I would have narrated a bit of queen breeding, then said "I was back in Saskatchewan, then back in Florida, back to Saskatchewan, Florida again, and then I sold queen cells to Ray." Another chronology example from the text is the bit about the Val Marie parade. I place it in 1978, near the beginning of this book, to help the reader acquire a sense for the small town - but Joe and I watched the parade march past us twice during the summer of 1980 - part of the celebration of Saskatchewan's 75th anniversary as a province. To assist the reader, I tried to group activities closely together, even if they are slightly out of sequence. But again, I have tried to be faithful to the veracity of the events themselves.

The story begins in 1978, when I purchased the Val Marie honey farm. But for seven years before that, I'd kept bees on the family farm in Pennsylvania, and in Wisconsin and Florida. By 1978, I'd already acquired some practical experience in the craft. I met Sandy in 1980; we married in 1981. I move the story quickly through several rather mundane seasons (1982, 1983, 1984), wrapping up the tale in the disastrous years of 1985-1987.

Not all the events happened in the places described, but all the events occurred as described. For example, the little contest at the bee meeting in Saskatchewan was from a different meeting, a different place, two years earlier. But even the most unbelievable events - my friend eating bee brood; the old gentleman in the yellow shirt vomiting while the speaker talked about nuclear bombs; me, hopelessly lost in my own beeyard - are honest accounts of the situations.

The characters presented are themselves, as best I remember them. Buzz and Mary, Earl and Josephine, Eleanor Dern. Various members of my family. A few minor characters have names I've lost. A few individuals are amalgamations of several characters. I was not especially satisfied with this construct, but there seemed no other way to reduce and focus this story. Hopefully, the reader may be assuaged with the knowledge that the things said and done were said and done as described.

Finally, this book is a memoir. A personal story. It is not a story about any particular character I met along the way. There is no malice or contrition, condescension or malevolence intended. I have tried to write the story as I lived it; told the tale as I have witnessed it.

Val Marie Scale Hive - Daily Gain in Pounds, Miksha for 1978-1986

date	1978 July	1978 August	1979 July	1979 August	1980 July	1980 August	1981 July	1981 August
20-Jun					7		2	
21-Jun					8		-1	
22-Jun					10		4	
23-Jun					3		-1	
24-Jun					-2		4	
25-Jun					8		11	
26-Jun					-1		10	
27-Jun					5		0	
28-Jun			6		8		-2	
29-Jun			7		13		-1	
30-Jun			5		6		7	
1		-4	4	8	8	0	5	4
2		0	10	4	7	0	6	0
3		0	16	2	0	0	7	3
4		0	-6	0	7	0	6	11
5		0	11	0	8	4	4	0
6	3	0	7	0	-1	2	7	8
7	5	1	7	0	7	0	5	8
8	2	0	9	11	6	8	0	8
9	8	2	5	0	7	-3	4	9
10	24	3	6	10	9	4	2	9
11	8	3	8	2	9	-2	12	8
12	9	3	3	8	9	3	15	8
13	24	0	1	2	15	4	-2	8
14	33	2	0	-4	14	3	8	8
15	18	4	10	23	-3	1	4	8
16	27	-2	12	12	14	2	11	8
17	-6	-2	16	15	12	5	7	6
18	-5	2	13	18	21	3	7	3
19	3	0	8	10	-3	7	-1	12
20	10	4	16	11	4	5	2	11
21	20	0	17	-3	19	0	1	14
22	15	5	4	0	10	3	8	9
23	23	1	3	7	5	3	7	20
24	8	5	0	0	1	4	-1	10
25	10	16	2	-1	5	0	1	12
26	0	0	8	6	3	-3	3	8
27	-3	0	14	0	2	0	2	7
28	-2	5	12	0	0	0	3	10
29	0	5	0	8	1	0	4	15
30	-6	0	13	6	3	-1	-1	-3
31	0	5	16	0	1	0	2	1
1-Sep		9		0		0		3
2-Sep		9		8		0		-1
3-Sep		12		15		0		0
4-Sep		18		0		0		-1

1978		1979		1980		1981	
June	0	June	18	June	65	June	33
July	228	July	245	July	200	July	138
August	58	August	155	August	52	August	243
Sept.	48	Sept.	23	Sept.	0	Sept.	1
year-->>	334	year-->>	441	year-->>	317	year-->>	415

APPENDIX: Scale Hives

1982 July	1982 August	1983 July	1983 August	1984 July	1984 August	1985 July	1985 August	1986 July	1986 August	date
										20-Jun
										21-Jun
								1		22-Jun
								1		23-Jun
								2		24-Jun
						0		1		25-Jun
						1		2		26-Jun
						3		3		27-Jun
						3		2		28-Jun
						2		3		29-Jun
						3		4		30-Jun
-1	0	2	4		0	4	-1	3	0	1
0	6	0	6		0	0	-1	3	0	2
0	4	0	7		0	2	2	0	2	3
-1	4	4	2	2	-1	4	0	0	0	4
0	3	6	2	1	0	2	-1	0	0	5
4	4	5	0	0	-1	2	-1	2	0	6
8	-2	7	0	2	0	7	0	7	0	7
4	-2	5	0	0	-1	0	0	10	0	8
4	4	-3	6	1	-1	7	0	0	-2	9
11	16	-2	10	4	0	5	-1	7	-2	10
7	6	3	4	3	0	5	-1	-1	-1	11
9	6	5	-3	1	0	4		4	-1	12
6	6	10	4	0	0	0		3	0	13
9	6	6	3	2	1	0		5	0	14
5	8	0	4	3	-1	0		5	0	15
-1	4	-2	3	0	0	-2		0	0	16
1	6	7	3	2	0	-1		-2		17
7	6	9	3	1	-1	-1		1		18
7	7	12	-1	1	0	0		2		19
9	7	7	4	0		0		3		20
12	7	5	5	0		0		1		21
4	5	9	-1	0		-1		0		22
4	0	9	2	0		-1		4		23
7	1	6	3	-1		0		3		24
19	2	19	4	-1		-1		2		25
7	6	6	6	-1		0		2		26
9	5	7	5	0		0		1		27
8	4	15	5	0		0		0		28
12	3	10	10	0		0		-1		29
9	0	15	4	-1		0		-1		30
22	1	10	3	-1		0		-1		31
	2		5							1-Sep
	7		-3							2-Sep
	8		0							3-Sep
	0									4-Sep

1982		1983		1984		1985		1986	
June	0	June		June	0	June	12	June	19
July	201	July	192	July	18	July	35	July	62
August	133	August	107	August	-5	August	-4	August	-4
Sept.	17	Sept.	2	Sept.	0	Sept.	0	Sept.	0
year-->>	351	year-->>	301	year-->>	13	year-->>	43	year-->>	77

Annual Summary for Scale Hive in Val Marie Saskatchewan

1978	1979	1980	1981	1982	1983	1984	1985	1986
334	441	317	415	351	301	13	43	77

Big River Scale Hive - Daily Gain in Pounds, Emde for 1971-1980

	1971 July	1971 August	1972 July	1972 August	1973 July	1973 August	1974 July	1974 August	1975 July	1975 August
June										
1	4	6		-2	-1	12	1	7		-2
2	3	9		4	0	-5	1	10	4	-2
3	3	15		2	0	-1	2	9	4	2
4	-2	13		1	0	1	0	9	4	8
5	5	23		2	-1	3	2	7	4	6
6	-3	8		6	0	1	-1	3	4	6
7	1	8		1	-1	1	4	4	0	13
8	-1	-3		9	1	2	5	3	4	-1
9	1	-4		2	6	5	2	-2	4	1
10	3	4		7	6	0	1	-1	4	1
11	-2	3		9	-2	4	2	-1	4	1
12	3	-3		-2	-1	1	-2	-2	4	0
13	3	0		9	-4	3	-2	-1	3	-2
14	7	2		3	11	5	5	-1	2	0
15	11	1		17	-3	7	0	-1	4	-1
16	1	7		13	3	1	3	-1	2	0
17	-2	-2	2	11	-1	1	0	-1	2	0
18	11	0	2	13	14	-3	6	-1	-1	-2
19	8	0	3	6	18	-2	4	-1	2	-2
20	4	2	7	-3	16	3	1	-1	0	3
21	6	2	2	3	15	6	0	-1	0	2
22	8	-1	4	9	11	-2	0	-1	0	0
23	8		-2	9	-1	-2	8	-1	7	-4
24	-5		4	8	3	-2	5	1	16	0
25	-1		3	6	5	-1	-1	-1	7	-3
26	-2		1	8	9	11	-2	-1	5	-1
27	0		12	4	6	6	2	-1	18	
28	0		8	3	-5	-2	6	-1	13	
29	0		2	10	8	1	8	-1	5	
30	11		-4	6	11	-2	12		7	
31	1		4	4	17		7		7	
Sept										
	84	90	48	178	140	52	79	31	139	23
year-->		174		226		192		110		162
	500 hives		500 hives		500 hives		500 hives		500 hives	
	Russia Aug 23		Holy Land Oct 4		South America Oct 8				France Sept 5	

APPENDIX: Scale Hives

	1976		1977		1978		1979		1980		June
	July	August	July	August	July	August	July	August	July	August	
	3	5	17	7	6	-3	14	5	18	16	1
	1	13	3	6	6	-2	3	0	20	-6	2
	9	22	4	9	6	2	3	1	11	-4	3
	6	15	-3	16	8	2	6	16	10	-1	4
	7	9	0	12	5	2	2	5	11	-1	5
	10	13	0	11	-1	2	5	9	0	0	6
	8	10	8	-3	-1	-2	5	0	7	0	7
	5	10	6	10	3	6	3	6	14	1	8
	10	7	-7	10	10	8	6	6	5	15	9
	-3	7	2	-4	11	8	3	11	5	3	10
	6	10	1	10	11	0	0	-7	-4	-2	11
	2	1	-4	-3	2	0	-2	5	5	2	12
	-2	0	0	4	-3	-3	-2	0	10	12	13
	-2	0	2	1	12	5	1	5	8	8	14
	8	13	0	-3	20	2	7	11	7	-1	15
	15	6	0	7	20	-3	12	24	0	6	16
	14	-2	10	13	-1	-2	13	6	5	6	17
	9	3	10	-2	-3	0	10	11	-2	-2	18
	3	13	4	10	0	-2	12	10	0	6	19
	9	-5	-1	18	2	0	11	11	6	0	20
	9	9	-7	13	10	0	9	0	31	-4	21
	2	16	-3	11	13	4	5	1	29	-1	22
	8	-4	-3	10	19	-4	10	8	6	1	23
	13	20	0	11	12	-1	-2	-5	0	3	24
	3	4	2	11	3	9	17	4	12	-3	25
	8	4	0	12	11	0	17		2	4	26
	-5	-2	0	2	-6	-1	20		5	5	27
	-3	-2	2	-3	3	3	16		12	-3	28
	9	-1	2	-2	-6	0	6		-4	6	29
	7	-2	-2	5	4	6	11		10	9	30
	7	-2	0	13	1	5	9		15	-6	31
						25					Sept
	176	190	43	212	177	66	230	143	254	69	
	year-->	366	year-->	255	year-->	243	year-->	373	year-->	323	

500 hives
S. Africa
swarmed August 14!!

500 hives
Australia

250 hives

250 colonies

250 colonies

Big River Scale Hive - Daily Gain in Pounds, Emde for 1981-1990

	1981		1982		1983		1984		1985	
	July	August	July	August	July	August	July	August	July	August
June										
1	3	-6	2	-6	0	3	2	23	1	10
2	7	-3	2	-3	0	6	2	20	1	13
3	10	0	2	0	5	12	2	18	2	14
4	12	3	8	3	2	4	10	14	10	13
5	8	1	-1	1	12	4	13	4	13	-5
6	12	1	4	1	19	4	8	6	18	-1
7	3	-3	15	-3	18	1	8	-3	0	2
8	-5	0	3	0	6	2	8	-2	-2.5	-4
9	19	0	0	0	7	2	8	9	-2.5	1
10	17	-1	2	-1	-2	2	25	5	12	0
11	12	5	15	5	11	2	22	10	14	0
12	22	-1	22	-1	7	0	9	4	8	-2
13	19	1	27	1	17	0	-4	2	-2	1
14	-4	0	18	0	9	0	6	-3	12	1
15	-2	6	-1	6	10	0	13	0	7	-1
16	9	1	15	1	6	2	12	4	13	-1
17	17	10	23	10	-3	0	19	3	8	-1
18	14	1	19	1	14	-2	9	2	12	1
19	13	0	14	0	29	0	23	0	0	1
20	-2	3	0	3	23	0	3	-2	11	2
21	17	0	13	0	-4	-1	10	1	10	0
22	13	-1	19	-1	11	-1	5	0	11	0
23	-3	-2	5	-2	24	-1	26	2	5	-1
24	0	-2	26	-2	10	0	23	0	-3	2
25	12	-2	20	-2	15	-1	24	0	8	
26	3	-2	35	-2	5	0	22	0	-5	
27	5	-1	21	-1	-6	-1	15	4	-3	
28	5	0	38	0	7	-1	12	-2	-1	
29	0	-1	1	-1	5	-1	4	-1	7	
30	-3	-1	19	-1	5	2	14	-1	12	
31	0	-1	22	-1	7	6	18	0	14	
Sept										
	233	5	408	5	269	43	371	117	190	45
	year-->	238	year-->	413	year-->	312	year-->	488	year-->	235
	275 hives		275 hives		218 hives		230 hives		319 hives	
	Mexico						California		Japan	

294

APPENDIX: Scale Hives

1986 July	1986 August	1987 July	1987 August	1988 July	1988 August	1989 July	1989 August	1990 July	1990 August	
		31						8		June
5	35	3	8	5	1		5	3	0	1
5	15	5	-2	7	-2		5	3	0	2
5	19	0	2	8	16		-2	-2	0	3
5	-4	0	4	10	10	6	-2	2	0	4
3	5	0	0	19	5	0	3	4	0	5
3	10	0	2	-3	-3	10	5	-1	4	6
3	0	2	2	0	1	12	6	5	2	7
24	3	8	0	0	3	-4	8	5	0	8
20	2	-2	0	1	2	4	8	7	0	9
-4	2	2	-1	1	0	7	6	8	0	10
0	2	2	-1	2	-2	-3	9	8	0	11
4	2	17	0	1	4	13	7	7	0	12
5	0	2	0	4	-3	14	1	8	-1	13
5	6	10	-1	4	-1	20	4	-2	1	14
4	0	5	-1	5	3	17	0	1	0	15
28	6	5	-1	2	-2	11	-2	1	0	16
5		8	2	6	0	16	0	-2	0	17
6		2	0	5	1	15	0	-2	0	18
16		-3	0	6	2	10	0	-1	0	19
22		11	-1	15	-2	13	-2	4	2	20
22		12	-1	11	0	11	-1	8	2	21
20		8	-1	7	-2	6	-1	8		22
15		3	-2	1	5	11	-1	3		23
9		18	0	11	-1	6		7		24
0		23	1	3	1	-1		7		25
0		11	-1	15		9		-2		26
0		24	-3	6		5		-2		27
0		3	-1	5		-4		-1		28
7		13	-1	4		8		4		29
0		-2		16		1		7		30
18		13		3		0		6		31
										Sept
255	103	234	3	180	36	213	56	109	10	
year-->	358	year-->	237	year-->	216	year-->	269	year-->	119	
24 hives		20 hives		20 hives		30 hives		30 hives Alaska		

295

BEEKEEPER'S GLOSSARY

Beekeepers have their own language, and it goes far beyond mumbling a few choice words at bees and bureaucrats. Here are a few terms to get you started at bee-talk.

BEESWAX I once met an educated young lady who thought 'beeswax' was a made-up word, something funny to tell children, as in "Get the beeswax out of your ears!" It took a while to convince her that bees make wax. They make it in tiny flakes which they extrude from the underside of their abdomen. Then the bees clump the flakes together into the combs upon which they live.

COMB Honey comb is made of seven-sided hexagonal pieces (seven-sided if you count the bottom - without a bottom the comb cell would be pretty useless). Bees have fashioned this wax into honey-comb for holding their honey, and into brood-comb for (any guesses?) holding their brood.

BROOD Beekeepers often sit and mope and whine and complain, but when the beekeeper is quiet and contemplative, we say he (or she) is 'brooding.' This is not much different from the use of the word 'brood' to mean a clutch of cluckers in a hen-house or a frame of eggs, larvae, and pupae in a bee-hive.

QUEEN The fully functional female, delicate, long and slender, with smooth skin and soft hair. She lays the eggs in the hive.

WORKER The non-functional female honey bee, often gruff in manners and too busy to care.

DRONE The fully functional male, but if he ever performs his function, he dies immediately. The only drone you will ever meet is a virgin. What's the point, we wonder?

HONEY BEE There would be very little honey produced without honey bees. And few honey bees would survive without honey to eat. We are stuck with a bit of a chicken-and-egg philosophical dilemma here, but amber-encrusted honey bees dating back forty-five million years seem to suggest the problem was resolved long ago. The honey bee is but one of an estimated 20,000 species of bees (scientists are not finished counting yet) but beekeepers will readily tell you that the honey bee is the most important species.

BEE IN HER BONNET Few women wear bonnets anymore, so this expression is getting harder and harder to defend. And if bees go the way of bonnets (which is certainly possible) we may have to drop the phrase from our vocabulary entirely.

Beekeeper's Glossary

BEEKEEPER   This is the guy or gal who keeps bees. But people are always saying to me, "Ron, isn't there another word for beekeeper?" Absolutely. One may wish to use the alternate   words 'Super-Hero' or 'Divine-Pollinator' although I've also seen the entirely too proper 'apiarist' used as a substitute.

APIARIST   Latin-inglish for beekeeper. From the Latino Abejo, abbreviated Apis in the text books, which means 'bee' then anglicized with the -ist ending, which means super-hero. The other contrived word which you never hear is from mellissa (Greek for honey or bee or honey bee or something) plus the versatile ending '-fier' which gives us the modern word mellissafier. Try these out on your friends when you're bored.

BEEKEEPER and BEE FARMER   These terms are commonly used in England to express the difference between the totally eccentric person who keeps a few hives of bees (the Beekeeper) and the raving lunatic who tries to make a living as a Bee Farmer.

GLOVES   These devices slip over the hands. Stylishly made of the sun-dried hide of a goat and snugly fitting up to the elbow, they are frequently worn on informal beekeeping outings.

VEIL   We are too brave to typically wear a veil as protection from bee stings, but since most of us beekeepers are a bit funny-looking, the bee veil gives us a chance to hide behind a shady screen.

WHITE SUIT   Beekeepers are white-collared farmers, donning a heavy set of overalls even on the hottest days of the year. A useful accessory is a ball cap with a pop-can holder and flexible straw assembly.

SMOKER FUEL   Smoke 'em if you got 'em, the chief apiary inspector's assistant's friend once told me. She used recycled hemp burlap bags to keep her bees mellow. Other beekeepers use cardboard, wood chips, pine needles, or dried cow dung. If you can't find any of these products on your own, a bee equipment saleslady will gladly sell you some prepackaged smoker fuel.

SMOKER   These special devices are simply steel smudge pots with leather bellows attached. You puff air through the bottom of the smoldering fuel, it gives off a cool white smoke that quiets most honey bees so you can rob their honey.

HIVE TOOL   This is the tool beekeepers invented to pry frames out of beehives and pop the lids from soda bottles. Home Hardware outlets now sell them - not in their 'Beekeeping Supply' aisle as you would expect, but as paint scrapers.

BOTTOM BOARD   As the term implies, this piece of beekeeping equipment is a board. It rests on the ground, providing a convenient place to set the first Brood Chamber.

BROOD CHAMBER Much more than a chamber for brood, this wooden box and set of combs holds developing bees (the brood), honey, pollen, and thousands of bees. This is the place bees meet, visit, and sometimes plan insurrections against royalty.

HIVE COVER Ever since earliest times, people have covered their hives. It keeps the rain out. We continue the tradition even into the twenty-first century.

BEE HIVE or **BEE-HIVE** or **BEEHIVE** Similar to Bee Yard, Bee-yard, and Beeyard, no one seems to know the correct form to use, so in this book I have randomly used all three variations at different times, just as the bee journals seem to do.

NUC Possibly an abbreviated form of nuclear or nucleon or nucleate or nucleogenesis. But I'm not sure. I've always thought it was a stand-alone word, one invented by my father in 1947 to mean 'tiny bee-hive'.

SUPER The honey-holding part of the beehive which sets on top the brood chamber and holds honey, if the bees are inclined to produce any. Actually, we still call the box a 'super' even if the bees have suffered a poor year, though it is then sometimes referred to as an 'empty-super'.

FRAME Think of a picture frame. Replace the seaside landscape with a chunk of beeswax comb. Throw away the matting, you don't need it. Replace the beveled and polished oak wood with spruce or pine, make it square and clunky. Attach ears (wooden ones) to the top edges of the frame, so your hands don't get sticky holding onto the honeycomb. Now you've got yourself a bee hive frame.

A Well-Used Frame

- From the May, 1902, <u>American Beekeeper Magazine</u>.
This 1902 frame is typical of the frames used
by beekeepers a hundred years later -
and is probably still being used by some poor beekeeper somewhere.

Suggested Reading

If you would like to learn more about the all-important subject of beekeeping, I warmly recommend these several books:

The Hive and the Honey Bee   You may enjoy the inexpensive reprint of Langstroth's original 1853 book. Other updates of <u>The Hive and the Honey Bee</u> have been published by Dadant and Sons and are excellent reference books, but bear little resemblance to the book written one gray winter one hundred fifty years ago. Langstroth's style is lively, at times hilarious. His practical discoveries and observations about bees are stellar. Reading his advice on bees and worldly affairs will educate and possibly amuse the modern reader.

ABC and XYZ of Bee Culture   This book, similar to revisions of the <u>Hive and the Honey Bee</u>, is an invaluable reference for the aspiring beekeeper. Originally prepared by A.I. Root in 1877, it has been continually updated and enhanced, expanding to almost a thousand pages with essays alphabetically arranged from After-swarming to Zinc.

Beekeeper's Guide Book   Professor Cook's 1883 <u>Manual of the Apiary: The Beekeeper's Guide</u> was probably the first North American college text book on beekeeping. The California professor based the first printing of 3000 copies on lecture notes he had prepared for his students.   Chapters have compelling titles: "Evils That Confront the Apiarist," "Italians and Italianizing" and "Working for Comb Honey."

Miller's 50 Years Among the Bees   This book by Dr. C.C. Miller was described as 'racy' when published in 1911.   One might still consider it a tell-all as Miller mixes his personal life story with his beekeeping discoveries.   C.C. was possibly the best commercial beekeeper of his time, producing huge crops through the simple art and practice of good beekeeping.

Honey Plants of North America   For those interested in the flowering plants that make the pollen and nectar that feed the bees, the finest book for the USA and Canada on this subject may be John H. Lovell's <u>Honey Plants</u>. Published in 1926 when nearly every North American farm had a hive of bees, it was an invaluable guide for the next fifty years.   Now it is a bit more of an historical document - Lovell writes glowingly about important honey plants that have become minor (buckwheat and fireweed, for example) and cites moisture conditions for 1910 in the Dakotas.   But it remains a fun read, still provides useful information, and is available as a reprint from the A.I. Root Company.

Bad Beekeeping

A Country Year and **A Book of Bees**, both by Sue Hubbell. Sue took up commercial beekeeping in the Ozark mountains. She's a brilliant writer, sharing incite and incident with poise and charm. She lives and works in coastal Maine these days, but her tales of beekeeping in the 1970s made her books international best sellers.

The Joy of Beekeeping The author, Dr. Richard Taylor, a metaphysicist and philosopher, kept 300 hives of bees in New York's Finger Lakes district. This is a book of practical beekeeping and spirited philosophy.

Following the Bloom Doug Whynott followed beekeepers across the United States, from Maine to Florida, in the Dakotas, and out to California, as the beekeepers hauled thousands of hives in and out of orchards, groves, and fields. These were specialized beekeepers, people who made most of their living pollinating crops. The book is well-written, well-researched, and tells the story of hard working, personable folks who live a nomadic life, shepherding bees from place to place.

The Archeology of Beekeeping Dr. Eva Crane has written a dozen scholarly tomes on beekeeping – its history, archeology, and impact on our lives. My favourite, The Archeology of Beekeeping, is littered with beekeepers' remnants – vase hives, bee boles, alpine huts, coins, medallions, sculptures and amulets – employed to trace the history of our habit.

The Illustrated Encyclopedia of Beekeeping Colourful and carefully selected drawings and photographs accompanying concise text entries edited by Roger Morse and Ted Hooper make this compendium a clear choice for beekeepers.

From Where I Sit This is an excellent book by Canada's leading entomologist. Mark Winston teaches and conducts research in British Columbia. He writes in a bright and clear style which entertains while it educates. Some of Dr. Winston's best essays on bees, honey, politics, beekeeping, and the art and science of research are collected in the book. Another fine book by Dr. Winston is his Biology of the Honey Bee. It was written fifteen years ago, but is scarcely out-of-date as bee biology really hasn't changed that much lately.

You may also enjoy the web site for this Bad Beekeeping book, www.badbeekeeping.com. The internet location contains a bit more about the book and has links to some of the author's other works.

Photo and Image Credits

All photographs and drawings in this book were produced by the author or members of his family, except as noted:

3. Perrault; 8. Unsigned, ancient Egyptians, from Crane; 11. Trottier; 12. Trottier promo photo; 20. Langstroth; 24. Moffett; 32. Cook; 46. Root; 50. Durer; 58. Breughel; 65. Public Domain; 72. American Beekeeper Magazine; 83. Root; 94. Root; 104. von Frisch; 107. Unsigned Paleolithics, from Crane; 119. American Beekeeper Magazine; 129. Cook; 132. Root; 133. Root; 138. Butler; 149. Root; 157. Miller; 160. Cook; 173. Cook; 178. Perrault; 183. Langstroth; 186. von Frisch; 194. From Crane; 196. Cook; 200. Moine; 205. Chandler; 208. Langstroth; 216. Cook; 225. Brother Adam; 226. American Bee Journal; 227. Government of Saskatchewan; 230. Cook; 240. Gruninger

About the Author

Not everyone gets to write a beekeeping book - an author should know something about the subject, though that hasn't stopped quite a few of us. Actually, I don't know much about the science of beekeeping. I have no beekeeper's degree, diploma, nor certificate. What I do have, though, is a little experience in the art and craft of bee culture. This was a gift from my father, a relatively good beekeeper during the 1950s and 1960s, and from my older brothers, who were extremely good beekeepers. But experience in beekeeping is mostly obtained through dirt under the fingernails and stings on the finger tips. This is what I know; this is what I write about.

Our family owned a farm in a part of America where farming was rare. My parents and my nine brothers and sisters worked on the property, and I would guess they all worked quite a lot harder than I did. The Miksha family's fifty acres in Pennsylvania produced potatoes, peppers, tomatoes, greenhouse flowers, and occasionally honey. With bees on the farm, my father rather rashly trusted three hundred hives to my care when I turned seventeen. That summer, I made fifteen thousand pounds of honey from buckwheat and goldenrod. It wasn't a big crop - fifty pounds per hive - but pretty good for that part of the USA. As pay, I got a third, worth about two thousand dollars. I enjoyed the work and enjoyed roaming around the countryside to the various apiaries. And the money was good. So I became a beekeeper.

My first winter out of school, I followed my oldest brother to Florida and learned a bit about queen breeding from him. I returned to Pennsylvania a few more summers, then Wisconsin, where the crops were a hundred pounds per hive. Then I heard about Saskatchewan, where beekeepers made two hundred pounds of honey from almost every hive, almost every year. So I went there.

I kept bees in Saskatchewan during summers, Florida in the winters. I was modestly successful, but worked pretty hard for very little money. If you've read the rest of this book, you know the details. After ten years, I decided to go back to school. Not to study beekeeping, but to learn about other sciences. I became a geophysicist and have spent the past fifteen years analyzing seismic, gravity, and magnetic data to help us all understand the earth a little better. But I continue to keep a few hives of bees.

I settled in Calgary, Alberta, Canada. I live here with my sons David and Daniel, my daughter Erika, and my wife Eszter. And, of course, five hundred thousand honey bees.

ISBN 141200627-9